W9-BBR-032

ANXIOUS POWER

SUNY Series in Feminist Criticism and Theory
Michelle A. Massé, Editor

ANXIOUS POWER

Reading, Writing, and Ambivalence in Narrative by Women

Edited by

CAROL J. SINGLEY

and

SUSAN ELIZABETH SWEENEY

State University
of New York
Press

Published by
State University of New York Press, Albany

© 1993   State University of New York

All rights reserved

Printed in the United States of America

No part of this book may be used or reproduced
in any manner whatsoever without written permission
except in the case of brief quotations embodied in
critical articles and reviews.

For information, address State University of New York
Press, State University Plaza, Albany, NY 12246

Library of Congress Cataloging-in-Publication Data

Anxious power : reading, writing, and ambivalence in narrative by
  women / edited by Carol J. Singley and Susan Elizabeth Sweeney.
        p.   cm. — (SUNY series in feminist criticism and theory)
     Includes bibliographical references and index.
       ISBN 0–7914–1389–6 (alk. paper) : $49.50. — ISBN 0–7914–1390–X
   (pbk. : alk. paper) : $16.95
        1. American literature—Women authors—History and criticism.
     2. English literature—Women authors—History and criticism.
     3. French literature—Women authors—History and criticism.
     4. Authorship—Sex differences. 5. Feminism and literature. 6. Sex
     role in literature. 7. Women and literature. 8. Narration
     (Rhetoric) I. Singley, Carol J., 1951–   . II. Sweeney, Susan
     Elizabeth, 1958–   . III. Series.
     PS152.A59   1993
     809'.89287—dc20
                                                            92–11504
                                                                 CIP

10 9 8 7 6 5 4 3 2 1

CONTENTS

PREFACE

This collection of essays follows from the insights of feminist theory that reading and writing are by no means gender-free acts. Patrocinio Schweickart speculates that the female reader may experience "grave psychic damage" because she must either read against herself or adopt a male point of view (41; cf. Fetterley xx); Sandra Gilbert and Susan Gubar argue that the female writer suffers "anxiety of authorship" (48–49). Although previous collections of essays explore gender, feminist theory, and feminist criticism, none has focused specifically on narrative representations of women's ambivalence toward language. This volume, addressing that gap, analyzes the conflicting feelings of anxiety and empowerment precipitated when woman, excluded from masculine discourse, "pluck[s] for herself the strange bright fruits of art and knowledge" (Woolf 204).

Our term, "anxious power," derives from Gilbert and Gubar's notion of "anxiety of authorship"; however, Gilbert and Gubar describe a general condition of nineteenth-century female authorship, whereas we explore language, gender, and power *specifically* in terms of ambivalence toward reading and writing and its distinctive representation in literature. In this volume, we apply the term primarily to narrative. Anxious power, then, refers both to women's perceptions of themselves and to the various formal strategies with which they express their anxiety about the power conferred by reading and writing.

Our interest in anxious power results not only from our individual research, but also from the work that the two of us—Carol and Beth—have done together. In a sense, we began collaborating on this topic when we started reading each other's writing seven or eight years ago. Discussing each other's work led to articulating our own anxiety about reading and writing as women, which led, in turn, to an essay which we wrote together on that very topic in women's narrative: "Forbidden Reading and Ghostly

Writing: Anxious Power in Wharton's 'Pomegranate Seed.'"
Writing this essay together, and confronting the differences in our
interpretations, theoretical approaches, and styles of composition
and argumentation, was itself an anxious as well as an empowering process. That essay, in which we first defined anxious power,
led to a panel of papers on the topic (at the 1989 Modern Language Association Convention) and to this book.

Several friends and colleagues have supported our progress
on *Anxious Power*. We especially thank Annette Zilversmit and
Clare Colquitt, whose early readings of our work helped us to
clarify the issues that became the foundation for this collection.
Dale Bauer, Shari Benstock, Patricia Bizzell, John Boyd, Laurie
Brown, Martha Crunkleton, Diane P. Freedman, Cynthia Jordan,
Carey Kaplan, Mark Mininberg, Jane Robinson, Ellen Cronan
Rose, Roberta Rubenstein, Anne Williams, and Josette Wisman
also provided spirited encouragement and useful advice. Daniel
Crawford, Jean Evanowski, Deborah Retzky, Ken Scott, and
especially Shirley Adams gave valuable assistance in preparing
the manuscript. Our husbands, Gordon Kinsey and Michael
Chapman, graciously accommodated themselves to the new
partnership formed by our collaboration, adjusting to myriad
telephone messsages, conference calls, and out-of-town writing
sessions. We are also grateful for Carol's Faculty Senate Research
Grants from The American University and Beth's Research and
Publication Grants from the College of the Holy Cross, which
endorsed our collaboration by providing practical support.

WORKS CITED

Fetterley, Judith. *The Resisting Reader: A Feminist Approach to American Fiction.* Bloomington: Indiana UP, 1981.

Gilbert, Sandra M., and Susan Gubar. *The Madwoman in the Attic: The Woman Writer and the Nineteenth-Century Literary Imagination.* New Haven: Yale UP, 1979.

Schweickart, Patrocinio P. "Reading Ourselves: Toward a Feminist Theory of Reading." *Gender and Reading: Essays on Readers, Texts, and Contexts.* Ed. Elizabeth A. Flynn and Patrocinio P. Schweickart. Baltimore: Johns Hopkins UP, 1986.

Woolf, Virginia. *Collected Essays.* Vol 1. London: Hogarth Press, 1966.

ACKNOWLEDGMENTS

"Forbidden Reading and Ghostly Writing in Edith Wharton's 'Pomegranate Seed,'" by Carol J. Singley and Susan Elizabeth Sweeney, is adapted from a longer essay entitled "Forbidden Reading and Ghostly Writing: Anxious Power in Wharton's 'Pomegranate Seed,'" which appeared in *Women's Studies* 20.2 (1991): 177–203. Copyright © Gordon and Breach Science Publishers S.A. Reprinted with permission.

A version of "Literary Tricksterism: Maxine Hong Kingston's *The Woman Warrior: Memoirs of a Girlhood Among Ghosts*," by Bonnie TuSmith, appeared in *Literature Interpretation Theory* 2.4 (1991): 249–59. Copyright © Gordon and Breach Science Publishers S.A. Reprinted with permission.

"Ambiguous Benefits: Reading and Writing in Feminist Metafiction," by Gayle Greene, also appears in her *Changing the Story: Feminist Fiction and the Tradition* (Bloomington: Indiana University Press, 1991). Reprinted with permission.

Excerpts from "Discourse as Power: Renouncing Denial," by Diane P. Freedman, appear in her *An Alchemy of Genres: Cross-Genre Writing by American Feminist Poet-Critics* (Charlottesville: University Press of Virginia, 1992). Reprinted with permission.

"In the Men's Room(s)," by Marge Piercy, *Circles on the Water: Selected Poems of Marge Piercy.* Copyright © 1982 by Marge Piercy. Reprinted by permission of Alfred A. Knopf, Inc., and the Wallace Literary Agency, Inc.

INTRODUCTION

Carol J. Singley and Susan Elizabeth Sweeney

Virginia Woolf says of Shakespeare's sister in *A Room of One's Own*, "a highly gifted girl who had tried to use her gift for poetry would have been so thwarted and hindered by contrary instincts, that she must have lost her health and sanity to a certainty" (49). This book is about those "contrary instincts" and their effect on the way women write. It argues, more precisely, that language itself evokes conflicting feelings of anxiety and empowerment in women; and that women's literature manifests this "anxious power," this ambivalence toward the very acts of reading and writing.

When women use their gifts to write or read narrative, in particular, how do they respond to language's alienating but compelling power? This book draws upon feminist literary theory, narrative theory, and reader-response criticism to answer that question. It examines anxious power in narratives by a variety of female writers; in a range of narrative genres; and from different historical, cultural, and theoretical perspectives. *Anxious Power* is the first collection of essays to address issues of ambivalence in narrative by women, trace those issues from the medieval period to the present, and outline a theoretical framework for understanding them.

Some essays in this volume examine British and American writers, both familiar figures in feminist criticism (Jane Austen, Charlotte Brontë, Edith Wharton, Willa Cather, Doris Lessing) and those who are less well known (Jane Barker, Mary Guion, Caroline Lee Hentz, Susan Warner, Sarah Grand, and Fanny Howe). Other essays examine European, Canadian, African American, South American, Latin American, and Asian American writers (Christine de Pizan, Marie-Catherine d'Aulnoy, Margaret Atwood, Carol Shields, Harriet Jacobs, Toni Morrison, Clarice Lispector, Sandra Cisneros, and Maxine Hong Kingston). The collection also considers various forms of women's narrative: narrative poetry; fairy tales; the oral tradition; diaries and autobiographies; novels and romances; ghost stories; *Bildungsromane, Künstlerromane*, epistolary fiction, and dystopic fiction; and cross-genre writing, which combines narrative with autobiography, poetry, and criticism. *Anxious Power: Reading, Writing, and Ambivalence in Narrative by Women* thus expands and further defines a rich female literary tradition.

Our four headings—"Anxieties of Authorship," "'My Book My Pen and My—Lover': Reading, Writing, and Romance," "Developing Narratives of Differences," and "Reading and Writing Empowerment"—trace the development and theoretical implications of anxious power in female literary history. Women who wrote during the Middle Ages, the Renaissance, and the eighteenth century are best characterized by their anxious authorship; nineteenth- and turn-of-the-century women, on the other hand, often expressed literary desire through the metaphor of romance. Modernist and contemporary women confront the power of discourse more directly; they also confront the important differences in color, class, ethnicity, or sexuality which lie within the common experience of female reading and writing. Experimental and postmodernist female writers continue to revise masculine discourse, even as they try to articulate an alternative feminist literary tradition.

In the opening essays, we explore what it means to experience anxious power and express it in narrative. We review relevant scholarship, provide a theoretical basis for the study of anxious power, and describe the nature of female identity and female narrative strategies. Carol J. Singley's essay, "Female Language, Body, and Self," argues that female ambivalence toward reading and writing is rooted in the concept of self, which in turn derives from women's biological and cultural roles. Traditionally, women have been thought innately incapable or unworthy of literature; not surprisingly, female writing is often experienced as unnatural and painful. In relationships with men—and especially in the roles of wife, mother, and daughter—women have also served others rather than the muse. Many female readers and writers, however, are actively redefining female identity in order to overcome the anxiety attendant upon gender. They celebrate writing through the body; find alternatives to masculine models of creativity; propose fluid or communal notions of self; and practice collaboration, a feminist enterprise whereby notions of solitary reading or writing—of knowledge as individually discovered and owned—are replaced by cooperation and mutuality. By these and other means, Singley concludes, women strive to make the power of language self-affirming rather than anxious.

Susan Elizabeth Sweeney's essay, "Formal Strategies in a Female Narrative Tradition: The Case of *Swann: A Mystery*," draws upon feminist theory, narrative theory, and reader-response criticism to show how women's narratives represent ambivalence toward reading and writing. In her reading of *Swann*, Carol Shields' satirical novel about the posthumous discovery of a female poet, Sweeney introduces narrative strategies discussed throughout this collection: interrupted, indirect, or dialogic narration; embedded texts (particularly ones that are hidden, lost, or illegible); self-reflexive depictions of a work's composition, publication, and interpretation; and ambiguous endings. These narrative strategies resemble the characteristics of women's contemporary experimental fiction, discussed in the last section of this volume and also illustrated by Shields' novel: dialogics, cross-genre writing, metafiction, and open endings. Women have consistently used such strategies to express their ambivalence toward language—a fact which suggests a distinctly female narrative tradition.

PART I
ANXIETIES OF AUTHORSHIP

Historically, woman's place is outside written discourse, excluded from the entitlement that acts of reading and writing confer. When women dare to break this silence and access the power of language, they often do so with profuse apologies and complicated strategies of indirection, substitution, and negation.

Although the phrase "anxiety of authorship" was coined to describe nineteenth-century women (Gilbert and Gubar 48–49), this section suggests that earlier female readers and writers also struggled with the appropriation of linguistic power. Do these women hide their literary talent so successfully that they reinforce the very power structures they would subvert? And despite their search for feminine modes of expression, are they still inscribed within masculine models of discourse? Essays in this section show how female writers in the fifteenth to eighteenth centuries developed elaborate means to speak as subjects, even as they tried to disavow that empowerment.

Writing within a powerfully misogynist medieval tradition, Christine de Pizan—subject of Christine Moneera Laennec's essay, "Christine *Antygrafe*: Authorial Ambivalence in the Works of Christine de Pizan"—adopts strategies which simultaneously disguise and express her desire for authorship. Laennec appropriates the term "antygraphie," defined as "writing-without-having-written," to describe de Pizan's narrative method. By disguising her signature in anagrams and attributing her work to allegorical superiors, de Pizan denies her own authority as a writer. While the rhetorical and poetic brilliance of these disclaimers attest to her narrative skill, they also serve only too well as models of the very misogynist discourse that she refutes. The result, Lanennec argues, has been de Pizan's relative obscurity. In light of contemporary theory, however, we may see her resistance to claims of authority as a particularly modern anxiety about the relationship between language and signification.

In "Our Bodies/Our Texts?: Renaissance Women and the Trials of Authorship," Wendy Wall analyzes the female body's relation to discourse, detailing how Mary Sidney's "To the Angell Spirit..." and Amelia Lanyer's *Salve Deus Rex Judaeorum* respond creatively to cultural prohibitions against female authorship. Male writers overcame social stigmas associated with publication by adopting strategies in which women's bodies served as tropes for writing. Wall argues that Sidney and Lanyer exploit those very strategies, "imagining the male body so as to renegotiate the relationship between writer, text, and reader." Sidney casts her late brother Philip as male muse by naming him the origin of her translation; she gains authority by figuring her text as his wounded body. Exploiting the socially approved role of woman as mourner in her retelling of Christ's passion, Lanyer becomes the object mourned, comparing herself to Christ, her text to the Word Incarnate, and infusing her narrative with religious authority. Both Sidney and Lanyer, Wall argues, forge a discourse of power and the body that alleviates the female writer's anxiety about literary production.

Patricia Hannon examines seventeenth-century French fairy tales in her essay, "A Politics of Disguise: Marie-Catherine d'Aulnoy's 'Belle-Etoile' and the Narrative Structure of Ambivalence." Hannon shows how Aulnoy's narration amplifies a conventional fairy-tale plot by embedding *mises en abyme*, inscribing contemporary allusions, and disrupting narrative sequence— what Hannon calls "writing by addition." While these strategies occasionally endanger the story's coherence, Hannon argues that they direct the reader's attention from the traditional fairy-tale plot and create an open space in between the story and the act of storytelling, wherein the writer can assert her own identity.

In "Galesia, Jane Barker, and a Coming to Authorship," Kathryn R. King studies authorial ambivalence in Barker's early eighteenth-century Galesia trilogy. Galesia's conflicts, and to some extent their resolutions, are expressed in patchwork analogies in the trilogy's central novel. Lacking a tradition of female novelists, and uncertain of her relationship to the masculine print culture, Barker seeks legitimacy by comparing the work of the pen to that of the needle. Her patchwork analogies also imply her desire for a sympathetic audience; her coming to authorship involves the double process of imagining a writing self *and* finding a rhetorical context in which that self can be heard. Barker does not simply valorize a female tradition, King argues; she also engages in the kind of revisionary, collaborative project that still occupies female writers today.

PART II
"MY BOOK MY PEN AND MY—LOVER":
READING, WRITING, AND ROMANCE

The next section describes a different kind of ambivalence, as nineteenth- and turn-of-the-century women attempt to resolve the apparent tension between independent reading, writing, and thinking, on the one hand, and a culture that emphasizes romance and marriage, on the other. Rather than simultaneously announcing and disguising their authorship, these women try to integrate linguistic power with traditional romance—whether in the texts they read and write or the lives they lead.

In "The Word as Battleground in Jane Austen's *Persuasion*," an essay that complements Hannon's analysis of ambivalent narration, Julia Giordano extends the theory that free indirect discourse developed as a means for early female novelists to establish narrative authority. Giordano shows, in particular, how Austen's use of free indirect discourse in *Persuasion*—which enables the narrator to identify with Anne Elliott and yet remain distant from her—undermines her heroine's apparent credibility and makes the novel more subversively ironic than it first appears. This irony explains why Anne's speech (illustrated by her accounts of her romance with Captain Wentworth) is so ambiguous, evasive, and ultimately unreliable: it reflects the same anxieties about feminine discourse that produce Austen's own indirect narrative strategy.

Martha Tomhave Blauvelt reads Mary Guion's diary in the context of American social history. The title of her essay quotes a phrase—"this altogather precious tho wholy worthless book"— which encapsulates Guion's ambivalence toward her diary. She felt that her diary was invaluable to her, yet meaningless to anyone else—an ambivalence poignantly expressed by her mingled fear and desire that someone might read it. However, Guion also saw her diary as a source of education, even empowerment. Another phrase from the diary that provides the title for this section, "my book my Pen and my—Lover," lists the most important things in her life: reading, writing, and the ideal husband she imagined. Guion's diary exemplified all three simultaneously. It allowed her to connect these aspects of her life, and to resolve differences between literature and life, between romance and reality. Blauvelt shows how Guion describes her suitors in terms borrowed from sentimental fiction, and practices with her diary the emotional and intellectual intimacy that she hoped to find in marriage. Complementing the analysis of prose fiction in other essays, Blauvelt's study in cultural criticism provides provocative evidence of the ambivalence toward reading and writing that ordinary women felt.

Debra Humphreys' essay, "Power and Resistance in Harriet Jacobs' *Incidents in the Life of a Slave Girl*," provides another glimpse of the complex relationship between sentimental fiction and women's lives. Using Foucault's theories about power, spatial configurations, and narrative strategies, Humphreys examines tensions between private and public places in *Incidents*. She argues, in particular, that Harriet Jacobs exposes the instability of such dichotomies—private and public, inside and out, black and white—by redefining the ambivalent space between them to empower her narrative. In the same way, Jacobs positions her autobiography within the sentimental romance tradition so as to resist both its conventions and its ideology. Humphreys' essay concurs with other essays about the considerable ambivalence with which a nineteenth-century woman compares her life to its fictional version. Humphreys suggests, however, that such ambivalence can be a source of power—especially for those excluded by race as well as gender.

In "Mirroring the Mother-Text: Histories of Seduction in the American Domestic Novel," Elizabeth L. Barnes also examines the influence of the sentimental romance. She argues that the nineteenth-century domestic novel is the child of the eighteenth-century seduction novel, and that it acknowledges this origin in its treatment of mothers and daughters. More specifically, Barnes shows how mothers and daughters struggle for narrative control in Caroline Lee Hentz's *Ernest Linwood*. The story of the mother's seduction, echoing seduction novels of the preceding century, is an embedded text which both frightens and seduces her daughter—who is paralyzed by her mother's story and the literary history it evokes. Establishing connections between two major genres of women's narrative, Barnes suggests a new paradigm for female literary influence.

In "Charlotte Brontë and Desire (to Write): Pleasure and Prohibition," Patricia E. Johnson provides a reading of Brontë's novels which links authorship, audience, and romance. Brontë's heroines do not seek true love, she argues, so much as self-expression and a sympathetic male audience. Johnson analyzes Brontë's narration, imagery, and embedded texts in order to trace a progression from *Jane Eyre*, in which desire to write is sublimated as sexual desire, to *Shirley*, in which writing and sexual desire express each other, to *Villette*, in which desire to write is unveiled as the heroine's true object. Johnson's essay provides a new interpretation of Brontë's oeuvre, and describes another way in which female writers express anxiety about authorship and interpretation through the medium of the romance.

Terri Doughty's essay, "Sarah Grand's *The Beth Book*: The New Woman and the Ideology of the Romance Ending," uses Anglo-American feminist theory to assess a complex relationship between fictional heroine, authorial persona, and an actual person—Frances Elizabeth McFall, the British feminist, "New Woman," and novelist. Doughty argues that both her heroine, "Elizabeth Caldwell Maclure," and her pseudonym, "Madame Sarah Grand," are in some sense wishful projections of McFall's real identity. *The Beth Book* was intended as feminist fiction about the life of a female writer and "woman of genius." However, although the novel resists the traditional romance ending, it finally and clumsily reinscribes it—a flaw that Doughty links to the romance ending's powerful ideology and to McFall's own ambivalence about her artistic career.

In "Forbidden Reading and Ghostly Writing in Edith Wharton's 'Pomegranate Seed,'" Carol J. Singley and Susan Elizabeth Sweeney draw on psychoanalytic theory, reader-response criticism, and feminist theory to explain the ambivalence toward reading and writing that haunted Wharton since childhood. The purloined love letter in "Pomegranate Seed" represents the power of language and generates the same series of triangular relationships that Lacan finds in Poe's "The Purloined Letter," with the important difference that all of Wharton's major characters are female. Along with the story's ambiguous plot and title, the "barely legible" letter—which is fearfully read by two women and written from beyond the grave by another—reveals Wharton's worry about becoming a writer. In this and other narratives, Wharton overcomes her ambivalence, purloining both the "letter" and the power it represents. But her anxiety remains—and turns the romance into a ghost story.

PART III
DEVELOPING NARRATIVES OF DIFFERENCES

In cultures that define subjectivity as masculine, to be female is already to be other. How is this attribution altered by a woman's added marginalization by sexuality, class, race, or ethnicity? Essays in this section explore differences among female writers, celebrate diversity, and suggest that there can be no universal theory of female creativity. Twentieth-century women no longer imagine themselves as literary transgressors, and they even recount stories other than the familiar one of husband, home, and children; but the pressing matter of one's identity remains, especially in contexts that pay only lip service to difference. These essays consider women who write sometimes subversively, always heroically, about the struggle to break old narratorial and ideological boundaries and claim new territories for themselves and their characters. Accordingly, several essays consider narratives of adolescent as well as literary development.

In her essay, "Willa Cather and the Fiction of Female Development," Judith Fetterley explores Cather's apparent rejection of the mothering that is so common in the female regionalist tradition. Fetterley argues that the ostensible misogyny in novels like *The Professor's House* reveals the high cost of Cather's male identification and her inevitable ambivalence about her development as a writer. This dissociation from gender poses an insoluable dilemma for the female artist. Fetterley finds possible exception, however, in *The Song of the Lark*, a novel of successful female development and a countertext to *The Professor's House*, a novel of failed male development. In *The Song of the Lark*, Fetterley argues, physical desire merges with the passion of art; the memory of foremothers creates a productive model of self-mothering; and irrepressible desire overcomes ambivalence toward successful artistic development. "Willa Cather and the Fiction of Female Development" complements Barnes' analysis of maternal legacies in the domestic novel and Gutiérrez-Jones' essay on gender and ethnicity in the *Bildungsroman*.

In "How Do We [Not] Become These People Who Victimize Us?: Anxious Authorship in the Early Fiction of Joyce Carol Oates," Brenda O. Daly explores the metaphor of "leaving home" to describe both Oates' efforts to flee the patriarchal house of fiction and her characters' attempts at self-authorship. Oates' early novels express her anxiety in the personae of suicidal adolescent men; she imagines authorship as masculine, dangerous, and even deadly. Later novels feature adolescent women—often young and poor as well as female—and envision ways for them not only to survive, but to redefine their relationship to self and world through alternatives to the romance plot. For Oates and her characters, however, the power of language still causes anxiety. Oates' dilemma remains the same: how to become self-authoring without exploiting others; how to tell her characters' stories without victimizing them.

Deborah J. Archer's essay, "Receiving the Other: The Feminine Economy of Clarice Lispector's *The Hour of the Star*," addresses the *écriture féminine* of a Brazilian novelist whose feminism has been overlooked until recently. Drawing on the theories of Cixous and Irigaray, Archer reads Lispector's novel in terms of a libidinal economy which reveals her self-consciousness about writing. In an essay that complements Daly's analysis of the relationship between author and character, Archer identifies Lispector's feminine modes of expression: hesitancy over speaking for the other, and uncertainty about the proper distance between herself and her protagonist. Lispector also reflects postmodernist concerns over the inadequacy of language, as she struggles to make words fit her heroine's reality without appropriating it. Archer's own essay replicates this struggle, as she strives to recreate Lispector's text in a way that leads readers beyond aesthetic appreciation to political and personal revelation.

Deborah L. Clarke considers women's ambivalence toward reading and writing in the context of black orality and white literacy in her essay, "'What There Was before Language': Preliteracy in Toni Morrison's *Song of Solomon*." Clarke shows how Morrison mediates the African American desire for a voice (which led Frederick Douglass to equate literacy with freedom) with women's hesitation to appropriate the conventions of white patriarchy. Clarke uses both feminist and narrative theory to demonstrate that Morrison upholds "prediscursive reality," in Irigaray's phrase, as an alternative to the written word. But whereas Irigaray identifies this prediscursive reality with feminine discourse, Morrison relates it to men as well as women: nature seems androgynous, and child's play, common to both sexes, transforms the masculine Bible into a simple alphabet from which a new language can be made. Although *The Song of Solomon* reveals Morrison's own ambivalence—it is a literate text that empowers an oral tradition—Clarke argues that it creates a new paradigm to replace the written discourse which has long kept African Americans from power.

Bonnie TuSmith explores the intersections of gender, ethnicity, and creativity in "Literary Tricksterism: Maxine Hong Kingston's *The Woman Warrior: Memoirs of a Girlhood Among Ghosts.*" Noting that the novel should be read as neither sociology nor history, TuSmith addresses the literary, rather than literal, issues that it raises about the individual and the community. Unlike those who read this text as conventional autobiography, TuSmith argues that Kingston's "memoir" challenges the optimistic, static assumptions of American autobiography in order to better represent the distinctive stories of ethnic women. Kingston's new form of autobiography replaces the notion of self as already constituted with the notion of self as continuity through change. Moreover, in the tradition of literary tricksterism, Kingston uses a "strategy of ambiguity" which engages readers in reconstructing appropriate contexts for the complexity of Chinese American life.

In "Different Voices: The Re-*Bildung* of the Barrio in Sandra Cisneros' *The House on Mango Street*," Leslie S. Gutiérrez-Jones reads Cisneros' novel in the context of Carol Gilligan's revisionary theories of psychological development and Michel de Certeau's analysis of the art forms of the disempowered. For Cisneros and other Chicana and marginalized writers, consumption of available literary genres can become a form of production: in *Mango Street*, Cisneros' narrator abandons the familiar pattern of adolescent rebellion and accession to a calm social order, so common to the *Bildungsroman* and *Künstlerroman* traditions, by returning to the barrio. Like Kingston, Cisneros revises the American mythology of the self-sufficient individual to envision a communal self involved with others. This reconceptualization of identity and development radically transforms the Bildungsroman into a novel of what Gilligan calls "identity as relationship." Attendant on this new model, however, is the anxiety with which women experience their individual creativity as alienation from the culture that fosters it. Gutiérrez-Jones argues that Cisneros, like other contemporary female writers, overcomes this anxiety by creating multiple narrative voices to balance the needs for connection and separation.

PART IV
READING AND WRITING EMPOWERMENT

Essays in the concluding section of *Anxious Power* address contemporary women's ambivalence toward reading and writing in a postmodernist (and postfeminist?) culture. In particular, these essays show that female writers of experimental fiction contine to revise patriarchal texts and masculine modes of discourse, even as they try to imagine what might take their place.

Gayle Greene's "Ambiguous Benefits: Reading and Writing in Feminist Metafiction" outlines a new literary history of recent experimental writing by women, beginning with the novels of Doris Lessing. Greene argues that feminist writers of the sixties, seventies, and early eighties used the self-reflexive strategies of postmodernism to depict the complex ways in which women are both limited and liberated by language. In a parallel to Doughty's essay on the New Woman and the ideology of romance, for example, Greene shows that these feminist writers also confronted the limitations of "happily-ever-after" endings—depicting those limitations even as they attempted to transcend them. She cites Margaret Drabble's *The Waterfall*, in particular, as an example of feminist metafiction which creates an alternative to the myth of romantic salvation.

In "Letters from Nowhere: Fanny Howe's *Forty Whacks* and Feminine Identity," Johnny Payne shows how contemporary female writers try to subvert male-authored discourse about women and articulate an alternative. Reading Howe's experimental epistolary novella in the context of biography and psychoanalysis, and comparing the heroine's letters to her psychoanalyst with Howe's own letters to her mentor, Payne suggests that correspondence with male discourse tends to efface feminine identity. "Letters from Nowhere" argues that a woman's participation in such discourse—whether it be psychoanalysis or intellectual exchange—places her in the powerless position of patient or protegé. Payne's essay also complements Singley and Sweeney's analysis of the purloined letter.

Margaret Atwood is a female writer who is always intensely aware of her heroines' relationship to language. In "Scripted, Conscripted, and Circumscribed: Body Language in Margaret

Atwood's *The Handmaid's Tale,*" Sheila C. Conboy examines the narrator's relationship to language at several levels. Drawing on analogies between the text and the female body (also evoked in Wall's essay on female publication in the Renaissance), Conboy shows the complicated connections between the narrator's textual and physical reproduction. In particular, Offred experiences her text—like her body—as "fragmented"; and she implies and even addresses an ideal female reader who will be able to reassemble it. Despite Offred's optimism, however, Atwood herself is ambivalent about the possibility of such sympathetic reading: Offred's actual reader, as depicted in the "Historical Notes" to her narrative, is a man who appropriates her text just as the Gilead regime appropriated her body.

The fictions of Lessing, Howe, Atwood, and other feminist writers suggest that, like their literary mothers, contemporary women are anxious about their relationship to a male literary tradition that describes their powerlessness. A new female literary tradition is clearly necessary, but it is difficult to imagine except in correspondence with male discourse. Even as feminist writers experiment with new fictional forms, then, they still reflect imprisoning endings, punitive mentors, and misogynist readers. Diane P. Freedman's essay, "Discourse as Power: Renouncing Denial," articulates an alternative feminist literary tradition. The tradition Freedman imagines is characterized by a blending of voices (like the narration of *The House on Mango Street*), rhetorical purposes (confessional and critical), and genres (poetry, fiction, journal, essay). Moreover, Freedman's essay itself illustrates this tradition. It includes an autobiographical account of her relationship to patriarchal language as well as an analysis of Adrienne Rich and other feminist "writer-critics." Indeed, it may be that the female writer's ambivalence—her sense of being both self and other, both writer and reader, both powerful and anxious—is the matrix for a distinctly female narrative tradition, in which voices and genres combine without cancelling each other out. *Anxious Power: Reading, Writing and Ambivalence in Narrative by Women* traces the gradual evolution of that tradition.

WORKS CITED

Gilbert, Sandra M., and Susan Gubar. *The Madwoman in the Attic: The Woman Writer and the Nineteenth-Century Literary Imagination*. New Haven: Yale UP, 1979.

Woolf, Virginia. *A Room of One's Own*. New York: Harcourt Brace Jovanovich, 1981.

Experiencing Anxious Power

Female Language, Body, and Self

Carol J. Singley

If the pen is a metaphorical penis (Gilbert and Gubar 3), then what is the site of female expression? Lacking the phallus, can woman write except through impersonation? Can she read except through an alienating mimicry of the male voice?[1] To examine the anxiety that women feel when they accede to the status of "writer" or "reader" and the power that those roles confer, we must begin by considering the concept of self and the self's relationship to language, body, and culture. We must also explore the sources of female ambivalence and suggest productive alternatives.

Writing and reading are gendered rather than neutral acts which are linked to the notion of self. The "I" is implicitly present in every act of writing and reading. Joan Didion, for example, explains that she likes the title of one of her essays, "Why I Write," because the sound of the words reiterates selfhood: "I I I...writing is the act of saying *I*, of imposing yourself on other people....It's an aggressive, even a hostile act" ("Why" 17). Writing, as Didion's imagery suggests, is associated with mastery and the masculine self, while reading evokes feminine receptivity. But we must resist facile distinctions. Writing is not necessarily masculine—women have been writing for centuries; and reading is not necessarily feminine—it can be seen as a masculine act in which the reader enters into or imposes herself upon the text in order to arrive at meaning.

Reading and writing do pose particular problems for women, whose status as autonomous beings capable of such assertions is historically and even ontologically in question. Text after text in western culture claims that women, lacking adequate selfhood, can neither read nor write; women who do so, then, must confront female textuality on male grounds. Aristotle, for example, defines the category "female" by virtue of its absence of male qualities; Thomas Aquinas in early times and Sigmund Freud in modern ones follow suit, proclaiming woman an imperfect or incomplete man. For Jacques Lacan, entry into language constitutes a split within the self, between the I that perceives and the I that is perceived. The female child, identified with the mother rather than split from her, lacks the desire and means for intersubjective communication and can only enter into the symbolic realm of discourse to the extent that she internalizes male desire and imagines herself as men imagine her. According to Lacan, woman is "an empty set," "a symptom" (167, 168). If women do read or write despite centuries of male utterances to the contrary, then what is the price of their mastery of language but a loss of identity *as woman*? How can woman write or read herself out of this empty set which defines her?[2]

I

To understand how women read and write, we must first understand how they address the term "woman," because language is so closely connected to selfhood. As Pamela Annas says, "Whenever a woman sits down to write, she is engaged in a complex political act in which the self and the world struggle in and through the medium of language" (362–63). One problem with "woman" is its generalization, as shown by the prohibitions of Aristotle, Aquinas, Freud, and Lacan. Important differences exist among women; essentialist thinking, striving for a universal definition, belittles or ignores issues of diversity produced by class, race, ethnicity, sexuality, age, or a multitude of other factors. For example, if white women are objectified by society, then women of color, poor women, and lesbian women face double objectification—even invisibility. The acts of "re-vision" by which, Adrienne Rich argues, women gain self-knowledge and empowerment ("When" 35), are themselves subject to re-vision. Barbara Christian notes that novels by and about African American women must refute the stereotypes of mammy, loose woman, tragic mulatta, and conjurer; Henry Louis Gates sets critical texts in dialogue with each other in order to define a female African American tradition.[3] Tillie

Olsen explains the "unnatural" silence of working-class women who lack the money or time to write (6). And feminists call for a lesbian theory of reading and writing that does not reinscribe the universality of heterosexuality.[4] Any exploration of female ambivalence toward language, then, must be sensitive to totalizing tendencies and inadvertent a priori definitions that spring from the terms of the investigation itself. Yet, as Diana Fuss notes, one may "deploy" rather than "fall into" essentialism, engaging it for its strategic or intervening value (20), or, as Gayatri Spivak suggests, as a temporary means toward a political end (205–07). Accordingly, this essay will employ the terms "female" and "woman" in order to facilitate female reading and writing and constructively change conditions under which women participate in language.

Feminist theory attempts to answer the question of how women's identity is affected when they write or read. Two attitudes, broadly defined as Anglo-American and French, form the grounds of contemporary debate. The former sees language as a more or less neutral medium through which women, once they begin to write, can represent their experience; the latter finds that experience is inseparable from language. According to the first, women need only to free themselves from ideological restrictions; according to the second, the speaking or writing subject is always masculine while its object is feminine. Feminist theorists point out that women's relationship to language is shaped by the female body; by the cultural roles women play as wife, daughter, and mother; and by the narrative forms which inscribe these roles.

The body—its functions and roles—is a crucial starting point for understanding female reading and writing, not only because woman is traditionally defined in terms of her body but because the body serves as the literal and figurative site of female pain, pleasure and production. In Isak Dinesen's story, "The Blank Page," a woman's daring assertion of self results in a blank page, as if to suggest that the female self and the female text are mutually exclusive. Yet, as Susan Gubar's essay shows, even this blankness speaks a language of its own: its uniquely absent markings protest the conformity expected of women. Male writers often see a woman's body and sexuality as metaphors for their own texts. However, because they experience their bodies "as the only available medium," women have less distance between themselves and their art, with the result that female creativity is experienced "as a painful wounding." The framed canvases in Dinesen's story are literally made out of their creators' blood, making "the creation of female art feel like the destruction of the female body" (296, 302). However persuasive this view, it is important not to see women's creativity only as a negative negotiation between language and body—which recapitulates antiquated thinking, such as the nineteenth-century view that excessive reading and writing made women infertile, and threatens to deny woman the full range of her being.

The body itself is an ambivalent source of identification for women, and may be seen positively or negatively. If men's creativity is shaped by the pleasure, pride, and privilege of the phallus, does women's creativity reside in some corresponding part? Hélène Cixous celebrates feminine difference, asserting that woman writes through the femaleness of her body: woman must recover "her organs, her immense bodily territories which have been kept under seal" to experience the textual and erotic pleasures which trangress the laws of phallocentric discourse (250). Luce Irigaray also theorizes female pleasure, or *jouissance*, anatomically, in the "two lips" which are *"neither one nor two"*— and which establish woman's doubleness and an alternative economy to the phallic one (*This* 26).[5] Yet despite claims by Cixous, Irigaray, and others, feminist theorists disagree about how women read or write in the mother rather than the father tongue.[6]

II

Female ambivalence toward reading and writing arises not only from the body per se, but also from the variety of cultural roles derived from woman's biology. These roles traditionally exclude women from acknowledged sources of power. Janet Sternburg notes that various societal "proscriptions" can make women "feel unworthy of literature" (xi). Didion recalls her alienation from the sphere of male experience: "wives, wars, big fish, Africa, Paris, no second acts"; "a woman who wrote novels had no particular role" (Interview 324). Reading and writing—"professions for women," to use Woolf's phrase—are still relatively recent and hard-won occupations.

If language expresses self, then women feel ambivalent if they conceive of writing and reading in terms of their most common roles as wife, mother, daughter. Wives occupy complementary rather than primary positions; countless helpmeets—Sonya Tolstoy, Dorothy Wordsworth, Zelda Fitzgerald, for example—fill dedications in male-authored texts, all women who subordinated their own talents and aspirations to serve as men's amanuenses, editors, and muses (Spender).[7] Reproductive and parental roles are also marked by gender difference. Following the ancients' belief that the father supplied the seed and life of the new being but the mother only the vessel, male writers often compare the writing process to male generativity or birth. To "father" a text connotes active creation; to "mother" connotes merely nurturance or maintenance—helping that which already exists to grow. And whereas paternal functions are contained in the act of conception, maternal functions extend endlessly, stealing time and energy from writing or reading.[8]

Women's roles as daughters also influence their relationship to language. Harold Bloom theorizes that male writers seek an Oedipal overthrow of their literary fathers, resulting in triumphant separation and autonomy—in Lacanian terms, a movement into the Symbolic. But the female child faces either the father's seduction which, as Jane Gallop shows, threatens to inscribe her further in the patriarchal order, or other manifestations of abuse or subjection (Boose and Flowers). She also experiences a double bind in relation to the mother. Identifying with her maternal aspects places her outside discourse, but severing the tie with the mother means denying some part of the self. According to Nancy Chodorow's understanding of gender, we might conclude that authorial aspiration, which seems to involve assertion or even aggression, contradicts female empathy and interdependence.

But women's cultural roles include not only those of wife, mother, and daughter, but relationships to men in general. Some feminist theorists, beginning with Simone de Beauvoir—who writes that "one is not born, but rather becomes a woman"

(301)—focus on social conditions that constrain women's self-hood. Gayle Rubin and Irigaray (*This*) each define woman as a mediated entity or means of exchange between men, rather than as agent in her own right. Laura Mulvey and E. Ann Kaplan focus on the dynamics of the observer and the observed, finding woman as "spectacle," dominated by the gaze of the male subject. And Julia Kristeva's term, "abject," is a fit description of the female condition of "non-being" (67). Women's lives, and therefore their narratives, fall outside the realm of male discourse—in the margin, on the fringe, in the "wild zone," or in some other unspecified site.

These gendered relationships are inscribed not only in society but in narrative itself. Vast quantities of romantic fiction—typically produced by female writers and consumed by female readers—subject women to ideological fantasies of masculine domination and feminine submission. Feminist critics debate whether these reenactments of women's experience serve only to entrap women further in cultural roles or facilitate their escape from them. The decision to write against this tradition—to find a narrative ending which is not marriage or death—does not always suggest clear alternatives. Subverting traditional roles and asserting creative powers may render a woman monstrous, as Barbara Johnson suggests, or mad, as Charlotte Perkins Gilman's "The Yellow Wallpaper" demonstrates. In gothic fiction, where boundaries are transgressed and one's deepest fears and desires indulged, the heroine, Claire Kahane argues, casts off her identity only to find herself still haunted by the spectral presence of the mother. Romance, the woman's genre, proves remarkably resistant to transformation, despite its many variations and critiques.[9]

III

The history of female reading and writing is a continuous effort to overcome the anxiety attendant upon the limitations of gender roles and narrative forms; but female readers and writers are working to alter history, first by articulating the sources of ambivalence. Anxiety, or fear, is at the root of ambivalence; in the best of cases, anxiety about being considered inadequate or trivial; in the worst, of being reviled, persecuted, or even extinguished. In its extreme, anxiety silences, blocks, or kills creativity. It also may express itself indirectly, in forms of politeness, circumlocution, deference, or denial. Thus Elizabeth Hardwick tells an interviewer that being a female writer poses "no special difficulty," but follows her comment with a paragraph-long enumeration of the punishments inflicted on presumptuous, know-it-all women (216). Female ambivalence is rooted in women's experience of such oppression. Successful literary women, inheritors of alien traditions they have had to make their own, understand both power and powerlessness. Working from a fragile sense of self and conscious of the courage that creative acts require, they hesitate to appropriate the voices of others as theirs have been appropriated, and to inflict their experience of alienation on others.

Other women are working to overcome anxiety through self-empowerment. Female writers and readers challenge their inscription within patriarchal discourse, finding forms of female creative expression which are more than a reaction to dominant male ideologies and forms. Some feminists, rejecting oppositional views of gender that see women as inferior or disadvantaged, redefine desire and celebrate a communal, fluid idea of the self which incorporates positive aspects of connection to the mother while also asserting female authority. Rich calls for a political as well as literary community to overcome the fragmentation of the feminine self ("When"). Contemporary novels such as *The Joy Luck Club*, *How to Make an American Quilt*, and *The House on Mango Street* are built of multiple voices and shared identities. In addition, Molly Hite recommends reading "otherwise" to recognize female-created violations of literary conventions as conscious and deliberate actions (3)—a practice that asks not what woman lacks, but under what conditions and through what strategies she participates in telling "the other side of the story." And Patricia Yeager replaces the image of the suffering or crazy female artist with an archetype of the "honey-mad woman," who, hungry for the power of language, climbs the honey tree to reach "a site of vision and liberation" (4, 7).

Still other women reject the notion that reading and writing are solitary acts—replacing the image of the isolated writer or reader with models of textual interaction and collaboration.

Many feminist collaborators view their relationship—with its commitments, challenges, and rewards—as a marriage of minds freed from hierarchies and prohibitions, a trust in the evolution of knowledge which alleviates anxiety. Collaborators Carey Kaplan and Ellen Cronan Rose, for example, describe their joint authorship as an "erotics of collaboration." By these and other means, female writers and readers seek to redefine the nature of language and identity, and to make the power of authorship self-affirming rather than anxious.[10]

NOTES

1. For Irigaray, femininity is a masquerade, with woman "acting out man's contraphobic projects, projections and productions of her desire" (*Speculum* 53). Atwood's handmaid, forbidden self-definition either as reader or writer, learns that female expression is impossible: "Pen is Envy" (241).

2. Feminist responses vary: Gardiner argues that while female gender identity is more fixed than male gender identity, "primary identity for women is more flexible and relational than for men"; thus female identity is a "process" (184). Because the categories "female" and "woman" are troubled and unstable, Butler recommends abandoning "questions of primary identity in order to get on with the task of politics" (xi).

3. While acknowledging the lack of African American feminist criticism, McDowell cautions, however, against easy generalizations about a distinctive female African American "consciousness," "vision," or "literary tradition" (195).

4. On lesbian identity, see also Rich ("Compulsory") and responses to her by Ferguson et al.; Stimpson; Lorde; Zimmerman; and Fuss.

5. Showalter ("Feminist" 250–51) and Jacobus ("Men" 62) are wary of using female anatomy as the identifying feature of feminism. Similarly, Miller advises seeking the body of women's writing, not the writing of the woman's body ("Women's" 271).

6. Homans addresses the question by arguing that because they are daughters, not sons, women are capable of two languages—the literal, which they learn from their mothers, and the figurative, which they learn from their fathers.

7. A variation on this theme is the "important male author and the aspiring lady writer" (Marchalonis xi).

8. Margaret Walker, author of *Jubilee*, explains why women are not more prolific: "It is humanly impossible for a woman who is a wife and mother to work on a regular teaching job and write" (24). Countless stories of demands on mothers' time are complemented, however, by Anne Tyler's statement that children, although they slowed down her writing, gave her "more of a self to speak from" (9). Suleiman protests the equation of motherhood with selflessness and calls instead for feminist interpretations of motherhood that include the mother as subject.

9. On romance as woman's genre, see Miller (*Heroine's*, "Emphasis"); Jacobus; Gilbert and Gubar; Showalter (*Literature*); and Radway.

10. I thank Susan Elizabeth Sweeney and Roberta Rubenstein for their helpful comments on this essay.

WORKS CITED

Abel, Elizabeth, ed. *Writing and Sexual Difference*. Chicago: U of Chicago P, 1982.

Agonito, Rosemary, ed. *History of Ideas on Woman: A Sourcebook*. New York: Putnam's, 1977.

Annas, Pamela J. "Style as Politics: A Feminist Approach to the Reading of Writing." *College English* 47.4 (1985): 360–72.

Aquinas, Thomas. "Woman as Derived Being." Agonito 83–90.

Aristotle. "Differences Between Men and Women." Agonito 43–56.

Atwood, Margaret. *The Handmaid's Tale*. New York: Fawcett, 1985.

Beauvoir, Simone de. *The Second Sex*. Trans. H. M. Parshley. New York: Vintage, 1952.

Bloom, Harold. *The Anxiety of Influence: A Theory of Poetry*. New York: Oxford UP, 1973.

Boose, Lynda E., and Betty S. Flowers. *Daughters and Fathers*. Baltimore: Johns Hopkins UP, 1989.

Butler, Judith. *Gender Trouble: Feminism and the Subversion of Identity*. New York: Routledge, 1990.

Chodorow, Nancy. *The Reproduction of Mothering: Psychoanalysis and the Sociology of Gender*. Berkeley: U of California P, 1978.

Christian, Barbara. *Black Women Novelists: The Development of a Tradition*. Westport, CT: Greenwood P, 1980.

Cixous, Hélène. "The Laugh of the Medusa." Trans. Keith Cohen and Paula Cohen. *New French Feminisms*. Ed. Elaine Marks and Isabelle de Courtivron. Amherst: U of Massachusetts P, 1980. 245–64.

Didion, Joan. Interview. Plimpton 319–36.

————. "Why I Write." Sternburg 17–25.

Dinesen, Isak. "The Blank Page." *Last Tales*. New York: Random House, 1957. 99–105.

Ferguson, Ann, Jacquelyn N. Zita, and Kathryn Pyne Addelson. "On 'Compulsory Heterosexuality and Lesbian Existence': Defining the Issues." *Feminist Theory: A Critique of Ideology*. Ed. Nannerl O. Keohane et al. Chicago: U of Chicago P, 1981. 147–88.

Freud, Sigmund. *New Introductory Lectures on Psychoanalysis*. Trans. James Strachey. New York: Norton, 1965.

Fuss, Diana. *Essentially Speaking: Feminism, Nature, and Difference*. New York: Routledge, 1989.

Gallop, Jane. *The Daughter's Seduction*. Ithaca: Cornell UP, 1982.

Gardiner, Judith Keegan. "On Female Identity and Writing by Women." Abel 177–92.

Garner, Shirley Nelson, et al., eds. *The (M)other Tongue: Essays on Feminist Psychoanalytic Interpretation*. Ithaca: Cornell UP, 1985.

Gates, Henry Louis, Jr., ed. *Reading Black: Reading Feminist: A Critical Anthology*. New York: Meridian, 1990.

Gilbert, Sandra M., and Susan Gubar. *The Madwoman in the Attic: The Woman Writer and the Nineteenth-Century Literary Imagination*. New Haven: Yale UP, 1979.

Gilman, Charlotte Perkins. *The Yellow Wallpaper*. Afterword by Elaine R. Hedges. Old Westbury, NY: Feminist P, 1973.

Gubar, Susan. "'The Blank Page' and the Issues of Female Creativity." Showalter, *New* 292–313.

Hardwick, Elizabeth. Interview. Plimpton 201–24.

Hite, Molly. *The Other Side of the Story: Structures and Strategies of Contemporary Feminist Narrative*. Ithaca: Cornell UP, 1989.

Homans, Margaret. *Bearing the Word: Language and Female Experience in Nineteenth-Century Women's Writing*. Chicago: U of Chicago P, 1986.

Irigaray, Luce. *The Speculum of the Other Woman*. Trans. Gillian C. Gill. Ithaca: Cornell UP, 1985.

———. *This Sex Which is Not One*. Trans. Catherine Porter. Ithaca: Cornell UP, 1985.

Jacobus, Mary. "The Buried Letter: *Villette*." "Men of Maxims and *The Mill on the Floss*." *Reading Woman: Essays in Feminist Criticism*. Ed. Mary Jacobus. New York: Columbia UP, 1986. 41–61, 62–79.

Johnson, Barbara. "My Monster/My Self." *A World of Difference*. Baltimore: Johns Hopkins UP, 1987. 144–54.

Kahane, Clare. "The Gothic Mirror." Garner et al. 334–51.

Kaplan, Carey, and Ellen Cronan Rose. "Strange Bedfellows: The Erotics of Feminist Collaboration." Women's Caucus Session. Northeast Modern Language Association Convention. Toronto, April 1990.

Kaplan, E. Ann. "Is the Gaze Male?" Snitow et al. 309–27.

Kristeva, Julia. *Powers of Horror: An Essay on Abjection*. Trans. Leon S. Roudiez. New York: Columbia, 1982.

Lacan, Jacques. "Seminar of 21 January 1975." *Feminine Sexuality and the 'école freudienne.'* Ed. Juliet Mitchell and Jacqueline Rose. Trans. Jacqueline Rose. New York: Norton, 1982. 162–71.

Lorde Audre. "An Interview with Audre Lorde." By Karla Hammond. *The American Poetry Review* March–April 1980: 18–21.

Marchalonis, Shirley, ed. *Patrons and Protegées: Gender, Friendship, and Writing in Nineteenth-Century America*. New Brunswick, NJ: Rutgers UP, 1988.

McDowell, Deborah. "New Directions for Black Feminist Criticism." Showalter, *New* 186–99.

Miller, Nancy K. "Emphasis Added: Plots and Plausibilities in Women's Fiction." *PMLA* 96.1 (1981): 36–48.

———. *The Heroine's Text: Reading in the French and English Novel, 1722–1782*. New York: Columbia UP, 1980.

———. "Women's Autobiography in France: For a Dialectics of Identification." *Women and Language in Literature and Society*. Ed. Sally McConnell-Ginet et al. New York: Praeger, 1980. 258–73.

Mulvey, Laura. "Visual Pleasure and Narrative Cinema." *Screen* 15.3 (1975): 6–18.

Olsen, Tillie. *Silences*. New York: Dell, 1979.

Plimpton, George, ed. *Women Writers at Work*. New York: Penguin, 1989.

Radway, Janice A. *Reading the Romance: Women, Patriarchy and Popular Literature*. Chapel Hill: U of North Carolina, 1984.

Rich, Adrienne. "Compulsory Heterosexuality and Lesbian Existence." Snitow et al. 177–205.

———. "When We Dead Awaken: Writing as Re-Vision." *On Lies, Secrets, and Silences: Selected Prose 1966–1978*. New York: Norton, 1979. 33–50.

Rubin, Gayle. "The Traffic in Women: Notes on the 'Political Economy' of Sex." *Toward an Anthropology of Women*. Ed. Rayna Rapp Reiter. New York: Monthly Review P, 1975. 157–210.

Showalter, Elaine. "Feminist Criticism in the Wilderness." Showalter, *New* 243–70.

———. *A Literature of Their Own: British Women Novelists From Brontë to Lessing*. Princeton: Princeton UP, 1977.

———, ed. *The New Feminist Criticism: Essays on Women, Literature, and Theory*. New York: Random House, 1985.

Snitow, Ann, et al., eds. *Powers of Desire, The Politics of Sexuality*. New York: Monthly Review P, 1983.

Spender, Dale. "Polish, Plagiarism and Plain Theft." *The Writing or the Sex? Or Why You Don't Have to Read Women's Writing to Know It's No Good*. New York: Pergamon, 1989. 140–94.

Spivak, Gayatri Chakravorty. "Subaltern Studies: Deconstructing Historiography." *In Other Worlds: Essays in Cultural Politics*. New York: Methuen, 1987. 197–221.

Sternburg, Janet, ed. *The Writer on Her Work*. New York: Norton, 1980.

Stimpson, Catharine R. "Zero Degree Deviancy: The Lesbian Novel in English." Abel 243–59.

Suleiman, Susan. "Writing and Motherhood." Garner et al. 352–77.

Tyler, Anne. "Still Just Writing." Sternburg 3–16.

Walker, Margaret. *How I Wrote* Jubilee. Chicago: Third World P, 1972.

Woolf, Virginia. "Professions for Women." *Women and Writing.* Ed. Michele Barrett. New York: Harcourt, 1979. 57–63.

Yaeger, Patricia. *Honey-Mad Women: Emancipatory Strategies in Women's Writing.* New York: Columbia UP, 1988.

Zimmerman, Bonnie. "What Has Never Been: An Overview of Lesbian Feminist Literary Criticism." Showalter, *New* 200–24.

Expressing Anxious Power

Formal Strategies in a Female Narrative Tradition: The Case of Swann: A Mystery

Susan Elizabeth Sweeney

> Formalism was part of the strategy—like asbestos gloves, it allowed me to handle materials I couldn't pick up barehanded.
>
> —Adrienne Rich, "When We Dead Awaken: Writing as Re-Vision"

> Doubled consciousness. Doubled understandings. How then could she neglect to invent a form which produces this incessant, critical, splitting motion. To invent this form. To invent the theory for this form.
>
> —Rachel Blau DuPlessis, "For the Etruscans"

My department, like many others, is debating how best to incorporate minority authors, marginalized texts, and unconventional genres into the canon—into the canon, that is, which we teach our sophomore majors in a two-semester course entitled "Traditions of English Literature." At a departmental discussion on whether to include Adrienne Rich in this syllabus, one of my colleagues, a narrative theorist and stalwart formalist, said he would gladly teach Rich's poetry in the context of her feminism—but only if he was persuaded that her feminism was expressed in the *form* as well as the *content* of her poetry.

I, too, am a formalist. I am also a feminist. I believe that women *do* write differently than men—because, as women, they respond differently to a literary tradition which is primarily composed by men, for men, and of men, and in which women appear often as muses and mistresses but seldom as readers or writers. Such a masculine tradition, Sandra Gilbert and Susan Gubar explain, prompts intensely divided emotions in a female writer: "feelings of alienation from male predecessors coupled with her need for sisterly precursors and successors…her need for a female audience together with her fear of the antagonism of male readers, her culturally conditioned timidity about self-dramatization, her dread of the patriarchal authority of art, her anxiety about the impropriety of female invention" (50). More important, a female writer may feel ambivalent toward language itself, toward the very acts of reading and writing—since they are both the measure of her powerlessness and the means for her to articulate it. And this ambivalence is expressed in the form and content of the narratives she writes.

Because, as Lawrence Lipking says, "a woman's poetics must begin…with a fact that few male theorists have ever had to confront: the possibility of never having been empowered to speak" (67), feminist theorists must first give a name to the silence surrounding female art. In "Toward a Feminist Poetics," Elaine Showalter coins the term "gynocritics" for such a poetics of women's writing.[1] Josephine Donovan warns that "a women's poetics" should reflect "a woman-centered epistemology" and an awareness of the diversity of women's experiences (98, 100); Jane Marcus describes a "feminist aesthetic" as the "obstinacy and slyness" with which women write for their silenced sisters, and overcome their own anxious authorship, "by keeping a hand in both worlds"—one of masculine discourse, the other of everyday feminine tasks (94). Rachel Blau DuPlessis defines a "female aesthetic" more precisely as "the production of formal, epistemological, and thematic strategies by members of the group Woman, strategies born in struggle with much of already existing culture." In women's writing, DuPlessis explains, these strategies include speaking in multiple voices, inviting the reader's participation, "not seeking the authority of the writer," and articulating a "both/and vision born of shifts, contraries, negations, contradictions" ("For" 275, 276). Susan Lanser calls for a feminist narratology which would address the surface and the subtext of such feminine texts, as well as the narrative frame that binds them. Reading an anonymous feminine text, Lanser points out that "beneath the 'feminine' voice of self-effacement and emotionality…lies the 'masculine' voice of authority that the writer cannot inscribe openly" (617).

Many feminist theorists, then, have helped to articulate a female aesthetic. I hope to extend their work by describing a female narrative poetics: specific narrative strategies with which women represent their ambivalence toward reading and writing.[2] Many feminist critics have helped to reconstruct a female literary history which demonstrates a female aesthetic; I hope to extend their work by showing how these narrative strategies define a distinctly female narrative tradition.[3]

Any female narrative poetics must take into account Virginia Woolf's artful essay *A Room of One's Own*, which began as a lecture on "women and fiction" (3). Woolf explains that the female writer usually produces novels, not poems or plays—because for centuries she could observe and record human nature only in the sitting-room, and because "the novel alone was young enough to be soft in her hands." In her novels, moreover, she developed a "natural, shapely sentence proper for her own use" (80), which Woolf elsewhere calls the "psychological sentence of the feminine gender": "capable of stretching to the extreme, of suspending the frailest particles, of enveloping the vaguest shapes." Men sometimes use such sentences, of course; but women design them specifically to "descend to the depths and investigate the crannies" of female consciousness ("Romance" 367). The feminine sentence—which expresses the most tenuous and shadowy extremes—shows how women manipulate narrative form in order to represent anxious power.

A Room of One's Own also imagines a female literary history, which ranges from "a lost novelist, a suppressed poet...some mute and inglorious Jane Austen" (51) to a series of women named "Mary": Mary Beton, Mary Seton, and finally Mary Carmichael, an experimental novelist like Woolf herself. In order to delineate the formal characteristics of a female narrative tradition, I would like to cite another Mary: Mary Swann, the shadowy heroine of *Swann: A Mystery*, Carol Shields' satirical novel about the posthumous discovery of a female writer. If the name "Mary" evokes women's common experiences, then "Swann"—with its Proustian allusion—suggests that which is lost or forgotten. Indeed, Shields uses her fictitious "suppressed poet" to reconstruct yet another female literary history—one that includes Emily Dickinson, to whom Swann is compared; Pearl Buck and Edna Ferber, her favorite writers; and a contemporary feminist critic, who discovers her. Like Woolf in *A Room of One's Own*, then, Shields describes women's ambivalence toward language in a fictive history of female reading and writing.

The content of *Swann* (what narrative theorists would call its *story*) concerns the problems of becoming a female writer and of being included in the literary canon. Mary Swann—already dead before her story begins, like many female writers in women's narratives—was a poor and abused farmer's wife, geographically and culturally isolated in rural Ontario, unschooled, and apparently unversed in any literary tradition except for the two popular romances she borrowed each week from her town library. The two most significant facts of Swann's life are that it ended when her husband shot her, dismembered her body, and then shot himself; and that she left behind 125 haunting poems whose compression, resonance, and use of common meter recall Emily Dickinson. Fifteen years after her death, when a young feminist scholar discovers her only book (a cheap pamphlet entitled *Swann's Songs*), Swann suddenly becomes a literary phenomenon—the inspiration for MLA sessions, *PMLA* essays, a Mary Swann Memorial Room in her hometown, even a Swann Symposium. Yet she remains elusive. Her biographer can find no useful information on her life; no two readers can agree on a poem's meaning; and even the few proofs of her existence (her photograph, her pen, her notebook, her unpublished love poems, the remaining copies of *Swann's Songs*) mysteriously disappear. The content of Shields' novel, then, expresses her anxiety about the production and interpretation of women's writing by recounting the life and posthumous reception of a female writer.

More important, the narrative form of *Swann* (what narrative theorists would call its *discourse*) reflects this same anxiety. In *Swann*, Shields uses formal strategies that reveal her ambivalence toward reading and writing: interrupted, indirect, or dialogic narration; mixed genres and embedded texts (in particular, feminine texts which are absent or illegible); depictions of a feminine text's composition, publication, and interpretation; and an ambiguous ending.[4]

The experimental narration of the novel's five sections reveals its ambivalence toward narrative authority. Each of the first four sections focuses on a different character (Sarah Maloney the feminist scholar, Morton Jimroy the biographer, Rose Hindmarch the town librarian, and Frederic Cruzzi the publisher of *Swann's Songs*); and each is narrated from a different point of view, organized in a different format, and written in a different prose style.[5] The narration of the fifth section is even more playfully self-reflexive: it takes the form of an imaginary screenplay, "The Swann Symposium," in which characters' voices become audible and inaudible in a cacophony of "random phrases" (251), "fragments of conversation," "overlapping voices" (252), and interrupted or misunderstood speech:

> GINGER PONYTAIL:...splitting headache—
> CRINKLED FOREHEAD:...was a trifle disturbed by his remarks regarding—
> BIRDLADY:...blatantly sexist—
> GREEN TWEED SUIT: Slash, slash—
> GINGER PONYTAIL: Jesus, the smoke in here's thick enough to—
> WOMAN IN PALE SUEDE BOOTS:...and the noise—
> SILVER CUFFLINKS:...sorry, I didn't catch— (288)

The extravagant multiplicity of narrative voices in the five sections of *Swann*—whether it takes the form of interrupted discourse, free indirect discourse, or dialogic narration—reflects, I think, a peculiarly feminine ambivalence toward narrative authority.[6] It is as if Shields divides responsibility for telling her story among as many narrators as possible. And yet such attempts to disguise or diffuse narrative authority actually draw attention to her own authorial power. This ambivalence is clearly articulated in the "Director's Note" that introduces the screenplay:

> *The Swann Symposium* is a film lasting approximately 120 minutes. The main characters...are fictional creations, as is the tragic Mary Swann, *poète naïve*, of rural Ontario. The film may be described (for distribution purposes) as a thriller. A subtext focuses on the more subtle thefts and acts of cannibalism that tempt and mystify the main characters. The director hopes to remain unobtrusive throughout, allowing dialogue and visual effects (and not private passsions) to carry the weight of the narrative. (231)

This self-reflexive passage reveals Shields' conflicting desires: "to remain unobtrusive throughout" the novel, on the one hand; and obtrusively to assert her authority as its "director," on the other.

Swann reveals Shields' ambivalence not only about narrative authority, but about narrative itself. It combines various forms of narrative (autobiography, biography, epistolary novel, romance, ghost story, detective story, university novel) as well as other genres (poetry and drama).[7] And it not only alludes to other texts that remain unwritten, such as Rose's letter to Morton Jimroy; it even embeds some of them, such as Frederic Cruzzi's "(Unwritten) One-Sentence Autobiography," "Short Untranscribed History of the Peregrine Press," and "Unwritten Account of the Fifteenth of December, 1965." *Swann* presents itself, then, as many different narrative and nonnarrative texts—but also as a text that cannot be written or, according to Kristeva's definition of the feminine, as "that which is not represented, that which is unspoken, that which is left out" (37).

In addition to mixing narrators, genres, and embedded texts, then, Shields reflects her ambivalence toward reading and writing by representing texts—in particular, feminine texts like Swann's poems—as "left out," illegible, blank, or altogether absent.[8] Swann's body of work is dismembered, like her physical body, during the course of the narrative. Her love poems, for example, are hidden beneath her kitchen linoleum, only to be appropriated by one scholar, stolen by another, and never published at all. Her other poems, published posthumously in *Swann's Songs*, are written in an ink called "washable blue"— which, when the poems are accidentally soaked, results in "a pale swimmy smudge, subtly shaded, like a miniature pond floating on a white field. Two or three such smudges and a written page became opaque and indecipherable, like a Japanese water-colour" (221–22). The novel thus represents the feminine text—Swann's manuscript—as an indecipherable image, a blank page, a missing sign.

Not surprisingly, Swann's inscrutable poems resist interpretation and confound her readers. Consider one poem whose meaning becomes less clear each time it is quoted:

> Blood pronounces my name,
> Blisters the day with shame,
> Spends what little I own,
> Robbing the hour, rubbing the bone. (51)

In a series of self-reflexive passages (what Gerald Prince would call "reading interludes"), several characters (whom Naomi Schor would call "intepretants") try to make sense of this embedded feminine text. Sarah Maloney, the feminist scholar, reads it as a poem about "the inescapable perseverance of blood ties, particularly those between mothers and daughters" (51–52). Morton Jimroy, the biographer, thinks it describes "the eating of the Godhead," "a metaphysical covenant with an inexplicable universe" (148, 150). Rose Hindmarch, the town librarian, thinks it concerns menstruation. And Frederic Cruzzi, the publisher, remembers deciphering the poem's almost illegible mansuscript with his wife on the day of Swann's death:

> The last poem, and the most severely damaged, began: "Blood pronounces my name." Or was it "Blood renounces my name"? The second line could be read in either of two ways: "Brightens the day with shame," or "Blisters the day with shame." They decided on *blisters*. The third line, "Spends what little I own," might just as easily be transcribed, "Bends what little I own," but they wrote *Spends* because—though they didn't say so—they liked it better. (223)

What Mary Swann wrote on the page—let alone what she meant to say—remains obscure. *Swann* also represents ambivalence toward reading and writing, then, in the fate of this embedded feminine text, whose transcription, editing, and publication is so unreliable, and whose readers' interpretations are so hopelessly contradictory.

When Swann's poems literally disappear at the end of the novel, it becomes clear that such feminine texts must be read differently than masculine texts. The last scene of "The Swann Symposium" shows a meeting room in a hotel, "but there is no one at the lectern and no one, seemingly, in charge. People are seated in a sort of circle, speaking out, offering up remembered lines of poetry, laboriously reassembling one of Mary Swann's poems" (310). The novel's ending describes the effects of reading the feminine text in this new way:

> The faces of the actors have been subtly transformed. They are seen joined in a ceremonial act of reconstruction, perhaps even an act of creation. There need be no suggestion that any one of them will become less selfish in the future, less cranky,

less consumed with thoughts of tenure and academic glory, but each of them has, for the moment at least, transcended personal concerns. (311)

The ending suggests, then, that reading a feminine text appropriately—unlike the earlier solipsistic interpretations of "Blood Pronounces My Name"—empowers readers by allowing them to transcend "personal concerns" and unite with others. Indeed, this collaborative reconstruction resembles the "intersubjective encounter" that Patrocinio Schweickart describes in her feminist theory of reading (52).[9]

Yet the novel also seems ambivalent about the validity of such feminist reading. Shields embeds this scene of collaboration within a series of unreliable narrative frames: Swann's absent text is reconstructed by a group of academics, who are played by hypothetical actors in a screenplay, which is produced only in the reader's imagination. More important, the text that results from this reading remains ambiguous. The poem that these readers reconstruct, line by line, is reprinted on the novel's last page under the heading: "LOST THINGS By Mary Swann." It comments ironically on Swann's life, her art, and the elusive feminine text:

> ...As though the lost things have withdrawn
> Into themselves, books returned
> To paper or wood or thought,
> Coins and spoons to simple ores,
> Lustreless and without history,
> Waiting out of sight
>
> And becoming part of a larger loss
> Without a name
> Or definition or form
> Not unlike what touches us
> In moments of shame. (313)

This meditation on "lost things" reflects the novel's sense of women's writing and provides a satisfying closure. Yet it is also an appropriately ambiguous ending: because the poem appears only as it was reconstructed, it may not be the poem Swann wrote. The ending of *Swann*, then, leaves us with another embedded feminine text that remains both absent and present—

thus raising additional questions about its interpretation and authorship, and about the nature of female reading and writing.

Carol Shields' self-reflexive narrative strategies suggest her ambivalence toward appropriating the power of language. Those same strategies recur throughout the history of women's narrative: disguised or deferred narrative authority (what in this volume Christine Moneera Laennec, after Christine de Pizan, calls "writing-without-having-written"); dialogic or interrupted narration (what in this volume Patricia Hannon calls "writing by addition" in seventeenth-century French fairy tales); mixed genres, modes of discourse, and *mises en abyme*; narrative codes, secrets, and subtexts (what Bonnie TuSmith describes, in this volume, as Maxine Hong Kingston's "strategy of ambiguity"); self-reflexive accounts of the composition, publication, or interpretation of a feminine text (such as the mother's story in Caroline Lee Hentz' *Ernest Linwood* or the handmaid's tale in Margaret Atwood's eponymous novel); descriptions of the dismemberment of female writing; embedded feminine texts that are both legible and illegible (such as the bewildering pattern in Gilman's "The Yellow Wallpaper," the white bedsheet in Dinesen's "The Blank Page," or the ghostly letters in Wharton's "Pomegranate Seed");[10] and unresolved or ambiguous endings. The formal strategies that Christine de Pizan, Marie-Catherine d'Aulnoy, Jane Barker, and other early female writers used to express their anxious power thus anticipated the characteristics of contemporary experimental fiction by Toni Morrison, Sandra Cisneros, Angela Carter, Kathy Acker, and others: dialogic narration, cross-genre writing, metafiction, and "writing beyond the ending" (as DuPlessis calls it). Indeed, the recurrence of these formal strategies—from de Pizan's fifteenth-century prose to Shields' 1987 novel—defines a distinctly female narrative tradition.

This reading of *Swann: A Mystery* not only confirms the existence of a female poetics, but outlines a narrative tradition in which women represent their ambivalence toward reading and writing. It also suggests that a combination of critical approaches (narrative theory, reader-response criticism, and feminist theory) can serve critics as the "asbestos gloves," in Adrienne Rich's phrase, with which to handle the question of woman's language about which feminist theory itself is so ambivalent.[11] Finally, in emphasizing the hidden authority of women's narrative, this reading of *Swann* indicates, as Lanser says, "that the powerless form called 'women's language' is...a potentially subversive—hence powerful—tool" (617).

And to return to my colleague's implicit question: yes, the female writer's struggle with the social construction of femininity does shape the *form* as well as the *content* of her writing. In narrative, it has even produced a female tradition of experimental, ambiguous, and self-reflexive narrative strategies—a tradition which is legible to anyone who can be persuaded to read "otherwise" (in Molly Hite's phrase), to heed voices that "never [have] been empowered to speak" (Lipking 67). That such persuasion remains necessary explains why women are still so anxious about the power of their words.[12]

NOTES

1. Unlike the "feminist critique" of male texts, "gynocritics" addresses "the psychodynamics of female creativity; linguistics and the problem of a female language; the trajectory of the individual or collective female literary career" (Showalter, "Toward" 128).

2. While I call such narrative strategies "female," I think they result from women's encounter with the social construction of femininity—not from the experience of female sexuality or the female body. I argue, then, that although these narrative strategies exhibit the multiplicity and heterogeneity of Kristeva's feminine semiotic order, they reflect anxiety about appropriating male discourse, not an essentially female *jouissance*.

3. See Spacks, Showalter (*Literature*), and Gilbert and Gubar. Critics also posit separate literary traditions by African American women (Walker, Carby) and by lesbians (Farwell). For accounts of women's narrative strategies, see Lanser on "feminist narratology," Warhol on representations of reading and writing in nineteenth-century novels, and Hite on methods by which contemporary female novelists tell "the other side of the story." See also Gayle Greene's essay on "feminist metafiction" in this volume.

4. Although *Swann* is Shields' most experimental work, her fiction is often self-reflexive. *Small Ceremonies*, her first novel, describes a bestseller whose plot is stolen from the narrator's unpublished

manuscript; she stole it, in turn, from someone's abandoned novel; "the chain of indictment might stretch back infinitely, crime within crime within crime" (106). Her next novel, *The Box Garden*, concerns a woman's correspondence with her spiritual adviser—an ex-husband disguising his identity. *Happenstance* is an ironic love story and a meditation on the nature of history, that which *"wasn't* written down" (120); the sequel, *A Fairly Conventional Woman*, describes a female artist. Shields' short stories refer more specifically to women's experience of language. *Various Miracles* includes tales of words, metaphors, letters, readers and writers; *Orange Fish* describes a woman who nightly "read herself out of her own life, leaving behind...a woman who swallowed her tongue, got it jammed down her throat and couldn't make a sound" (51). For an introduction to Shields, see the special issue of *Room of One's Own* edited by Wachtel.

5. "Sarah Maloney" contains twenty numbered first-person present-tense meditations; "Morton Jimroy" is a third-person, past-tense narration with free indirect discourse, organized chronologically in unnumbered sections; "Rose Hindmarch" is divided into third-person present-tense vignettes with facetious titles and an intrusive narrator; "Frederic Cruzzi" consists of embedded texts which parody various forms of discourse. Significantly, the reader has no access to Swann's consciousness—except for her cryptic poems and a few terse entries from her notebook.

6. Lanser remarks that "polyphony is more pronounced and more consequential in women's narratives and in the narratives of other dominated peoples" (618). See also Bauer.

7. In content (the difficulties of female authorship, illustrated by an imaginary writer's life and posthumous reception) and form (dialogic narration, mixed genres, embedded texts), Byatt's *Possession* resembles *Swann*. It also recalls other contemporary novels about dead female artists, such as Lurie's *The Truth About Lorin Jones*. *Swann* thus represents not only a female narrative tradition, but a specific genre: the feminist fictitious critical biography.

8. On absent texts in women's narrative, see Gubar; on hidden subtexts in women's narrative, see Lanser.

9. Schweickart asks what it means "for a woman, reading as a woman, to read literature written by a woman writing as a woman?" (51). What it means, according to her reading of Adrienne Rich reading Emily Dickinson, is an "awareness of the double context of reading and writing" which preserves the subjectivity of both reader and

writer (52). See also Fetterley and Kolodny, who each analyze representations of reading in women's narrative.

10. See Treichler, who argues that the yellow wallpaper's unresolvable pattern is an ambivalent representation of feminine discourse; Gubar, who reads the white bedsheet as an emblem of female creativity; and Carol J. Singley and Susan Elizabeth Sweeney ("Forbidden"), in this volume.

11. This ambivalence about woman's relationship to language reflects the epistemological differences between Anglo-American and French feminism (power versus pleasure, Marx versus Freud, cultural criticism versus essentialism). Showalter speculates that feminist theory's divided nature reflects, in turn, "our own divided consciousness": "We are both the daughters of the male tradition...a tradition which asks us to be rational, marginal, and grateful; and sisters in a new women's movement which engenders another kind of awareness and commitment" ("Toward" 141).

12. I am grateful to Patricia Bizzell, Maurice Géracht, Cynthia Jordan, and Carol J. Singley for their comments on this essay.

WORKS CITED

Bauer, Dale. *Feminist Dialogics.* New York: State U of New York P, 1987.

Benstock, Shari, ed. *Feminist Issues in Literary Scholarship.* Bloomington: Indiana UP, 1987.

Byatt, A. S. *Possession.* New York: Random House, 1990.

Carby, Hazel V. *Reconstructing Womanhood: The Emergence of the Afro-American Woman Novelist.* New York: Oxford UP, 1987.

Donovan, Josephine. "Toward a Women's Poetics." Benstock 98–109.

DuPlessis, Rachel Blau. "For the Etruscans." Showalter, *New* 271–91.

———. *Writing Beyond the Ending: Narrative Strategies of Twentieth-Century Women Writers.* Bloomington: Indiana UP, 1985.

Farwell, Marilyn. "Toward a Definition of the Lesbian Literary Imagination." *Signs* 14 (1988): 100–18.

Fetterley, Judith. "Reading about Reading: 'A Jury of Her Peers,' 'The Murders in the Rue Morgue,' and 'The Yellow Wallpaper.'" Flynn and Schweickart 147–64.

Flynn, Elizabeth A., and Patrocinio P. Schweickart. *Gender and Reading: Essays on Readers, Texts, and Contexts*. Baltimore: Johns Hopkins UP, 1986.

Gilbert, Sandra M., and Susan Gubar. *The Madwoman in the Attic: The Woman Writer and the Nineteenth-Century Literary Imagination*. New Haven: Yale UP, 1979.

Gubar, Susan. "'The Blank Page' and the Issues of Female Creativity." Showalter, *New* 292–313.

Hite, Molly. *The Other Side of the Story: Structures and Strategies of Contemporary Feminist Narrative*. Ithaca: Cornell UP, 1989.

Kolodny, Annette. "A Map for Rereading: Gender and the Interpretation of Literary Texts." Showalter, *New* 46–62.

Kristeva, Julia. "La femme, ce n'est jamais ça." Trans. Marilyn A. August. *New French Feminisms*. Ed. Elaine Marks and Isabel de Courtivron. Amherst: U of Massachusetts P, 1980. 137–41.

Lanser, Susan S. "Toward a Feminist Narratology." *Feminisms: An Anthology of Literary Theory and Criticism*. Ed. Robin Warhol and Diane Price Herndl. New Brunswick, NJ: Rutgers UP, 1991. 610–29.

Lipking, Lawrence. "Aristotle's Sister: A Poetics of Abandonment." *Critical Inquiry* 10 (1983): 61–81.

Lurie, Alison. *The Truth About Lorin Jones*. Boston: Little, Brown, 1988.

Marcus, Jane. "Still Practice, A/Wrested Alphabet: Toward a Feminist Aesthetic." Benstock 79–97.

Prince, Gerald. "Notes on the Text as Reader." Suleiman and Crosman 233–46.

Rich, Adrienne. "When We Dead Awaken: Writing as Re-Vision." *On Lies, Secrets, and Silence: Selected Prose 1966–1978*. New York: Norton, 1979. 33–50.

Schor, Naomi. "Fiction as Interpretation / Interpretation as Fiction." Suleiman and Crosman 165–82.

Schweickart, Patrocinio P. "Reading Ourselves: Toward a Feminist Theory of Reading." Flynn and Schweickart 31–62.

Shields, Carol. *The Box Garden*. Toronto: McGraw-Hill Ryerson, 1977.

———. *A Fairly Conventional Woman*. Toronto: Macmillan, 1982.

————. *Happenstance*. Toronto: McGraw-Hill Ryerson, 1980.

————. *The Orange Fish*. Toronto: Random House, 1989.

————. *Small Ceremonies*. Toronto: McGraw-Hill Ryerson, 1976.

————. *Swann: A Mystery*. 1987. New York: Viking, 1989.

————. *Various Miracles*. Toronto: Stoddart, 1985.

Showalter, Elaine. *A Literature of Their Own: British Women Novelists from Brontë to Lessing*. Princeton: Princeton UP, 1977.

————, ed. *The New Feminist Criticism: Essays on Women, Literature, and Theory*. New York: Random House, 1985.

————. "Toward a Feminist Poetics." Showalter, *New* 125–43.

Spacks, Patricia Meyer. *The Female Imagination*. New York: Knopf, 1975.

Suleiman, Susan R., and Inge Crosman, eds. *The Reader in the Text: Essays on Audience and Interpretation*. Princeton: Princeton UP, 1980.

Treichler, Paula A. "Escaping the Sentence: Diagnosis and Discourse in 'The Yellow Wallpaper.'" Benstock 62–78.

Wachtel, Eleanor, ed. Carol Shields Issue. *Room of One's Own* 13.1–2 (1989).

Walker, Alice. "In Search of Our Mothers' Gardens." *In Search of Our Mothers' Gardens*. New York: Harcourt Brace Jovanovich, 1984. 231–43.

Warhol, Robyn. *Gendered Intervention: Narrative Discourse in the Victorian Novel*. New Brunswick, NJ: Rutgers UP, 1990.

Woolf, Virginia. "Romance and the Heart." *The Essays of Virginia Woolf*. Ed. Andrew McNeillie. Vol. 3. San Diego: Harcourt Brace Jovanovich, 1988. 365–68.

————. *A Room of One's Own*. New York: Harcourt Brace Jovanovich, 1981.

PART 1

Anxieties of Authorship

Christine Antygrafe:
Authorial Ambivalence in the Works of Christine de Pizan

Christine Moneera Laennec

Christine de Pizan (ca. 1365–1430) is now well known as Europe's first professional female writer. This role was, by its very nature, a problematic one. Because authorship was considered a male domain, de Pizan faced the challenge of defining herself as an author and thus of redefining authorship to include women. While she enjoyed international acclaim in her own time, her writings also reveal a certain ambivalence with respect to her status as an author. In her mystical allegory, *Lavision-Christine*, de Pizan writes that she has been appointed by Philosophy as an "antygrafe" (77). This evocative word (from the Latin *antigrafus* meaning "recorder") not only indicates de Pizan's authorship, but invites us to consider it as "anti-writing"—a concisely formulated description of how, in some of her writing, she affirms her authorship while simultaneously denying it. This procedure might indeed be described as a kind of "antygraphie," a form of writing-without-having-written. In several works, for example, de Pizan creates a character, Christine, who is identified as the author—but who, far from having authority for her work, is portrayed as guided by allegorical superiors.[1] In *L' Epistre au Dieu d'Amours*, her earliest anti-misogynist polemic, de Pizan's authorship is signaled only by an anagram of her name at the end: "CREINTIS" ("fearful") (27).[2]

It is generally recognized that while de Pizan adheres to the literary conventions of her time, the very fact that she wrote means that she was in conflict with these conventions.[3] By disclaiming authority for her writing, she circumvents, on the narrative level, the difficulty inherent in being a female writer. This disavowal also allows her to display—at a rhetorical remove from the explicit themes of her text, and with great irony—considerable poetic mastery and skill; the assertion of authorial incompetence ultimately functions to emphasize her talents as a writer.[4] However, the rhetorical devices in her polemic texts are similar to those employed by the misogynists she is criticizing.[5] This raises several questions: can she effectively argue for women in a way which does not conform to misogynist discourse? How can she conduct a polemic while refusing to admit an active role as author? And what is the fear expressed by the dismemberment of the signature? This essay will address these questions by looking at how "antygraphie" functions within several of de Pizan's works.

SIGNATURES

The proper name is an essential part of what Foucault terms the "author-function": it denotes the origin of the text and thus designates the text's authority, the guarantee of its truth.[6] In de Pizan's works, the use of the proper name reveals ambivalent authorship: the character named "Christine" both invites us to identify her as the author, and at the same time displaces responsibility for the polemic from the author named Christine de Pizan.[7] Yet de Pizan was far from being an anonymous author, or even a retiring one (she supervised the production of her manuscripts and created several "anthologies" of collected works for presentation to patrons).[8] She was responsible for publishing the letters which make up *Le Débat sur le Roman de la Rose*, thereby transforming a private correspondence into a public polemic. She frequently cross-references her own work, referring to other writings by name and even, obliquely, by date.[9] It is clear that she is working with a received idea of the author as an identifiable individual responsible for his or her work: this can be seen by the fact that in the *Débat* she criticizes both *Le Roman de la Rose* and Jean de Meun himself.

L' *Epistre au Dieu d'Amours* takes the form of a letter whose authorship is attributed to Cupid,[10] with the anagram "CREINTIS" following Cupid's proclamation ordering men to cease their abuse of women. The choice not only to scramble the letters of her name, but to transform them into this particular word, is a provocative gesture. De Pizan signals to the reader that the author of the letter is not in fact Cupid, yet she also refuses to acknowledge her own authorship openly. De Pizan's works often include such permutations of the proper name. In *Le Livre de la Mutacion de Fortune*, she gives her name as "Christ + I.N.E." (20). In her lyric poetry (but not in *L' Epistre au Dieu d'Amours*) she invites the reader to look for her encoded name: "But in the last verse I want to say and tell what my name is, whoever wishes to draw it out" (*"Mais au dernier ver vueil dire et retraire / Quel est mon nom, qui le vouldra hors traire"*) (*L'oeuvre* 2:157). While her name is encoded, it is nonetheless clearly meant to be decoded: in the refrain of one of her ballads she tells the reader, "I have put my name in writing," or more literally, "I have put my name in the word 'escrit'" (*"En escrit y ay mis mon nom"*) (*L'oeuvre* 1:100).[11] In this last instance, the anagram functions on two levels: "escrit" reveals "criste," which leads by association to "Christine."

The persistence of these anagrams, of names hidden within names, derives from a tradition going back to the Latin poets, but more is at stake here: one wonders *what* she is afraid of. At the most literal level, the disguise of a proper name undoubtedly points to a dissociation of identity; de Pizan consciously fragments her identity to protect her anonymity and thus deflect criticism of her as a female writer. At a deeper level it reveals a more fundamental split between authorship and authority, a split which the misogynist tradition mandates in declaring that women cannot have access to truth, and therefore cannot have textual authority, because they are created not in God's image but in man's.[12]

THE AUTHOR AS APPRENTICE

This dissociation of authorship and authority is manifest not only at the rather discrete (but strategically significant) level of the signature, but also in works where de Pizan creates a character, Christine, who has no authority—although she obediently undertakes the task of writing the work—because she needs the correction and enlightenment of allegorical teachers. *Le Livre de la Cité des Dames* is one of several texts which, on one level, avoid responsibility or authority for their polemic message by using this narrative structure. In the *Cité*, Christine[13] is guided by Reason, Rectitude and Justice (the "Three Ladies"), who come to her when she is plunged in despair after reading a book by the misogynist author Matheolus. They help her to build the City of Ladies, made up of the anecdotal examples of women's accomplishments and noble qualities. Eloquent in its appeal and bitingly critical at points, the polemic of the *Cité* is in fact always an indirect one: Christine is subordinate to other fictional characters and concedes to their anger rather than expressing any on her own behalf. It is Justice and not Christine who expresses outrage at the treatment of women; Christine merely agrees with the arguments put forth by her interlocutors: "Now my lady, I indeed understand more than before why you spoke of the enormous ingratitude, not to say ignorance, of these men who malign women" (80) ("*Ha! dame, or apperçoy par ce que vous dittes, plus qu'oncques mais, la tres grant ingratitude et descongnoissance d'iceulx hommes qui tant mesdient des femmes*" [751]).

Christine is convinced by her allegorical superiors, just as de Pizan wishes her readers to be convinced. But the authority for the content of the book, the forceful arguments against misogyny, comes not from Christine but from her allegorical teachers. Only in the final chapter, "The end of the book: Christine addresses the ladies" (254) ("*La fin du livre, parle Christine aux dames*" [1031]), does Christine speak directly to her readers. Her speech, however, is a summary of the Three Ladies' teachings, and ends with an exhortation to women to put up even with physical mistreatment from their husbands. This advice, if anything, detracts from the force of the preceding chapters: while the Three Ladies tell Christine stories of women's physical and intellectual accomplishments, Christine appears to undercut their arguments by telling women to let themselves be subjugated.

The same narrative technique is evident in *Le Livre des Fais d'Armes et de Chevallerie*. In this work, a war manual written for noblemen, de Pizan uses the device of the master and apprentice in the last half of the book. Here the abdication of authorial responsibility is used both to distance herself from her text and to minimize the problem of its obviously "unsuitable" authorship. Only by emphasizing her own lack of authority and her dependence on the knowledge of others does she have a chance of being taken seriously. In the first half of the work, de Pizan defers to classical authors for her subject matter but then introduces a teacher who personifies the authority of the classical writers. Christine's "master"—who is described as "a weighty ancient wise man, a judge of authority" (*"un pesant ancien saige auttorisié juge"* [184])—tells her that he will help "to found part of your edifice, in the making of which I, as the master, will help you, as the disciple" (*"fonder partie de ton dit ediffice, auquel parfaire je comme maistre et tu soyes disciple, y seray en ton ayde"* [185]). The second half is structured around a series of questions which Christine poses and her "master" solves, again apparently allowing de Pizan to abdicate authority for her own work.

In these works, the text itself is constituted by the responses of Christine's teachers, who uphold the authority and responsibility for its content. De Pizan portrays Christine the apprentice as a mere scribe, writing only with the aid of figures more informed than she, who have themselves provided the substance for the work. Christine's lack of authority in the narrative structure is emphasized by constant references to her intellectual deficiencies. Reason, for example, is careful to point out things which Christine may not have grasped: after recounting the story of the Creation, she says of Eve, "I don't know if you have already noted this: she was created in the image of God" (23) (*"Je ne sçay se tu le nottes; elle fu fourmee a l'image de Dieu"* [651]).[14] In the *Cité*, even Christine's role as scribe is presented as one which she passively accepts rather than initiates (11 [630]).

De Pizan seems further to disclaim responsibility for these texts by feigning intellectual weakness. She emphasizes the superiority of the allegorical teachers to the character Christine. It is startling to note the extent to which de Pizan humiliates her textual representative, who constantly belittles herself and excuses herself for speaking. Near the end of the *Cité*, for example, she says, "I would like to ask you several questions, if I were sure that they would not bother you" (*"moult voulentiers vous feroye aucunes demandes, se je savoye que anuyer ne vous deust"*), to which Rectitude patiently replies, "Friend, ask what you like, for the disciple who must ask the master questions in order to learn ought not to suffer reproof for inquiring about everything" (186) (*"Amye, dis ce qu'il te plaira, car le disciple qui pour apprendre demande au maistre ne doit estre repris se il enquiert de toutes choses"* [926]).

This intellectual weakness, rather than a peripheral thematic element, is central to the very possibility of writing in the first place. The claim of weakness provides the catalyst for writing: when Christine falls into a deep depression after reading Matheolus, Reason rebukes her, saying, "simple-mindedness has prompted you to hold such an opinion" (8) (*"simplesce t'a meue a la present oppinion"* [625]). The entire book which follows is essentially a correction of Christine's mistaken initial reaction to her reading of Matheolus. In this work as in others, authorship and authority are effectively split on the narrative level: Christine the narrator acknowledges authorship, but not authority, for the work. The mastery and authority implied by authorship reside entirely with the allegorical teachers.

De Pizan's relegation of her representative in the text to a passive conveyor of a polemic expressed by beings much wiser than herself ultimately reveals an adept and complex assertion of narrative competence. Furthermore, she employs her fictional teachers to legitimize not only the particular work in which they appear, but to authorize all of her writing. In *Lavision*, she asks Opinion to tell her if she has been mistaken in past works: "may it please you to tell me whether, in the things engendered by you that are written in my compilations and volumes, I have erred in any way" (*"plaise vous me certifier. se es choses par vous engendrees qui en mes compillacions et volumes sont declairiees se en aucune chose yay erre"* [143]). Dame Opinion answers, not surprisingly, in the negative. This disingenuous doubt serves to justify not only *Lavision*, but de Pizan's entire *oeuvre*.

MISOGYNIST DISCOURSE

That the apparent evasion of authorial responsibility is an important strategy becomes clear in the context of the target of de Pizan's polemic, namely, defamation of women. A close look at her anti-misogynist texts shows that, paradoxically, her own writing in many ways fits her definition of misogynist discourse (such as her use of quoting and examples). This may explain to some extent de Pizan's reluctance to assume responsibility for a text which conforms to the kind of writing that it condemns. The fear implicit in "CREINTIS" might be interpreted as reflecting both de Pizan's trepidation at undertaking a polemic against the misogynist tradition, and her anxiety about conforming to this tradition.[15]

De Pizan discusses the nature of "diffamation" (a word she uses to refer specifically to attacks on women) in *L'Epistre au Dieu d'Amours* when describing how misogynists attack women:

> Several clerks put the blame on them [women]. They write compositions, rhymes, prose and verse, defaming their morals with various words....In verses they tell how Adam, David, Sampson, Solomon and many others were deceived by women....And this is what clerks do morning and night, first in French and then in Latin. And they base their claims on who knows what books, books that tell more lies than a drunkard.

> *De pluseurs clers qui sus leur mettent blasmes,*
> *Dittiez en font, rimes, proses et vers,*
> *En diffamant leur meurs par moz divers*
> . . . .
>
> *En vers dient, Adam, David, Sanson,*
> *Et Salemon et autres a foison*
> *Furent deceuz par femme main et tart*
> . . . .
>
> *Et ainsi font clers et soir et matin,*
> *Puis en françois, leur vers, puis en latin,*
> *Et se fondent dessus ne sçay quelz livres*
> *Qui plus dient de mençonges qu'uns yvres.* (9–10)

These "diffamateurs" are men who write: *clercs* who ceaselessly heap abuse on women in every possible literary form, in both French and Latin. The force of their discourse is guaranteed by the authority of books (even if de Pizan breezily dismisses them as "books that tell more lies than a drunkard"). Textual authority—of paramount importance for the success of de Pizan's own polemic against the misogynists—is established in two closely related ways: by giving examples (Adam, David, Sampson and Solomon), and using quotations. These two classic scholastic practices are rhetorical strategies which de Pizan characterizes as misogynist, but they are also at the heart of her own polemic against the misogynists. Examples constitute the very narrative fabric of the *Cité*, and de Pizan relies heavily on the power of proof by illustration. After a litany of no less than thirty-two examples, Justice refers the reader to Vincent de Beauvais' *Speculum Historiale*: "If you want more examples, there you will find a great many" (234) (*"se plus en veulx avoir...la assez en trouveras* [1000]). This technique is not limited to the *Cité*; in *Lavision*, Opinion tells Christine: "you could never in all your life...hear all the examples, they are so many and so varied" (*"ne pourroies en ta vie...tous les exemples ouir / tant en ya et si divers sont"* [142]).

It is also interesting to note that there are points at which de Pizan refuses to acknowledge the admissibility of the examples used by the misogynists, such as those in Matheolus' book. In the *Epistre au Dieu d'Amours*, she states that women are peace-loving and says that examples to the contrary are exceptions and therefore invalid:

> And whoever wishes to disprove my argument with stories or the Bible, giving me examples of one or two women, or of several together who have been wicked and bad, all the same, these women are not normal.

> *Et qui vouldra par hystoire ou par bible*
> *Me rampronner, pour moy donner exemple*
> *D'une ou de deux ou de pluseurs ensemble*
> *Qui ont esté reprouvées et males,*
> *Encore en soit celles mais enormales* (21)

"Bad" women in the *Cité* are likewise explained away as "monsters in nature" (18) (*"monstres de la nature"* [643]). This merely shows that de Pizan's use of examples does not differ from that of Matheolus, for each side can deploy a multitude of examples to "prove" his or her point.

Furthermore, de Pizan is inconsistent in her use of examples. Even though they are meant to provide conclusive, authoritative proof, it is clear, even upon a casual reading, that examples do not function as stable referents in these texts: the same stories are recounted with widely divergent plots. Furthermore, she also modifies the stories of well-known legendary figures, using them to her own purposes. Medea is a striking illustration: she appears in the *Cité*, the *Epistre au Dieu d'Amours*, and the *Epistre d'Othea* as an example of a resourceful, powerful woman betrayed by a man, but de Pizan conveniently omits any reference to Medea's famed infanticide.[16] Quotations and examples function similarly in her texts: both are used by misogynists and by de Pizan to reinforce their arguments.[17] If the *Cité* is essentially composed of examples, the *Livre des Fais d'Armes* is similarly made up of quotations either from the classical authors or from Christine's master. The importance of quotation as a means of conferring an authority on her work which it would otherwise lack is made explicit in the *Livre des Fais d'Armes*, in which de Pizan defends her use of quotation. Here the master tells Christine:

> if anyone murmurs, as gossips will do, saying that you have gone begging [for material for your book], I say to them that it is a common practice among my disciples to give to one another and share the flowers that they take from my gardens....Did not Jean de Meun, in his *Romance of the Rose*, borrow from Guillaume de Lorris' writings? And it is the case with the others as well. So it is not a cause for reproach, but rather for praise when sources are well and properly applied: therein lies mastery, and it is a sign of having seen and read many books.

> *se aucuns murmurent selon l'usaige des mesdisans, disant que autre part mendies, je leur respons que c'est commun usaige entre mes disciples de eulx entredonner et departir des fleurs que ilz prennent en mes jardins....Comment, ne s'ayda pas Jehan de Meun en son Livre de la Rose des diz de Lauris, et semblablement d'autres? Sy n'est point de reprouche ains est louenge quant bien et proprement sont appliquiez. Et la gist la maistrise et est signe d'avoir foison veu et visité mains livres.* (185)

The similarities between de Pizan's writing and that of her adversaries is brought out very forcefully in this passage. Not only does she justify her use of other authors by citing Jean de Meun—whom she condemns for different reasons in the *Débat*—but she openly admits that quoting (one of the cornerstones of misogynist discourse according to the *Cité*) serves to show how much an author has read.

In addition to using examples and quotations, de Pizan describes several other qualities of misogynist writing which are related to textual authority and which she exhibits in her own work. In the *Cité*, Reason explains the misogynists' need to demonstrate that they are well read in their attacks against women: "In order to show they have read many authors, [they] base their own writings on what they have found in books and repeat what other writers have said and cite different authors" (19) ("*pour monstrer que ilz ont biaucoup veu d'escriptures, se fondent sur ce qu'ilz ont trouvé en livres et dient aprés les autres et aleguent les autteurs*" [643]). The defensive gesture of displaying one's erudition is certainly true of de Pizan as well as of the misogynists, and is a corollary to the strategy of lending textual authority by using examples and quotation. Reason also tells Christine that the misogynists' anger is caused by impotence: "Nature, which allows the will of the heart to put into effect what the powerful appetite desires, has grown cold in them.... They do not know how to overcome their sadness except by attacking women" (18–19) ("*nature est reffroidie en eulx qui ne sueffre a la voulenté du couraige mettre a effect ce que l'appetit sans puissance vouldroit....Sy ne scevent comment evaporer et mettre hors leur tristesce fors par blasmer les femmes*" [644]). Reason clearly refers here to sexual impotence, but a parallel can be seen in de Pizan's own polemic. In portraying Christine the apprentice-narrator as helpless, and in taking an indirect authorial stance in both the *Epistre au Dieu d'Amours* and the *Cité*, she may be motivated by exactly the same kind of impotent rage as Matheolus.

De Pizan is thus both at odds with the misogynist tradition and at the same time inescapably part of it. She uses the same rhetorical techniques as the misogynists to argue against them. One has to wonder, therefore, whether there is an alternative open to her, other than that of remaining silent. Reading her polemic texts as an attempt to criticize her opponents' conclusions, while borrowing their methods, would explain the profoundly ambivalent attitude toward authorship and authority in her works: in her use of allegorical superiors, examples and quotation, de Pizan distances herself from her own discourse, and is able thereby to avoid the implications of the conflict between what she is writing and how she is writing. Certainly she expresses insecurity regarding her authority in the text, but she ultimately uses it to confirm this authority. Although her own strategy resembles that of misogynist texts, insofar as both base their claims on acknowledged textual authority, she also undermines this tradition both explicitly (by criticizing the patriarchal system which upholds it) and implicitly (by affirming the ironic paradox of her own authorial ambivalence).

Just as in the *Livre des Fais d'Armes* Christine's teacher brings up the possibility of "gossips" accusing her of begging for material for her books, so in *Lavision* Opinion mentions that some people accuse her of not writing her books herself. Despite such accusations, Opinion at least recognizes their value:

> Some say that clerks or monks forge your works for you, and that they could not come from the mind of a woman. But those people who say this are fools...others say that your style is too obscure and difficult to understand, and thus it is not enjoyable....I advise you to continue writing as you have, for your work is good.
>
> *les aucuns dient que clers ou religieux les te forgent / et que de sentement de femme venir ne pourroyent. Mais ce sont les ignorans qui ce dient...les autres dient ton stille estre trop obscur et que on ne lentent si nest si delictable....Si te conseil que ton euvre tu continues comme elle soit iuste[.]* (143–44)

This thorough rebuttal of the criticism of de Pizan's work is a brilliant and ironic demonstration of poetic mastery: the mention of readers who complain of her obscurity and difficulty, immediately following the charge that her works could not have been written by a woman, is an especially humorous assertion of her erudition and accomplishments.

To have placed this vindication of her work in the mouth of a fictional figure of authority is also highly ironic. It no doubt confirms de Pizan's real lack of authority in the eyes of many of her less generous male readers, but it ultimately proves her poetic mastery. It is telling that these evocations of challenges to her authority—doubting not only her knowledge and mastery of the subject, but her having written the works at all—revolve around the question of quotation, for she is accused of having passed off other texts as her own work. She suggests that the scholastic, institutionalized device of using quotation and examples might be turned against her simply because she is a woman. And indeed, de Pizan works both to uphold and resist such a reading: while her complex narrative structures tend to undermine her authority, they ultimately affirm her talents—and these complexities would have been well appreciated by a medieval audience.

READING ANTI-WRITING

The drawback of refusing responsibility for one's work is that one risks being denied credit for it. While de Pizan uses the pose of helplessness to reinforce her arguments in a strategically effective manner, such that she thwarts any intentions her opponents might have had of ignoring either her presence or her ability as a writer, at the same time her strategy of authorial ambivalence may have worked only too well. Although internationally known in her own time, she was soon forgotten and is only now being rediscovered. "CREINTIS" could be read as signifying not simply fear of revealing her female identity to a hostile readership, but fear of the consequences of dismembering that identity. De Pizan thus expresses a very modern anxiety about language itself, an anxiety precisely about the relationship of language to what it signifies. Her ambivalent authorial stance points to the impossibility of being in control of language, and thereby to the impossibility of having "authority" (in all the textually weighted meaning of the term)—an illusion, some would say, which is symptomatic of a masculine and logocentric concept of language. Christine de Pizan is embraced by modern readers as one of the first authors to speak for and to women of all time. But at what price did she speak? And how was her speech shaped by factors outside her control? Contemporary feminist scholarship shows that we live in a gendered world and that language itself is gendered: de Pizan's authorial ambivalence indicates that, five hundred years ago, she was well aware of this fact.[18]

NOTES

1. Such works include the *Livre du Chemin de Long Estude,* the *Livre de la Cité des Dames,* the *Livre des Trois Vertus, Lavision,* and the second half of the *Livre des Fais d'Armes.*

2. All translations are mine, except for Richards' translation of *The Book of the City of Ladies.*

3. Critics who study how de Pizan situates her work vis-à-vis her predecessors and contemporaries include Bell, Blumenfeld-Kosinski, Delany, Phillippy, and Quilligan.

4. Brownlee argues that in de Pizan's last work, a tribute to Joan of Arc, she validates her status as author by portraying herself as part of an important historical moment.

5. As Richards says, "The success of her advocacy of sexual equality depended somewhat ironically on her mastering a clerical tradition permeated with misogyny" (23).

6. Foucault specifically mentions the need for such an authorial guarantee in the Middle Ages (149).

7. While it is true that earlier medieval authors commonly referred to themselves by first name only ("Chrétien" and not "de Troyes"), by the late fourteenth and early fifteenth centuries this practice had begun changing to the use of last name only ("Machaut," "Villon"). It is interesting to speculate whether referring to oneself by first name alone is a feminine practice; it certainly seems to be accepted when others refer to women (why do we speak, for instance, of "Abélard and Héloise" rather than "Pierre and Héloise"?).

8. See Dulac, and Willard 45ff, 100, 107.

9. See, for example, *The Book of the City of Ladies* 165, 43; *Lavision-Christine* 135, 142, 164; *The Treasure of the City of Ladies* 31, 98; *Le Débat sur le Roman de la Rose* 17.

10. The "au" in the title of this work means "from": it is an epistle written by (and not to) Cupid, the God of Love.

11. For other instances of anagrammatical signatures, see Cerquiglini's excellent introduction to de Pizan's *Cent ballades d'amant et de dame* 23.

12. Saint Paul states quite explicitly: "I permit no woman to teach or to have authority over man; she is to keep silent. For Adam was formed first, then Eve" (Timothy 1, 2:12–13). On this topic, see Bloch.

13. I distinguish between the character/narrator and the author by referring to the former as Christine and the latter as de Pizan.

14. De Pizan here refutes Paul's words (see n.12) and thus can be said to claim—indirectly—the right to authorship.

15. Margolis argues that de Pizan believed that "one learns from 'within the system' and by serving 'the enemy' before liberating oneself from it" (362). A conscious decision to learn the enemy's ways would not exclude the possibility of feeling anxiety about undertaking this task.

16. Delany also makes this point (84). Another interesting modification appears in the *Epistre au Dieu d'Amours*, in which Cupid argues that in the true story of the creation, Eve was made first, not Adam (607–08).

17. The link between quotation and authority is clearly evident in the fourteenth-century word *"auctorité,"* which means both "authority" and "quotation".

18. I am very grateful to Claire Nouvet for her help and encouragement in reading "antygraphie."

WORKS CITED

Bell, Susan Groag. "Christine de Pizan (1364–1430): Humanism and the Problem of a Studious Woman." *Feminist Studies* 3 (1976): 173–84.

Bloch, R. Howard. "Medieval Misogyny: Woman as Riot." *Representations* 20 (1987): 1–24.

Blumenfeld-Koskinski, Renate. "Christine de Pizan and the Misogynistic Tradition." *Romanic Review* 81 (1990): 279–92.

Brownlee, Kevin. "Structures of Authority in Christine de Pizan's *Ditié de Jehanne d'Arc.*" *Discourses of Authority in Medieval and Renaissance Literature.* Ed. Kevin Brownlee and Walter Stephens. Hanover: UP of New England, 1989. 131–50.

Delany, Sheila. "Rewriting Woman Good: Gender and the Anxiety of Influence in Two Late-Medieval Texts." "'Mothers to Think Back Through': Who are They? The Ambiguous Example of Christine de Pizan." *Medieval Literary Politics: Shapes of Ideology.* Ed. Sheila Delany. Manchester: Manchester UP, 1990. 74–87, 88–103.

de Pizan, Christine. *The Book of the City of Ladies.* Trans. Earl Jeffrey Richards. New York: Persea, 1982.

———. *Cent ballades d'amant et de dame.* Ed. Jacqueline Cerquiglini. Paris: Union Générale d'Editions, 1982.

———. *Le Débat sur le Roman de la Rose.* Ed. Eric Hicks. Paris: Champion, 1977.

———. *L'Epistre au Dieu d'Amours. L'oeuvre* 2:1-27.

———. *Lavision-Christine.* Ed. Sister Mary Towner. Washington, DC: Catholic U of America P, 1932.

————. *Le Livre de la Cité des Dames.* Ed. Maureen C. Curnow. Diss. Vanderbilt University, 1975.

————. *Le Livre de la Mutacion de Fortune.* Ed. Suzanne Solente. Paris: Société des Anciens Textes Français, 1959-66.

————. *Le Livre des Fais d'Armes et de Chevallerie.* Ed. Christine Moneera Laennec. Diss. Yale University, 1988.

————. *L'oeuvre poétique complète de Christine de Pisan.* Ed. Maurice Roy. 3 vols. Paris: Didot, 1886-96.

————. *The Treasure of the City of Ladies or the Book of the Three Virtues.* Trans. Sarah Lawson. Middlesex: Penguin, 1985.

Dulac, Liliane. "La figure de l'écrivain dans quelques traités en prose de Christine de Pizan." *Figures de l'écrivain au moyen âge (Actes du Colloque du Centre d'Etudes Médiévales de l'Université de Picardie).* Goppingen: Kummerle Verlag, 1991. 113-23.

Foucault, Michel. "What Is an Author?" *Textual Strategies: Perspectives in Post-Structuralist Criticism.* Ed. Josué V. Harari. Ithaca: Cornell UP, 1979. 141-60.

Margolis, Nadia. "Christine de Pizan: The Poetess as Historian." *Journal of the History of Ideas* 47 (1986): 361-75.

Phillipy, Patricia A. "Establishing Authority: Boccaccio's *De Claris Mulieribus* and Christine de Pizan's *Le Livre de la Cité des Dames.*" *Romanic Review* 77 (1986): 167-94.

Quilligan, Maureen. "Allegory and the Textual Body: Female Authority in Christine de Pizan's *Livre de la Cité des Dames.*" *Romanic Review* 79 (1988): 222-48.

Richards, Earl Jeffrey. "Christine de Pizan and the Question of Feminist Rhetoric." *Teaching Language Through Literature* 22 (1983): 15-24.

Willard, Charity Cannon. *Christine de Pizan: Her Life and Works.* New York: Persea, 1984.

Our Bodies / Our Texts?: Renaissance Women and the Trials of Authorship

Wendy Wall

Historians and literary critics have amply demonstrated that women in early modern England persistently found themselves constrained by the norms of acceptable feminine behavior. Strictures against education for women, coupled with a cultural obsession with female modesty, worked to privatize women (Kelso 59–60; Stallybrass). In *The Instruction of Christian Women*, Juan Vives characteristically advises: "it neither becommeth a woman...to live amonge men, or speake abroade...it were better to be at home within and unknowen to other folkes" (sig. C6r; qtd. in Lamb 114). Given such widespread injunctions, it is hardly surprising that few women would dare to *write*, to enter the frighteningly sexual and political world of textual circulation. It is inadequate, however, to say that women's anxieties about authorship were solely the product of their gender; men also felt compelled to offer elaborate justifications for their texts. In the sixteenth-century socio-literary system, privilege was afforded to writers who circulated their works privately within elite circles; all writers risked estrangement from the social sources of power when they chose to publish (Saunders). Public writing was aligned with the increasingly more mobile social groups who posed a threat to the institution of patronage. It was not just female modesty, but aristocratic practice, that discouraged authorship.

This is not to say that gender is not at issue. On the contrary, as a means of asserting their literary authority within a social milieu resistant to publication, male writers often justify their works through highly gendered language. Nancy Vickers

describes the Petrarchan reflexes of reification and fragmentation that were popular in sixteenth-century culture, strategies
by which sonneteers articulated desire by linguistically dismembering the female body through the blazon. Vickers's argument can be extended to the text's materiality. Writers and publishers eagerly seized upon the logic of the "blazon" (meaning
in one definition "to publish") as a ground for textual presentation: the representation of book as female body allowed the
writer to deprivatize himself by re-privatizing the woman; he
could thus solidify a shaky textual authority by an appeal to a
more established hierarchy (Wall).

For women, the general problems of writing were exacer-
bated by the male-coded ideology of authorship fueled by concerns over social mobility. When women wrote, privately or
publicly, they had to confront forms and figures that alienated
them from the position of speaking subject. If women felt anxiety about their status as authors, it was not a hazy psychological
concern over their exclusion from literary history, but an awareness that their task transgressed both gender boundaries and
the decorum of literary presentation. If women were tropes necessary to the process of writing, with what authority could a
woman publish? How could she become an author if she was
the Other against which "authors" differentiated themselves? If
she was the body of the text?

Mary Sidney's prefatorial poem to her translation of the
Psalms, "To the Angell Spirit of the Most Excellent Sir Philip Sidney," and Amelia Lanyer's *Salve Deus Rex Judaeorum* document
how the female writer grappled with the gender code subtending literary paradigms. What Sidney and Lanyer do in these
religious works is startling: they devise novel ways of imagining the male body so as to renegotiate the relationship between
writer, text, and reader. Their works stage the anxieties of
female writing by playfully reconstructing the techniques of
corporeal representation dear to authorial presentation. Ann
Rosalind Jones has called attention to the importance of seeing
Renaissance women's writing as "situational": "Prohibitions on
women's intercourse with the literary world were not as paralyzing as they were intended to be. Their effect was not to
silence women but to provoke them into complex forms of
negotiation and compromise" (92). I want to argue that Lanyer

and Sidney create symbolic modes ("bricolages" of social dictates, in Jones' terms) that intervene in the emerging concept of authorship. In other words, they write within and against an ideologically problematic discourse, revising the representations of the female body fueled by Petrarchism that positioned them as written text rather than writing subject.

THE BROTHER'S CORPSE/CORPUS:
THE CASE OF MARY SIDNEY

Because of their guilty lineage from Eve, women were frequently exhorted to meditate, pray and read the scriptures. As Elaine Beilin points out, women took these injunctions to heart, publishing works that sought to define the ideal of Christian life and to glorify "female" Christian virtues. The title of Margaret Hannay's recent collection of Renaissance women's writing, *Silent But for the Word*, encapsulates the exceptional nature of religious publications as legitimate projects for women. And Margaret Tyler's preface to her translation of French romance calls attention to the genre-specific interdictions on women's writing; she mentions detractors who would "enforce me necessarily either not to write or to write of divinitie" (sig. A4v). Mary Sidney was one writer who chose to write a text that was not only traditional in its religious subject, but also a mediation of another, more masculine text—a translation of the *Psalms*.[1] In translating biblical verse, Sidney asserts an authority exemplary of prescribed piety and protected by its mediated status.

Although Sidney translated other works by Philip de Mornay and Petrarch, the *Psalms* are the only text in which we see how she would present her writing for readers. Though the work was never published, she carefully designed it for presentation to the Queen, prefacing the poems with two verse dedications, "To the Angell Spirit" and "Even now that Care" (also referred to as "To the Thrice Sacred Queen Elizabeth"), that explained and justified her status as author. The *Psalms* went on to become highly public texts, circulating widely enough to be read by Donne, Lanyer and Herbert, and surviving to be disseminated in the next centuries. Her other works, those without prefatorial justifications, interestingly did not achieve such fame.[2]

The *Psalms* were a particularly appropriate text for Sidney because they both signalled an allegiance to her brother and provided a religious version of secular literary forms associated with the Sidney family. Mary Sidney coauthored the text with Philip, revising his forty *Psalms* and writing ninety of her own after his death. In the poetic and formal challenges they offer, the *Psalms* constitute a religious version of the Petrarchan love complaint popularized largely by Philip Sidney's *Astrophel and Stella*. David's poems not only provide a discourse mobile enough for probing a range of intense emotions—grief, exaltation, desolation—but enable metrical and stanzaic experimentation through the generation of multiple, serial personae. By rehearsing the eloquent and often eroticized submission to a higher authority found in David's language, Sidney explores the issue of sovereignty/subjection central to the discourse of love. The *Psalms* bemoan loss, offering a poetic description of what David calls the "downcast state." It is telling that Philip Sidney turned to these translations when banished from court. The mingled voices of Sidney and David note that enemies level bitter words at them "as if not words but shafts they were" (M. Sidney 117). Through this mediated verse, Sidney imitates the speaking position in "male" symbolic modes, one which turns on controlled subjection and embattled rescue through the appropriated shaft of language.

In her introductory poems, Sidney makes clear that the authoritative ground for the text is not its divine subject, but her brother. Philip Sidney's hand in the project sanctioned the collaborative enterprise: "he did warpe, I weav'd this webbe to end" ("Even" 89). Through the metaphor of weaving, Sidney denotes her role as perfunctory, his as imaginative. She further effaces her authorial role in an address to Philip in which she lauds him as her source:

> To thee pure sprite, to thee alones addres't
>   this coupled worke, by double int'rest thine:
>   First rais'de by thy blest hand, and what is mine
> inspird by thee, thy secrett power imprest. ("Angell" 92)

Although Philip did not publish his own works when alive, his death authorizes the publication of his texts, as well as those of others who discursively mourn his demise. The apocalyptic moment of the final departure overshadows any social repercussions generated by public display. Here Mary Sidney uses that authorization in her private text. While her insistence on a circumscribed audience is reiterated in her declaration to Philip that her work "hath no further scope to goe / nor other purpose but to honor thee," her modest claims ironically proved her an accomplished and public poet, "imprest" with secret power and a broad "scope." Sidney's prefatorial poem thus names Philip as the origin of her *Psalms* and the rationale for their circulation. When she admits that the "coupled work" is now a solo performance (telling the Queen: "Which once in two, now in one Subject goe / The poorer left, the richer reft awaye"), her words emphasize the trace of the "richer" one in the text that validates the work (88). From the grave, "reft awaye," Philip is able to project his (and her) voice to a reading audience. Seemingly mediating this ethereal projection, Sidney appropriates his "secrett power," one that vindicates her literary endeavor and disguises the transgression of her writing.[3]

In casting Philip as the text's "richer" origin, Sidney's poem regenders and literalizes the concept of the Muse itself, an icon often evoked in eroticizing the moment of literary production. When Milton notes that his heavenly muse visits him nocturnally in bed, he plays off a traditional depiction of literary texts as the progeny of male writer and female muse. In his "Epigram on the Court Pucell," Ben Jonson amplifies this notion when he guardedly praises Cecilia Bulstrode's writing as "equall with the best" although "with Tribade lust she force a Muse" (*Underwood* 44:222). "Tribade," according to the OED, suggests "the unnatural acts women perform upon one another." Jonson's use of this homoerotic term places the female writer in a socially awkward position. If the writer and muse conventionally dally together in creating a text, then the conventional gender of the muse makes authorship a masculine business. Yet by making Philip into her muse, Sidney disrupts conventional sexual metaphors for textual production, particularizing the abstractions that traditionally fueled writing.

"To the Angell Spirit" plays upon this tradition by depicting the "muse" as interactive, casting the ensuing work as the product of an erotic entanglement. Her muse and Philip's "combine" to produce a child: that text which is first "raised" by Philip's hand and later described as well "borne" (in the sense of carried forth and birthed). The elegaic mode allows an impassioned outpouring of love that frames Sidney's place in the writing process. By tantalizingly disclosing her muse as a conjugal duo, Sidney attaches free-floating anxieties about the sexualizing effect of writing to this (barely suppressed) promiscuous mingling; sexuality is contained within the sibling relationship. She hints at the provocative nature of this coupling: "So dar'd my Muse with thine it selfe combine." The Muse is not only literalized, but its textual erotics is staged within the family.

Sidney's address is couched in amplified Petrarchan language: she gathers her thoughts like tributaries to the sea, she performs an accounting of the "strange passions" in her heart, she proclaims the limits of language. "To his Angell Spirit" blends broken bodies, monetary language, eternizing conceits, and hyperbolic praise—in short, it trades heavily on typical Petrarchan poetic conventions. Like other Renaissance writers, Sidney also uses the intensified Petrarchan image of textual corporeality to introduce her work. Many Renaissance writers employed the analogy of the text as female body—holding forth a ravished maiden to be mastered by its author or a blazoned body to be admired by its reader. In his preface to *Tancrede and Gismund* (1591), for instance, Robert Wilmot tells his friend: "I am bold to present Gismund to your sights, and unto yours only, for therefore have I conjured her…that she waxe not so proud of her fresh painting, to straggle her plumes abroad, but to contein her self within the walls of your house" (Gebert 77). Wilmot's trope highlights the more pervasive but tenuous associations made between text and woman in poetic forms such as the sonnet sequence.

Sidney's text sallies forth as a wounded body, painfully aware of its loss of male author.[4] In calling her work a "half maim'd peece" with "deepe wounds enlarg'd, long festered in their gall / fresh bleeding smart," Sidney draws upon the conventional body metaphors associated with the violent metaphors of Petrarchan emotion (92). But her language is peculiarly emphatic about the text's injuries:

> …Theise dearest offrings of my hart
> dissolv'ed to Inke, while penns impressions move
> the bleeding veines of never dying love:

> I render here: these wounding lynes of smart
> sadd Characters indeed of simple love
> not Art nor skill which abler wits doe prove. (95)

Her evocation of "wounding lynes" conflates her own grief at her brother's loss with David's grief and with Philip Sidney's wounds on the battlefield. In describing the maimed text through a series of adjectival clauses, the poem creates a set of imprecise grammatical associations, a string of modifiers that refer to Philip's body (called forth at the beginning of the stanza). Philip's body blends with that of the *Psalms*—both wounded, bereft, and incomplete. Rather than constructing the mastery of the curative editor, the text authorizes itself through the piecemeal body of a culturally resonant, dead man. Philip's death enables his representation as the physical and textual commodity. Mourning is the public operation, one perhaps even more authorized for women than men, that allows Sidney to rewrite Petrarchan codes of power. Sidney thus revises the strategy of presenting the displayed "weak" text by holding up her martyred brother's heroic wounded body to deflect attention from the bravado of her act of writing. Philip's body stands as a sign of her ambivalent position as female writer, registering as well as assuaging the anxiety of writing.

Another of Sidney's central tropes, that of clothing, alters the resonances of the body metaphor. As a series of "holy garments" alternately worn by David, the reader, and Elizabeth, and as an artifact stitched, warped, weaved, and attired, the text seems to shroud the broken body, to drop a veil over the corporeal object through a craft that is decidedly aristocratic, domestic, and female. The text thus revels in its ability to call forth the body and make pieces of limbs become "peec't" cloth. In this way, the work names itself as wounded body only to evoke its ability to cover over its own textual lack. The poem's formulation is particularly interesting given the Freudian gloss on weaving as the labor of compensation for the "lack" inherent in woman. The work may manipulate the readerly "gaze" in displaying the aristocratic male body, but it problematizes that staging by enshrouding the body in elegiac text; by alternating self-referential metaphors, the poem both regenders and disrupts the poetics of corporeal display central to male writers' self-authorizing rhetoric. The poem may represent "the gratitude and discomfort [Sidney] felt at having to use [Philip's] example to find her own means of expression," as Beth Wynn Fisken notes (266); but it also reveals how Sidney is able to use a debilitating discourse for her own purposes, expressing emotions—piety and grief—in a literary form that clears a space within the ideology of authorship for an alternative poetics of display.

Sidney's poignant self-erasure in this process of revision may disturb modern readers. At one moment, she claims that her project is to immortalize Philip by making him a twinkling star—her "stella," in effect—by relegating herself to blackness: "thou art fixt among thy fellow lights, my day put out." The self-abnegation evident in this invisibility, however, takes on new meaning when it is stylistically dramatized in the next stanza. As if to demonstrate this seeming erasure, the stanza omits the subject "I," instead piling up a stack of language that finally reveals her place in the process of building Philip's corpus:

> As goodly buildings to some glorious ende
>   cut of by fate, before the graces hadde
>   each wondrous part in all their beauties cladde,
> Yet so much done, as Art could not amende;
>   So thy rare workes to which no witt can adde,
>   in all men's eies, which are not blindely madde,
> Beyonde compare above all praise, extende. (94)

The last verb hangs alone, demanding that the reader retrospectively apply a subject to the stanza that can govern these clauses. Although ambiguously related to the subject "rare workes" (which enact a moment of self-extension), this verb points as well to the subject "I," which is never spoken, but governs not only the rhetorical structure, but the act of poetic extension (I extend these works, which seem sufficient so as to need no aid, but only a mere expansion). The dislocated final verb forces the reader to reconstruct the dense grammatical organization of the stanza to *find* that subject. The mastery of this stylistic erasure/disclosure, which exemplifies her "day put out," paradoxically serves to foreground her poetic presence. Philip's absent body, like his missing poems (both cut off by fate, both full of "wondrous parts"), enables her mystified but persistent presence.

Sidney garnered authority from the cultural legend that she helped to create, a legend that authorized her production of Philip's works as well as her own. In revising and presenting publicly the text he named for her, *The Countess of Pembroke's Arcadia*, Mary Sidney was in all probability responsible for "bowdlerizing" the romance: she erases an attempted rape and an adulterous night of passion (Ringler). In doing so, she appropriates editorial and creative power in the service of cleansing the text. In the preface to the 1593 edition, Hugh Sanford notes that "it is now by more than one interest *The Countess of Pembroke's Arcadia*: done, as it was, for her: as it is, by her" (60). To this Renaissance publisher, by editing the work Sidney shifted her position from that of dedicatee to author. If manuscript circulation fostered a view of textuality that generally blends subject and object,[5] the female writer capitalized on this in becoming her own titled text. John Aubrey even asserts, in a history of the Sidney family, that Mary Sidney wrote the poems in the *Arcadia* since "they seem to have been writt by a woman" (qtd. in Waller, *Mary* 4). While Aubrey's justification is hardly convincing, his confusion stems from the unique authority she had over the text. She appropriated her brother's power as she edited his language. Aubrey's further salacious speculations, that the siblings' devotion extended to the bedroom, seems a perverse but not completely unsolicited response to this "coupled work" (qtd. in Waller, *Mary* 100). Aubrey's words are ironically appropriate; from her stance as religious devotional poet and mourning sister, Sidney established a dialogue with the fashionable poetics of erotic writing, revising the embodied figures that become visible in textual commodification. She was not sexually but authorially "coupled," with Philip's body an important icon in her construction of authorial identity. Sidney's legacy for female writers is, finally, an elegiac poetic corpus predicated upon the absent and therefore representable male body.

THE BODY OF CHRIST: AMELIA LANYER'S PASSION

In 1611, Amelia Lanyer published a very different religious poem, *Salve Deus Rex Judaeorum*, which enacted its own brand of corporeal representation as it poetically presented the Passion of Christ and counteracted popular condemnations of women.[6] Unlike Sidney's poems, the *Salve Deus* foregrounds gender as it revises traditional myths that fueled misogynist views of women's weakness. Lanyer's text portrays biblical women as the instruments of God sent out to counter sinful men. She fervently praises Pontius Pilate's wife, for instance, for her heroic attempt to prevent the crucifixion; Pilate's wife assumes the voice of the text, judging the sin of Eve (foremother to female weakness) to be less egregious than that of Christ's male crucifiers. That murder, she announces, comprised a fall more horrendous than the initial loss of Eden: "Let not us Women glory in Mens fall," she states (102). In describing the crucifixion, Lanyer classifies the spectators' responses according to sexual difference: thieves, sergeants, and hangman stood passively while, she states, "the women cri'd" (109):

> When spightfull men with torments did oppresse
> Th'afflicted body of this innocent Dove,
> Poore women seeing how much they did transgresse,
> By teares, by sighes, by cries intreat, nay prove,
> What may be done among the thickest presse,
> They labour still these tyrants hearts to move;
>   In pitie and compassion to forbeare
>   Their whipping, spurning, tearing of his haire. (110)

Although the women try to soften the "tyrants hearts," their labors are in vain; the men's "malice hath no end." Lanyer presents a group huddled around the cross, divided into camps by gender: the men inflict pain upon the body of Christ while the mourning daughters of Jerusalem beg for his release from persecution. The crucifixion, then, becomes the site of a contest between the sexes, an agonistic moment in history that makes woman's virtue visible.

In a review of *Do the Right Thing*, Spike Lee's controversial film about racial tensions in twentieth-century America, Ellen Goodman complains about the absence of the female viewpoint from the debate about racially motivated violence: "women are often victims of one kind or another. They may be perpetrators as well but for the most part they suffer the losses. Murder may be the greatest cause of death among young African-American men. But women are the mourners, the mothers, the sisters, wives"

(11). While I hesitate to essentialize the female position as that of victim (as Goodman does), it seems evident that women have historically been forced into and thus allowed the social position of mourning—excluded from public violence, instead governing ensuing domestic casualties. Lanyer taps into this ascription of gender difference, as does Sidney in mourning Philip's death; both women speak from the socially approved female role of mourner in their attempt to legitimize female speech.

That this is Lanyer's project seems evident from the "proto-feminist" statements in her work. Through the heterogeneous portions of the text—the numerous dedications, the meandering poetic tale, the final country-house poem—Lanyer variously configures women's relationships to each other and to mythology: her list of female dedications is a litany of the most educated aristocratic women in her time; her discussions of biblical women provide a mytho-historical basis for a defense of women's nature; and her nostalgic view of her childhood home portrays a Edenic environment in which girls frolicked in harmony with nature. The numerous dedications to women that preface the text, as Barbara Lewalski points out, create a female community of readers poised against a flawed community of biblical men. Lanyer's work is figured almost obsessively as an interactive mirroring of female virtues, a redemptive textual space in which women might find the image of themselves and of other devout women, and in which they might purify their sight (67). When Christ is called the "mirrour of Martyrs" (99), it becomes apparent that Lanyer offers female readers the story of Christ as model for, and an extreme example of, female godliness. Her text takes on a strange character. The governing persona spends roughly the same amount of textual space in her prefaces (she opens with ten separate verse dedications and a prose address to the reader) as in the "central" portion of her work devoted to its religious subject. When she does turn to Christ's passion, her praise for her potential patroness keeps interrupting the devotional piece. The pious subject matter becomes inextricably linked with the defense of women.

The power of this textual community seemingly compensates for Lanyer's sense of social disenfranchisement, which she presents in a Petrarchan complaint of loss and desire. She compares herself to a hurt bird

Whose untun'd voice the dolefull notes doth sing
Of sad Affliction in an humble straine;
Much like unto a Bird that wants a wing,
And cannot flie, but warbles forth her paine:
  Or he that barred from the Suns bright light,
  Wanting daies comfort, doth comend the night.

So that I live clos'd up in Sorrowes Cell,
Since great Elizaes favour blest my youth;
And in the confines of all cares doe dwell,
Whose grieved eyes no pleasure ever view'th:
  But in Christs suffrings, such sweet taste they have,
  As makes me praise pale Sorrow and the Grave. (44)

Although she sets up the analogy between her suffering and
Christ's only to differentiate them (his pain can relieve hers), the
temporary identification is solidified later in the work. The
Petrarchan image of the wounded bird with the "untun'd"
voice is here employed to connect Christian suffering with
social alienation, and to hold up Christian devotion as a remedy
for social distress.

Lanyer's public narrative work, obviously quite different
from Sidney's more privatized lyric translations, nevertheless
applauds Sidney's "holy sonnets" in a prefatorial poem dedicated to the Countess, the longest dedication Lanyer offers. It is
thus no coincidence that Lanyer's text also draws upon and
revises the rhetoric of embodiment in its textual presentation.
Lanyer grounds her poetic authority in her divine subject, which
she metamorphizes as her animate text. In explaining the
"poverty" of her skill to Ladie Margaret, Lanyer quotes Peter:
"Silver nor gold have I none, but such as I have, that give I you:
for having neither rich pearles of India, nor fine gold of Arabia,
nor diamonds of inestimable value...I present unto you even our
Lord Jesus himselfe" (66). The lavish materials she evokes in this
statement of "humility" are resonant when we consider that
these objects of comparison were typically used in poetic
descriptions of the mistress's body. Lanyer presents the unblemished rich jewel of Christ who surpasses all metaphors of wealth.
In calling him up for representation, Lanyer in effect performs an
anti-blazon upon his body: "no Dove, no Swan, nor Iv'rie could
compare / With this faire corps, when 'twas by death imbrac'd; /

No rose nor no vermillion halfe so faire / As was that pretious blood that interlac'd / His Body" (70). This technique of negation reflects upon her previous presentation of "even our Lord Jesus himselfe": Christ's body, first offered as a substitute for poetic and material riches, becomes defined by what it is not: gold, ivory, jewels. Her descriptions, then, invert the blazon— alluding to its deficient strategy in lieu of presenting the "thing itself," which she acknowledges as nonrepresentable but imagines as coherent.

The corporeal metaphor commonly used by writers in characterizing their books becomes transformed under Lanyer's pen; for her text becomes the word Incarnate. When she tells Mary Sidney that "it is no disparagement to you, / To see your Saviour in a Shepheards weed, / Unworthily presented in your viewe, / Whose worthinesse will grace each line you reade," she humbly suggests her own inadequacy in presenting such an important subject (64). But the effect of this conflation—making Christ the poorly-dressed book—suggests the Divinity within her own work. Her words thus constitute an ambitious gesture that protects and announces her project. The incarnation is the Word made flesh; Lanyer strategically plays upon this by calling attention to the fleshliness of her own representation of the Word.

This pattern of reification again surfaces when Lanyer instructs Ladie Arabella: "cast your eyes upon this little Booke, / Although you be so well accompan'ed / With Pallas, and the Muses, spare one looke / Upon this humbled King, who all forsooke" (52). The audacity of suggesting that her reader merely "spare" a look for the Deity (a gesture also evident when she presents "our Lord Jesus himselfe" because she lacks other gifts of value) announces the importance of her "little booke" imagined as the animate "King." In the folds of this language, her published text *becomes* Christ. She solicits Ladie Susan to do more than cast her eyes upon the kingly text: "Receive your Love whom you have sought so farre, / Which heere presents himself within your view; / Behold this bright and all directing Starre, / Light of your Soule that doth all grace renew: / And in his humble paths since you do tread, / Take this faire Bridegroome in your soules pure bed" (54). Agency is redirected from the displaying author to the divine subject who "presents himself." What better way to insure a good reception for the published work than to defer responsibility to the savior? By figuring the book as the spiritualized and eroticized body of Christ, Lanyer forges a vocabulary through which to present her work.

In couching the presentation of her book in language that suggests that she is delivering the savior to female readers, Lanyer inverts the textual dynamic in which the writer asserts control over his book by figuring it as in need of governance. Deriving authority from the commodified presentation of the animated text, she draws upon the text's superior subject matter rather than its unruly or deficient nature. She authorizes herself through the divinity of her subject. The savior as book—walking, embracing, knocking on the reader's hearts—should by definition be accepted and admired. Lanyer's indebtedness to Sidney is thus made apparent. Sidney justified her work by pointing to its inevitable reception by Queen Elizabeth: "A King should only to a Queen be sent: / God's loved choice unto his chosen love: / Devotion to Devotion's President" (68). The poem urges a favorable textual reception through the metaphor of royal marriage between text and reader. Sidney's language craftily dramatizes this reciprocity through the chiasmic structure ("loved choice...chosen love"). Drawing upon Sidney's mode of presentation, Lanyer personifies her text in order to empower both writer and recipient; both women's texts come to life in the interconnected language of salvation and marriage.

The *Salve Deus* is represented more specifically as a bridegroom, a deified and physically desirable lover. Lanyer exhorts her female readers not only to feast in a female community, but also to join in marriage: "Put on your wedding garments every one, / The Bridegroome stayes to entertaine you all" (48). This erotic metaphor, common in medieval and Renaissance devotional works, is amplified throughout the text and becomes especially resonant when accompanied by protofeminist polemic. Christ becomes the erotic Other on display, the thing dissected, displayed, and described. This strategy imitates the male blazon of the mistress's body—the use of reification, commodification, and display as a means of inscribing authority and controlling a threatening, desirable, and elusive force. The blazon, as described by Vickers, is a gesture of display and an assertion of possession. It is a tool used to proclaim, to publish, to unfold to view; it is an articulation of control. In Lanyer's words, Christ's dying body is lovingly detailed in a blazon, his face compared to snow, his eyes to doves, his head to gold and his lips to dripping honey:

> This is that Bridegroome that appeares so faire,
> So sweet, so lovely in his Spouses sight,
> That unto Snowe we may his face compare,
> His cheekes like skarlet, and his eyes so bright
> As purest Doves that in the rivers are,
> Washed with milke, to give the more delight;
>> His head is likened to the finest gold,
>> His curled lockes so beauteous to behold;
>
> Black as a Raven in her blackest hew;
> His lips like skarlet threeds, yet much more sweet
> Than is the sweetest hony dropping dew,
> Or hony combes, where all the Bees doe meete;
> Yea, he is constant, and his words are true,
> His cheekes are beds of spices, flowers sweet:
>> His lips like Lillies, dropping downe pure mirrhe,
>> Whose love, before all worlds we doe preferre. (120)

Of course, the Song of Songs provides the model for describing the union of Christ and Church in erotic terms. In fact, because the secular blazon is an offspring from the canticles, Lanyer's rescripting constitutes a movement toward origin. Through her critique of the blazon in popular love lyrics, she ironically returns it to its history. In the vocabulary of the Canticles, Lanyer figures her readers as the holy Church, which accepts Christ as lover by dis-covering his "rare parts" (71). "This rich Jewell," the speaker tells her female patron, "I present (deare Lady) to your view" (118). In a characteristically Petrarchan reflex, the speaker admits her failure in describing the ineffable and exhorts the reader to find Christ's image engraved *within* the heart: to read it, kiss it, meditate upon it. The text's construction of a female gaze provides an acceptable means for a woman to become a desiring subject.

The power of assuming this position is tempered by, although enabled by, the stance of mourning which takes place in the moment of death. The language of eroticism evident in this scene pervades the texture of the entire poem. Christ is described as a "dying lover" (65), a "Lover much more true / than ever was since first the world began" (69), "the husband of [the reader's]

Soule" (87) and the subject who "imbrace[s]" the soul of Ladie Arabella "in his dying armes" (52). The female reader is exhorted to welcome "this faire Bridegroome in [her] soules pure bed" (54). Christ is thus portrayed as a lover, whose attempt to "unlock" the door to the Countess of Bedford's heart is fraught with sexual overtones. Throughout the poem, Lanyer figures spiritual transformation as courtship, urging her readers to evaluate Christ as a potential suitor: "if deserts a Ladies love may gaine, / Then tell me, who hath more deserv'd than he?" (76); "judge if ever Lover were so true" (118); he is "all that Ladies can desire" (71). At the conclusion of the poem, Lanyer contrasts Cleopatra's faulty love for Antony with the Countess's virtuous desire for Christ. This comparison acts merely as the culmination of the depiction of Christ as questing lover, who offers his spiritual grace and salvation to female believers by an appeal to the body. Redemption is persistently figured in sexual terms.

It would be a mistake to think that Lanyer's work constitutes an act of blasphemy or sacrilege. Leo Steinberg points out the pervasive eroticism in Renaissance pictorial representations of Christ, arguing that such configurations participated in a sanctioned theological discourse about the Incarnation. He documents hundreds of Renaissance works that stress Christ's sexuality, both as an infant and during the crucifixion, in order to exempt him from genital shame and emphasize his humanity. Interestingly, these postures occur particularly at moments of threshold—the Incarnation and the Passion—moments when the mystery of a divine body would need to be fully articulated.[7]

Lanyer's portrayal of Christ as lover and her focus on his body's "rare" and eroticized parts draws upon this pictorial tradition; but in doing so, she destabilizes the dynamic operative in traditional poetic acts of linguistic dismemberment and display. In *Salve Deus*, subject and object blend so that the speaker does not merely derive power by differentiation—by gazing upon the reified body of Christ—but also encodes that position as female. In this way, the positions of Other and Self, encoded male and female, are deconstructed. While Lanyer obviously follows traditional devotional poetry in depicting the particulars of Christ's body, her emphasis on his dismembered and bloodied "feeble limbs" reveals a peculiarly strong empathy:

> His joynts dis-joynted, and his legges hang downe,
> His alabaster breast, his bloody side,
> His members torne, and on his head a Crowne
> Of sharpest Thorns, to satisfie for pride:
> Anguish and Paine doe all his Sences drowne. (115)

The reader is made aware that Christ is the object of a staged display when the text retreats to frame this poignant scene by orchestrating the Countess of Cumberland's gaze: "This with the eie of Faith thou maist behold / Deere Spouse of Christ…here both Griefe and Joy thou maist unfold, / To view thy Love in this most heavy plight" (115). This framed tableaux seems a powerful if not perverse answer to the images of female dismemberment and display layered within idyllic praise in secular love poetry. Lanyer offers a religious version of the blazon through the anatomized but heroic body of Christ.

The *Salve Deus* does not merely reverse the dynamics of the blazon—female dissecting male—but also deconstructs its relationship between subject and object. The speaker and displayed subject exchange positions throughout the text, so that the eroticized Other, Christ, *also* occupies the same position of powerlessness as the speaker. Christ is represented in the socially inscribed female position as well as the eroticized position of Otherness. Both martyred saviour and cloistered female share the space of restriction and virtue. Lanyer makes this clear when she details Christ's virtues in terms of the values prescribed to women in contemporary conduct books—constancy, faith, patience, sobriety, grace, piety, chastity, meekness, obedience. Even the title page's inventory of contents insists on this conflation, as it lists the subjects of the poem: "The Passion of Christ," "Eves Apologie in defence of Women," "The Teares of the Daughters of Jerusalem," and "The Salutation and Sorrow of the Virgine Marie" (40). And in her prose defense of women, Lanyer explicitly calls attention to a shared victimization, linking men who criticize women with those who put Christ to death (77). By associating women's struggle against misogynist traditions with Christ's entrapment by male authorities, she feminizes Christ and renders women holy. In this way, the *Salve Deus Rex Judaeorum* refashions Petrarchan strategies into a female poetics, one which disrupts the conventional authorial and textual codes that alienated women from publication and from the public sphere.

When male authors constructed elaborate discursive techniques for assuaging their own anxieties about publication, they generated a gendered ideology of authorship largely dependent upon the potent social and political rhetoric of Petrarchism (Marotti; Armstrong and Tennenhouse 4–10). Enjoined to remain silent within the domestic spheres, these female Renaissance writers mobilized the Petrarchan forms and tropes offered to them, forging a discourse of power and the body that countered the articulation of authorial power through displayed female objects. When women began to write publicly, they had to sidestep representations of their own scattered and reified corporeality, what Waller calls "the logic of love poetry," which turns on a highly gendered gaze ("Struggling" 250). They did so by shrouding the visibility of their own gendered embodiment, reassigning female associations with the material by presenting male objects of display. By creating alternative projections of their own blazoned bodies, their texts disrupted the language of commodification found within Renaissance poetry. Such a disruption perhaps allowed the female writer to articulate and to overwhelm anxieties about wandering into the forbidden realm of literary production. First Mary Sidney, in her more private text, and then Amelia Lanyer, in her more polemical and public work, contested the emerging late sixteenth-century concept of authorship. It may not be to modern taste to watch Sidney stylize her career in self-deprecating terms, or to see Lanyer name her own authority by depicting women as martyrs and mourners. But within the perimeters of writing at the end of the sixteenth century, these texts are astonishing not only for their poetic accomplishment, but for their reworking of popular discursive structures. In Lanyer's reference to Sidney, then, we see a trajectory—significant not because it constituted a discourse of female difference, or because it rivaled the male tradition, but because it served as a sign of that tradition's strategies of exclusion and modes of silencing.

NOTES

1. Florio derides the art of translation as "defective...since all translations are reputed femalls, delivered at second hand" (sig. A2r).

His assessment seems unusual, however, in that humanist education encouraged translation and imitation as modes of discursive learning. In fact, original and imitative works as a categorical opposition is largely absent in the Renaissance. Florio's statement nevertheless points to the "coveredness" that translation offered male and female writers. And while his negative comment may be exceptional, his use of gender as a means of denigrating its autonomous status was not; after all, legally women were *femmes coverts*, "covered" by a male guardian (qtd. in Lamb 116).

2. Freer explains that the *Psalms* were "known to a good number of churchmen, and selections were reprinted in anthologies of religious lyrics during the eighteenth and nineteenth centuries. Her other works fell into comparative obscurity" (489).

3. Donne describes the Psalms by reemploying Sidney's language, noting that the "cloven" nature of the work (union of God/man) is carried through in the double authorship "'so thou hast cleft that spirit, to performe / That worke againne and shed it, here, upon / Two, by their bloods, and by the Spirit one; / A Brother and A Sister" (qtd. in Rathmell ix).

4. For examples of other works that are described as wounded or maimed, see the prefatory material to Beaumont and Fletcher's *Philaster*, in which the printer states that the main characters have "laine so long a bleeding, by reasons of some dangerous and gaping wounds which they received in the first Impression, that it is wondered how they could go abroad so long" (Gebert 251). The 1623 Shakespearean *Folio* also presents a text "cur'd and well limb'd."

5. Daniel, for instance, tells Mary Sidney that his text, *Delia*, is "begotten by thy hand and my desire." The exchangeability of her hand and his points to a peculiar conception of poetic property, one in which the dedicatee can "own" the work.

6. Although Lanyer admits a "Womans writing of divinest things" is "seldome seene" (41), she boldly offers a polemical counternarrative to biased accounts of women and bibical history: "I have written this small volume, or little booke, for the generall use of all virtuous Ladies and Gentlewomen of this kingdome...this have I done, to make knowne to the world, that all women deserve not to be blamed" (77).

7. For example, Steinberg notes the groin-touching by the dying or dead Christ, the outlined erection of Christ in moments of sorrow, the erotic "chin chuck" between infant and Mary and the general gestures that emphasize Christ's physicality and sexuality. He argues that

such depictions, part of mainstream theology, point to both Christ's exemption from genital shame and his power in mastering sexual desire (84–87).

WORKS CITED

Armstrong, Nancy, and Leonard Tennenhouse. Introduction. *The Ideology of Conduct: Essays on Literature and the History of Sexuality.* New York: Methuen, 1987. 1–24.

Beilin, Elaine. *Redeeming Eve: Women Writers of the English Renaissance.* Princeton: Princeton UP, 1987.

Daniel, Samuel. *Delia and the Complaint of Rosamond,* STC 6254 (1594).

Fisken, Beth Wynne. "'To the Angell Spirit...': Mary Sidney's Entrance into the 'World of Words.'" Haselkorn and Travitsky 263–75.

Freer, Coburn. "Mary Sidney: The Countess of Pembroke." *Women Writers of the Renaissance and Reformation.* Ed. Katharina M. Wilson. Athens: U of Georgia P, 1987. 481–90.

Gebert, Clara, ed. *An Anthology of Elizabethan Dedications and Prefaces.* Philadelphia: U of Pennsylvania P, 1933.

Goodman, Ellen. "Missing: The Influence of Black Women." Rev. of *Do the Right Thing* by Spike Lee. *Boston Globe* 18 July 1989: 11.

Hannay, Margaret, ed. *Silent But for the Word: Tudor Women as Patrons, Translators, and Writers of Religious Works.* Kent, Ohio: Kent State UP, 1985.

Haselkorn, Anne M., and Betty S. Travitsky, eds. *The Renaissance Englishwoman in Print: Counterbalancing the Canon.* Amherst: U of Massachusetts P, 1990.

Jones, Ann Rosalind. "Surprising Fame: Renaissance Gender Ideologies and the Women's Lyric." *The Poetics of Gender.* Ed. Nancy K. Miller. New York: Columbia UP, 1986. 74–95.

Jonson, Ben. *Works.* Ed. C. H. Herford and Percy and Evelyn Simpson. 11 vols. Oxford: Clarendon P, 1925–1952.

Kelso, Ruth. *Doctrine for the Lady of the Renaissance.* Urbana: U of Illinois P, 1956.

Lamb, Mary Ellen. "The Cooke Sisters: Attitudes toward Learned Women in the Renaissance." Hannay 107–25.

Lanyer, Amelia. *Salve Deus Rex Judaeorum.* STC 15227. London: 1611.

Rpt. *The Poems of Shakespeare's Dark Lady*. Ed. A. L. Rowse. New York: Clarkson N. Potter, 1979. 39–136.

Lewalski, Barbara. "Of God and Good Women: The Poems of Ameilia Lanyer." Hannay 204–23.

Marotti, Arthur. "'Love is not love': Elizabethan Sonnet Sequences and the Social Order." *ELH* 49 (1982): 392–428.

Rathmell, J. C. A. Introduction. *The Psalms of Sir Philip Sidney and the Countess of Pembroke*. New York: Anchor, 1963. xi–xxviii.

Ringler, William. Notes. *Sir Philip Sidney: Poems*. Oxford: Clarendon P, 1962. 1–99.

Saunders, J. W. "The Stigma of Print: A Note on the Social Bases of Tudor Poetry." *Essays in Criticism* 1 (1951): 139–64.

Sidney, Mary. *The Triumph of Death and Other Unpublished and Uncollected Poems*. Ed. Gary Waller. Salzburg: Universität Salzburg, 1977.

Sidney, Sir Philip. *The Countess of Pembroke's Arcadia*. New York: Penguin, 1984.

Stallybrass, Peter. "Patriarchal Territories: The Body Enclosed." *Rewriting the Renaissance*. Ed. Margaret Ferguson, Maureen Quilligan and Nancy Vickers. Chicago: U of Chicago P, 1986. 123–42.

Steinberg, Leo. *The Sexuality of Christ in Renaissance Art and in Modern Oblivion*. New York: Pantheon, 1983.

Tyler, Margaret. *A Mirrour of Princely Deedes and Knighthood*. STC 18859. London: T. East, 1578.

Vickers, Nancy. "Diana Described: Scattered Women and Scattered Rhyme." *Writing and Sexual Difference*. Ed. Elizabeth Abel. Chicago: U of Chicago P, 1986. 95–110.

Wall, Wendy. "Disclosures in Print: The 'Violent Enlargement' of the Renaissance Voyeuristic Text." *SEL* 29 (1989): 35–59.

Waller, Gary. *Mary Sidney, Countess of Pembroke: A Critical Study of her Writings and Literary Milieu*. Salzburg: Universitat Salzburg, 1979.

———. "Struggling into Discourse: The Emergence of Renaissance Women's Writing." Hannay 238–56.

A Politics of Disguise:
Marie-Catherine d'Aulnoy's
"Belle-Etoile" and the Narrative Structure
of Ambivalence

Patricia Hannon

INTRODUCTION

Seventeenth-century France witnessed an unprecedented flour-ishing of works by female writers. During the latter part of the century, women's increased participation in literature resulted in a proliferation of novels and memoirs which sought a new realism in the depiction of sentiment (Hipp 457-520; Demoris 264). Yet this novelistic production was not the only expression of the emerging sense of female identity; alongside these works valorizing a certain realism, female writers surpassed their male counterparts in the publication of supposedly unrealistic fairy tales.[1] When in 1690 Marie-Catherine d'Aulnoy embedded the first literary fairy tale, "The Island of Happiness," in her novel *The Story of Hypolite*, she at once heralded a century-long literary vogue and initiated the mixing of genres which was to mark women's tales between 1690 and 1700.[2]

This first vogue of fairy-tale writing provides a unique cor-pus for the study of the female writer: not only did women pre-dominate in the genre by publishing two-thirds of the tales in comparison to one-third published by men, but both women and men wrote separate versions of similar tale types.[3] These thirteen tales consisting of male and female versions of the same plot constitute an ideal sample for comparing men's and women's writing in a given historical context.[4] The male and female versions differ in their use of literary conventions and their production of meaning. Lucien Dällenbach's theories of textual reflexivity, and especially of the *mise en abyme*,[5] serve as a valuable tool in locating the ambivalent female writer in the interstices of her text—in between the story (that is, the espousal of linear narration) and the act of storytelling (that is, the disrupting and rejecting of linear narrative by referring to its construction).

According to *Webster*'s definitions of ambivalence as "continual fluctuation (as between one thing and its opposite)" and "uncertainty as to which approach to follow," the female writer's interstitial position in between the story and the processes that construct it conveys her ambivalence toward the dominant ideology from which stories are derived. Whereas linear male-authored tales are characterized by antithetical structures and generalizations that reflect dominant cultural values, female-authored tales are marked by the disruption of sequential narrative through self-reflexive amplifications. Following a general strategy which can be described as "writing by addition," the female writer both amplifies her tale and interrupts the linear plot by alluding to the narrational situation of enunciation—that is, the dynamic between writer, reader, and the time and place of writing and reading. These indirect references to the enunciatory situation may take several forms: *mises en abyme*; inscriptions of the contemporary scene; and disguised or metamorphosed characters. They not only deconstruct the story by fostering the reader's awareness of a break between the representation (story) and the act of representing (writing the story), but also construct it by amplifying the text: the *mise en abyme* doubles a textual part such as the story or the enunciation process; the inscription of the seventeenth-century scene conflates contemporary and fairy-tale time; and disguised or metamorphosed characters write one identity over another. Since a preference for amplification is a hallmark of ambivalence (both/and versus either/or), one might speak of a complicity between narrative structure and the writer's stance with regard to her work of fiction; by amplifying her text, the female writer expresses her reluctance to articulate a binary representation of reality. The much criticized length of the women's tales, which are approximately three times longer than those written by men, partly results from their exceptional degree of amplifying self-reflexivity.[6]

Rather than directly criticize conventional plots, the female writer, like many of her heroines, subscribes to a politics of disguise: what appear to be additions to the story are really its undoing, since these amplifications demystify the fictional illusion by diverting the reader's attention from the storyline. Although writing by conflation enables the ambivalent female writer to avoid an either/or choice—on the one hand, between the story and a disclosure of the processes that produce it, and on the other, between active and passive female characters—her interstitial position implicitly criticizes both the story and its point of origin, the dominant culture. The female fairy-tale writer disrupts the story's linearity and says "I the writer," by underlining her own and the reader's role in textual composition. She thus distances herself from plots that are not in her favor, while suggesting that such plots are fictional and therefore arbitrary. Even though writing by conflation denotes her ambivalence toward literary and other conventions, the female writer does not unconditionally offer a counterplot; rather, her active heroine exists alongside the traditionally passive one. Nonetheless, by insistently suggesting the processes underlying the work of fiction, she creates open textual spaces that are receptive to new gender identities and new stories.

Madame d'Aulnoy's eighty-seven-page fairy tale, "The Princess Belle-Etoile and the Prince Chéri" (1696), represents other female versions of fairy tales.[7] I will preface my analysis of moments in the narration that reveal the female writer's ambivalence—both toward her writerly role and her active heroine—with a plot summary. In the preliminary story, a destitute princess moves to the countryside and supports herself and her three daughters by becoming a cook. The main story commences when the daughters marry and accompany their husbands to the same kingdom: Blondine marries the king, Brunette the king's brother, and evil Roussette an admiral. When Blondine gives birth to Belle-Etoile, Beau Soleil, and Heureux, and when Brunette begets Chéri, the jealous Roussette, who wishes to marry the king, joins forces with the king's evil mother, who despises Blondine. The evil queen mother orders her wicked lady-in-waiting Feintise to cast all four children out to sea; however, the children are found by a reformed pirate and his wife who raise them. The remainder of the story recounts how Belle-Etoile and her cousin Chéri (who believe themselves to be brother and sister) fall in love, and how all the children set out in search of their identities. Their quest is hindered by Feintise, who persuades Belle-Etoile to send Chéri off on three quests. The first two ventures are successful; however, the third proves disastrous for all three male heroes. Finally, Belle-Etoile usurps the hero role and saves the day. The tale ends as the children are reunited with their parents, and Belle-Etoile and Chéri are married.

REVEALING DISGUISES

Disguise—be it of character, social role, or literary genre—is a prominent characteristic of this tale, which is primarily concerned with the identity quest. Indeed, the fact that fairy tales often recount the coming-of-age scenario explains the female writer's prominence in the fairy-tale genre in the seventeenth century. The genre is particularly suited to express the emerging sense of female identity which characterizes women's writing at this time. Since disguise implies a second identity beneath the apparent one, it demands unmasking and thus inherently favors the search for identity. At the same time, it implies a problematics of representation: the reader becomes aware of two levels of representation—what the character feigns and what the character is—and, indirectly, of the narrator responsible for representing both levels. "Belle Etoile"'s first disguise concerns a princess banished from her kingdom by poverty. This fallen princess dons the mask of a self-sufficient cook only after her royal identity is reduced to the synecdochic trappings of sovereignty:

> Once upon a time there was a princess who possessed nothing of her former glory except for a sofa and a lock; one was made of pearl-embroidered velvet, the other of gold decorated with diamonds. She kept them as long as she could, but the extreme poverty to which she was reduced forced her from time to time to detach a pearl, a diamond, an emerald, and these gems were sold in secret to maintain her lifestyle.

> *It était une fois une princesse à laquelle il ne restait plus rien de ses grandeurs passées que son dais & son cadenas; l'un était de velours,*

en broderie de perles, & l'autre d'or, enrichi de diamants. Elle les garda tant qu'elle put; mais l'extrême nécessité où elle se trouvait réduite, l'obligeait de temps en temps à détacher une perle, un diamant, une émeraude, & cela se vendait secrètement pour nourrir son équipage. (179)

In women's tales, poverty is positively marked; it is an open door leading from the passive enthroning of woman in the kingdom, to the active status attainable only beyond kingdom borders. Like the princess in "Belle-Etoile"'s preliminary story, the female writer's often dethroned heroines accede to authorial status by moving outside the royal domain and inventing new identities for themselves.[8] The industrious princess-cook articulates the duality common to other disguised heroines, while setting a precedent for Belle-Etoile's later usurpation of the hero role. Her assumed appearance is a mask announcing the initial discordance between appearance and reality. This discourse logically culminates in the split between fiction and reality—expressed, as we shall see, by the tale's two *mises en abyme.*

The narrator's predilection for disguise is lexically signalled throughout the text by a network of forty-five terms belonging to the same signifying block—"to feign" *(feindre)*—and its synonyms. The princess-cook, and later her granddaughter Belle-Etoile, try on identities like so many disguises on the way to inventing new conceptions of selfhood. Indeed, the princess may have learned her deceptive powers of invention from the court, whose dissimulation is epitomized by the aptly-named Feintise, the wicked queen's ally who casts the children out to sea. The wise princess-cook here refuses to accompany her daughters to the court where they are to be married:

> The king invited his mother-in-law to follow him, and promised that she would be regarded with the utmost distinction. But she immediately thought that the court is always a troubled sea. Sire, she told him, I have too much worldly experience to leave the calm that I have achieved only with much difficulty....The king admired the intelligence and moderation of a woman who thought and spoke like a philosopher.

> *Le roi convia sa belle-mère à le suivre, & lui promit qu'elle serait regardée avec toute sorte de distinction. Mais elle pensa aussitôt que la cour est une mer toujours agitée. Sire, lui dit-elle, j'ai trop*

d'expérience des choses du monde pour quitter le repos que je n'ai
acquis qu'avec beaucoup de peine....Le roi admira l'esprit & la mod-
ération d'une femme qui pensait & qui parlait comme un philosophe.
(186–87)

The feints of the court are matched not only by the princess's, but also the narrator's. Her valorizing of the princess-cook's intellect takes on a larger significance in light of the frame story, *Le Gentilhomme bourgeois*, which interrupts the tale at midpoint with a feminist comment that defends women's learnedness and ability to hold high office.[9] Embedding may here be understood as a kind of disguise through layering; the narrator hides her defense of women for the reader to discover.

"To feign" can signify not only the dissimulation involved in false appearances, but also the largely hidden work of poetic invention. As we shall see, the two *mises en abyme* in Aulnoy's tale suggest the reader's and the writer's participation in the process through which the literary text is created. Paradoxically, the narrator breaks the fictional illusion by writing one genre into another—that is, by inscribing a romantic couple borrowed from the sentimental novel within the fairy-tale structure. This adding of one genre to another occurs in yet another space of the tale outside the kingdom, the retreat where the pirate and his wife raise Blondine and Brunette's marvelous children. One day Chéri observes Belle-Etoile reading:

> They still had no idea of the extent of their tender feelings for one another, nor did they recognize the exact nature of this tenderness, when one day Belle-Etoile was given several new books; she took the first one within her reach: it was the story of two young lovers, whose passion had started at a time when they believed themselves to be brother and sister, then they were recognized by their parents [to be cousins], and after infinite trials and tribulations they were married.

> *Ils ignoraient encore jusqu'où allait leur tendresse, & ils n'en con-*
> *naissaient point l'espèce, lorsqu'un jour on apporta à Belle-Etoile*
> *plusieurs livres nouveaux; elle prit le premier qui tomba sous sa*
> *main: c'était l'histoire de deux jeunes amants, dont la passion avait*
> *commencé en se croyant frère et soeur, ensuite ils avaient été recon-*
> *nus par leurs proches, & après des peines infinies ils s'étaient*
> *épousés.* (200)

Belle-Etoile gives the book to Chéri, who reads to her while she finishes her needlework: "He read that adventure and it was with a great deal of uneasiness that he saw a true depiction of all his feelings. Belle-Etoile was no less surprised; it seemed as if the author had read everything that was going on in her mind" (*"Il lut cette aventure & ce ne fut pas sans une grande inquiétude qu'il vit une peinture naïve de tous ses sentiments. Belle-Etoile n'était pas moins surprise; it semblait que l'auteur avait lu tout ce qui se passait dans son âme"* [200]). Subscribing to Gerald Prince's definition of *mise en abyme*—"a miniature replica of a text embedded within that text; a textual part reduplicating, reflecting, or mirroring (one or more aspects of) the textual whole" (53)—this inscription of a novelistic couple, whose story reflects that of the fairy-tale couple, qualifies as a *mise en abyme* or replica of the story. According to Dällenbach, the *mise en abyme* signifies the text's consciousness of itself as literature while disrupting narrative line. This disruption of linearity makes the reader aware of the text as fiction, and locates the narrator in between the story and the act of storytelling, in between the novel and the fairy tale.

Indeed, the couple's shock of recognition is well-founded, since the author of the book they are reading will shortly prove to be none other than Aulnoy herself. Aulnoy asserts her writerly identity by representing herself as a writing subject in an allusion to her own intertext. Chéri, who mistakenly believes Belle-Etoile to be his sister, compares their situation as ill-fated lovers to that of the novelistic couple: "'Ah, my sister,' he cried while looking at her sadly and letting his book fall! 'Ah, my sister, how lucky for Hypolite that he was not Julie's brother!'" (*"Ah, ma soeur, s'écria-t-il en la regardant tristement & laissant tomber son livre! ah, ma soeur, qu'Hypolite fut heureux de n'être pas le frère de Julie!"* [201]). It so happens that Hypolite and Julie are the main characters of Aulnoy's *The Story of Hypolite*, the novel which, it will be remembered, embedded the first published fairy tale. *Hypolite* is representative of the sentimental novel in vogue at this time: a pair of lovers are beset by all manner of obstacles, only to be finally reunited. To the reader familiar with Aulnoy's work, the allusion to the characters Hypolite and Julie functions as her signature. Thus the *mise en abyme* of the story— "it seemed as if the author had read everything that was going on in her mind"—is immediately followed by a *mise en abyme* of the enunciatory situation: Aulnoy's signature via her intertextual characters suggests both the author's and the reader's participation in creating the text.[10] The space in between the representation and the act of representing widens as the reader's attention is directed toward the processes of writing and reading. Given that Aulnoy's signature occurs at the point where the text articulates a *mise en abyme*, one might say that she signs her *mise en abyme*. Such a signature says "I the author" while underlining the writer's and, by extension, the reader's critical distance from the story being told. It is significant that Aulnoy indirectly refers to her first fairy tale, rather than her later work. She thus highlights the female writer as initiator, as originative source; woman is represented here not merely as writer, but as originator of a genre.[11]

However, the genre founded by this female writer defies conventional definition. The reader no sooner recognizes the novelistic couple Hypolite and Julie than she finds herself caught in a reversed mirror play of intersecting genres: her critical distance from the story becomes all the more acute when she realizes that *The Story of Hypolite* reverses "Belle-Etoile"'s embedding of novelistic characters by instead embedding the fairy-tale characters of "The Island of Happiness." Moreover, since the moral of this *unhappy* fairy tale is recited by none other than the sentimental lover Hypolite himself, Aulnoy deconstructs her character by writing contradictory identities over one another. The fairy-tale genre—unlike "The Island of Happiness," whose very title is a disguise of sorts—by definition ends happily.[12] Thus, just as the ending problematizes Hypolite's identity as romantic lover, so too it questions the identity of the genre. To question what constitutes identity is to doubt the validity of the established definitions on which identities are founded and by which conventional fictions are written. The reader, relegated to a critical space outside tale boundaries, finds herself with no firm story ground to stand on; the reversed mirror play here deflects the implied criticism of Hypolite onto Belle-Etoile and Chéri, the couple whose situation reflects his own.

When it is remembered that "Belle-Etoile" itself is embedded in a novelistic frame story, Aulnoy's preference for indeterminate generic boundaries becomes apparent; rather than respect the boundary separating novel from fairy tale, this tale amalgamates the two genres. The unsure identity of literary genres, together with the princess-cook's dual social identity and the court's duplicity, articulate a problematics of disguised identities and, indirectly, a problematics of representation: how does the artist portray a reality that she has defined as double? Perhaps this question can best be answered by examining the last part of the tale, in which a disguised Belle-Etoile usurps the traditionally masculine hero role; the heroine's dual gender role clearly relates to the question of her identity. The desire for self-knowledge impels Belle-Etoile to quest after the green bird, the key to solving the question of the children's origins. Thanks to the enterprising Chéri, the princess now possesses the dancing water and the singing apple; nevertheless, she must have the green bird if her true identity is to be known: "what good can come of the water and the apple since I do not know who I am, who my parents are, and by what twist of fate my brothers and I were exposed to the dangerous sea?" ("*de quoi me servent les avantages que je reçois de l'eau et de la pomme, puisque j'ignore d'où je suis, qui sont mes parents, & par quelle fatalité mes frères et moi avons été exposés à la fureur des ondes?*" [246]). However, the narration of Belle-Etoile's identity quest will not unhesitatingly dispatch the heroine to capture the green bird. Instead, the narrator's reluctance to portray a woman as the initiator of action expresses her doubt about what is narratable according to literary conventions. This hesitation, marking her ambivalence, relates to her politics of disguise: the narrator emphasizes the expected linear hero plot only to disrupt it more remarkably. What at first appears to be adherence to convention proves in the end to be a maneuver to circumvent it.

The narrator's tracing of Belle-Etoile's identity quest challenges linearity—which is related to the reader's conception of the hero role—and underlines its failure. Dominant literary ideology requires that a hero, namely Chéri, undertake this knightly adventure. The narrator admittedly sends not one, but three male heroes off to seize the oracular green bird; nonetheless, each knight's failed quest progressively silences the traditionally male hero and challenges the presuppositions of literary conventions. Belle-Etoile's lover Chéri is the first candidate for hero:

He was so close to the green bird that he thought he had it,
when all of a sudden the rock opened up and he fell, *immobile
as a statue*, down into a spacious room; *he could neither move nor
lament* his deplorable adventure. *Three hundred knights*, who,
like himself, had set off on this quest, *were in the same state*;
they looked at one another, that was the only thing permitted
them.

*Il se voyait si proche de l'oiseau Vert, qu'il croyait le prendre,
lorsque le rocher s'ouvrant tout d'un coup, il tomba dans une spa-
cieuse salle, aussi* immobile qu'une statue; il ne pouvait ni
remuer ni se plaindre *de son déplorable aventure*. Trois cents
chevaliers *qui l'avaient tentée comme lui*, étaient au même état;
ils s'entreregardaient, c'était la seule chose qui leur était permise.
(248–49, emphasis mine)

This group of three hundred knights who have encountered the
same fate emphasizes that it is the hero *type* that is immobilized;
the narrator literally objectifies the socio-literary concept of the
hero by transforming its masculine representatives into statues.
The hero's uncharacteristic passivity is accompanied by loss of
speech when Petit Soleil repeats the aborted adventure: "he fell
into a large room; the first thing that caught his eye was Chéri,
but he was unable to speak to him" ("*il tomba dans la grande salle; la
première chose qui arrêta ses regards, ce fut Chéri*, mais il ne put lui
parler" [249, emphasis mine]). The third and penultimate itera-
tion of the quest script is likewise doomed to failure, when
Heureux meets the same fate as his brother:

he fell like a statue into the room, where he recognized the
princes he was seeking, *without being able to speak to them*; they
were all arranged in nooks of crystal; they never slept, did not
eat, and remained enchanted in a very sad manner, since they
were free only to dream and lament their adventure.

*il tomba comme une statue dans la salle, où il reconnut les princes
qu'il cherchait* sans pouvoir leur parler; *ils étaient tous arrangés
dans des niches de cristal; ils ne dormaient jamais, ne mangaient
point, & restaient enchantés d'une manière bien triste, car ils
avaient seulement la liberté de rêver & de déplorer leur aventure*.
(250, emphasis mine)

The narrator's silenced and immobilized representation of masculinity indirectly criticizes stories in the dominant culture

where man is written as active and woman as passive. The paralyzed hero expresses a critique of gender-marked situations such as those found in the male-authored version of this tale.

THE HEROINE REVISITED

After all three heroes are safely ensconced in their "nooks of crystal," the emboldened narrator sends off a disguised Belle-Etoile to join the list of heretofore masculine adventurers: "she took a man's outfit, thinking that there was less risk for her thus disguised on her travels, than if she set off to explore the world as an adventuress" (*"elle prit un habit d'homme, trouvant qu'il y avait moins à risquer pour elle, ainsi travestie dans son voyage, que si elle était allée en aventurière courir le monde"* [251]). Not only is there "less risk" for the heroine, but also for the narrator, who must negotiate the literary and social conventions that deny active status to female characters. Belle-Etoile's disguise is proof that active and passive roles are sexually distributed in the kingdom. Certainly, this disguise reflects the narrator's doubt as to the acceptability of writing woman as the initiator of action. The heroine thus assumes authorship of her own story, but only through a mask that places her *in between* male and female identity. Disguise may here be considered a kind of writing by addition that confounds the exclusivity or one-dimensionality of definitions; writing "woman" and "man" together jumbles definitions, as one shuffles a stack of cards. Since two signifiers ("heroine" and "heroine disguised as man") now refer to the same signified (man), disguise challenges the representational system by obscuring the relations between signified and signifier. If one envisages the mask as disordering conventional modes of representation, one might here assume that writing man and woman together challenges a system based on binary division: what is masculinity if it can be assumed by donning a set of clothes?

Woman is therefore written as the space where conflation is practiced.[13] However, even though the heroine succeeds in disenchanting her lover and the other immobilized knights, her disguise keeps her at a distance from the heroic role she seemingly espouses:

> it was necessary to touch the eyes and lips of all those *she* wished to disenchant with the red feather: *she* rendered this service to several kings, and particularly to our three princes.... Touched by so great a favor, they all threw themselves at *his* feet, naming *him* the liberator of kings.

> *il fallait avec la plume incarnate frotter les yeux & la bouche de tous ceux qu'elle voudrait désenchanter:* elle *rendit ce bon office à plusieurs souverains, & particulièrement à nos trois princes.... Touchés d'un si grand bienfait ils se jetèrent tous à ses genoux,* le *nommant le libérateur des rois.* (254, emphasis mine)

This pronominal expression of the heroine's duality places her squarely in between two sexual identities, just as it places the reader's deciphering activity (what the heroine is, "she"; what the heroine feigns to be, "he") in between the story and an awareness of its construction. Indeed, the narrator keeps the reader at attention throughout her careful preparation of Belle-Etoile's role as the "liberator of kings." First of all, nearly half the tale is devoted to the quest episodes and the events engendering them. Such an emphasis on the heroic enterprise awakens the reader's expectations; the three failed masculine quests all the more clearly engrave the hero scenario in the reader's consciousness as she awaits its final realization. When Chéri and the two brothers are unsuccessful, there is a break in the series of exploits constituting the hero's actions; this is at once a break in linearity and in the hero's identity. In a manner of speaking, Chéri's failure leaves an open space in the hero role. The reader is prepared to pay the maximum attention to Belle-Etoile's performance, since this role rightfully belongs to Chéri or the brothers. This break in the heroic series challenges linearity and, at the same time, enables the heroine's achievement of active status. One can thus speak of a complicity between disrupting narrative conventions and empowering the female characters.[14]

However, the narrator is markedly ambivalent toward her heroine's accomplishment. Although Belle-Etoile succeeds in the hero's task, she refuses to avail herself of the rights that literary convention grants to the proven knight. After she has disenchanted the knights,

> each one told her of his particular adventure, and offered to accompany her wherever she wished to go. *She responded that*

> *although the laws of chivalry gave her some rights over the liberty*
> *she had just given them, she had no intention of claiming these*
> *rights.*

> *chacun lui dit son aventure particulière, & s'offrirent à l'accompag-*
> *ner partout où elle voudrait aller.* Elle répondit qu'encore que les
> loix de la chevalerie puissent lui donner quelque droit sur la
> liberté qu'elle venait de leur rendre, elle ne prétendait point
> s'en prévaloir. (254–55, emphasis mine)

Belle-Etoile rejects not only the laws of chivalry but also the literary conventions responsible for stories in complicity with the
dominant culture. In fact, her rejection of those conventions
reflects the narrator's own evasion of the literary code which
founds generic identities; just as the heroine rejects a privilege
of dominance dictated by the chivalric novel, so too does the
narrator refuse those literary conventions that would, for example, draw the boundary between fairy tale and novel. If one con-
ceives the kingdom as representing codified law—including
that of the literary establishment—then the narrator figures the
symbolic rejection of that law by describing the dispossessed
kings, forced to return on foot to their royal domains:

> All four [Belle-Etoile, Chéri and the brothers] mounted on
> their horses and left the emperors and kings on foot; because
> during the two or three hundred years that they had been
> there, their horses had long since perished.

> *Ils montèrent tous quatre à cheval, &* laissèrent *les empereurs & les*
> *rois à pied; car depuis deux ou trois cent ans qu'ils étaient là, leurs*
> *équipages avaient péri.* (255)

The narrator's phrase, "during the two or three hundred years,"
suggests that even if the forgotten kings do reach their home-
lands, their courts will have long since disappeared. And yet,
even though Belle-Etoile refuses to play by the old set of (chivalric) rules, she does not emulate her grandmother by opting for a
space apart from the kingdom; she chooses a place in the very
center of the royal domain. Nevertheless, before the tale's
inevitable reintegration of the heroine into the dominant culture
(characteristic of female writers' ambivalence), it suggests
another realm beyond the kingdom's "laws of chivalry," where
the heroine might act and speak for herself. This domain out-

side the rule of law is expressed not only diegetically, in the princess-cook's move to the countryside, but also structurally, in the disruption of linearity and the writing by addition which figure so prominently in this tale's disguises of character, social roles, and literary genres.

THE AMBIVALENT INVENTOR

Aulnoy's preference for indeterminate boundaries, both generic and characterological, suggests that she hesitates to discard existing narrative conventions and the ideology subtending them. If one were to locate the narrator in her text, it would be in that interstitial space in between the two realities which the dominant culture defines as masculine and feminine. This interstitial position expresses her fundamental ambivalence about which reality is preferable, and translates textually into a disruption of linearity and symmetry through amplifications indirectly referring to textual production. Rather than directly contest literary and other conventions, Aulnoy adheres to a politics of disguise wherein amplifications discourage a linear and binary figuration of reality. Thus her invention, which also challenges convention, is properly hidden; the princess is hidden under cook's clothing, Belle-Etoile is masked in men's attire, and the fairy tale masquerades as a novel. Such narrative strategies recall the tale's dominant signifier "to feign"—which, according to Pierre Richelet's 1680 *Dictionnaire françois*, "is said in particular of poetic invention, of the art of imagining feints" ("Il se dit on particulier en de l'invention poétique, de l'art d'imaginer des feintes").[15] One might surmise that Aulnoy's invention is fostered by her interstitial position, a space of not deciding between two givens. Such ambivalence promotes creation, since the female writer, in between two realities, may seek to invent a third one. Just as the princess-cook abandons the kingdom for a space apart where she invents her own identity, so too does this writer create from an interstitial space—in between the story and the act of storytelling, in between the active and passive female character. Both the female writer and the heroine occupy the space of feints, which is one of invention as well as disguise.

NOTES

1. Although the vogue of fairy-tale publication might appear to counter the new novelistic realism, many of the tales abound in references to contemporary reality.

2. All translations are my own.

3. Robert delineates two vogues of fairy-tale production, one extending from 1690 to 1700, the other from 1730 to 1758 (131). This essay is concerned with the first period.

4. Miller independently advocates such "reading in pairs" (49).

5. Dällenbach defines the *mise en abyme* as "any sign having as its referent a pertinent continuous aspect of the narrative (fiction, text or narrative code, enunciation) which it represents on the diegetic level" (*Mirrors* 10).

6. Both seventeenth-century and twentieth-century critics complain about the length of the women's tales. See Villiers 75 and Robert 7.

7. The male version, Le Noble's "L'Oiseau de Vérité," is a short seven pages in comparison.

8. For example, in the preliminary story of Aulnoy's "Finette Cendron," a king and queen are forced out of their kingdom by poverty. The inventive queen accedes to authorial status by conceiving the new plot (new social roles) that she and her husband will enact (472–503).

9. In this story, a group of men and women recite fairy tales, a common practice in literary salons of the times. A woman addresses a man who has just uttered a phrase in Latin: "women are presently as learned as men; they study and are capable of everything, it's a great shame that they cannot hold office, a parliament composed of women would be the loveliest thing imaginable" (*"les femmes sont à présent aussi savantes que les hommes; elle étudient, & sont capables de tout; c'est dommage qu'elles ne puissent être dans les charges, un parlement composé de femmes serait la plus jolie chose du monde"* [222]).

10. Most fairy tales written between 1690 and 1700 were signed in semi-anonymous, abbreviated form, for example, "Madame la Comtesse Dxxx" for "Madame la Comtesse de Murat."

11. Lhéritier traces the origins of fairy tales back to "a very educated lady" who learned them from the ancient troubadours.

12. Propp's definition of the fairy tale emphasizes the primacy of events which occur in orderly succession and rectify an initial injustice (122). Robert defines it as a narrative that centers around the reparation of a misdeed and valorizes a heroic couple (36–37).

13. Disguise and metamorphosis, both of which may be considered a kind of writing by addition (one identity added to another), are markedly more common in women's than in men's versions of the tales.

14. DuPlessis discusses the relation between "breaking the sequence" and criticizing the dominant ideology (x).

15. Richelet's dictionary was one of the authoritative lexicons of the century.

WORKS CITED

Aulnoy, Marie-Catherine le Jumel de Barneville, Comtesse d'. "Finette Cendron." *Les Contes des fées*. 4 vols. Paris, 1697. Rpt. *Nouveau Cabinet des Fées*. Vol. 3. Genève: Slatkine Reprints, 1978. 18 vols. 472–503.

———. *Histoire d'Hypolite, Comte de Duglas*. Paris: Louis Sevestre, 1690. Rpt. Genève: Slatkine Reprints, 1979.

———. "La Princesse Belle-Etoile et le Prince Chéri." *Les Contes nouveaux ou Les Fées à la mode*. 4 vols. Paris: Veuve de Théodore Girard, 1698. Rpt. *Nouveau Cabinet des Fées*. Vol. 5. Genève: Slatkine Reprints, 1978. 18 vols. 179–266.

Dällenbach, Lucien. *The Mirror in the Text*. Trans. Jeremy Whitely with Emma Hughes. Chicago: U of Chicago P, 1989.

———. *Mirrors and After: Five Essays on Literary Theory and Criticism*. New York: CUNY Graduate School, 1986.

Démoris, René. *Le Roman à la première personne, du Classicisme aux Lumières*. Paris: Librairie Armand Colin, 1975.

DuPlessis, Rachel Blau. *Writing Beyond the Ending: Narrative Strategies of Twentieth-Century Women Writers*. Bloomington: Indiana UP, 1985.

Hipp, Marie-Thérèse. *Mythes et réalités: Enquête sur le roman et les mémoires (1660–1700)*. Paris: Librarie C. Klincksieck, 1976.

Le Noble, Eustache. "L'Oiseau de vérité." *Le Gage touché*. Paris: 1700. *Il Etait une Fois des Fées: contes des XVIIe et XVIIIe siècles*. Ed. Raymonde Robert. Nancy: Presses Universitaires de Nancy, 1984. 81–90.

Lhéritier de Villandon, Marie-Jeanne. "Les Enchantements de l'éloquence ou les effets de la douceur." *Oeuvres meslées*. Paris: J. Guignard, 1696. *Contes de Perrault*. Ed. Gilbert Rouger. Paris: Garnier Frères, 1967.

Miller, Nancy K. "Men's Reading, Women's Writing: Gender and the Rise of the Novel." *Yale French Studies* 75 (1988): 40–55.

Prince, Gerald. *Dictionary of Narratology*. Lincoln: U of Nebraska P, 1987.

Propp, Vladimir. *Morphologie du conte*. Paris: Editions du Seuil, 1965.

Richelet, Pierre. *Dictionnaire françois*. 2 vols. Genève: Jean Herman Widerhold, 1680. Rpt. Genève: Slatkine Reprints, 1970.

Robert, Raymonde. *Le conte de fées littéraire en France, de la fin du XVIIe à la fin du XVIIIe siècle*. Nancy: Presses Universitaires de Nancy, 1982.

Villiers, Pierre, l'Abbé de. *Entretiens sur les contes de fées et sur quelques autres ouvrages du temps, pour servir de préservatif contre le mauvais goût*. Paris: Jacques Collombat, 1699.

Galesia, Jane Barker, and a Coming to Authorship

Kathryn R. King

I

The story told by the poet and novelist Jane Barker, in three autobiographical narratives about her struggle to fashion an identity as a writing woman, is inevitably a study in ambivalence. It is impossible that a woman coming to writing in England in the 1670s and 1680s would not be anxious about her own acts of authorship. But it is hardly surprising that such a woman, talented and stubbornly intelligent, living in relative isolation in rural Lincolnshire, would turn to writing as a way of maintaining, perhaps inventing, a sense of self. Nor is it surprising that she would fantasize about achieving the kind of acclaim enjoyed by a small but visible number of female poets in the generation before her, most conspicuously Katherine Philips ("Orinda"), whose verse seems to have aroused in the teenaged Barker her first desire for literary fame.[1] What *is* surprising is that the three autobiographical novels in which Jane Barker recounts her early history as a writing woman should remain so little known.[2]

The anxieties of authorship exposed in the Galesia trilogy—*Love Intrigues* (1713), *A Patch-work Screen for the Ladies* (1723), and *A Lining for the Patch-Work Screen* (1726)—belong to a cultural moment when, for the first time, the work of an appreciable number of English women began to be published. It is estimated that between 1640 and 1700 the writings of as many as four hundred women found their way into print.[3] These included devotional works, educational theories, religious polemics, lives and letters, household advice, plays, poetry, prose fiction. By the early decades of the eighteenth century, growing numbers of women were adding to the increasingly busy traffic in novels and, in ways which we are only now beginning to recognize, shaping the emerging novelistic discourse. Eliza Haywood, Mary Davys, Penelope Aubin, and Mary Hearne (and before them Aphra Behn and Delariviere Manley) were just a few of the women who, spurred by the expansion of the print trade and the new moneymaking possibilities of authorship, lived (at least in part) by the proceeds of novel writing.

Though Barker was herself an innovator in the novel, she came to writing in a less print-aggressive age. She appears to have begun composing verse for her own pleasure while living with her family in rural Lincolnshire, perhaps as early as the late 1660s, and then circulating her work in manuscript among a circle of friends. In 1688, in her mid-thirties, a collection of her verse was published as the first part of *Poetical Recreations*. Not until 1713, a quarter of a century later, would Barker's writing again see print. By then relations among writers, readers, and texts had altered dramatically. In the previous century women rarely wrote for print or for money. (Barker later claimed that the poems in *Poetical Recreations* were published without her consent.)[4] In the manuscript culture to which Barker and other seventeenth-century writers belonged, verse writing was a genteel accomplishment and a sociable act, the products of which were to be shared with friends, in Barker's case a group of Cambridge students. But by 1713, when Barker published her first prose narrative, *Love Intrigues*, professional writers, male and female, sought unknown readers through the impersonal mechanisms of the commercial book trade. The discomforts attendant upon this entry into the marketplace are one source of Barker's ambivalence, which makes her autobiographical Galesia fictions unusually rich texts for the study of anxieties of authorship in an early professional female writer.

The pages which follow focus on the problem of audience in one of these fictions, *A Patch-work Screen for the Ladies* (1723), as a way of charting some of these anxieties. The discussion draws upon Nancy K. Miller's practice of reading narrative as figurative of the "symbolic and material process entailed in becoming a (woman) writer" (129); it argues that *A Patch-work Screen* encodes within itself the story of its own creation and, by implication, the story of how one early eighteenth-century professional writer managed to construct for herself the conditions, psychological and discursive, that made addressing an impersonal readership possible. More specifically, it argues that the complex layerings of female auditors built into the framing fictions of *A Patch-work Screen for the Ladies* attempt to ease the anxieties of authorship thematized in its core narrative.

II

In a brilliant series of essays, Miller demonstrates that the process of coming to writing is usefully understood as a problem of location. Constructing an authorial identity entails locating a place from which to "imagine and image a writing self" (109); it entails also finding a place within the range of public discourses from which to speak and be heard. For women, the process is complicated by two familiar conditions: discourses are gendered, and gender matters for women in ways that it often does not for men. A woman of Barker's generation knew that she could gain approval by confining herself to female discourses— to "lofty Themes of useful Houswifery, / Transcribing old Receipts of Cookery," as in 1703 Sarah Fyge mockingly put it— but she also knew that such approval carries its own dismissal. The dynamic is hilariously invoked in the late eighteenth century by Elizabeth Moody, whose "Sappho," having burnt her books and replaced poetry with cultivation of the culinary arts, discovers that "none but cooks applaud her name [and] naught but recipes her fame."[5] But departures from recipes and the like might arouse contempt, ridicule, or hostility—dismissal of a ruder sort.

In *A Patch-work Screen* the perplexities of location haunt the narrator, Galesia, who looks back on her younger versifying self with the ambiguous feelings of one who grounds her identity in acts of writing but questions the legitimacy of literary activities for women in general. Barker's preoccupation with the female writer's uncertain and contradictory relation to male culture is adumbrated in *Love Intrigues*, the first of the Galesia trilogy. The story, which recounts Galesia's entanglement in a strange and finally unreadable courtship, is centrally concerned with relations between language and interiority as well as with issues of female self-identity. Galesia is forced to mask "with an outside Indifference" (*Love* 19) the realities of her inner life; her speech is broken, false, guarded, faltering. And thus the importance for her of poetry. Poetry offers a space in which to exercise control over the linguistic forms which break apart under the pressure of a code of propriety that requires her words be kept "close Prisoners" (34). In poetry—a private space—she can articulate the desires she must guard against revealing to the world and her unaccountable lover. The privateness of poetry offers momentary release from the bleak disciplines of duplicity, but its separation from public discourses means that Galesia ends up colluding in her own silencing.

The condition of being at once present in, and split off from, one's own acts of writing is more fully developed in *A Patch-work Screen*, especially in those moments when Galesia brings a text before a reader or group of readers. An exemplary instance is the episode concerning her literary correspondence with the group of Cambridge students who offer the intellectual companionship missing in her immediate environs. The scene evoked in a letter from one of these students hints, however, at the problematics of using writing to supply a lack:

> We all return you Thanks for your *Ballad*; to which our Friend *Sam. Setwell*, put a Tune, and we sung it in a Booth merrily, 'till the *Proctor* had like to have Spoil'd the Harmony. But he finding no Female amongst us, drank the innocent Author's Health, and departed. (31)[6]

In this assemblage, Galesia's text is present ("put [to] a Tune") and its author noisily toasted. But the woman herself is not only absent from the scene but firmly excluded; indeed, only upon condition of her continuing exclusion ("he finding no Female amongst us") does authority, in the person of the Proctor, permit the merriment to continue. To the extent that a Cambridge songfest can be thought of as standing for the male-constituted cultural establishment, this scene of collegiate roistering figures the (familiar) relegation of the writing woman to the cultural margins, as well as her split relation to a dominant male culture that celebrates her work but excludes *her* from its precincts.[7]

Another instance of such exclusion is found in Galesia's account of her experience writing within male medical discourses. Her pride in her knowledge of botany, anatomy, physiology, and Latin (still used to encode medical knowledge) reaches a pitch when she discovers that she can pass off as the texts of university-trained doctors prescriptions she has written herself in the male-specialized Latin code—"this being," she notes with satisfaction, "particular in one of my Sex" (4).[8] But she longs, understandably enough, to enjoy recognition for this and other medical accomplishments, as shown in her remarkable poem, "*On the* Apothecaries *Filing my* Recipes *amongst the* Doctors":

> The *Sturdy Gout*, which all Male-Power withstands,
> Is overcome by my soft Female Hands.
> Not *Deb'rah Judith*, or *Semiramis*,
> Cou'd boast of Conquest half so great as this;
> More than they slew, I save, in this Disease. (57)

That Galesia's boast of the triumph of her "soft Female Hands" over "all Male-Power" is, at best, a fantasy of female power becomes clear from the narrator's ironic comment:

> Thus, Madam, as People before a Looking-glass, please themselves with their own Shapes and Features, though, perhaps, such as please no body else; just so I *celebrated my own Praise*, according to the Proverb, *for want of good Neighbours to do it for me.* (59)

Galesia's invisibility (except within the self-regarding mirror of her own verse) reproduces in another key her absent presence vis-à-vis the Cambridge students. If literary authority involves the ability to be seen and to be heard in the realm of public discourse, then Galesia's authority is strictly limited: it enacts itself "before a Looking-glass."

Whether Galesia writes *as if male*, using the language and discourses of university-trained men, or *as female*, disengaged from public modes of discourse, the effect is much the same: the female subject is herself invisible, absent, or excluded. Positioned in the contradiction between her inner needs for personal expression and external recognition and a discursive realm that renders her invisible, Galesia experiences divisions that amount at times almost to self-cancellation. Her story is shot through with images of exile, loneliness, alienation, and even dismemberment (most memorably in her tale of a murdered man whose body is hauled up "Piece-meal" from a ditch [sig. A9r]); and her consciousness of herself as a writer oscillates between fantasies of literary achievement and the recognition, by turns sardonic, wistful, resentful, self-mocking, and bemused, of the real slenderness of what she has achieved. Toward the end of *The Lining of the Patch-Work Screen*, the final novel in the trilogy, Galesia relates a bizarre dream. She is led up to the summit of Parnassus to see her poetic idol Orinda (Katherine Philips) crowned "Queen of Female Writers" (174). But Galesia, who had earlier yearned to rise to "fair ORINDA's Height" (*Love* 14), arrives too late to witness the ceremony, and after hiding awhile in the corner is discovered and sent away. Belatedness, banishment, failed aspiration: the vision is a fitting image of an abortive struggle to come fully into authorship.

III

But this is only part of the story. If the story Galesia tells of herself as a writing woman exposes the split between language and interiority, between desire for power and actual powerlessness, the larger narrative in which it is embedded, *A Patch-work Screen for the Ladies*, declares the possibility of patching together the pieces. Crucial to my reading of the narrative as a whole is the framing fiction which comes toward the end of the preface. It stages a reunion between an exiled poet named "Jane Barker" and her old friend Galesia. This meeting of two poets, each an alter ego of the historical Jane Barker (or more precisely, that part of Barker which defined itself as a woman writing), is at once a meeting of two versions of the writing self and of two styles of authorship. Galesia, now a seasoned, wry commentator on her earlier self, represents a style of authorship with its roots in the manuscript culture of the seventeenth century when young women wrote verse for themselves and a circle of friends. The "Jane Barker" who appears in the preface is very much a woman of 1723—urban, briskly ironic, disinclined to indulge in "Romantick" fancies about the poetic vocation. She belongs, indeed, to the new breed of writer, the novel-writing woman who casts a commercial eye on that new breed of reader, the novel-buying public. Galesia emerges as "Jane Barker"'s precursor; and the *other* Jane Barker, the historical author who stages this meeting between two fictionalized alter egos, stands screened somewhere behind it all, simultaneously rehearsing and rewriting her own history as a woman coming to authorship.[9] The conception is dazzling, and as I will now show, contains within itself a radical reimagining of the conditions in which a coming to authorship takes place.

The image of writer-as-Icarus which appears both in Galesia's story and in the framing fiction of the Preface provides an entry into this act of reimagining. In the cautionary tale offered by Galesia's mother in the core narrative, Icarus is a figure for the folly of literary aspirations ("idle Dreams on *Parnassus*, and foolish Romantick Flights") as well as their dangers (his "waxen Wings fail'd him so as to let him fall into the Sea" [79-80]). The Preface invokes just such folly when "Jane Barker" concedes (with considerable irony) that her own "high Flight in Favour of the Ladies" has made a "mere *Icarus* of me, melted my Wings, and tumbled me Headlong down, I know not where" (vi). The episode of banishment which now follows strongly resembles—but only up to a point—the scenes of alienation and isolation reiterated within Galesia's narrative. Discovered to have manuscripts of verse in her pockets, "Jane Barker" is thrust out of the "joyful Throng" into which she had tumbled, "every one hunching and pushing me, with Scorn and Derision" (vii). But what comes next brings an end to exile, isolation and freakishness. The banished poet, fleeing this jeering crowd, now comes upon Galesia, who again takes up the life story she began in *Love Intrigues*. And *that* story contains yet another: the story of how Galesia told her story to a kindly aristocratic lady. Working outwards, what we have, finally, is this: Galesia's life story, as told to a fictive Lady, as told to a fictionalized "Jane Barker," as fashioned by a professional author named Jane Barker into a patchwork narrative published under the title *A Patch-work Screen for the Ladies*—a recursive layering of sympathetic listeners which, by framing a space in which tale, teller, and told are at last brought together, revises the plot of female exclusion and isolation in which young Galesia remains confined.

That the release from isolation is linked to a new conception of female authorship is strongly implied by the patchwork analogies which introduce a pattern of needlework symbolism common to women's writing at this time. Similar text/textile equivalences can be traced back at least to 1599, when Mary Sidney, in "To the Thrice-Sacred Queen Elizabeth," described her collaboration with her brother on a translation of the Psalms as a shared textile production: "he did warpe, I weav'd this webbe to end" (89). A half century later another aristocratic writer, Margaret Cavendish, likened the writing of poetry to a "*Spinning with the braine*"; while at roughly the same time, on the other side of the Atlantic, Anne Bradstreet sent forth her poems trimmed in "home-spun Cloth." Metaphors such as these, which assimilate an emerging form of female work (authorship) to a familiar domestic one, assert continuities between writing and traditional forms of women's work. By associating the work of the pen with that of the distaff and needle, these early writers found a way to authorize their own acts of authorship.

Read within this intertextual field, the patchwork analogies situate the Galesia/Jane Barker story within the larger story of emergent female authorship. Such, at any rate, is the implication of the preface's enigmatic final paragraph, in which Galesia walks into the text (and perhaps literary history) with legs cramped from "long sitting at her Work." The paragraph, which appears to develop an allegory about a collective female coming to authorship, deserves full quotation:

> When I was got out of this Throng into the open Field, I met with the poor *Galesia*, walking to stretch her Legs, having been long sitting at her Work. With her I renew'd my Old Acquaintance; and so came to know all this Story of her *Patch-Work*: Which if you like, I will get the remaining Part of the *SCREEN*; for they are still at Work: And, upon my Word, I am glad to find the Ladies of *This Age*, wiser than *Those* of the *Former*; when the working of *Point* and curious *Embroidery*, was so troublesome, that they cou'd not take *Snuff* in Repose, for fear of soiling their Work: But in *Patch-Work* there is no Harm done; a smear'd Finger does but add a *Spot* to a *Patch*, or a *Shade* to a *Light-Colour*: Besides, those curious Works were pernicious to the Eyes; they cou'd not see the *Danger themselves* and *their Posterity might be in, a Thousand Years hence, about I know not what*. (viii)

The passage develops a contrast between the work performed by Barker's own generation (patchwork/novel-work) and women's work of the generations before her. (Until our own century, it should be recalled, the word *work* in a female context meant needlework.) The work of these earlier women—"*Point and curious Embroidery*"—was elegant but also finicky, anxious, and "pernicious to the Eyes," as opposed to the sloppy but on the whole agreeable work undertaken by Barker's contemporaries, which admits of a smudge (of ink?) here and there: "a smear'd Finger does but add a Spot to a Patch."[10] The allegory remains perplexing in places—I would like to know what is meant by the final assertion that these earlier women "cou'd not see the *Danger themselves* and *their Posterity might be in*," for example—but it seems evident that its implicit conception of authorship moves beyond a preoccupation with the isolated writing self to assert a larger unity with other writing women and to affirm connections between authorship and shared female experience.

The patchwork frame may also imply new relations between the female author and her reading public. Barker's technical and thematic concern with relations between teller and told—and, by implication, writer and readership—is discernible in the framing device she used ten years earlier in *Love Intrigues*. Galesia tells her story to a companion, Lucasia, who projects the character Galesia's need for an auditor, but in a broader sense the text's need for a sympathetic readership. In choosing to call her by the name used by Katherine Philips to address her best-known female friend, Barker places her narrative within the tradition of chaste female authorship. The choice of name may also point toward Barker's desire to imagine for her work a readership of literary women. The multilayered as-told-to structure of *A Patch-work Screen* suggests that the writer is reaching beyond a single listener (Lucasia) to an entire community of auditors—a public comprised in large part of a distinct female readership.

The patchwork screen, arranged by a group of women out of the patches derived from the shared materials of female life, may thus inscribe a distinctively female set of conditions for coming to authorship. Certainly the layering of teller-told relationships constructed in the framing fiction affords the narratorial Galesia the kind of sympathetic audience that proved unavailable or problematic in the context of the life story she now rehearses. If coming to authorship involves a double process of imagining a writing self and finding a discursive place from which that self can speak and be heard, then *A Patch-work Screen for the Ladies* symbolically reenacts such a process, as Galesia finds within an imagined community of patchworking women an end to ostracism, exclusion, loneliness, and self-division, and then goes on to tell her story to her literary successor, "Jane Barker." *A Patch-work Screen* is finally a story of empowerment, of becoming present, of patching together the pieces.

IV

That said, I begin to wonder if my own high flight in favor of *A Patch-work Screen for the Ladies* has made a "mere Icarus" of me. Am I burdening a simple framing device with more than is "really" there? Constructing out of what amounts to a narrative convention a Utopian vision of gynocentric creativity? Sentimentalizing women and professional authorship in ways that Barker herself would fail to comprehend or appreciate? Possibly. The view of women she presents is in fact anything but sentimental: Galesia is sharply critical of female frivolity, vanity, shallowness, indifference to the life of the mind, and is happy enough to dissociate herself whenever possible from the general run of womankind. And my impulse to celebrate Barker's coming to authorship is tempered by the reflection that Barker herself may have felt something less than rapture at finding herself late in life (she was at least seventy when she published *A Patch-work Screen*) required to face the indignities of the London book trade, especially as carried on by her publisher, the notorious Edmund Curll, already known for his "scurrilous and sensational publications" (McBurney 386). Barker may have derived considerably less satisfaction from the patched-together screen she placed between herself and possible economic distress than we take in her accomplishment.

Jane Barker's feelings about her role as a professional writer remain finally unknown, but from her texts we have much to learn about what it has meant historically for women to come to writing. I would suggest by way of concluding that Myra Jehlen's understanding of the process by which women writers "create their creativity" accounts for some of the resonance of the Galesia fictions. Jehlen argues that the female coming to writing, often thought of in largely psychological terms, is "also a conceptual and linguistic act: the construction of an enabling relationship with a language that of itself would deny [women] the ability to use it creatively" (583). We might, following Jehlen, think of *A Patch-work Screen* as a text revelatory of the activities undertaken prior to its creation, a record of the process by which its author imagined a network of enabling relationships—with language, but also with traditions of female culture as they authorize writing, and with female audiences as they offer a place in which to speak and be heard. It would be too simple to say that Barker argues for sexual separatism or valorizes a distinct female subculture—though it seems clear that literary empowerment is for her unimaginable outside of female contexts and the connectedness they provide. Rather, in *A Patch-work Screen* she claims her own creativity by imagining the conditions under which her work is to be produced and read. This too is a revisionary project, and perhaps a collaborative one as well: the screen, as Barker says in her preface, is not yet finished, the patchworkers are "still at Work."[11]

NOTES

1. For a valuable discussion of Philips and the literary contexts of seventeenth-century poetry by women, see Mermin.

2. Jeslyn Medoff discovered that Barker was baptized in 1652; she was thus in her sixties and seventies when the Galesia fictions were published (Greer et al. 354). For introductory discussions of the fictions, see Spencer 62–70 and Williamson 244–51. The perception that Barker is a key figure for the study of women's entry into the literary culture is beginning to gain currency; see Donovan for an important account of the role of *A Patch-work Screen* in the emergence of the novel.

3. Wilson and Warnke xi. For an account of female publication in the seventeenth century, see Crawford.

4. See Medoff's note in Greer et al. 361. *Poetical Recreations* is briefly discussed in Hobby 159–62 and Williamson 102–07.

5. The Fyge citation is from "The Liberty" (Greer et al. 347). Moody's 1798 poem, "Sappho Burns her Books and Cultivates the Culinary Arts," includes this invocation to the "Goddess of Culinary Art": "Teach me more winning arts to try, / To salt the ham, to mix the pie" (Lonsdale 406). The versified recipe is one of many poetic genres represented in *A Patch-work Screen*. My favorite of these "Receipts," one for French soup, begins with this splendid line: "Take a large Barn-door Cock, and all his Bones break" (109).

6. Here and in a few other passages, I silently reverse italics for ease of reading.

7. The Proctor suggestively prefigures the Beadle in Woolf's *A Room of One's Own*. I owe the notion of duality developed here to Jacobus's discussion of Woolf 59–61.

8. The original erroneously reads "being in particular."

9. This pattern, Mason argues, is fundamental to female autobiographies: such splitting and doubling appears to construct the audience which disclosure of female self-identity depends upon. Recent studies have arrived at similar conclusions. See the essays collected by Brodzki and Schenck, and Benstock (especially Friedman).

10. This detail may also point toward ambivalence about the sullying effects of writing for the marketplace. It is perhaps pertinent that when Galesia is banished from Parnassus in her dream, she is given a bag of gold.

11. I thank Ruth Looper, Jes Medoff, Sarah Palmer, and Ellen Wright-Vance for their very useful responses to this essay.

WORKS CITED

Barker, Jane. *The Lining of the Patch-Work Screen: Design'd for the Farther Entertainment of the Ladies*. London: Printed for A. Bettesworth, 1726.

———. *Love Intrigues*. Ed. Josephine Grieder. New York: Garland, 1973.

———. *A Patch-work Screen for the Ladies*. Ed. Josephine Grieder. New York: Garland, 1973.

Benstock, Shari, ed. *The Private Self: Theory and Practice of Women's Autobiographical Writings*. Chapel Hill: U of North Carolina P, 1988.

Brodzki, Bella, and Celeste Schenck, eds. *Life/Lines: Theorizing Women's Autobiography*. Ithaca: Cornell UP, 1988.

Cavendish, Margaret. *Poems and Fancies*. Menton, Yorkshire: Scolar P, 1972.

Crawford, Patricia. "Women's Published Writings 1600–1700." *Women in English Society 1500–1800*. Ed. Mary Prior. New York: Methuen, 1985. 211–82.

Donovan, Josephine. "Women and the Rise of the Novel: A Feminist-Marxist Theory." *Signs* 16 (1991): 441-62.

Friedman, Susan Stanford. "Women's Autobiographical Selves: Theory and Practice." Benstock 34–62.

Greer, Germaine, et al., eds. *Kissing the Rod: An Anthology of Seventeenth-Century Women's Verse*. New York: Noonday-Farrar Straus Giroux, 1988.

Hobby, Elaine. *Virtue of Necessity: English Women's Writing 1649–88*. Ann Arbor: U of Michigan P, 1989.

Jacobus, Mary. "The Difference of View." *The Feminist Reader: Essays in Gender and the Politics of Literary Criticism*. Ed. Catherine Belsey and Jane Moore. New York: Basil Blackwell, 1989. 49–62.

Jehlen, Myra. "Archimedes and the Paradox of Feminist Criticism." *Signs* 6 (1981): 575–601.

Lonsdale, Roger, ed. *Eighteenth-Century Women Poets: An Oxford Anthology*. Oxford: Oxford UP, 1989.

Mason, Mary G. "The Other Voice: Autobiographies of Women Writers." Brodzki and Schenck 19–44.

McBurney, William H. "Edmund Curll, Mrs. Jane Barker, and the English Novel." *Philological Quarterly* 37 (1958): 385–99.

Mermin, Dorothy. "Women Becoming Poets: Katherine Philips, Aphra Behn, Anne Finch." *ELH* 57 (1990): 335–55.

Miller, Nancy K. *Subject to Change: Reading Feminist Writing*. New York: Columbia UP, 1988.

Sidney, Mary. *The Triumph of Death and Other Unpublished and Uncollected Poems*. Ed. Gary Waller. Salzburg: Universität Salzburg, 1977.

Spencer, Jane. "Creating the Woman Writer: The Autobiographical Works of Jane Barker." *Tulsa Studies in Women's Literature* 2 (1983): 165–81.

————. *The Rise of the Woman Novelist: From Aphra Behn to Jane Austen.* New York: Basil Blackwell, 1986.

Williamson, Marilyn L. *Raising Their Voices: British Women Writers, 1650–1750.* Detroit: Wayne State UP, 1990.

Wilson, Katharina M. and Frank J. Warnke. Introduction. *Women Writers of the Seventeenth Century.* Ed. Katharina M. Wilson and Frank J. Warnke. Athens: U Georgia P, 1989. xi–xxiii.

PART 2

"My Book My Pen and My—Lover": Reading, Writing, and Romance

The Word as Battleground in
Jane Austen's Persuasion

Julia Giordano

There is often danger for a woman in the act of speaking or writing. Jane Austen hid her manuscript when anyone entered the drawing room where she wrote; Anne Elliot, in Austen's novel *Persuasion*, couches her observations in circumlocutions which make them more palatable to her family: female author and fictional heroine alike choose to hide the content of their minds from the people with whom they share their lives. Certainly "to speak one's mind" involves an assumption of power which has made women uneasy. To speak risks the danger of response; the response may be overwhelming, or contradictory, or annihilating. All women have engaged in the kind of self-disguise which minimizes this risk through subterfuge, speaking in the third-person masculine when we mean the first-person feminine, using "everyone" or "all women" to cloak our own personal experience for self-protection. We learn to proceed cautiously, not to make assumptions which might be easily challenged. Part of the curious appeal of *Persuasion*, Jane Austen's last novel, lies in its masterful portrayal of this anxious power which attends Anne Elliot's every effort to find and speak the truth of who she is. This essay aims to show that the author achieves her mastery through the same kind of silence which Anne uses to survive in her hostile family: where Anne uses circumlocution and denial to avoid voicing the unpleasant truth she sees, Austen uses free indirect discourse to force her reader to a judgment without using the words of judgment herself.

I

Let me begin my examination of *Persuasion* with a puzzle, a slight inconsistency of character of the sort in which Austen delights. Early in the novel, after Anne meets Frederick Wentworth again, she learns from her sister Mary that he thought "'You were so altered he should not have known you again'" (85). To this judgment Anne submits "in silent, deep mortification" as she repeats his words to herself: "'So altered that he should not have known her again!' These were words which could not but dwell with her." The repetition reinforces the importance of Wentworth's words, although the text itself undercuts their truth-value by immediately connecting his judgment to a long-held resentment: "He had thought her wretchedly altered, and had spoken as he felt. He had not forgiven Anne Elliot. She had used him ill; deserted and disappointed him" (86). Nevertheless, his perception is acknowledged to be sincere, and serious: he spoke as he felt. This time the operative verb is modified by an adverb which emphasizes the depth and direction of the change (she is "wretchedly altered"). Wentworth believes that something has changed in Anne, something important enough to make her unrecognizable, unknowable to the man who once loved her.

But the minor inconsistency of character seems to belong to Wentworth, and it is revealed only after he and Anne finally renew their engagement at the end of the novel. After a revolution the victors rewrite the history books, and one of the first things the couple does together in their new happiness is to rewrite their recent history in order to transform the story of their estrangement into one of their reconciliation. Certainly the change in the status of their connection qualifies as a revolution in their lives, but, significantly, here again the novel returns to the change in Anne: was that change also a revolution? Wentworth mentions a visit to his brother Edward, who "'asked even if you were personally altered, little suspecting that to my eye you could never alter.'" Again that word "alter" echoes in the text and recalls his earlier words even before we are told of Anne's smile at his "blunder." She "could never alter"; in his present happiness he has changed his mind retroactively, so that he erases his previous words; history is rewritten. Her evaluation of this reversal of his feelings is fond, tender: "the value of such homage was inexpressibly increased to Anne, by comparing it with former words, and feeling it to be the result, not the cause of a revival of his warm attachment" (245).

Anne has decided what happened: in the first fondness of his returning feelings for her, Wentworth persuaded himself that he always loved her, just as earlier his resentment persuaded him that she had changed so much as to be unrecognizable. But what if Anne is wrong? Certainly in the fervor of his present feelings Wentworth has propelled his judgment back in time to make it retroactive. But what if both judgments are accurate at the time they are formed? What if the Anne whom he first met at Uppercross had indeed changed so radically that she had become unknowable? And let me then posit another change, signalled by the reversal of Wentworth's feelings. Let us suppose that Anne has changed again, in the course of the novel, to resemble more closely the Anne with whom he first fell in love, eight years previously. If we accept Anne's judgment of the situation, the change in Wentworth's opinion is only a slight inconsistency in his character, understandable and even endearing given the circumstances; the narration itself reinforces this view. The alternative scenario, which makes Wentworth's evaluation of Anne seem less "persuaded" by his own emotions, infinitely complicates Anne's character as well as the narration's reliability. This novel presents Anne as its center of narrative authority, someone whose ideas and opinions are definitely to be trusted, an island of sanity in "the sameness and the elegance, the prosperity and the nothingness" of her family (40). If this evaluation of Anne is incorrect or partial, then the narrator's voice[1] and the whole tenor of the novel become subversively ironic. In this novel, which almost exclusively depicts the thoughts and opinions of its heroine, the distance between narrator and heroine may be wider than it first appears.

II

Margaret Anne Doody makes an interesting historical observation in her analysis of free indirect discourse, the technique which Jane Austen uses effectively in all her novels and almost exclusively in *Persuasion*: "A peculiar difficulty confronted women novelists of the eighteenth century, an obstacle so enormous that the wonder is that they made any headway in getting over it: a woman is not supposed to be judgmental. The tone of judgment coming from the lips of a woman was thought unpleasant, unnatural" (280). This prohibition had overwhelming consequences in women's lives, of course; we will soon see the kind of circumlocution it engenders in Anne's attempts to speak. But more specifically the unnaturalness of a judgmental woman dictated how women wrote novels: the development of an authentic voice for a female writer began with the novel-as-letters or the novel-as-journal, forms in which characters themselves functioned as narrator. Female writers slowly moved out of this restrictive silence and, with a variety of indirect quotation in free indirect discourse, found a more effective posture as narrator. By representing a character's voice without enclosing it in quotation marks, the female writer might now use words as if the character were speaking, thus both maintaining and blurring the distinction between narrator and character.[2] With this technique of speech representation characters assist in narration; but the presence of the author becomes more tangible, since there is always an implied gap in the words themselves, "a discrepancy between a character's thoughts and authorial re-speaking of them" (Doody 288). The narrator's (still never spoken) judgment of a character emerges slowly, as the reader comes to understand the character from the inside and then begins to find the shadowy outline of a judgment within the words themselves.

Doody's analysis places the origin for this style of narration within a social conflict grounded in the fact of sexual difference. For female novelists the way out of this conflict was the way around, a circuitous route of creative avoidance. Even as female writers learned to speak in the novel—learned to break the silence of the blank page—their method was born of silence. They used their characters' language at once to hide and to reveal their own judgments and thereby avoided the risk of making those judgments aloud, in an unequivocal and univocal language of their own. They triumphed over a society that attempted to silence their voices, by apparently obeying rules of feminine propriety which concealed the essentially subversive nature of the female act of narration.³ Even as these female writers assumed the word's inherent power to define and delineate reality, they adhered to the social fiction of their own silence: such power as they assumed was anxious, precariously rooted in the success of their charade (whether conscious or unconscious) and maintained with an uneasy glance over the shoulder.

The narrative style thus developed embodied within it this tension between silence and speaking, a tension which was itself a direct analogue of the social impropriety of combining the words "female" and "novelist." If the female author can speak only in the voice and words of the character, then within those words she must somehow establish her own authority, at times subverting, at other times supporting the character's outlook on reality. Austen is a master of this style of narration, which assumes a character's voice even as it sabotages that character's assumptions about the world. She opens *Persuasion* in the style of a character we soon come to despise: "Sir Walter Elliot, of Kellynch-hall, in Sommersetshire, was a man who, for his own amusement, never took up any book but the Baronetage; there he found occupation for an idle hour, and consolation in a distressed one" (35). The sarcasm inherent in this picture of a book which provides occupation and consolation (not the Bible, as we might expect, but the Baronetage) signals immediately an implicit and savage judgment of Sir Walter. The narrator is at war with her character, and the battlefield is his own utterance.

Bakhtin describes the process by which a social conflict might become embodied in an utterance which is no longer univocal: "two socio-linguistic consciousnesses, two epochs...come together and consciously fight it out on the territory of the utterance" (360). Free indirect discourse is one form of incorporating social conflict into the novel through dialogization, a concept developed by Bakhtin for the essential multiplicity of voices ("heteroglossia") which characterizes the novel as a genre. When Austen uses Sir Walter's voice as the vehicle for her own covert judgments, the word itself becomes part of a dialogue. Its relationship to the object it attempts to depict is never a straightforward one-to-one correspondence:

> When we seek to understand a word, what matters is not the direct meaning the word gives to objects and emotions—this

> is the false front of the word; what matters is rather the actual
> and always self-interested *use* to which this meaning is put
> and the way it is expressed by the speaker....*Who* speaks and
> under what conditions he speaks: this is what determines the
> word's actual meaning. All direct meanings and direct expres-
> sions are false, and this is especially true of emotional mean-
> ings and expressions. (Bakhtin 401)

The word cannot be trusted at face value: it has become a battleground whose reference is determined more by the logistics of
war than by truth or correspondence to reality. The word itself is
the site of a struggle for power: whoever controls the word controls the world.[4] But of course such a struggle can never be
finally resolved. The power assumed maintains its character as
anxious power simply because the war is never over.

This ideology of the word results from the cultural resistance to the very idea of female novelists which faced Austen
and others of her time. For a woman to assume the power of
narration, to attempt to define a world, threatened the assumption that men controlled social reality. Bakhtin's analysis of the
link between discourse and power suggests the enactment of
this cultural conflict in the narration itself; certainly, the inner
tension of free indirect discourse is a struggle between author's
and character's voice for the power of the word. This style
avoids any direct statement by the narrator, so when at the end
of *Persuasion* the narrator enters her novel in the first person, the
violation of third-person anonymity is in itself a shock. But
more than this, she enters the novel expressly to subvert the
reader's identification with Anne, an identification established
throughout the novel and now at its height in the successful resolution of her love for Wentworth:

> Who can be in doubt of what followed? When any two young
> people take it into their heads to marry, they are pretty sure
> by perseverance to carry their point, be they ever so poor, or
> ever so imprudent, or ever so little likely to be necessary to
> each other's ultimate comfort. This may be bad morality to
> conclude with, but I believe it to be truth; and if such parties
> succeed, how should a Captain Wentworth and an Anne
> Elliot, with the advantage of maturity of mind, consciousness
> of right, and one independent fortune between them, fail of
> bearing down every opposition? (250)

The initial question trivializes the marriage which ends the novel's central conflict, even as it ostensibly negates the doubt that such a marriage will occur. The following statement then questions the wisdom of the institution of marriage and, by implication, the triumph over social opposition which this specific marriage would celebrate. The narrator thus, within the exposure of the first person, establishes her opposition to any end to the conflict her text has engaged, even as she goes on to problematize the nature of that conflict.[5] Anne and Wentworth encounter very little resistance from her family: Anne obviously matters too little to her father and sister for either to be roused to active opposition. Yet the narrator has implied, by her "bad morality," the inadequacy of any solution to the conflict her novel has addressed; if this is the case, surely that conflict must be larger and deeper than this easily resolved dispute over whether the marriage should take place.

This final narrative impasse recalls the particular skirmish in the war between the sexes which created free indirect discourse, a cultural conflict which was not resolved but only circumvented by the resourcefulness of female writers. Plot will not be tamed by dénouement; the tension of sexual difference does not disappear with increased opportunity for women. Both narrative and cultural indeterminacy are mirrored in the battle between narrator and character for possession of the word, another contest where victory is never won. As we return to *Persuasion* to investigate the nature of this narrative conflict which resists resolution, and the nature of the change in Anne, we must remember that dialogization of the word dictates a tension within the utterance that belies any easy identification of character (even as sympathetic a character as Anne) with narrator.

III

Certainly Anne is the most sympathetic character in this novel full of vain, greedy, shallow or misguided people, some of whom have allowed their failings to progress toward outright evil. But she is also an enigmatic character, a mystery. She has kept her sanity and her integrity by concealing her emotions from the people who might have been her intimates. In the early parts of the novel she is an attentive listener who makes short, astute comments which are immediately overwhelmed and negated by her family's replies. Her own conversation is simply not recorded; Anne's voice is silent. And she is not only unheard, she is also unseen, "nothing" to her sister, to her father. She is literally fading away, losing "her bloom" (37). In this alien environment, Anne at no time tells the whole truth of what she feels because exposure would be too dangerous. She speaks only when she must, and she couches whatever she says in the lies, attitudes and tone of voice which will make it least offensive to the people around her. When all the Hayters complain to her about each other, "she could do little more than listen patiently, soften every grievance, and excuse each to the other, give them all hints of the forbearance necessary between such near neighbours, and make those hints broadest which were meant for her sister's benefit" (72). The characteristically reticent construction which surrounds and constricts each of the verbs ("could do little more than listen...soften...excuse...give...make") emphasizes the danger of direct reply or action in Anne's situation. She is treating her family as the enemy: she acts only when she must, and then does as little as she possibly can.[6]

Her feelings for Captain Wentworth have also been a secret from most of her family, revealed only at the time to Sir Walter, Lady Russell, and Elizabeth, and never mentioned again in the eight years since the engagement ended. So when Wentworth tells a story of a dangerous situation at sea happily averted, "Anne's shudderings were to herself alone" (90) because no one else knows about her special interest in his safety. Even to the reader, the engagement is a beginning which remains outside the novel's action, a "distant and difficult originating event" (Tave 273) denied significance by the narrator's irony: "he had nothing to do, and she had hardly any body to love," and so they fell "rapidly and deeply in love" (55). The novel built on Anne's perspective would of course keep Anne's secret.

The narrator surrounds Anne's every attempt to speak or act with circumlocutions which at once mirror Austen's own dilemma as a female novelist and Anne's belief that such self-definition betrays her safety. Even Anne's inner emotions are expressed in the same kind of tortuous avoidances which characterize her spoken feelings: "Anne could not but be amused" at the idea of herself preaching patience to Captain Benwick, "nor could she help fearing" that her own conduct belied her message (122); "she could not be insensible of" Mr. Eliot's admiration when he sees her in Lyme (125); a look on Captain Wentworth's face "Anne was sure could never be forgotten by her" (132). Danger is present to Anne not just in the expression of emotions, but in their very existence; she acknowledges feelings to herself as unwillingly as to anyone else. When she has first seen Captain Wentworth again after their long separation, "she would have liked to know how he felt as to a meeting....He must be either indifferent or unwilling. Had he wished ever to see her again, he need not have waited till this time; he would have done what she could not but believe that in his place she should have done long ago" (83–84). Anne has no feelings in the active voice. The first sentence expresses the possible consequence of a hypothetical condition: she doesn't want to know, she "would have liked to know." But no condition is stated, and so the possibility of such a desire is left vague and indefinite. Even her attempt at a judgment is forced upon her (he "must be") and then lost in the uncertainty of choice ("either indifferent or unwilling"). And the painful conditionality of the final sentence allows her to avoid the bleak and unavoidable judgment even as she at once states and denies her own desire ("what she could not but believe...she should have done"). It is a short step from treating the visible expression of emotion as dangerous, to seeing emotion itself as the problem: if she didn't feel emotions, she would not have to police her expression of them.

In a novel so dominated by Anne's perspective, the combination of her startlingly acute perceptions of others and her desperate avoidance of any direct statement of her own feelings, even to herself, seriously subverts narrative reliability. Anne knows more than any other character in the book about the thoughts and feelings of those around her, and so when she acknowledges her own feelings we may consider her to be just as reliable. But this is not the case. Certainly it is obvious that her own evaluation of her feelings about Wentworth cannot be trusted: "Anne found herself by this time growing so much more hardened to being in Captain Wentworth's company than she had at first imagined she could ever be, that the sitting down to the same table with him now, and the interchange of the common civilities attending on it—(they never got beyond) was become a mere nothing" (120–21). Anne is lying to herself here. The parenthesis, demonstrating the limits of her narrative authority, points to a careful monitoring of the extent of their interaction which belies her casual and cruel dismissal of her own feelings: seeing Wentworth "was become a mere nothing." If Anne lies to herself once, she may again; and a liar's participation in the narration must make its reliability suspect.

IV

"Liar" is a strong word; perhaps it would be better to describe Anne as an expert at the art of concealment, just as many women have learned to conceal the essential power of their natures, to hide behind lies and evasions, to work at being beautiful, helpful, dumb; and just as the female novelist who created her was an expert at the art of concealment within her character's voices, a master of free indirect discourse. But the obvious difference between Anne and her creator is that Anne seems to have lost any freedom of movement or expression. The narrative circumlocutions which surround and overwhelm her every thought, utterance, and action only highlight the seminal fact of Anne's existence: her world is dangerous, and to cope with it she has perfected the art of concealment until it is second nature, involuntary, and almost beyond her power to stop.

More important than the fact that the world which surrounds her may actually be dangerous is Anne's struggle to overcome the techniques of effacement which she has used for survival, and thus finally to speak her own nature. She does so within the context of a love story, where speaking her truth means admitting her feelings to the man she loves. Certainly the erotic power generated in the final part of the novel is largely the result of Anne coming to life again after a long paralysis, awakening to her own power as she becomes aware that she still holds power over Wentworth.[7] The scene where she first meets Wentworth again deserves as much attention as the later, more often noted meeting in which they covertly declare their love in the Hayters' hotel parlor. In a Bath teashop, "Anne, as she sat near the window, descried, most decidedly and distinctly, Captain

Wentworth walking down the street" (185). The overwhelming alliteration (*window*, *descried*, *decidedly*, *distinctly*, *Wentworth walking down*) emphasizes the uncharacteristic vigor of Anne's glance. She commits herself wholeheartedly to a concentration of energy and attention which implies great risk in the dangerous world she inhabits. The difference between this description and the earlier circumlocutions which couched her every move in subterfuge and concealment is underscored by the tumultuous emotions Anne now experiences:

> For a few minutes she saw nothing before her. It was all confusion. She was lost....She now felt a great inclination to go to the outer door; she wanted to see if it rained. Why was she to suspect herself of another motive? Captain Wentworth must be out of sight. She left her seat, she would go, one half of her should not be always so much wiser than the other half, or always suspecting the other of being worse than it was. She would see if it rained. (185)

Sedate Anne Elliot is overcome by her emotions to the point where she cannot concentrate on the situation before her. Desperate poise in the presence of danger has been the characteristic which determined her movements, or rather her stasis; now she releases herself quite consciously from her normal self-watchfulness. A young woman moves to the door of a teashop in Bath; an insignificant occurrence, surely, and yet the world has changed for Anne. She has overcome her fear of action. Here she acknowledges her fear as sexual excitement, her motives as suspect, even as she denies the knowledge and allows her desire to determine her actions. She assumes the power to dialogize her own inner conversation and thereby undermines the authority of concealment as an instinctive strategy. Here and later, in her efforts to speak her mind to Wentworth, she does nothing less than overturn the logic on which she has based her world. The risk is earthshaking, and she takes it.

In the climactic scene where Anne's conversation with Captain Harville finally prompts Wentworth to write her his letter of proposal, the same mechanisms of denial and covert acknowledgement which sent her to the door of the teashop again govern her actions. Engaged in a discussion with Harville on the relative constancy of men and women, Anne hears Wentworth at a nearby desk drop his pen: "Anne was startled at finding him nearer than she supposed, and half inclined to suspect that the pen had only fallen, because he had been occupied by them, striving to catch sounds, which yet she did not think he could have caught." Her two halves are again at war, and her final assertion is so uncertain as to be disingenuous. Certainly she goes on as though her conversation with his friend might also be a conversation with Wentworth. Harville speaks of the fickleness of women in books, and she replies, "'no references to examples in books. Men have had every advantage of us in telling their own story....The pen has been in their hands'" (237). She quite pointedly replies to Wentworth's action here even as her words are ostensibly directed toward his friend: she is dialogizing her own word. She is writing her own story, telling Wentworth that the story he wrote of their relationship was wrong, that he must now listen to her story and her claim (for women) "of loving longest, when existence or when hope is gone" (238). Anne here uses her skills at concealment as a consummate artist, playing the game of silence even as she uses silence to speak. Propriety dictates that as a woman she cannot speak her feelings to Wentworth, and Anne herself would be extremely uncomfortable with any direct exposure of her feelings. But because her words are directed to Harville and not to Wentworth, she permits herself to say things only Wentworth would understand, if he were listening. Her specious assertion that he is not listening supports this tottering structure of social intercourse, as does her belief that he would not break the rules of propriety by eavesdropping. Of course both propositions are false, but the technique of simultaneous belief and disbelief here meshes perfectly with the technique of simultaneous concealment and exposure to produce effective communication. Within the rules of the game the word is spoken, and heard.

V

I do not mean to suggest a simple opposition between the Anne of earlier parts of the novel and the Anne who is finally able to speak her mind to Captain Wentworth. Certainly it is true that when Anne does speak she uses the same techniques of concealment which have become second nature to her, but it is also possible that Anne would never have been able to speak at all had she not been silent for so long. I have suggested already that her extreme reticence began as a measured refusal to speak rather than as an inability to speak. That refusal implies activity even as it dictates silence, for it depends on the adroit circumvention of the dominant mode of discourse in her society.[8] Anne's decision to withdraw into silence remains problematic, the discovery of its exact nature thwarted by the secrecy in which the novel shrouds its originating event, the end of her engagement to Wentworth eight years before the novel begins. The reader may posit the despair she felt at the collapse of her dreams of marriage and the difficulty of readjusting to her family's indifference. But the novel refuses to satisfy any curiosity about her decision to retreat from the world around her or the pain which must have attended such a withdrawal. Anne's silence remains as complete as she obviously needs it to be.

In the face of this secrecy, the inner conflict which dictated Anne's strategy of concealment and silence may best be illuminated by another outsider's decision to flee the essential savagery of what passes for civilized social interaction. In the *Adventures of Huckleberry Finn*, Huck, like Anne, despairs of finding acceptance in a society which coerces conformity to empty, hypocritical rules. But unlike Anne, Huck attempts to subvert society's power over him by using the dominant discourse of the civilization he wants to escape: he lies. By lying, he hopes to achieve an identity for himself through mastery of the rules which govern his society, but he dooms his attempt at escape simply because he has brought civilization with him in his instinctive reliance on lying. He participates in society even as he attempts to escape its power, and this participation dictates his final return to "sivilization" and angry silence: "so there ain't nothing more to write about, and I am rotten glad of it, because if I'd 'a' knowed what a trouble it was to make a book I wouldn't 'a' tackled it, and ain't a-going to no more" (283).

Anne, on the contrary, attempts neither subversion nor mastery. She neither leaves her family nor tries to conform to its rules. Instead, she protects herself with evasion and concealment whenever she is forced to participate in the language of social interaction, because she rightly senses that her very survival depends on divorcing herself as much as possible from the incarnation in language of the prevailing organization of power in her family and her society. Only when she senses the possibility of an alternative society opened to her by the discovery that Wentworth may still love her, does she again attempt to speak her feelings. And only then does the novel evince a headlong erotic power as it frees itself from the circumlocutions which have characterized Anne's indirect discourse. Here, then, is the conflict which would indeed be trivialized by any "happy" ending, any reconciliation of the outsider back into society. Just as there was no resolution to the social conflict which dictated a woman's silence except through a novelistic discourse which embodied conflict within itself, so too there can be no escape from Anne's dilemma except through her own dialogization of the word. She finds such a solution when she speaks her heart to Wentworth in the guise of conversation with his friend.

When the final words of the novel describe Anne's marriage, the description begins as a definition of conventional married bliss, then veers alarmingly:

> Anne was tenderness itself, and she had the full worth of it in Captain Wentworth's affection. His profession was all that could ever make her friends wish that tenderness less; the dread of a future war all that could dim her sunshine. She gloried in being a sailor's wife, but she must pay the tax of quick alarm for belonging to that profession which is, if possible, more distinguished in its domestic virtues than in its national importance. (254)

As this description begins, the word is univocal: the truth Anne struggled to express has been spoken and Anne has become emotion itself, she is tenderness, and that feeling is totally reciprocated by her husband. But conflict is introduced into the word immediately: the danger of his profession makes her friends wish her tenderness less, and by definition her "Anne-ness" less also, since "Anne" now equals "tenderness." Even within this commonplace there exists a shadow of the threat which other people have always posed for Anne, but the words then open up to a greater danger. The place which Anne has found for herself through her disavowal of the landed society into which she was born is itself a place of conflict, both military and personal:

a conflict between her happiness and the concern of her friends to limit that happiness for her own safety, between society's devaluation of her husband's (and thus her own) profession and the reality of its worth, between sunshine and the dimness of future war. There is no end to hostilities here, no happily-ever-after. The identity of signifier with signified ("Anne was tenderness itself") is immediately threatened, and dialogism as a technique of self-protection may be imminent. For a woman to speak her heart so openly as to become the word she speaks might well mean danger in a world which has forced female writers into the self-protection of indirect narration. Anne has found her rightful place, the place where her emotions can be expressed, but it is not without danger.

The reconciliation with which comedy traditionally ends proves to be a problem for both Twain and Austen. Twain subverts Huck's repatriation with his yearning to escape again, this time to uncharted territory which might support the freedom he learned on the raft with Jim. For Austen, the conventional dénouement betrays the novel enough for the narrator to break her anonymity and point ironically to the inadequacy of the only solution open to her. To suggest that Anne's profound discontent with her society might be solved by marriage would mean solidarity with the same society which sought to silence Austen's own voice as a novelist. Yet the genre of comedy dictates the ending. Austen's solution employs the same strategy which led to the development of free indirect discourse: a radical dialogization of the word which enables her to obey the rules of genre even as her narrator speaks her own first-person discontent with the institution of marriage as a solution to the problems of the married parties. Since the only words she can say are false, the narrator dialogizes them and points to their fraudulence as she speaks. Even in the novel's resolution there is no end to the struggle for the power of the word: the novelist fights the dictates of genre, the narrator implies the inadequacy of her generic solution, and Anne herself cannot expect quite so happy an ending as her prospects might imply.

NOTES

1. Throughout this essay I use the term "narrator" as the author's persona in the novel—not identical with the author herself, yet also female.

2. Bakhtin calls such a technique "double-voiced discourse. It serves two speakers at the same time and expresses simultaneously two different intentions: the direct intention of the character who is speaking, and the refracted intention of the author....And all the while these two voices are dialogically interrelated, they...know about each other (just as two exchanges in a dialogue know of each other and are structured in this mutual knowledge of each other); it is as if they actually hold a conversation with each other" (324). Such a conversation goes on within a word which is still one word but no longer single; it has become, in Bahktin's words, "internally dialogized" and so can express the conflict between its two speakers.

3. Kirkham analyzes feminism in the burgeoning of female writing at the time Austen began her career: "it will not do to approach the female authors of this period and divide them into genuine feminists versus the rest, for at this period to become an author was, in itself, a feminist act" (33).

4. Tanner points to the dialogism within even the one-word title, *Persuasion*: "In previous titles using abstract nouns Jane Austen had deployed pairs. This time the debate, the struggle, the contestation, the contrarieties and ambiguities are all in the one word" (208).

5. Gilbert and Gubar point to the duplicity of Austen's happy endings: "the implication remains that a girl without the aid of a benevolent narrator would never find a way out of either her mortifications or her parent's house" (169).

6. Trilling underlines the importance of Anne's approach to these apparently trivial interactions when he proposes "that our attitude toward manners is the expression of a particular conception of reality" (207).

7. Yaeger examines the significance of this "traditional heterosexual plot" in her essay on Kate Chopin's *The Awakening*, where the emancipatory nature of the text rests in "a conflict articulated as a struggle between men's normative language and something unvoiced and enigmatic—a clatter, a 'language which nobody understood'" (211–12).

8. I second Harding's opinion that Austen offers in *Persuasion* "a

more mature interpretation of the [Cinderella] theme, one no longer presenting the heroine as a passive sufferer of entirely unmerited wrongs." But where Harding stresses Anne's "mistaken decision" to break the engagement as the proof that her wrongs were not "unmerited," I would rather stress the activity of Anne's decision to withdraw into silence as proof that she is no "passive sufferer" (9).

WORKS CITED

Austen, Jane. *Persuasion*. Harmondsworth: Penguin, 1975.

Bakhtin, M. M. "Discourse in the Novel." *The Dialogic Imagination*. Ed. Michael Holquist. Trans. Caryl Emerson and Michael Holquist. Austin: U of Texas P, 1981. 259–422.

Doody, Margaret Anne. "George Eliot and the Eighteenth-Century Novel." *Nineteenth-Century Fiction* 35 (1980): 260–91.

Gilbert, Sandra M. and Susan Gubar. *The Madwoman in the Attic: The Woman Writer and the Nineteenth-Century Literary Imagination*. New Haven: Yale UP, 1979.

Harding, D. W. "Introduction." Austen 7–26.

Kirkham, Margaret. *Jane Austen, Feminism and Fiction*. New York: Methuen, 1986.

Tanner, Tony. *Jane Austen*. Cambridge: Harvard UP, 1986.

Tave, Stuart M. *Some Words of Jane Austen*. Chicago: U of Chicago P, 1973.

Trilling, Lionel. "Manners, Morals, and the Novel." *The Liberal Imagination*. New York: Scribner's, 1976. 205–22.

Twain, Mark. *Adventures of Huckleberry Finn*. New York: New American Library, n.d.

Yaeger, Patricia S. "'A Language Which Nobody Understood': Emancipatory Strategies in *The Awakening*." *Novel* 20 (1987): 197–219.

"This Altogather Precious tho Wholy Worthless Book": The Diary of Mary Guion, 1800–1852

Martha Tomhave Blauvelt

At the turn of the nineteenth century, Mary Guion (1782-1871), a seventeen-year-old living in rural Westchester County, New York, began to keep a diary. Like many young women, she began with brief, unrevealing entries; but her journal, unlike most, burgeoned into 387 closely written pages, 340 of them covering her courtship years from 1800 to 1807.[1] Guion chronicled the everyday life of a young woman of the early American republic in almost overwhelming detail: who came to tea, what they said, where she went, whom she danced with, how she spent her day. It is impossible to read this flood of words without asking why Guion needed to record her life in such detail. What did writing mean to her? Did she experience the ambivalence or "anxious power" so common to female writers?

As an historian interested in women's writing, I believe that we can find its meaning in precisely those details of everyday life which Guion's diary described. Texts can be understood only in terms of context: the experience of writing had specific meaning in the early nineteenth century, in America, for a woman, and for those engaged in courtship. An examination of Guion's 1800–1807 courtship diary suggests the origins of both the anxiety and the power of writing. At first, Guion's journal functioned as an educational tool: it represented her desire to "improve" her intellectual abilities at the same time that it raised fears that her diary lacked "geniues." But as Guion entered her twenties and made marriage her central concern, her diary gained a new function: it became a means of empowerment that helped her to analyze men's motivations and strengthened her resolve in relationships with them. In sum, the meaning of writing changed as the circumstances of Guion's life changed.

Directly related to the role of writing in Guion's education and courtship is the role of reading. Throughout her journal, books—especially novels—both invited Guion to write and set the literary standards she anxiously tried to imitate. At the same time, their plots provided warnings about men's behavior and advice essential to successful courtship. In Mary Guion's case, "anxious power" characterized reading as well as writing. Both "precious" and "worthless," her diary captures the interplay of reading and writing in the context of everyday life in early nineteenth-century America.

That Mary Guion began a diary at all suggests that she possessed an important initial power: the freedom to write. Her particular class, family, and historical era provide the immediate context in which we must interpret her writing. Born in 1782 into a prosperous North Castle, New York, family, she enjoyed the leisure both to read others' literary creations and to produce her own. In her diary Guion records periodic spinning, wool-carding, milking, candle-making, knitting, and sewing, yet she regularly spent nights at balls, and days immersed in reading or writing, without any suggestion of their interference with important tasks. Undoubtedly the fact that she had four sisters lessened the household labor of each. Within two days' journey from New York City, the Guion family could also purchase many goods rather than make them; Guion's journal itself may have been purchased in the city.

If the Guion family's class and location provided leisure time, its atmosphere also encouraged writing. Guion's father and mother were, as she said, "the best and most indu[l]gent of Parents" (160). They willingly provided the material needs for writing by buying her pen and paper and granting her privacy. At a time when many parents discouraged their daughters' interest in literary enterprises, her father and brothers regularly borrowed novels for Guion and joined her in reading them aloud. Happily situated in a circle which mirrored the family ideal of the early republic, Guion enjoyed great latitude, from how she behaved with men to whether she went to church and how she spent her time. Her family's respect and love for her is reflected in Guion's conviction that her life merited a book.

Leisure and encouragement created the possibility for writing, but the fact that Mary Guion grew up during the late eighteenth century gave the practice of writing particular meaning. The early republic was an era of enthusiasm for women's education, an enthusiasm that had significant implications for diary keeping. This educational reform movement was not motivated by any overriding concern for women's right to develop their minds: rather, they were to learn in order to become better companions to their husbands and better mothers to their sons (Lewis 701–03). Nor did it transform educational practice. The irregular spelling, erratic capitalization and idiosyncratic punctuation of Guion's journal—not uncommon in women's writing of the time—suggest the limits of female education during this period. Yet the early republic had a marked effect on female education in that it validated women's desire for self-improvement. "Improvement," with its image of progressive attainment of knowledge, was a favorite word of both educational theorists and young women such as Mary Guion. Guion apparently spent few years in school, but she maintained that "it would be impossible for any to prise an education higher than I" (251) and was proud of her past academic performance. "I was envied by all the little misses at school for receiving the premium at the expiration of the Quarter" (160), she recalled in 1804. And long after she finished her formal education, Guion sought opportunities to polish her basic skills. In 1801, for example, she began studying grammar with her brother James (37). Two years later, at age twenty, she went back to school to study arithmetic. Her comment that "the Schollars were all quite small so they had not power to draw my attention from [m]y book" (80) suggests both the incongruity of her situation and her determination to learn. It is unclear how frequently she attended school, but as late as 1806 she went to night classes, set aside days to study geography and ciphering (252), and vowed "to improve every moment to some kind of useful study" (251).

Writing was an integral part of Guion's effort to continue her education beyond school. It provided a freedom of subject, style, and structure which encouraged self-expression as well as literary expertise. For young women eager to "improve" themselves, journals also promised privacy in education; through them women could polish their writing without school or correspondent. Guion may have known that journal keeping, with its habits of daily writing and observation, was a common assignment in female academies; by keeping a diary she privately participated in a practice of the most elite schools of her time (Kerber 214). She noted that "the less I practise the worse I write" (217), and over time her prose became more polished and her entries more reflective. A penchant for self-improvement through writing was partly responsible for the marked increase in the number and quality of diaries by women such as Guion during the early national period.

Equally important in encouraging Guion and other women to write was the early republic's expanding book market, as Cathy Davidson notes (chap. 2). At the turn of the century imports and American editions were available in higher numbers than ever before. Recognizing that many of the most avid readers were young women who could not afford to purchase books, entrepreneurs founded lending libraries where for a modest fee local patrons could borrow books of all kinds. Mary Guion and her family regularly borrowed volumes from these libraries, as well as from literary friends. "I wish it was as customary for every family to have a good library as it is to have a bed in their house" (276), she wrote in 1806. Reading was an integral part of Guion's social life: she and her brother regularly read out loud to each other, and Guion delighted in a "smart confab" (85) over books with her suitors. Between 1800 and 1807 Guion read an amazing number of works, including novels such as *The Children of the Abbey, The Fool of Quality, Charlotte Temple*, and *The Man of Feeling*; sentimental poetry such as Young's *Night Thoughts*; popular philosophy; and many magazines.

The novels Guion read were especially important in encouraging her and other women to become writers. Dale Spender estimates that female novelists outnumbered male authors by two- and perhaps three-to-one during the century before Jane Austen, as the female author became a public figure for the first time (6). More important is the frequency with which eighteenth-century literature, especially sentimental fiction, represents women at their writing desks, composing letters or keeping diaries. More than in any other period, the fictional heroine of the eighteenth century is a writer. Often her writings carried the plot, and women's private compositions became public fiction: a substantial proportion of English and American novels were epistolary works which prominently featured women's letters, and many epistolary novels included diary entries as a narrative device (Black 8, 23). Even third-person narratives often had the fragmented quality of letters and diaries; as Janet Todd notes, "missing chapters, torn sentences or mutilated letters" form gaps in the prose, as if the novel were a private manuscript, a diary-like fragment of private life (6). In all these cases, women appear in the act of writing and often tell their own stories.

Sentimental heroines not only told their own stories, but told them well. As Davidson points out, novels demonstrated "that an unblemished prose style was as proper to a would-be heroine as a spotless reputation or a winsome smile" (73). The sentimental heroine was as well-educated as she was well-spoken. Fictional heroines regularly engaged in philosophical asides and talked knowingly about the works of Locke, Hume, and Rousseau (Davidson 72). Readers such as Guion had ample reason for believing that "people might very much improve the understanding by a sereous attention to" novels (76). Sentimental fiction in effect provided an education in how to write about oneself and how to write well. Guion was only one of many female readers who attempted to imitate the prose of sentimental fiction in their private first-person narratives.

But if both the diary and the novel promised Guion "improvement," the process of writing itself raised doubts about her intellectual abilities. Her diary mirrors this ambivalence. On the one hand, a journal is preeminently a "book of the self" (Fothergill 44), and in its inception, scope and detail, Mary Guion's diary is an overt assertion of self. It is based on the assumption that her life is worth recording, deserves to be remembered, and merits a second existence on paper. But the creation of another self put her in a peculiarly painful situation. In a word she used repeatedly, it "exposed" her. Above all, it exposed her relative lack of education and called into question her intellectual self-worth. Guion often deprecated "this Silly Simple nonscence" (14) which gave "but a very imperf[e]c't idea to what I should wish it might be" (121). Guion repeatedly called herself "illiterate" (228, 251) and lamented, "I really wish I was in possession of an education or a geniues sufficeint to inscribe something that would afford if to no one els' to myself a real pleasure and satisfaction" (217). With these mixed feelings, she characterized her journal as "this altogather precious tho wholy worthless book" (119).

Guion's embarrassment and pride in her other self are reflected alternately in her fear that someone would read her book and her hope that it would find an audience. She went to great lengths to assure that no one would see her diary and typically wrote when her family was asleep. When others were near, she wrote in fear of interruption: "am siting by the fire all a lone writeing expecting every moment some intruder to discover me & expose my work" (118). When company came she often "stole" outside with her journal, and when visiting relatives she withdrew to a "hovel for retirement" to write (145). On one cold November day in 1803, she summed up her secrecy with the words: "al alone writeing for no one to read" (116). Yet Guion clearly expected someone to read her diary. She frequently prefaced entries with "if there ever is a reader to this paper" or "what will the candid reader thinck of me." Occasionally she playfully invited the reader to guess with whom she had danced (126) or what her feelings were (315). Several times she expressed the hope that she would "entertain" her reader, although she typically despaired of edifying anyone.

Usually Guion's references were to future readers, but occasionally she also offered opportunities for contemporaries to study her diary. Her behavior suggests that her references to readers were not simply a literary device. One night after retiring she realized she had left her journal by the fire, where her brothers might find it. In what seems an extended flirtation with exposure, she decided to wait until morning to retrieve it. "I believe it ran in [my] thots all night for I had a curious sort of Dream and awoke with the first dawn of day," she reported. On going below, she found "it had not been disturbed" (185). It is hard to tell if she was disappointed or relieved at this discovery.

Guion had escaped "exposure" that time but, inevitably, someone read her journal: her adored older brother James. In a long account dating from late July 1801, Guion described her intense reaction to this self-revelation (25). At that point she had been writing her diary for over a year. She began with an acute juxtaposition: "Friday I was a Scrubing the floor   James was In the study   he stepd in the Parlour & said to me Polly I never know[n] you kept a Journal befor." Rising to stop him, Guion wished she "had never a wroat it" and was filled with "Shame," especially for a lovesick acrostic she had written. She told James that she had meant no one to read her diary, but he replied he could see no harm in it. At this point Guion "said no mor" despite "a kind of febleness & trembleng thoro Shame." Her desire to know what he thought of her diary had overcome her initial reluctance to be exposed. Fortunately, her first reader "seemd to aplaud it" and offered to buy her a new journal so she could continue writing. Torn between pleasure and embarrassment, Guion ended her account on an ambivalent note: she found "great satisfaction" in her brother's reaction, but judged it "undeservingly" bestowed.

Guion's mixed feelings towards her literary creation never entirely abated. A desire both to assert and improve herself had motivated her writing, but even as the process of writing expressed her self-worth, the seemingly inadequate result undercut her self-confidence. Emotionally, the diary was "precious" to her; intellectually, it seemed often insufficient and even "worthless." In many ways Guion's deprecation of her intellect was similar to that of contemporary female English autobiographers. Like Mary, they engaged in self-presentation, belittled their intellects, and both feared and desired an audience. What distinguishes the reactions of diarists such as Guion from those of female autobiographers of her time is how gender intersects with their respective literary forms. The autobiography, as a public form, exposed female writers to the gender expectations of a public audience and ignited fears of deficiency. As Patricia Meyer Spacks shows, female autobiographers were acutely aware that in simply publishing their life histories, they had revealed themselves as unfeminine (*Imagining* 78–82).[2] They compensated for this outrageous act by writing defensively and belittling themselves. By contrast, Guion, facing at best a private or future audience, feared intellectual deficiency more than feminine deficiency. Private writing did not assume male privilege the way public writing did, and her self-criticisms typically appear in the context of a desire for more education and greater intellectual ability, rather than an effort to appear deferential. She had not escaped the oppression of gender—it had limited her educational opportunities—but no "angel in the house" seems to have suggested that writing was inappropriate for her sex. Instead, Guion offered her writing on its own terms: a flawed literary creation that others might not find worth reading, but which she, in her struggle for improvement, found worth writing.

The desire to be educated and the fear that she was not provide the basic ambivalence in Mary Guion's diary. But her journal served another function: an instrument to help her decide whom to marry. As such, it took her diary in new directions. Novel reading, which had encouraged her writing, provided themes and a self-understanding which shaped her courtship. At the same time, her diary became a representation of the ideal man she sought in courtship. As she moved toward marriage in 1807, Guion lost her fear of self-exposure and began to use her diary to expose the machinations of men. In the complex interplay of these factors, Guion's diary empowered her as she negotiated her way in a patriarchal society.

When she began her diary at age seventeen, Guion was already well launched on the search for a spouse. In a pattern of advance and retreat that characterized the dance figures of her day, dozens of young men move through her diary. Guion captured the pairing and unpairing in a brief entry from June, 1800: "I went to Meeting   two Young Gentlemen came home with us staid & drank tea   one of them went away and another took his pla[c]e in the evening" (3). As many historians have observed, courtship was the most crucial period of a woman's life, and she had best choose a partner carefully. Under common law husbands controlled family money, and women had few legal rights; a wrong choice meant not only personal unhappiness but possible economic disaster. Guion's own family provided a telling example of the dangers of marrying the wrong man. Her sister Sally's husband not only neglected Sally when she was sick and ridiculed her before others (240–41), but blamed his wife when someone tried to rape her (321–22), trafficked in stolen goods (196), and spent his earnings on drink, leaving his family in poverty (364). "How much do I pity her hard lot—!" Guion exclaimed; "much sooner would I meet with Death than live with a person of th[a]t discription" (322). Her brother James, on the other hand, was a supremely considerate husband. Guion understandably wondered which would be her fate, and as a result, hers is primarily a courtship diary in which she compared suitors.

Women had undoubtedly always wondered whom they would marry, but courtship diaries such as Mary Guion's were not common until the rise of a reading public in the late eighteenth century. Guion and her contemporaries were avid readers of a sentimental fiction which was often written specifically for female readers and typically focused on a young woman whose name furnished the book's title. Variously subjected to handsome rakes, nasty husbands, and money-hungry parents determined to marry her to a brute, the heroine made her way to a fate of either seduction and death, or virtue and bliss. These seemingly farfetched plots accurately captured women's vulnerable social and economic position, in which unwed pregnancy meant social if not literal death, and a wise marital choice was crucial to happiness. Guion's sister Sally's life offered ample proof of these fictional themes. In this sense these novels were, as their authors maintained, "founded on fact." As such, they provided their female readers opportunities to consider appropriate responses to male courtship and marital behavior without suffering the consequences.[3]

Sentimental fiction inevitably influenced another form of literature "founded on fact": the diary.[4] The realism of these novels, and their focus on women, encouraged female readers to incorporate elements of plot and theme into their own "books": diarists quickly assumed the place of fictional heroines, made their own courtships the chief subject of their entries, and acutely analyzed male behavior. Novel reading was especially important in encouraging women to continue journal writing once they had started. Frequently women became discouraged over the fragmented nature of diary keeping; if they could not find a pattern to their entries, they often quit. As extraordinary a diarist as she was, Guion occasionally became mired in lists of who came to tea and periodically abandoned her journal. The plots of novels both provided shape to the sprawl of everyday life and endowed the domestic with literary significance. Guion recognized the influence of fiction when she, much like a novelist, included conversations in her entries. Originally fiction had appropriated the letter and the diary; in a complex dialogue of reinterpretation and reinforcement, the diary reappropriated the novel and fostered the journal of courtship.

Guion's diary recalls sentimental fiction in its plot (whom will she marry?), characters, and themes. Immediately recognizable to any novel reader was the man to whom she devoted many entries: Captain Jasup, a wealthy middle-aged widower who, despite his protestations of innocence, turned out to be a shameless rake. Guion and Jasup met at a wedding in 1804 where, Mary breathlessly reported, Jasup "seamed to wish to be very familiar took his seat next me & even ventured to put his arm round me wich quite ambaresed me" (158). On meeting again, Jasup shocked Guion by openly embracing her, "teling me at the same time he wanted me to know him next time I seen him what must I thinck of his fredom did he not behave thus to se if I had wit suficient to resent it." Significantly, Guion drew on a favorite sentimental novel in her reaction: "I thot of it several times of makeing the same speach to him as Evelina did to Clement [in Fanny Burney's 1778 novel] 'Your fredom Sir were you are more acquainted may perhaps be better accepted' but did not speak it" (159).

Despite her reservations, Guion, like the heroine of any seduction and betrayal novel, was quite taken with Jasup. She danced with him, went sleighing, allowed him to visit her, and flirted. But having recently read *Charlotte Temple*, she decided to investigate his character. Guion discovered that Jasup drank, gambled (189), had "strange transactions" with his housekeeper and "had contracted an acquaintance with a fashionable tho despisable disorder" (215). He was, in short, a villain. "I believe the Gentlemen thinck it an honour to then to tell as many Fictious stories to the Ladies as their imagination can invent," Guion remonstrated. "Adieu! Adieu! for ever, I will endevour to never write, speak, and even thinck, of him more" (194). In this account Guion cast herself in the role of innocent heroine, a potential victim to the villainous fictional males over whose escapades she had wept. But in her diary she had an opportunity to rewrite the often unhappy endings of sentimental novels. Here novel reading and diary writing at first parallel each other, but then diverge: her familiarity with novels warned

Mary Guion away from her seducer and in her book women escape their literary fate.

Throughout her diary the question of whom Guion will marry is intimately related to a theme prominent in sentimental fiction: whom can a woman trust? Her journal provided the means to distinguish reality from flattery, words from intentions. The theme that men's words are false appears on the first surviving page of Guion's journal. There a young gentleman, Jotham Smith, promised to take her to a ball but never came for her. Over the next few years "the inconstant young Sycopha[n]t" (55) repeatedly promised to visit Guion at certain appointed times but failed to appear. Occasionally she retaliated by snubbing him (72, 75), but more typically she accepted his excuses and fell into his trap: "after all this I once more concented for him to come again wich I hartily repent of," Guion wrote in wonderment, "how strange it is I shoul[d] act so different to my Reason" (57). Other men treated her no better.

By the time Guion met Captain Jasup in 1804, she had concluded that "two fac[e]d Gentlemen are quite common now a day" and wondered, "can an inocent female account for the meaning of so much discimulation in the other sex?" (152). Even before she investigated Jasup's character, she suspected his intentions. When Jasup proposed that they write to each other, Guion knowingly reported, "to that I would not consent for I am very sensible it is an easy matter for the pen to write expresions that the heart never experienced…and as I detest flattery so much I would not with my own consent indulge him with so fair an oportunity of that kind" (173). Looking back at their relationship, Guion concluded that it was only Jasup's age which had lent credibility to "the reality of his words" (203).

Guion was no more sure of her own feelings than those of her suitors. She repeatedly used her diary to puzzle over whom she loved best and therefore should marry. This question was especially difficult because Guion could not settle what role feelings should play in her decision. She found herself caught between two "companions": "reason" and "fancy." In her philosophical moments she usually favored reason and cited the republican truism, "let reason be my guide." Reason told her that Jasup was too old for her and that no "sober woman" wanted a rake (189). "But I have another companion that I call

Fancy wich is apt to intrude itself unless I keep a wachful eye," she realized (174). "Fancy" seemed to have a strong sexual component: her entries on Jotham Smith and Captain Jasup, the men to whom fancy drew her, emphasized the former's looks and the latter's outrageous advances. With both Smith and Jasup she had allowed fancy momentarily to triumph, only to be deceived and ill-treated. Not unlike the heroines of sentimental fiction, she found passion left her a victim.

Guion resolved her conflict between fancy and reason by deciding that the proper basis for marriage was friendship, which incorporated the warm, affective element of fancy without its sexual dangers and recognized the good sense of reason without its coldheartedness.[5] Like many early republicans, she idealized marriage as the union of kindred, feeling souls living in harmony, equality, and sympathy, "'where every thought is anticipated before it escapes from the lips; where advice, consolation, succour, are reciprocally given and received'" (179–80). Guion glimpsed such a relationship in her brother's union, but it was her sister Sally's unhappy marriage which cemented her firm belief that "those who list in the conjugal state are designed as help mates for each other not as tirants" (241).

Yet as Mary Guion discovered during her courtship, even when she had determined her true feelings, it was not always possible to express them. How was she forthrightly to convey her feelings when the entire community scrutinized her courtships? Guion frequently reported rumors that she would marry whichever young man was currently visiting her (45, 58, 114), a practice that made her reluctant to open her heart to anyone. A too frank preference for one man might also endanger her reputation (247). The customs of the period similarly set limits to honesty in courtship. After entertaining an unwanted suitor, Guion complained, "the Gentlemen have much the advantage of the Ladies for they need only go were they choose but we must stay at home and pretend to be pleased with the company of such persons whose absence would be a releif to us" (257).

Guion found this situation particularly painful. Throughout her diary she characterized herself as "partial to plain dealing" (187) and "candid." During her years of courtship she became more and more desperate in her search for a man she could trust. Drawn more to men than to her own sex, Guion lacked the close female friendships which sustained other women in her position. As she suffered repeated disappointments, her affection grew for her one trusted confidante: her diary. During the years from 1800 to 1807 Guion increasingly recognized the role her journal played in her life. "Wen I amuse myself with my pen or a book I always find that I have very agreeable & entertaining company & that wich never Cloys," she wrote in 1804 (141), undoubtedly thinking of the tedious young gentlemen she had been compelled to entertain. The following year, when she struggled with her feelings for Captain Jasup, she repeatedly praised her diary. "I believe my pen will always expose my thots   what a tell tale has it ever been and still continues to be…by placing them in so external a point of vieu that I can read them at leisure, wich tho simple as they are often afford me real pleasure" (175). "I conseal nothing from this paper," she maintained (241). "So different am I from many others that I find a real pleasure in it when my mind is animated, and a sympathising freind when dejected" (235). "My two reall friends," Guion concluded in 1805, were "my boock & pen" (209).

In short, with her diary Guion developed the affectionate, confiding, egalitarian relationship she idealized for husbands and wives. If novels warned her away from villains, her journal embodied the alternative. In that sense, she anticipated the relationship she finally developed with the man she would marry: Samuel Brown. Brown first appeared in Guion's diary in December 1800 (13) and by 1802 she reported rumors that they would marry (45). At this point she was drawn to him, but Smith, Jasup, and others caught her fancy. When she gave up Jasup in 1805, her attention returned to Brown. In him she at last found "candid speach" (253) and "a reasonable and a constant heart" (247). But by then she was herself reluctant to speak frankly. For two years she temporized, unable to either refuse or accept Brown, overcome with anxiety at the prospect of making a wrong choice. In a striking metaphor, she felt she stood "upon a precipice," hardly knowing "which path to chuse" (201). Acutely aware that on her decision would depend her "happiness or misery" (336) and unsure which way to turn, she "artfully…disguised my fealings and every emotion of my heart when in [Brown's] company" (329), confining her feelings to her faithful journal.

Bit by bit, Brown broke down her reticence, and Guion in

March 1807 "at last determined [to] marry none but him" (308). But this marked no unthinking capitulation. Guion had spent the last two years "observeing his discourse and behaveour for before marriage people can hardly be too critical" (241). Having given reason its due, Guion could then allow fancy some leeway. In the months prior to her wedding she and Brown engaged in much sexual banter: clearly he had won her heart as well as her head. Guion recognized his place in her life by characterizing him in exactly the same terms she had described her journal in 1805. Brown was, she felt, "a Sympathsi[zing] friend" (331). Guion now had not two but three friends: "my book my Pen and my—Lover" (330).

Guion's grouping of her book, pen and lover captures for us the intertwining of reading, writing and courtship that were crucial for her diary. As I have shown, there are many parallels between the plots, themes and subjects of novels and diaries. But the relationship between reading and writing can be understood in a different, more ironic sense if we focus on the process common to both: the interplay of fiction and reality. The novels Guion read were fictional constructs of reality. That was part of their appeal: from the safety of her seat by the fire, Guion could analyze imagined aspects of her own life. The warnings embedded in that fiction potentially enhanced her safety: they told her of the dangers of certain types of behavior and men. In this sense, sentimental fiction was a reading of and a guide to reality. But throughout her diary, Guion understood fiction in another sense: the "Fictious" words of men whose intentions were dishonorable. This type of fiction had portended ruin for her sister. Sally had mistaken "appearances" (196)—fiction—for reality, and disaster had ensued. Throughout her years of courtship, it was Mary Guion's aim to avoid a similar fate. To do so, she must distinguish the fictions around her and accurately "read" men's behavior.

Guion solved this problem of reading through writing. In turning to a diary she in a sense created yet another fiction, in that her journal was a partial vision of reality and often an echo of sentimental literature. But she recognized that her journal placed her thoughts "in so external a point of view" that she could read them "at leisure." Her diary helped distance her from life, from reality, much as novels did, so that she could safely analyze its meaning and choose how to act. In a sense, her diary made her both author and audience, writer and reader.[6] In those roles she could both vent her emotions and explore them, be the subject of an often unmanageable life and control that life, recognize her fancies and counter them with reason. Her creation of that partial fiction, that rereading of her life, helped bring her courtship to a happy conclusion.

But if the interaction of book, pen and lover helped Mary Guion through the perils of courtship, that same combination led to the decline of her journal: after her marriage, Guion would never again keep her diary with the faithfulness that had characterized her single years. Only forty-seven pages cover the years from 1807 to 1852. The particular circumstances of daily life which had initially encouraged her to write— leisure time, a supportive family, the influence of novels and the freedom to "improve" herself—ended with marriage and motherhood. Submerged in care for her husband and four daughters, Guion gave up novel reading, embraced religion, and became a devout matron. Context hastened the decline of her journal, just as it had shaped its beginning. But Guion did not forget how essential writing had been to her happiness. In 1822, at the age of forty, she reread her courtship diary and was at first so appalled by its seeming triviality that she began to burn it. But in a final assertion of her writing's worth, she could not bring herself to destroy the entire manuscript. Although writing would never again occupy a central place in her development, this last reluctance to burn her literary creation suggests that Guion recognized that her journal was more "precious" than "worthless," and that it had once been a source of power in her life. Its surviving pages remind us how the concrete details of everyday life shape the meaning of writing for women.[7]

NOTES

1. The New-York Historical Society holds the original diary. In my quotations I preserve the original spelling, grammar, capitalization and punctuation, with the exception that I lower superscripts and eliminate the dashes and commas Guion sometimes used between sentences. To separate apparent sentences, I insert three spaces. For

alternative views of Guion's life, see Rothman (Part I) and Brown 170–72, 177–78.

2. In "Female Rhetorics," Spacks also finds self-deprecation in eighteenth-century Englishwomen's letters. I find that autobiographies, letters and diaries are ranged on a public-private continuum. The more private the literary form, the greater the freedom from public gender expectations, although gender expecatations may be expressed in quite different ways, as with Mary Guion.

3. Here I follow Davidson (chap. 6).

4. On the relationship between diaries and fiction, see Lensink.

5. On this period's concept of marriage as friendship, see Lewis.

6. Culley characterizes "a dislocation from the self, or a turning of subject into object" in diary keeping as a "double consciousness" (10).

7. I would like to thank Hilde Lindemann Nelson, Annette Atkins, and the College of Saint Benedict Feminist Studies Discussion Group for their comments, and Cherie Spall for her research assistance. Permission to quote from Mary Guion's diary courtesy of the New-York Historical Society.

WORKS CITED

Black, Frank Gees. *The Epistolary Novel in the Late Eighteenth Century: A Descriptive and Bibliographic Study*. 1940. Folcroft, PA: Folcroft P, 1969.

Brown, Richard D. *Knowledge is Power: The Diffusion of Information in Early America. 1700–1865*. New York: Oxford UP, 1989.

Culley, Margo, ed. *A Day at a Time: The Diary Literature of American Women from 1764 to the Present*. New York: Feminist P, 1985.

Davidson, Cathy N. *Revolution and the Word: The Rise of the Novel in America*. New York: Oxford UP, 1986.

Fothergill, Robert A. *Private Chronicles: A Study of English Diaries*. London: Oxford UP, 1974.

Guion, Mary. Diary. 1800–52. New-York Historical Society.

Kerber, Linda K. *Women of the Republic: Intellect and Ideology in Revolutionary America*. Chapel Hill: U of North Carolina P, 1980.

Lensink, Judy Nolte. "Expanding the Boundaries of Criticism: the Diary as Female Autobiography." *Women's Studies* 14 (1987): 39–53.

Lewis, Jan. "The Republican Wife: Virtue and Seduction in the Early Republic." *William and Mary Quarterly* 44 (1987): 689–721.

Rothman, Ellen K. *Hands and Hearts: A History of Courtship in America.* New York: Basic Books, 1984.

Spacks, Patricia Meyer. "Female Rhetorics." *The Private Self: Theory and Practice of Women's Autobiographical Writings.* Ed. Shari Benstock. Chapel Hill: U of North Carolina P, 1988. 177–91.

———. *Imagining a Self: Autobiography and Novel in Eighteenth-Century England.* Cambridge: Harvard UP, 1976.

Spender, Dale. *Mothers of the Novel: 100 Good Women Writers Before Jane Austen.* London: Pandora, 1986.

Todd, Janet. *Sensibility: An Introduction.* London: Methuen, 1986.

Power and Resistance in Harriet Jacobs' Incidents in the Life of a Slave Girl

Debra Humphreys

In her powerful African American autobiography, *Incidents in the Life of a Slave Girl*, Harriet Jacobs documents the oppression of female slaves by white slaveholders and recounts how she and other slave women resist this oppression by manipulating the power structures that constrain them. While not always confident in exerting her own power, Linda Brent[1] makes use in the story of various liminal spaces, those neither wholly public nor wholly private—including her grandmother's house, the black church and cemetery, and even the town jail—in order to reverse the power structures that enslave her.

In examining power relations and their spatial configurations in this narrative, I map out how Jacobs manipulates public and private spaces that reveal and subvert these power relations. Through her complex configuration of spaces, Jacobs reveals not only how networks of power relations are "local and unstable" and resisted at many points, as Foucault suggests (93), but also how power rests on ideologically determined dichotomies that confer meaning on various spaces. The meanings ascribed to these spaces shift throughout the narrative, and Jacobs exposes the instability of dichotomies (private and public, inside and outside, black and white) by demonstrating how liminal or marginal spaces are appropriated, redefined, and rendered empowering. In her narrative, the discursive boundaries between spaces can never hold up under the pressure of the extended community that empowers Jacobs and that cuts across public and private delineations.

Employing the theories of Foucault, I read the narrative, then, primarily through its complex network of power relations;

by mapping out the spatial configurations Jacobs sketches, one can see how her narrative challenges both an ideology of true womanhood and an ideology of "proper" spaces that supports the domestic ideology of the time. *Incidents* calls into question the discursive system on which the hierarchy and power relations of slavery rest, and the "ideo-spatial" configurations used to control and uphold the dichotomies between public and private, slave and master.[2]

Jacobs' narrative exhibits how in some matrices of power, individuals exert control only ambivalently and tentatively and thereby resist the power structures that oppress them via "loopholes of retreat." Valerie Smith analyzes how Jacobs employs this complex figure:

> Jacobs' phrase "the loophole of retreat" possesses an ambiguity of meaning that extends to the literal loophole as well. For if a loophole signifies for Jacobs a place of withdrawal, it signifies in common parlance an avenue of escape....the garret, a place of confinement, also renders the narrator spiritually independent of her master, and makes possible her ultimate escape to freedom. (29)

This essay examines how Jacobs finds loopholes of retreat by reversing traditional power relations enacted through mechanisms of discipline and surveillance. By so doing, she reveals the ambivalence inherent in these particular power structures.

Early in the narrative Brent describes a scene that exemplifies how these power structures can be manipulated. She recounts how her grandmother became not only free from slavery but an owner of property in the small town of Edenton, North Carolina. After their "good" mistress dies, her son-in-law, Dr. Flint, attempts to sell Linda's grandmother, Aunt Martha. Since he and the whole town knew that his mother-in-law had promised to free Aunt Martha upon her death, Flint attempts to conduct the sale in private to avoid the town's judgmental gaze. On the appointed day of the "public sale of negroes, horses, etc.," Flint informs Aunt Martha "that he was unwilling to wound her feelings by putting her up at auction and that he would prefer to dispose of her at *private* sale." Seeing through his hypocrisy and knowing that "he was ashamed of the job," she insists that he enact the sale in the public sphere, on the auction block: "If he was base enough to sell her, when her mistress intended she should be free, she was determined the *public* should know it." The narrator tells us that on the day of the sale, Aunt Martha *"took her place* among the chattels." The public outcry was swift: "Shame! Shame! Who is going to sell you, Aunt Marthy? Don't stand there! That is no *place* for you" (11, emphases mine). Aunt Martha stood *her* ground on the auction block, a public space in which masters ordinarily exert the most complete control over slaves. No one would bid for Aunt Martha but her deceased mistress's seventy-year-old sister, who knew of her sister's intentions and Aunt Martha's faithful service. She not only purchased her for fifty dollars with no competing bids, but "gave the old servant her freedom" (12).

One can read Aunt Martha's remarkable appropriation and redefinition of the auction block as the first in a series of appropriations of spaces (mostly by women) in order to slip through the cracks in the power network that otherwise restricts their movements. The protective action of the white woman who buys Aunt Martha is just the first in a series of actions by both white and black women who make up this tightly-knit community network that cuts across lines of kin and lines of the public and private.

Another important issue that the auction block scene raises, and that can be traced throughout the narrative, is the danger of the "purely" private realm. Unlike writers wedded to a domestic ideology that regards the private as a safe haven from the threatening public realm, Jacobs portrays the private as a dangerous place—dangerous because it is outside a somewhat protective public gaze that exerts power over both slaves and masters. Knowing that in a private sale Dr. Flint can dispose of her as he pleases, but that social pressures constrain his public behavior, Aunt Martha uses the public space of the auction block to appropriate a public gaze in a way that subverts his power over her. Similarly, throughout the narrative Linda tries to avoid being trapped in private with Flint—fearing that behind a curtain of privacy he would rape her. As long as they are in public, the doctor's public persona and fear of reprisal protect her. As Jacobs comments: "Bad as are the laws and customs in a slaveholding community, the doctor, as a professional man, deemed it prudent to keep up some outward show of decency" (29). This power of surveillance in both private and public realms figures prominently throughout *Incidents*.

By appropriating the public space of the auction block, Aunt Martha is able to obtain a home which functions in the narrative as a protective space not only for Brent but for others in need who are not kin. This first and central domestic space of Aunt Martha's house is both protective and protected—not, however, because it is separated from the public sphere, as in traditional sentimental fiction, but because Aunt Martha runs her business there; the public persona and community ties that she develops through her business interactions make her and her space very powerful.

Hazel Carby interprets Jacobs' use of sentimental conventions as challenging a domestic ideology that cannot account for a slave woman's experiences. As Carby points out, Jacobs' narrative differs in significant ways from the sentimental novel and from ideologies of domesticity. She demonstrates that slavery not only denies her the opportunity to have a private, domestic space, but calls into question the domestic ideal itself. After all, it is the grandmother's house—a liminal space between the public and private—rather than a more traditional domestic space, that seems to be Jacobs' ideal.

While Carby has already noted Jacobs' use of but ambivalence toward sentimental convention, I will focus instead on the differences between Jacobs' narrative and the discourse of domestic feminism. While sentimental novels may have reconfigured the public and the private, they were also part of a discourse of domesticity that subscribed to the more "traditional" separation of spheres. Whether they conceived of the private as a haven from the cruel, competitive public—"a sacred refuge from an increasingly competitive, fragmented, and transitory society" (Kelley 437)—or as a morally effective realm that could "domesticate" or morally cleanse the public arena (as in Harriet Beecher Stowe), sentimental novelists preserved the separation between these spheres. In Jacobs' narrative, however, survival depends on a lack of divisions between public and private spaces.

One space Jacobs purposefully juxtaposes to her grandmother's house is the plantation house. She describes how the plantation house becomes a corrupted domestic space primarily through the master's sexual abuse of female slaves. Jacobs also contrasts with her grandmother's home "the lonely cottage" that Flint threatens to build for her on the outskirts of town, in which she fears he will sexually abuse her: "He told me that he was going to build a small house for me, in a secluded place, four miles away from the town....*to give me a home of my own, and to make a lady of me.* Hitherto, I had escaped my dreaded fate, by being in the midst of people" (53, emphasis mine). Jacobs purposefully uses the language of domesticity ironically. She knows that this threatened domestic isolation will certainly not make her a lady. Indeed, the distant cottage is the worst possible place Jacobs can envision not only because she fears being sexually abused there, but because it is outside her protective community. She explicitly links this space to the isolated plantation (a figure employed similarly in other slave narratives, including Frederick Douglass') where the slave's work and abuse was always greater.

Unlike these corrupted domestic spaces, the grandmother's house gains its meaning and power not from isolation but from connection to the community, from its marginal position between slavery and freedom, between public and private. Linda is further protected by her grandmother's public persona and by many of her grandmother's public aquaintances, including a white slaveholding woman who hides Linda in her attic when she first escapes. The space of the grandmother's house is not only central but highly charged with meaning for Jacobs— meaning which shifts throughout the narrative. The marker of this shifting meaning is the sound of the gate swinging open and closed. At one point, it signals protection from Flint, but after she confesses her affair with Sands to her grandmother, it signals her feeling of exclusion from this protective space because of her grandmother's harsh judgment. When Aunt Martha turns her out, Brent must leave that haven behind.

The grandmother's house, however, is only part of the intricate web of social spaces and power relations that Jacobs presents. The web of spaces, gazes, and power that Jacobs describes can further be illuminated by employing the insights in Foucault's writings on modern disciplinary forms of power. Unlike some other slave narratives such as Mary Prince's or Douglass', which document the brutal exercise of power by the master over the slave, Jacobs presents a network of much more subtle power relations—akin to the disciplinary power structures that Foucault argues become increasingly important during the nineteenth century.

Foucault's analysis of modern power structures helps us to decipher the power structures that Jacobs reveals. The subject of *Discipline and Punish* can be loosely described as the Western world's transition to modernity—from a society of spectacle and monarchy to one characterized by surveillance and normalization—which appears most fundamentally as a transformation in the modality and technology of power. According to Foucault, disciplinary power functions through a play of asymmetric glances that the objectified individual ultimately internalizes. It is a modest form of power, ubiquitous but invisible; discipline hides its own exercise yet subtly exerts enormous control over bodies and spaces.

Foucault points out that sovereign power glorifies and makes visible the ruler, while "in discipline, it is the subjects who have to be seen. Their visibility assured the hold of power that is exercised over them. It is the fact of being constantly seen...that maintains the individual in his subjection" (*Discipline* 187). Foucault takes his model of disciplinary power from Bentham's "Panopticon," a model prison in which the captive is seen but does not see. The disciplines "have the precise role of introducing insuperable assymetries and excluding reciprocities [and are] a series of mechanisms for unbalancing power relations definitely and everywhere" (*Discipline* 223). But for Foucault, "where there is power, there is resistance" (*History* 1: 95). Power is never a global, seamless, totalitarian structure; it is always local, unstable, and open to resignification. As Foucault explains,

> Power must be understood in the first instance as the multiplicity of force relations immanent in the sphere in which they operate and which constitute their own organization; as the process which, through ceaseless struggles and confrontations, transforms, strengthens, or reverses them; as the support which these force relations find in one another, thus forming a chain or a system, or on the contrary, the disjunctions and contradictions which isolate them from one another; and lastly, as the strategies in which they take effect. (*History* 1: 92–93)

Jacobs' narrative reflects these two Foucaultian themes—the power of the gaze, and the instability of power that makes it possible for the subjugated to reappropriate its techniques. Jacobs reveals how slavery in the South involved not only the exercise of explicit and violent power exerted institutionally and spectacularly from above, but also involved more "modern" forms of control including surveillance and self-policing. At the same time, it is paradoxically through the dissymmetry of the gaze that Jacobs' loopholes of retreat emerge as powerful forces which subvert the surveying apparatus. Jacobs' narrative reveals the imbalances and instabilities in power relations that open up these spaces of resistance and loopholes of retreat.

The most explicit loophole of retreat is within the grandmother's house, where Linda waits secretly for an opportune moment to escape to the North with the assurance that her children will be safe. For seven years, she hides within a nine-by-seven-foot crawlspace above a shed adjacent to her grandmother's house. While the crawlspace is the most confining space that Linda occupies, she appropriates and redefines it as an empowering one as well. From this space, which is neither private nor public, neither legitimate nor illegitimate, Brent reverses the controlling gaze that Flint and her mistress had exerted over her as she places him under her own powerful gaze.

Linda knows from her own experience how a gaze can control and torment. When Flint first starts harrassing her, she describes her torture as one of being constantly under his eye: "My master met me at every turn....If I went out for a breath of fresh air...his footsteps dogged me. If I knelt by my mother's grave, his dark shadow fell on me even there" (28). Brent's jealous mistress also exerted a controlling gaze over her, making her sleep in a room adjacent to her own: "She spent many a sleepless night to watch over me. Sometimes I woke up, and found her bending over me" (34).

In her loophole of retreat, Brent reverses this gaze and watches Flint and those hired to look for her plotting in the street: "I peeped at him as he passed on his way...[sat] at the *loophole* to watch the passers by. Southerners have the habit of stopping and talking in the streets, and I heard many conversations not intended to meet my ears" (116–17, emphasis mine). She enables her psychological well-being and survival by watching through the peephole. She gets pleasure from watching her children, and especially from watching, without his knowledge, Flint's vain attempts to find her. Brent uses the knowledge she gains from watching and listening to devise a plan for sidetracking Flint's efforts to locate her: sending him letters, purportedly from her, mailed from New York by friends to give him the impression that she has already escaped. Even while in her first hiding place in the home of her grandmother's generous white friend, she exerts this powerful gaze—watching the public sphere from within a loophole of reappropriated domestic space.

Other liminal or marginal spaces in the narrative are also appropriated and redefined—reinvested with enormous power, as the auction block was by Aunt Martha. The first of these spaces is the black church or meeting house. Jacobs tells us that this public black space, autonomous but deemed illegitimate because it was outside the white community's control, was a highly threatening space that the whites destroyed after the Nat Turner rebellion. The church was a public space where the slave community could meet outside the watchful white gaze. Jacobs relates how the whites violently suppressed this threat after Turner's capture: "The slaves begged [for] the privilege of again meeting at their little church in the woods, with their burying ground around it. It was built by the colored people, and they had no higher happiness than to meet there and sing hymns together...the church was demolished" (67). In part, the whites met the threat that Turner's uprising posed by bringing black parishoners back under their gaze. Not only did they destroy the black church, but they attempted to force blacks into white churches where their movements could be better monitored, their spaces clearly delimited, and their ideas controlled.

Bands of white marauders plundered blacks' homes, but once again, Aunt Martha's public persona protected her home from being robbed or invaded: "Colored people and slaves who lived in remote parts of the town suffered in an especial manner....The dwellings of the colored people, unless they happened to be protected by some influential white person, who was nigh at hand, were robbed of clothing and every thing else the marauders thought worth carrying away." Brent and her grandmother knew that their home would be protected "because [they] were in the midst of white families who would protect us" (64). Once again, the lack of privacy protects Brent and her kin, and the private sphere is revealed to be a potentially dangerous place.

One can read the graveyard adjacent to the destroyed black meeting house as another metonymically connected marginal space. The black graveyard, which is public but not considered as legitimate as white controlled spaces, figures prominently. Linda goes there to visit her parents' graves as she is making the decision to escape: "I went to make this vow at the graves of my poor parents, in the burying-ground of the slaves. 'There the wicked cease from troubling, and there the weary be at rest. There the prisoners rest together; they hear not the voice of the oppressor; the servant is free from his master'" (90). Brent describes the graveyard as a kind of haven, much as sentimentalists routinely depict the domestic space. The graveyard appears as a privileged, sanctified place because there the oppressor's gaze is rendered impotent. In the solitary scene that Linda describes, the space accrues further significance: "never had it seemed…so sacred as now" (90). The graveyard, linked in this scene to two other marginal spaces, the black church and the jail, and explicitly to freedom, can be read as another loophole of retreat. Brent says, "As I passed the wreck of the old meeting house, where, before Nat Turner's time, the slaves had been allowed to meet for worship, I seemed to hear my father's voice come from it, bidding me not to tarry till I reached *freedom or the grave*" (91, emphasis mine).

Another incident lends further significance to this black public space. While Brent is in hiding, her Aunt Nancy, who had been a faithful servant to the Flints, dies. Although Mrs. Flint wants Nancy buried in the Flint family plot, Aunt Martha insists that she be buried with her own community in the black cemetery—that highly charged place next to the old black meeting house. Brent refers to those buried in the cemetery as prisoners, but prisoners freed from the gaze and whip of the slave master.

This reference to the dead as "prisoners" links the cemetery to the jail—another marginal space that Jacobs' narrative reappropriates and redefines. Although jail is usually thought of as the most punitive of public spaces, Jacobs portrays it as a relatively protective environment. When Linda's uncle Benjamin is jailed for trying to escape, the jailer enables Linda and her grandmother to visit him and care for him. The jail accrues further meaning after Linda's children, brother, and aunt are placed there to coax her out of hiding. Linda's daughter, Ellen, revolts when taken from the jail and back to Dr. Flint's: "Poor little Ellen cried all day to be carried back to prison. The instincts of childhood are true. She knew she was loved in jail" (102). For Jacobs, confinement and subjection to a watchful public gaze in jail seem to compare favorably to dangerous isolation in the big house.

Brent's most threatening and powerful act of appropriation is taking a white lover to get back at Dr. Flint. Although she feels uneasy about recounting this liaison, she redefines this "private" act in terms of her own "public" freedom from "private abuse." Jacobs expresses her uneasiness about this act both by condemning it and by suggesting that the moral standards white readers might use to criticize her liaison are inappropriate to the life of a slave woman. Nevertheless, Jacobs interprets her relation to Sands as yet another loophole to freedom. She believes that it helped her to end Flint's harrassment and later gain her children's freedom. She explicitly links this more public, if "shameful," affair to her own freedom: "There is something akin to *freedom* in having a lover who has no control over you, except that which he gains by kindness and attachment" (55, emphasis mine).

Despite redefining her illicit affair as politically significant and potentially liberating, Jacobs' ambivalence prevents her from giving it a defined place in her narrative. Even though we know that the affair lasted for several years, since she had two children by Sands, she never even hints when it occurred. Sands' home is never located in the narrative. This marginal space may be the most threatening one of all; it lurks entirely within the cracks and silences of the narrative.

Jacobs is acutely aware of the mores of her intended readers—the white, middle-class Northern women accustomed to reading sentimental novels. She knows that her readers' gaze—a gaze of moral judgment—may be the most powerful of all. Through repeated emphasis upon the differences between her material conditions and those of her readers, Jacobs calls into question the applicability of traditional standards of female behavior to black women's experiences. If she is skeptical about the applicability of white women's standards to black behavior, however, Jacobs seems equally unwilling to conform to the conventions of the sentimental novel—middle-class white women's standard reading fare. As I have noted, Jacobs often uses the language of sentimentality ironically. Further, as Carby notes, *Incidents* does not offer the sentimental novel's conventional happy ending: Brent never achieves her dream of a safe domestic space of her own and remains "bound" to a white mistress. As she does throughout the narrative, Jacobs explicitly juxtaposes her circumstances to those of her readers and of the sentimental novel: "Reader, my story ends with freedom; not in the usual way, with marriage....The dream of my life is not yet realized. I do not sit with my children in a home of my own....Love, duty, gratitude, also bind me to [my employer's] side" (201).

Jacobs' relation to her employer and to her own public and private spaces constrained the writing of her narrative. Jacobs wrote *Incidents* in private, at night, in a domestic space. But this was not *her* domestic space; it was her work space. After she escapes to the North and even after she officially gains her freedom, Brent continues to work as a domestic servant, this time in the home of Mr. and Mrs. Bruce. Jacobs reappropriates this domestic/work space in which she is confined as yet another site of empowerment, one where she performs the powerful public act of writing. One can read her appropriation and redefinition of this space as analogous to Aunt Martha's appropriation of the auction block for her own empowerment. Even after she is nominally free, Jacobs still faces discrimination and exploitation in the North and must continue to find loopholes to freedom.

Jacobs never finds a "pure" private space in which she is not bound in some way to a master. The only positive, purely private spaces in the narrative appear in its first and last chapters. She discusses her early home in fairly traditional terms, as an idyllic one where she lived with both parents and didn't even realize that she was a slave. But in this first chapter Jacobs describes even this space as precarious because of their status as property. In nearly every sentence, she uses the language of propertied relations to expose the precariousness of this domestic space and to distinguish it from her readers' more protected homes. The narrative really begins with her realization that because she can be exchanged, her domestic space is not secure. The private domestic space in the final chapter, on the other hand, is an ideal and utopic one that is constantly deferred and to which she never has access. Between these two framing chapters, the public and private are not maintained as separate spheres, or, when they are separated, the private is devalued as the more dangerous place.

Jacobs also collapses the public and private simply by writing a politically motivated autobiography—making public her private life, and legitimating and defining her most private act (her sexual liaison) as one motivated by personal necessity and politically significant to the abolitionist cause. Jacobs was not unaware of the ideals of true womanhood that her narrative clearly violated. She was also aware, however, that her powerful story could further the abolitionist cause and challenge the assumptions about slavery held by many of her white middle-class readers.

One of the abolitionists' principle objections to slavery was that it ruined both slave and slaveholding families. The abolitionist rhetoric suggested, however, that slavery threatened the sanctity and integrity of these separate spheres. Stowe remarked that the "worst abuse of the system of slavery is its outrage upon the family"; another abolitionist declared that "the family is the head, the heart, the fountain of society...and it has not a privilege that slavery does not nullify, a right that it does not counteract, nor a hope that it does not put out in darkness" (qtd. in Walters 95). While Jacobs would certainly agree that slavery prevented her from having a "decent" family life and corrupted even the households of the slaveholders, the most powerful spaces and actions in her narrative are ones of community and extended family that cut across these rigidly defined distinctions between private and public. Jacobs' narrative thus offers a radical critique of the power relations of the South and of other regimes of power that control through the use of space. It also offers a powerful feminist message about the strength that derives from extrafamilial community networks, and the danger that lies in domestic isolation and isolation from a sense of community in general.

NOTES

1. When referring to the main character in the narrative, I use "Linda Brent," the name Jacobs gives to the character representing herself in the narrative. When referring to the author of the narrative, I use "Harriet Jacobs."

2. I coin the phrase "ideo-spatial" to indicate an interaction and dialectical relation between the ideological (superstructural) sphere that defines appropriate spaces and the material constraints that spatial configurations exert.

WORKS CITED

Carby, Hazel. *Reconstructing Womanhood: The Emergence of the Afro-American Woman Novelist*. Oxford: Oxford UP, 1987.

Foucault, Michel. *Discipline and Punish: The Birth of the Prison*. New York: Vintage, 1979.

———. *The History of Sexuality: Volume 1: An Introduction*. New York: Vintage, 1980.

Jacobs, Harriet A. *Incidents in the Life of a Slave Girl Written by Herself*. Ed. Jean Fagan Yellin. Cambridge: Harvard UP, 1987.

Kelley, Mary. "The Sentimentalists: Promise and Betrayal in the Home." *Signs* 4 (1979): 434–46.

Smith, Valerie. *Self-Discovery and Authority in Afro-American Narrative*. Cambridge: Harvard UP, 1979.

Walters, Ronald G. *The Anti-Slavery Appeal: American Abolitionism After 1830*. Baltimore: Johns Hopkins UP, 1979.

Mirroring the Mother Text: Histories of Seduction in the American Domestic Novel

Elizabeth L. Barnes

America's post-Revolutionary period marks the emergence of a literature written predominantly by, for, and about women. The popular eighteenth-century novel of seduction, typically chronicling the single woman's fall from grace and family into the snare of her seducer, not only points to a newly-emerging bourgeois culture's uneasiness with issues of authority and individual desire, but questions woman's place in that culture. Divorced from the political and economic systems meant to motivate male citizens to "virtue,"[1] women came to represent what most threatened the young republic: the "lawlessness" of those whom the law excluded. By the mid-nineteenth century, however, the focus of sentimental literature shifts from the letter to the spirit of the law. The sentimental heroine undergoes a similar conversion. Once the representative of criminality and deviance, the sentimental heroine of nineteenth-century domestic fiction serves as a model of middle-class femininity. Stripped of corporeal but invested with religious significance, she exemplifies the superiority of heartfelt sacrifice over mere physical satisfaction. Consequently, in the nineteenth-century version of the single woman's story, the heroine's success is measured by her effectiveness at *interior* housekeeping: if she can adequately cleanse her body and heart of all impurities, she will have proven herself up to the task of regulating the larger and more material space which will someday encompass her family. Yet the conversion of the woman's story from seduction to domesticity is more than a rewriting of the woman's character; it is a rewriting of her des-

tiny. For it is the happy ending, the marriage to the ideal or converted male, that forms the cornerstone of the domestic tale, just
as it is the heroine's romantic success which validates the narrative renovations of the female space—a space which not only
shelters but constructs, then defines, the woman.

Houses are not without their ghosts, however, and the spec-
tre of betrayed and disillusioned womanhood returns to haunt
the pages of the domestic dwelling, to shake the very founda-
tions, in fact, on which the domestic story is laid. This spectral
presence attests to the limitations of the nineteenth century's
reconstruction of femininity, where essential elements of the
woman's story of love are necessarily suppressed. The move
from dangerous to "true" love—"maternal" love that is other-
directed and self-effacing—indirectly links the new heroine
with her past, the domestic scene with the seduction story. The
eighteenth-century woman's story of betrayal and misreading,
ostensibly expurgated from the more civilized nineteenth-century plot, is brought home to the domestic novel through the
conventional image of security—the mother. In positing the
maternal as the womanly ideal, then, the domestic novel aims
its daughter-heroine in the direction of her mother, that figure
from the past whose own story undercuts the convenient moral
the domestic novel would uphold. The mother's story, as
recounted within the daughter's tale, not only reenacts the
mother's own victimization, but implicates her daughter in the
seduction. Rather than supporting the myth of an ideal world in
which mothers domesticate and thus regulate their environment, the mother-figure in the domestic novel actually calls into
question the reigning ideology of maternal love, feminine
nature, and a cooperative network of female relations.[2]

While the nineteenth-century daughter's goal is to become
the perfect mother, the mother, via her narrative, is cast as the
daughter-figure of the earlier era. The return to the mother as
daughter-heroine makes the mother and daughter rivals—not
so much for possession of the man as for control of the script of
woman's history. The return of the mother's story also aligns
her with the male lover in the novel: her "seduction" of the
daughter—that is, her ability to penetrate and appropriate the
daughter's ego as well as her story—is analogous to the future
lover's subsumption of the heroine's identity in his own. This

triangulated network of desire expands and complicates the initial symbiotic bond between mother and daughter, exposing the problematic nature of love relationships at the heart of this genre. While the mother's story attests to the duplicitous nature of romantic attachment (and "womanhood" itself), it also sublimates this knowledge. By confining the pain to her mother and her era, the domestic plot continues to deny the part betrayal may play in the daughter-heroine's destiny.

I

When Gabriella Lynn, the heroine of Caroline Lee Hentz's *Ernest Linwood*, gazes into the mirror and sees for the first time a beautiful woman there, she feels a sense of triumph, power, and destiny. However, as she herself goes on to say, "The moment of triumph was brief. A pale shadow seemed to flit behind me and dim the bright image reflected in the mirror. It wore the sad, yet lovely lineaments of my departed mother" (81). Gabriella's vision of her mother in this scene highlights a central tension in the novel, and in many nineteenth-century domestic novels—the daughter's physical and emotional tie to the figure whom she most closely resembles and yet whose fate she fears. Since Gabriella's birth, she and her mother, Rosalie, have lived alone on the outskirts of town, Rosalie suffering the effects of her seduction into an apparently bigamous marriage, Gabriella attempting to fill the emotional void in her mother's life left by the father's absence. The two have become bound together in relative isolation, and Gabriella has learned firsthand the emotional, physical, and financial costs of disappointed love. It is no wonder, then, that as Gabriella looks in the mirror she sees her mother's figure cast its shadow over the brightening future; she intuits that her entrance into womanhood, for all its glory and influence, also opens her up to the disappointment and disillusionment of her mother's life.

Gabriella's tuition in the lessons of womanhood is afforded by the visible example of her mother's isolation but, perhaps more important, by Rosalie's written record of her mysterious and unhappy past which she bequeaths to Gabriella on her deathbed. "My Mother's History," as Gabriella terms it in her narrative, tells her mother's story of passionate but misguided love to a duplicitous man whose own sordid past blights any hope for their future happiness. According to Rosalie, her history is meant as both an explanation and a warning to Gabriella, to be read at that time when Gabriella's own heart "awakens to love." But as the novel illustrates, this is exactly when a warning comes too late. Rosalie's history proves ultimately designed to foretell her daughter's future rather than divert it: since it is woman's "destiny" to love, Gabriella is doomed to repeat the past in her own unique way. And she does this, in fact, by falling hopelessly in love with the intensely moody Ernest Linwood, an emotional tyrant whose jealousy soon turns Gabriella's dream of domestic bliss into nightmare. The product of these intense attachments is Gabriella's autobiography—and the connection between mother and daughter narratives is only too clear. Gabriella's written record of her own "heart's history," the novel we presently read, not only includes the mother's story of seduction and betrayal, but becomes its own version of the story. The reader is thus left to question whether the daughter's attempt to write her own story can ever result in anything but a resurrection of the past.

This anxiety over preestablished modes of writing can be viewed in a larger context as well, where similar but individualized subgenres intersect in a growing literary market. The relationship between what I term "mother" and "daughter" texts of the late-eighteenth and mid-nineteenth centuries provides a grid onto which we can map changing and somewhat contradictory cultural attitudes about women. In framing the relationship between the seduction and domestic novel in terms of the mother-daughter relationship, I mean to emphasize not only the actual historical connection between female writers and their cultural descendants, but the literary relationship between successive subgenres that legislate a woman's character, the nature of her attachments, her role in the community, and her destiny in light of these factors. If viewed in connection with seduction fiction, domestic fiction is traditionally read as a new and improved version of the eighteenth-century story. In it, the victimized woman and the threat of appropriation is ostensibly laid to rest. Motherhood is heralded as the ideal, and daughters aspire to self-sufficient vulnerability and moral steadfastness.

While such a change in storyline may signal a positive shift in the way women view and represent themselves, novels like *Ernest Linwood* and Susan Warner's *The Wide, Wide World* demonstrate that the threat to female autonomy remains; it has simply gone underground. Haunted by her mother's image, the domestic daughter strives to fulfill the maternal ideal while avoiding her own mother's model. For the most part, the domestic heroine is a woman divided.

One of the sources of ambivalence in domestic fiction is its tendency to glorify "maternal" values even as it locates the source of pain and weakness in the mother's character. What the daughter-heroine cannot explicitly acknowledge, the narrative consistently makes clear: the heroine's mother fails as a model for successful romance. In fact, the mother comes to represent those aspects of failed femininity against which the domestic heroine is constructed. As Nina Baym points out, the domestic heroine fashioned herself against two types of femininity: "the 'belle,' who lived for excitement and the admiration of the ballroom," and "the passive woman—incompetent, ignorant, cowed, emotionally and intellectually undeveloped." Such types are considered by domestic writers to be anachronistic. And, Baym notes, the heroine's mother is often just such a type.

Yet it is not merely within the confines of the domestic plot that the daughter attempts to assert her individuality. For what Baym does not note in her analysis is that one can find the prototypes for these two aspects of the failed feminine in the two most popular seduction novels of the early national period: Susanna Rowson's *Charlotte Temple* and Hannah Webster Foster's *The Coquette*. Although bestsellers in their day, neither novel confined itself to its own historical period but in fact continued its success well into the nineteenth century amid the growing popularity of the new domestic fiction. *The Coquette* reached the height of popularity between 1824 and 1828, when it was reprinted eight times, while *Charlotte Temple* boasted over two hundred editions by 1905 (Davidson, Introduction xxviii). Susanna Rowson's domestic sequel to *Charlotte Temple*, *Charlotte's Daughter*, was published posthumously in 1828, marking a literary intersection of "mother" and "daughter" texts in the mid-nineteenth century. Domestic writers were not simply writing against abstract types of womanhood, but against particular

models of femininity which had once cornered and still continued to infiltrate the literary market. While the specter of the
mother's story may have conjured up anxieties concerning literary competition, more importantly it threatened to perpetuate
disturbing images of women and their futures. Its presence in
the culture forced domestic writers to question whether women
could be different, could write themselves differently than their
mothers did—and if so, to question how they were to do so in the
shadow of a previous paradigm, especially when that paradigm
had been set by one's creator.

In writing themselves into a new tradition, then, domestic
authors experienced anxiety not only over their bold intrusion
into a patriarchal culture, as Sandra Gilbert and Susan Gubar
argue, but over their inheritance of a literary and imaginative
space that had not been fully deserted by the mother. Such an
image is centrally figured in a novel like *Ernest Linwood* where
the mother's story, Rosalie's "heart's history," literally appropriates the space of the daughter's autobiography for several chapters in order to tell its own story. Nor is *Ernest Linwood* an
anomaly in the domestic tradition: popular novels, ranging from
Catharine Sedgwick's *Redwood* (1824) to *The Wide, Wide World*
(1850), foreground the mother's history, which mirrors the
seduction story in its portrayal of the victimized female and her
misguided passion. The intrusion of the mother's story into the
daughter's narrative signals a return of repressed knowledge in
the domesticated version of the woman's story. And it is a lesson
which reflects on its own textual nature. The mother often dies
early in the domestic novel, leaving behind a text—a Bible, a letter, a "history"—which functions as a substitute for the mother
and her wisdom. This text testifies to the sacrificial and, more
often than not, painful nature of "true womanhood." It serves
also to reify, and to universalize, the traits associated with womanhood which the daughter inherits. And which she not simply
inherits but internalizes—the daughter is to inscribe her
mother's precepts upon her heart. By the mid-nineteenth century, associations between mother and text render them practi-
cally interchangeable: not only does the domestic novel feature
the mother-as-text, it becomes itself an example of the text-as-
mother, with the daughter figure now playing the mother's leading role.

II

The relation among mothers, texts and the disciplinary function of novels is one of the subjects of Richard Brodhead's "Sparing the Rod: Discipline and Fiction in Antebellum America." Brodhead explores the shift in mid-nineteenth-century America from corporal punishment to a less visible and more effective form of disciplinary action which he refers to as "disciplinary intimacy, or simply discipline through love" (69). According to Brodhead, this new kind of disciplinary model first requires that authority "put on a human face." It then regresses into a symbolization of personal authority, whereby the person in authority is no longer visible yet has the same disciplinary effect. Using Warner's *The Wide, Wide World* as an example, Brodhead gives shape to the nineteenth-century theory that by "enmeshing the child in strong bonds of love," the parent introduces its charge "to its imperatives and norms. What the parent figure believes in comes across to the child indistinguishably from his love, so that the child imbibes what the parent stands for in a moral sense along with the parent's physical intimacy and affection" (72).

There is no question that Warner's novel exemplifies the "disciplinary intimacy" of its day, both in terms of the mother-daughter relationship it depicts and what it hopes to accomplish as parent figure to its readers. The young heroine, Ellen Montgomery, is led to religion through her mother's example and influence. Similarly, readers sympathetic to Ellen's struggles are to be *converted* by their sympathy. In other words, good readers will become better people. Yet what remains unexplored in this discussion is the role of textual mediation and literary convention within the novel, as well as its relationship to maternal influence. It is not religion alone through which Ellen internalizes her mother's authority, but religion and language. Consequently, the two tools with which Ellen's mother equips her when they must separate are a Bible and a writing desk. Moreover, the Bible which Ellen receives from her mother is not simply a reminder of her mother's beliefs; it acts as a literal convenant between mother and daughter. At Ellen's request, Mrs. Montgomery signs Ellen's name on the front cover of her Bible. She then pens a Biblical quotation which has significance only in terms of Ellen's *future* conduct:

> Mrs. Montgomery wrote Ellen's name, and the date of the gift. The pen played a moment in her fingers, and then she wrote below the date: "I love them that love me; and they that seek me early shall find me." This was for Ellen, but the next words were not for her; what made her write them?—"I will be a God to thee, and to thy seed after thee." (42)

The first inscription echoes not only God's promise to his children, but the disciplinary ideology of the day: "I love them that love me" is sounded in subtle and not-so-subtle ways by mother-figures throughout nineteenth-century literature. The inscription which follows is a sign of how far and how deep that ideology runs, for it is, as the narrative tells us, not only a covenant with Ellen, but with Ellen's future—it points toward both the woman Ellen will become and the children she will bear as a result of her maturity.

Mrs. Montgomery also buys her daughter a writing desk; and as Helen Papashvily observes, the purchase of this desk is one of the most unforgettable scenes in Warner's novel:

> letter paper, large and small, with envelopes and note sheets to match, an inkstand, steel and quill pens, a little ivory knife and a leaf cutter, sealing waxes in red, green, blue and yellow, lights, wafers, a seal, a paper folder, a pounce box, a ruler, a neat silver pencil, drawing pencils, India rubber, and sheets of drawing paper.
>
> Many readers have confessed that yearning over these delightful objects they quite missed the intended poignancy and would have counted a mother well lost for such a desk gained. (7–8)

Papashvily's somewhat ironic comment hits the mark, since it is the desk, as well as the Bible, which is meant to bridge the gap, in some real sense, between mother and daughter. But for nineteenth-century readers the list of objects on which the narrative dwells would be a matter of some distinction. By the dawn of the Civil War, countless handbooks on epistolary etiquette had flooded the market, offering hundreds of sample letters to exemplify the art of polite correspondence. Karen Halttunen writes that "Polite men and women were...advised to use good paper and fine wafers to seal their letters and to keep their handwriting neat"; after all, "just as personal appearance reflected character in face-to-face social relations, the appearance of a letter reflected character at a distance." Letter writers were warned that in sending even a note, you left "'written evidence of either your good sense or your folly, your industry or carelessness, your self-control or impatience.'" Letters were nothing if not acts of "emotional self-expression" (121). They were also, however—and paradoxically—a means by which one's gentility was evaluated. The goal became to express oneself sincerely, but with good taste; to write within the boundaries of prescribed epistolary etiquette, and yet to be completely genuine.

How both to express one's true self and yet conform to the dictates of social responsibility and respectability is the contradiction negotiated by Mrs. Montgomery's assertions to her daughter about the benefits of epistolary education. Her motivation in buying Ellen the desk and materials is to insure that Ellen will always be "neat, and tidy, and industrious; depending upon others as little as possible; and careful to improve [herself] by every means, and especially by writing to" her mother (31–32). Though Mrs. Montgomery seems to subscribe to the Victorian belief that by reading her daughter's letters she will be able to discern the state of her heart, she also implies that by writing these letters at all, in the privacy of her own room and in possession of her own materials, Ellen will become a better person. The relationship of writing to independence, improvement, and maternal influence spelled out here is telling. It indicates that through her mastery of literary convention Ellen will be able to master both language and herself. This idea is reinforced a few pages later, when Mrs. Montgomery cautions Ellen about the psychological cost of the desk and its contents: "'my gifts will serve as reminders for you if you are ever tempted to forget my lessons. If you fail to send me letters, or if those you send are not what they ought to be, I think the desk will cry shame upon you'" (37). These two sentences move from the idea of the mother's gifts as reminders of her presence to their substitution for it. Ellen's writing desk, the instrument of her self-expression, assumes the mother's role as moral detective, indicting her should she waver in her spiritual struggle. "Self-expression" thus becomes the representation of internalized maternal authority—the words of the daughter's heart will become the law that convicts her. In this way personal sincerity and social respectability once again intersect as Ellen becomes both the author and the moral interpreter of her own internal struggles.

Although the Bible seems at first glance to function as a source of cultivation in Ellen's personal and private life, and the writing desk to initiate her improvement in the public sphere, the ideology of epistolary etiquette reminds us that for a nineteenth-century woman the two spheres are virtually inseparable: as Mary Kelley has shown, the woman's story is a story of the heart made public. Mrs. Montgomery's admonishment to Ellen early in the novel that she "try to compose [herself]" speaks to the dilemma that lies within the metaphor: it is an injunction to repression dressed in the language of articulation. Ellen is literally being told to "put herself together,"[3] and she is to do so in sensual as well as in narrative terms. Paradoxically, to "compose" oneself comes to mean curbing those physical, emotional, and psychological urges which inhere in self-expression. The proof of the woman's integrity, in both senses of the word, is then made visible through its narrativization. In the domestic novel, daughters are taught by their mothers to regulate themselves, and this is achieved by their internalization of both the mother's precepts and her method of transmitting them. What the mother bequeaths to her daughter, then, is essentially a version of herself, and the impression she leaves upon her is the stamp of literacy as well as love.

III

The nature and extent of the domestic heroine's self-possession remains ultimately ambiguous and undecidable. Although taught to be her own *moral* guide, the protagonist is still left in the physical and psychological possession of others. In *The Wide, Wide World*, for instance, Ellen Montgomery fulfills the contract between herself and her mother by becoming the embodiment of the perfect Christian woman—pious, contemplative, and, most important, submissive. Her religious training, initiated by the mother, is then taken over by a "brother" figure whose own seminary schooling equips him for the job. By the time she has learned to put self-interest aside and to love and obey this minis-

ter as she did her mother, she is old enough—and worthy
enough—to marry him. In *Ernest Linwood* the line between education and psychological seduction is made more manifest. On
her deathbed, Gabriella's mother leaves her with a dying injunction: "If you live to years of womanhood, and your heart awakens to love,—as, alas, for woman's destiny it will,—then read my
life and sad experience, and be warned by my example'" (57).
Just as the seduction narrative is said to foster those very desires
in the telling of the story that it purports to suppress, so the
mother's confessions to her daughter ironically invoke a future
they are trying to forestall. As the daughter "reads" her mother's
desire, she is taught to desire what she should avoid. In a repetition of the seduction novel's dilemma, what is meant as education becomes a form of seduction.

A near-perfect example of the mother's seduction—the
seduction of and by the mother—occurs when Gabriella finally
reads her mother's history and loses herself in the story: "Thus
far had I read, with clenching teeth and rigid limbs, and brow
on which chill, deadly drops were slowly gathering, when my
mother's shriek seemed suddenly to ring in my ears,—the knell
of a broken heart, a ruined frame,—and I sprang up and looked
wildly round me. Where was I? Who was I?" (184). Gabriella
reads the manuscript literally hunched over her mother's grave,
and when she finishes, she finds herself in another world: "I did
not become insensible, but I was dead to surrounding objects,
dead to the present, dead to the future. The past, the terrible, the
inexorable past, was upon me, trampling me, grinding me with
iron heel, into the dust of the grave" (185). Gabriella becomes so
involved in her mother's seduction that she loses all sense of
her own body, mind, and even personal history. After reading
the narrative Gabriella questions why she should wish to live,
as if it were her own future, and not her mother's past, which
she has just been reading. In this, as in so many domestic stories, we see that the attempt to put violation behind one proves
to be unsuccessful—the past may always return, if not through
the body of the mother herself, then through the text with which
she momentarily engages her daughter-reader.

The seduction of the daughter is not confined to metaphor,
however. In reading her mother's history, Gabriella becomes
absorbed in the story of desire, and her temporary swoon into

the past leaves her ripe for present seduction. This is evidenced by the immediate arrival of Gabriella's future lover, Ernest Linwood. Linwood lifts the heroine up off the grave and out of the past with an assurance that her history is nothing, a clouded name is nothing; his name can absorb it. And absorb it he does. For the autobiography Gabriella writes is under the lover's name, *Ernest Linwood*, subtitled vaguely, "or, The Inner Life of the Author." Linwood offers Gabriella a new name—his own—and thus ostensibly a new destiny: the mother's "sad history of wrongs and disgrace" will be subsumed in the lover's identity. The mother's text is thus replaced by the lover's text which bears his name, and it is a story which proves equally engrossing. For Linwood's entrance into the mother-daughter dyad prompts Gabriella's turn from her mother to her new lover, where, now seduced by *his* words, Gabriella admits that she "forgot the sad history of wrongs and disgrace which [she] had just been perusing; [she] forgot that such words had breathed into her mother's ear, and that she believed them" (188). Gabriella is ready to take her own place in the family circle of seduction.

The fact that Gabriella legally marries Linwood serves mainly to legitimate the seduction model which informs their relationship. Her husband's desire to "enshrine [Gabriella] like a crystal vase in his heart," to fashion her after one of his classical statues and paint her into the image of the flower-girl whose portrait hangs in his study, attests to Linwood's proficiency in the objectification of women so central to nineteenth-century lovemaking. And it reveals that this is yet another relationship meant to keep Gabriella's self-boundaries permeable and her identity undeveloped. Housed within her husband's fortress of marble and burnished gold, Gabriella dwells as Ernest Linwood's most priceless object. As if to emphasize that such a state is the necessary outcome of becoming a woman, Gabriella describes the setting of her leisure space as that room "lined with mirrors, where I could not turn without seeing myself reflected on every side; and not only myself, but an eye that watched my every movement, and an ear that drank in my every word" (244). When taken to the extreme, domestic ideology proves more of a prison than a sanctuary; and the romantic lover, a panoptic disciplinarian who can penetrate not only the woman's every deed, but her every thought as well: "'Beware then, Gabriella,—I may be one of the genii, whose terrible power no mortal can evade, who can read the thoughts of the heart as easily as the printed page. How would you like to be perused so closely?'" (243). Once the daughter-reader of her mother's text, she is now turned into a text by her lover, a text for him to read and read into whatever his jealous and paranoid imagination may conjure up.

Gabriella's reduction to textual object reconfirms the uneasy alliance between mother and daughter. But as if to underscore the point, Gabriella's long-lost father, Henry Gabriel St. James, mysteriously appears. His entrance into Gabriella's life signals a resurfacing of her mother's unhappy past, yet it is also the necessary precondition to a happy *domestic* ending. The repressed past must be brought to light and dealt with before the new daughter-heroine can go forward in her story.[4] Since the domestic novel aims to convert the seduction story to its own ends, all criminal actions of the past must be rectified and the damage contained; order must be restored. And this, ironically, is managed through the familiar plot device of the evil twin brother. It was, it turns out, St. James' profligate brother who married and deserted the woman in New Orleans, not Gabriella's father. The news is doubly significant: in rewriting the mother's history, even after her life has ended, there is an attempt to presage the daughter's felicitous end, since Gabriella's fate has all along been inextricably linked with the mother's. However, what this plot twist succeeds in doing on another level is to drive home the paradigm of the duplicitous nature of love, as well as the duplicitous nature of men. The man you marry, like the mother you adore, has two faces; this is a fact that Gabriella, as well as the reader, has seen all too clearly in the charismatic but unpredictable Ernest Linwood.

In her attempt to write the woman's end differently from the old eighteenth-century story, the nineteenth-century woman is confronted again and again by her mother's image, often in the shape of herself. An illustration is furnished by yet another of our heroine's encounters with her own reflection, this time coming after she has read her mother's history and pledged her future to Ernest Linwood: "As I passed and repassed the double mirror, my reflected figure seemed an apparition gliding by my side. I paused and stood before one of them, and I thought of the time when, first awakened to the consciousness of personal influence, I gazed on my own image." This time the mother's face is absent from the reflection; it is Gabriella herself who forms the double, foreshadowing her own coming struggle to reconcile the image she holds of herself with the way she is read by others, particularly her husband. However, in standing between the double mirror and mirroring a reflection of herself, Gabriella also constitutes herself as the reader of her own story, and so as a daughter to herself. Her gaze recalls the figures of absorbing influence—the mother and the lover—and drama- tizes in disturbing fashion her own participation in, or rather her own assumption of, the model. As Gabriella repeatedly searches into the mirror for some answer to her own identity, she dramatizes her position as both subject and object of admi- ration, as both watcher and watched. It is neither past nor future, neither mother nor lover, which holds her attention now—it is the vision of what she has become that enthralls her.

The domestic novel's idealization of womanhood finally leads us back to earlier, repressed modes of viewing and dealing with feminine "charms." In its reconstruction of the mother's genre, its rewriting of her story with a new and improved hero- ine, domestic fiction brings us yet deeper into the heart of the problem: desire repressed returns with a vengeance. For although Gabriella's destiny is to be a happy one by conventional nineteenth-century standards, and her struggle for individuation amid the seductive manuevers of lover and mother resolves itself into a picture of domestic peace in the last chapter, there is a lin- gering uneasiness. In the final scene the heroine's and husband's struggle for identity and understanding is neither affirmed nor denied; it is in fact eclipsed by a third figure—the new-born baby girl into whose eyes they gaze. The question of whether or not the daughter can escape her mother's fate is ultimately left to the reader's imagination, but we have seen how intricately the pat- tern of seduction is woven, and how far its ties extend. It suggests that while the mother may offer an example of how to write one's story, she cannot tell how to avoid being imprisoned by it: the shift of "female type" from body to text, from flesh to word, may only serve to render the woman an object of a different kind. Rather than initiating or reflecting an ideal world of female relations, then, the domestic novel helps to show how women are taught to objectify themselves and each other. Its self-contained world of domestic intimacy, no matter how seductive, suggests the frightening possibility that for the woman enshrined within, there is no way out of the house of mirrors.

NOTES

1. For a look at the relation of "virtue" to American republicanism, see Wood, Pocock, and Bailyn. For a discussion of republican "virtue" in the context of gender relations, see Smith-Rosenberg ("Domesticating") and Davidson *(Revolution)*. For a persuasive and ground-breaking feminist reading of contractualism in pre-Revolutionary America, see Pateman.

2. The idea of a cooperative network of female relations is most persuasively argued by Smith-Rosenberg, who emphasizes the close bond between mothers and daughters and between sisters in the nineteenth century. Her research and analysis, taken mainly from diaries and letters of eighteenth-and nineteenth-century women, reveals the existence of a "female world" in which women enjoyed with each other great intimacy, love, and passion, characteristics often missing in their relationships with men. My reading of domestic fiction attempts to complicate Smith-Rosenberg's findings, to demonstrate the extent of the emotional ambivalence which arises from such a closed world.

3. The word "compose" comes from the Latin *componere*, literally meaning to "put together": see Partridge 515.

4. In Sedgwick's *Redwood*, as in *Ernest Linwood*, the heroine faces her mother's past before she can pledge herself to her beloved. Ellen Bruce must read her mother's letter and be assured of her "virtue" before she can contemplate marriage. Her mother's story assures Ellen of her legitimacy, but also reveals the deception and betrayal that lay at the heart of that marriage.

WORKS CITED

Bailyn, Bernard. *Ideological Origins of the American Revolution.* Cambridge: Harvard UP, 1967.

Baym, Nina. *Women's Fiction: A Guide to Novels by and about Women in America, 1820–1870.* Ithaca: Cornell UP, 1978.

Brodhead, Richard. "Sparing the Rod: Discipline and Fiction in Antebellum America." *Representations* 21 (1988): 67–96.

Davidson, Cathy N. Introduction. *Charlotte Temple*. New York: Oxford UP. 1986. xi–xxxiii.

———. *Revolution and the Word: The Rise of the Novel in America*. New York: Oxford UP, 1985.

Gilbert, Sandra M. and Susan Gubar. *The Madwoman in the Attic: The Woman Writer and the Nineteenth-Century Literary Imagination*. New Haven: Yale UP, 1979.

Halttunen, Karen. *Confidence Men and Painted Women: A Study of Middle-Class Culture in America, 1830–1870*. New Haven: Yale UP, 1986.

Hentz, Caroline Lee. *Ernest Linwood*. Boston: John P. Jewett, 1856.

Kelley, Mary. *Private Woman, Public Stage: Literary Domesticity in Nineteenth-Century America*. New York: Oxford UP, 1984.

Papashvily, Helen Waite. *All the Happy Endings*. New York: Harpers, 1956.

Partridge, Eric. *Origins: A Short Etymological Dictionary of Modern English*. New York: Macmillan, 1966.

Pateman, Carole. "The Fraternal Social Contract." *The Disorder of Women: Democracy, Feminism and Political Theory*. Cambridge: Polity P, 1989. 33–57.

Pocock, J. G. A. *The Machiavellian Moment: Florentine Political Thought and the Atlantic Republican Tradition*. Princeton: Princeton UP, 1975.

Sedgwick, Catharine Maria. *Redwood: A Tale*. [anon.] New York: E. Bliss & E. White, 1824.

Smith-Rosenberg, Carroll. "Domesticating 'Virtue': Coquettes and Revolutionaries in Young America." *Literature and the Body: Essays on Populations and Persons*. Ed. Elaine Scarry. English Institute New Series 12. Baltimore: Johns Hopkins UP, 1988. 160–84.

———. "The Female World of Love and Ritual." *Signs* 1 (1975): 1–30.

Warner, Susan. *The Wide, Wide World*. New York: Feminist P, 1987.

Wood, Gordon. *The Creation of the American Republic, 1776–1787*. Chapel Hill: U of North Carolina P, 1969.

Charlotte Brontë and Desire (to Write): Pleasure, Power, and Prohibition

Patricia E. Johnson

In a well-known passage from *Jane Eyre*, Jane directly addresses her readers in an effort to explain the desire that drives her narrative. As she describes her habit of pacing on the top of Thornfield Hall, she says:

> Who blames me? Many, no doubt; and I shall be called discontented. I could not help it: the restlessness was in my nature….Then my sole relief was to walk along the third story, backwards and forwards…and allow my mind's eye to dwell on whatever bright visions rose before it…to let my heart be heaved by exultant movement, which, while it swelled it in trouble, expanded it with life; and, best of all, to open my inward ear to a tale that was never ended—a tale my imagination created, and narrated continuously; quickened with all of incident, life, fire, feeling, that I desired and had not in my actual existence. (95–96)

This passage has correctly been read as a feminist manifesto, demanding a wider scope of action for women. I wish, however, to focus on a related but slightly different topic: this passage's emphasis on writing as the answer to Jane's restless desires. For "best of all" to her is "a tale that was never ended—a tale my imagination created, and narrated continuously." My interpretation of Brontë's three novels—*Jane Eyre*, *Shirley*, and *Villette*—argues that their heroines' ultimate object of desire is writing. Despite the importance of female characters in nineteenth-century literature, relatively few novels of the period have female narrators. Brontë's novels are notable exceptions in that two are narrated entirely by their heroines. Even *Shirley*, Brontë's only foray into omniscient narration, quotes an entire essay by Shirley

Keeldar. It is as if Brontë cannot resist showing her heroine's writing, even if she has to bend the form of her novel to do so.

Why, then, has female writing as a thematics been so little emphasized in critical discussions of Brontë's work? I believe that there are two interrelated reasons for this omission, and that both are related to the particular ways that Brontë's novels manifest anxiety about authorship. First, any expression of desire in the novels has been interpreted as sexual desire. However, placing Brontë within a different economy of desire—an "erotics of art" (Brooks xv)—emphasizes how much pleasure in the novels relates to female creativity and self-expression. Brontë's novels progress from *Jane Eyre*, where the desire to write is coded as sexual desire, through *Shirley*, where writing and sexual desire represent each other, to *Villette*, where the desire to write is finally unveiled as having been the true object all along.

Yet how can a Victorian woman openly admit not only that she desires pleasure, but that she finds that desire most satisfied through writing? This question leads us to the second reason that writing as a thematics has been neglected in Brontë's work: the Victorian woman's desires often cannot be directly named. The prohibition against such desires and ambitions was one that all Victorian women felt, but Brontë met with it in an unusually blunt form. To illustrate, one need only recall poet laureate Robert Southey's infamous response to Brontë's poems:

> Literature cannot be the business of a woman's life, and it ought not to be. The more she is engaged in her proper duties, the less leisure will she have for it, even as an accomplishment and a recreation. To those duties you have not yet been called, and when you are you will be less eager for celebrity. (qtd. in Peters 54)

Southey's prohibition is a powerful one. It invokes both gender and class as enforcers of the "proper duties" of the proper lady, and it prohibits writing on a number of levels: the imagination and fantasy leading to writing are a sick indulgence; writing takes time away from duty; and the desire for publication ("eager for celebrity") is seen as particularly dangerous and unladylike. Brontë's continuing significance for female readers and writers has its hidden source in her novels' dramatic enactment of the female desire to write despite such cultural prohibitions.

Jane Eyre is powerfully narrated by its heroine, yet how and why she comes to write her story is never described. Instead, Jane's literary aspirations are coded in three specific ways: as lying in the Gateshead and Lowood sections; as painting in the Thornfield section; and finally as letter-writing. All of these codes mask Jane's ambitions in ways that make them more acceptable to a Victorian audience; and through them, Jane points to the sources of her anxiety about writing.

Why is Jane thrust out of Gateshead, thus beginning the series of conflicts that is her life story? The plot begins, significantly, when Jane is found reading a book which John Reed claims belongs to him. If Jane would silently submit to punishment, there would be a plot of victimization. But Jane does not. She not only reads, but *tells* stories. She confronts John Reed's tale of herself and her beggary—"You have no business to take our books; you are a dependent"—with a competing tale of her own: John Reed is a cruel and sadistic tyrant like the Roman emperors of old (8). From this moment on, Jane tells her story—to the apothecary, Mr. Lloyd; to the servant, Bessie; and, finally, twice, to Mrs. Reed herself. This is her introduction to narration, and she is severely punished for it. In fact, she is cast out of Gateshead for it. When Mrs. Reed describes Jane's character to Mr. Brocklehurst, it is not Jane's violence or wildness that she attacks as unbearable; according to Mrs. Reed, Jane's "worst fault" is a "tendency to deceit" (28). It is this label that she also receives at Lowood school, when held up to exposure by Mr. Brocklehurst:

> Teachers, you must watch her: keep your eyes on her movements, weigh well her words, scrutinise her actions, punish her body to save her soul: if, indeed, such salvation be possible, for (my tongue falters while I tell it) this girl, this child, the native of a Christian land, worse than many a little heathen who says its prayers to Brahma and kneels before Juggernaut—this girl is—a liar! (58)

In these scenes the forces of class values, proper womanhood, and religious fundamentalism combine to condemn and punish Jane's storytelling. As she moves into the female-dominated world of Miss Temple's Lowood school, however, Jane finds that her version of events is taken seriously, and another stage of her artistic development begins.

In the Thornfield section of the novel, a second code for writing makes its appearance. Four scenes describe Jane's painting in detail: (1) the well-known scene where Rochester examines her paintings; (2) a scene at Thornfield where Jane disciplines herself by painting contrasting portraits of herself and Blanche Ingram; (3) a scene at Gateshead where Jane paints while awaiting the dying Mrs. Reed's summons; and (4) the scene in which Jane paints Rosamond Oliver and discusses that painting with St. John Rivers. The four scenes taken together underline some points which are not always evident. First is the fact that painting appears throughout the novel. Indeed, Jane's paintings link the separate sections of the novel. For example, at Lowood Jane painted the pictures that Rochester looks at; they reflect, in turn, her childhood reading and experiences at Gateshead. Similarly, Jane paints a portrait of Rochester as she awaits her aunt's death in the forbidding, haunted atmosphere of Gateshead. Finally, Jane's sharing of her portrait of Rosamond Oliver with St. John Rivers provides him with the secret of her identity because she has written her real name on the paper that she uses to protect the portrait. Yet, although her painting emblematizes Jane's creativity, it also has its limitations in representing "the tale that her imagination endlessly created."

The self-protective limitations put on the interpretation of the paintings are clear in the first scene in which they are introduced. Rochester examines Jane's paintings in the midst of a cross-examination to which he subjects her at their first formal meeting. From the beginning, then, the paintings are subordinated to Jane and Rochester's relationship. As her employer, Rochester exercises his right to question her credentials as a governess. He quizzes her on her background and education, and then orders her to play the piano for him. Thus, painting appears unthreateningly as part of a governess's qualifications and a proper lady's accomplishments. Jane, too, is modest about her work. Rochester has first seen the paintings because her pupil, Adele, showed them off, and the portfolio is produced only at his command. In a manner that Southey would have approved, Jane explains that she painted only during her vacations at Lowood "when I had no other occupation" (109).

Given these limitations, however, the paintings do, in important ways, represent Jane's writing. First, while she claims that they are in some sense failures, "nothing wonderful," and "but a pale portrait of the thing I had conceived" (110), they are powerful and disturbing—a drowned corpse glancing through green water; the Evening Star imaged as a woman; a colossal head resting on an iceberg. As Rochester says in unusual understatement, "the drawings are, for a schoolgirl, peculiar." Originality and forcefulness are as much a part of their "peculiarity" as the traumas that form their psychological background. Second, Jane identifies her creativity with intense pleasure. She describes painting the pictures as "one of the keenest pleasures I have ever known." Third, Rochester effectively begins his courtship of Jane by being the perfect audience for her work. He is not flattering but critical. When Jane admits, "In each case I had imagined something which I was quite powerless to realise," he answers, "Not quite: you have secured the shadow of your thought but no more, probably. You had not enough of the artist's skill and science to give it full being." His criticisms are sharp but encouraging, suggesting that the "schoolgirl" could develop more "artist's skill and science." Significantly, nowhere does he suggest that her work is unfeminine or that gender limits her in any way. The concluding questions in his cross-examination express wonder at what she has achieved: "How could you make [the eyes of the Evening Star] look so clear, and yet not at all brilliant? And what meaning is that in their solemn depth? And who taught you to paint the wind? Where did you see Latmos?" (111).

These questions are left unexplored. From this point onward in the novel, painting will be domesticated and subordinated to courtship, no longer reflecting, however palely, the artist's dreamworld in Jane's mind, but instead reflecting the relations of aspiring lovers. Three succeeding scenes describe Jane in the act of painting representational portraits. Two themes continue from the group of Lowood paintings: Jane feels pleasure in her work—she describes an "artist-thrill" when painting Rosamond Oliver, for example (325)—and she paints in close association with women. In the first scene, she bases her portrait on Mrs. Fairfax's description of Blanche Ingram; in the second, her cousins, Eliza and Georgiana Reed, examine and comment on her work; and in the third, she paints at the request of her model, Rosamond. The paintings, however, lack the power of her earlier ones. In harnessing them to courtship motifs, she has lost her "peculiar" vision. They do not even retain the power to move sexual desire. When she shows Rosamond's portrait to St. John Rivers, for example, she uses it to force him to admit his desire for Rosamond, but in the end, he rejects her offer of a "copy" for himself. This sequence of reproductions, ending with a copy of a copy of Rosamond Oliver, shows the danger of acceding too much to the drama of male desire. Once Jane harnesses her paintings to courtship, they lose their force and originality—their power, specifically, to represent *her* desires.

It is significant, therefore, that while St. John does not accept the offer of a copy of Rosamond's portrait, he does take a small scrap of paper on which Jane has unconsciously written her real name. While writing's significance is hidden in this text, it is still, as St. John discovers, the key to the mystery of Jane's identity. For example, it is easily forgotten that the traumatic revelation of Bertha Mason Rochester's existence actually depends on the letter that Jane writes to her Uncle Eyre announcing her impending marriage to Mr. Rochester. This disclosure also sheds light on the reason that *Jane Eyre* ends not with Jane's words, but with a quotation from a letter by St. John Rivers. Jane has gained money, social station, marriage, and love by the end of her story; but, as St. John's letter signifies, there is something else she desires that she has still not laid claim to.

In *Jane Eyre* the desire to write channels itself into the traditional female plot of ambition and advancement through marriage, but as the novel's conclusion suggests, that handling of desire is not altogether satisfactory. In *Shirley* and *Villette*, therefore, the plots alter and the codes change. In other words, they both resist the marriage plot and thematize female writing more openly through the use of schoolroom essays as well as letters. *Shirley* makes a particularly interesting instance because the use of Shirley Keeldar's essay in the novel disrupts its dominant pattern of omniscient narration. Shirley is unusual in other ways as well because the narrator makes greater claims for her as an artist than modest Jane Eyre makes for herself. For example, Shirley is often involved in discussions of poetry and literature. Furthermore, she criticizes male writers' representations of female characters. Witness her attack on Milton's Eve, whom she argues is not a portrait of the first woman but a portrait of

Milton's "cook" (314). Finally, not only is Shirley well-read, but in her inspirations and feelings, she is a poet: "A still, deep, inborn delight glows in her young veins; unmingled—untroubled; not to be reached or ravished by human agency, because by no human agency bestowed: the pure gift of God to His creature, the free dower of Nature to her child" (374). Here Shirley experiences the "keen pleasure" of the imagination that Jane Eyre felt, and the narrator makes the additional claim that, contra Southey and Mr. Brocklehurst, this delight comes from God.

Why is Shirley not subject to the censorship, the code, as Jane Eyre is? The reason is that she has no aspirations to publish; she is not "eager for celebrity"; she feels no need to share her visions:

> Had she a little more of the organ of Acquisitiveness in her head—a little more of the love of property in her nature, she would take a good-sized sheet of paper and write plainly out, in her own queer but clear and legible hand, the story that has been narrated, the song that has been sung to her, and thus possess what she was enabled to create. But indolent as she is, reckless as she is, and most ignorant, for she does not know her dreams are rare—her feelings peculiar: she does not know, has never known, and will die without knowing, the full value of that spring whose bright fresh bubbling in her heart keeps it green. (374)

Shirley can only be praised as a poet because she does not act upon her inspirations. But the narrator's attitude is mixed. The desire to save what she has imagined, to "possess" it through writing it down or even publishing it, is negatively associated with a kind of greed—"Acquisitiveness" and "love of property." On the other hand, if she is not greedy, she is lazy and careless. Yet, finally, the narrator mourns Shirley's lack of ambition more than she envies or criticizes it. For Shirley will die without ever having fully explored the most unique and nourishing part of herself, her imagination.

Shirley Keeldar and Louis Moore make plain the writing as desire motif that was hidden in *Jane Eyre*, for it is through Shirley's essays for her tutor Louis, and his commitment of them to memory, that their desire for each other is revealed. In their relationship Brontë tries to imagine a noncompetitive artistic partnership between a man and a woman. Louis Moore draws pictures and keeps a diary just as Shirley writes essays. Each explores the mind of the other by examining these productions. Sometimes they are even produced as pairings, as when Shirley writes a description of a snow-scene and then Louis draws it (437).

This search for a sexual and artistic partnership culminates when Louis recites an old essay of Shirley's entitled "La Première Femme Savante" or "The First Blue-Stocking." It is set in the dawn of time, and its title character is a young girl who seeks the meaning of life:

> She asked, was she thus to burn out and perish, her living light doing no good, never seen, never needed,—a star in an else starless firmament,—which nor shepherd, nor wanderer, nor sage, nor priest, tracked as a guide, or read as a prophecy? Could this be, she demanded, when the flame of her intelligence burned so vivid; when her life beat so true, and real, and potent; when something within her stirred disquieted, and restlessly asserted a God-given strength for which it insisted she should find exercise? (457–58)

The first "femme savante" asks the same question that the Victorian female writer would like to pose: why was she given these desires and talents and yet forbidden to exercise them? And she seems to find the answer when she meets a Son of God, who plays Genius to her Humanity, combining the roles of lover and male Muse. The femme savante rejoices and feels power in her union with him. But what comes after? Shirley cannot tell. Like Rochester's response to Jane Eyre's paintings, her essay ends in more questions: "Who shall rehearse the tale of their after-union?" (459). Certainly not Shirley, because when reality replaces myth, Shirley loses her powers of vision. Without ambition or acquisitiveness herself, she cannot imagine the conflicts that the femme savante will undergo in a fallen world. She can only vaguely list the internal and external struggles that await the female writer in the world of historical time: the "deadly plots," "the long strife," "the polluted cup," "the debased emotion," and "the agony of the passage." The concluding question of her essay is "Who shall, of these things, write the chronicle?" (459–60). The answer is: Lucy Snowe.

After the smooth first-person narrative of *Jane Eyre* and the attempted romance of artistic partners in *Shirley*, the fractured, difficult, untrustworthy first-person narrative of *Villette* comes as a surprise. Yet while *Villette* is often described as a narrative about the effort to repress desire, I would like to suggest that it is fractured and conflicted precisely because it strives for the first time to name directly the desire that had been buried in the preceding novels. In *Villette* the reader is aware of the narration, of its power to trick or to withhold information. Like Jane Eyre, Lucy is called a liar—but by her readers, not by Mrs. Reed. The direct thematization of writing in Lucy's narrative is the cause of these conflicts, conflicts that are no longer projected onto others but are identified as internal to the female narrator herself. *Villette* enacts this thematization of female writing in three ways. First, Lucy admits, though indirectly and ambivalently, the power as well as the pleasure that she experiences through writing. Second, Lucy twice describes herself in the act of writing: as she composes her first letter to Graham Bretton and as she writes an essay during an examination. Third, *Villette* enacts Lucy's conflicts with a (male) audience through her relationships with Graham Bretton and Professor Paul Emmanuel.

Two important scenes that describe Lucy's writing occur in response to Graham Bretton's letters. The first scene describes Lucy's internal battle at the mere idea of writing to Graham. Reason coldly tries to rein in Lucy's excitement by demanding, "If he *should* write, what then? Do you meditate pleasure in replying?" Lucy responds that she frequently talks to Graham, and Reason has not scolded. Reason explains, "Talk for you is good discipline. You converse imperfectly. While you speak, there can be no oblivion of inferiority—no encouragement to delusion: pain, privation, penury stamp your language—." Reason does not complete her statement, but the implication is clear. When Lucy speaks, her language is imperfect, but when she writes, pain turns into pleasure, privation into fullness, penury into wealth. Writing, in short, is power; but, Reason warns, "At your peril you cherish that idea, or suffer its influence to animate any writing of yours!" (207).

Lucy's first scene of writing shows that she obeys the dictates of Reason ambivalently. When she sits down to write her response to Graham, Lucy confesses, "To speak truth, I compromised matters: I served two masters...I wrote to these letters two answers—one for my own relief, the other for Graham's approval." The first letter she writes with "eager pen," "deep enjoyment," and "sincere heart." But Reason, mindful of the writing's audience, bursts in and proceeds to "snatch the full sheets, read, sneer, erase, tear up, re-write, fold, seal, direct, and send a terse, curt missive of a page" (230). Here Lucy enacts for the reader the conflict that the female writer undergoes—first inspired by her imagination, but then led to censor her own production, to hide her pleasure and power, in order to present it in a form that the world will accept.

In Graham Bretton and then Paul Emmanuel, Lucy turns to the audience that provokes these conflicts. And, for the first time, the male audience is seen in its full reality, as readers and teachers, but also competitors and censoring judges, of female writing. Graham belongs to the medical profession; but his character is based on Brontë's publisher, George Smith, and an early scene in the novel presents him writing. This scene shows Paulina Home, who will become Graham's wife, interrupting him at his schoolboy studies. Paulina asks, "What are you doing?" and Graham responds, "Writing." When Paulina finds that he is "too busy" with his writing to come to breakfast, she brings his breakfast to his writing table. As a reward, Graham praises her and tells her that if she shows any "culinary genius" when she grows up, he will reward her by making her "his cook" (17). This scene, with its echoes of Milton's cook, quite obviously represents the cultural inequality of men and women, men relieved even from looking after their own wants as they pursue culture, women rewarded for their servitude to such men by even more servitude. Lucy's Reason, then, is perhaps not so unreasonable in suggesting that she not attempt to exercise her power over such an audience. In fact, while Lucy cherishes Graham's letters, he never endangers his cultural superiority by commenting on hers.

On the other hand, Paul Emmanuel proves to be a much more responsive audience. Paul's continuing involvement in Lucy's education allows her to probe the sources of her ambivalence while she plays against every kind of male cultural attitude towards female writing. During the course of their relationship, Paul forbids Lucy to write, encourages her to do so, accuses her of plagiarism, accuses her of pride, and, finally, forces her to write in an examination before two professors who have accused her of forgery. But because Paul is naked in his desire to control her writing, Lucy is better able to respond. Furthermore, she can forgive much of his attitude because she discovers its source. Paul himself desires to write, and that is the reason that he envies and tries to control Lucy's writing. He is a brilliant speaker and storyteller, yet he confesses to Lucy, "I could not write that down…I hate the mechanical labour; I hate to stoop and sit still. I could dictate it, though, with pleasure to an amanuensis who suited me. Would Mademoiselle Lucy write for me if I asked her?" (347).

Here Lucy comes to a possible resolution of her struggles. Instead of competing with men, usurping their assigned place in culture, she could subordinate her abilities to their desires. Lucy's conflict over her writing reaches its climax when this possible resolution is put to the test. Paul arranges, without Lucy's knowledge, an examination where she will demonstrate her skill to two professors from a nearby university. In a chapter entitled "Fraternity," Lucy is brought into a classroom to be "tested." Torn between anger and nervousness, Lucy performs poorly in the oral section of the examination, and the professors comment that she is an "idiot" (364). For her writing test Lucy is given the genderless, classless topic, "Human Justice." As she considers rejecting this assignment, she has a flash of insight that illuminates the scene as an emblem of female writing. It is impossible to join the fraternity with its "universal" topics. And she identifies another basis for that fraternity when she recognizes the professors as two men who had sexually harassed her, a lone woman in the street, on the night of her arrival in Villette.

But Lucy does not throw down her pen and leave the room, as she is tempted to do. Instead, in anger, she writes an essay that treats "Human Justice" not as an ideal abstraction, but as deeply implicated in the gender and class relations of her society. In Lucy's essay Justice is not a dignified and blindfolded "proper lady." She is a "beldame," a witch, who rejects the poor and rewards the rich (366). What is striking here is that, after Lucy's long struggle with the issue, there is no escape to an imaginary world, like the one occupied by Shirley Keeldar's *femme savante*, where pleasure and power exist without prohibition. Writing is always deeply implicated in its historical moment and its gender and class relations. There is no escape through it to an unfallen world ruled by a beneficent "human justice." Rather there is a guilty rediscovery of the writer's continual collusion with this world and its injustices. What is finally even more important is that, despite the set-up, Lucy does not refuse to write. She follows her desire, as Charlotte Brontë had always done, by enacting her conflicts.

This scene of Lucy writing while being observed by Paul Emmanuel and two professors is a plain challenge to Southey's "literature cannot be the business of a woman's life," a recognition that female writing must finally confront those who prohibit it. Through her teaching, her letters to Paul, and her narrative, Lucy will make literature her business. This scene also measures the distance that Brontë has travelled since Jane Eyre described her "restlessness" and fears of condemnation—"Who blames me?"—as she paced the battlements of Thornfield Hall (95). Jane had excused her desire to tell a tale because she did not have "incident, life, fire, feeling" in her "actual existence" (96). In *Jane Eyre*, writing could be seen as mere replacement for women who did not have "proper duties." But in *Villette* writing itself is "incident," pleasure, and power. Charlotte Brontë herself will continue to be signally important to female writers and readers: first, because she struggles with cultural prohibition, but, second, and more essentially, because she discovers her pleasure and power in writing despite it.

WORKS CITED

Brontë, Charlotte. *Jane Eyre*. Ed. Richard J. Dunn. New York: Norton, 1971.

———. *Shirley*. Eds. Andrew and Judith Hook. New York: Penguin, 1974.

———. *Villette*. New York: Dutton, 1974.

Brooks, Peter. *Reading for the Plot: Design and Intention in Narrative*. New York: Random House, 1984.

Peters, Margot. *Unquiet Soul: A Biography of Charlotte Brontë*. New York: Atheneum, 1986.

Sarah Grand's The Beth Book: The New Woman and the Ideology of the Romance Ending

Terri Doughty

The New Woman is a well-known figure from the 1890s, but only as male authors construct her. Most studies of New Woman fiction focus upon male writers, especially Hardy and Gissing; female writers, like Sarah Grand, Mona Caird, or "Iota," are ghettoized as "minor" figures because their writing is not as experimental as that of their male counterparts. They are considered too concerned with polemics, and their only received contribution to literature is their willingness to deal with taboo subject-matter (Cunningham; Stubbs; Boumelha; Showalter 31; Rubinstein 33). However, these female writers' formal conventionality is ideologically important because it signifies not female lack of creativity, but female anxiety about writing women's lives in fictional plots. Many female writers of New Woman fiction uneasily weigh their independence as authors against the necessity of satisfying their audience.

The Beth Book: Being a Study of the Life of Elizabeth Caldwell Maclure, A Woman of Genius (1897), a semi-autobiographical novel by Sarah Grand, herself a New Woman, vividly and daringly portrays the protagonist's rebellion against the traditional female marriage plot, yet its romantic ending fails to sustain resistance. Writing in an autobiographical vein, Grand *rewrites* her own life: Beth, Grand's alter ego, finds both a career and a lover. Either Grand is expressing a secret desire, or she is somehow unable to reinscribe her own independence in the text. In an April 1932 letter to Gladys Singers-Bigger, Grand attempts to distance herself from *The Beth Book*: "I can't think why you

185

should suppose it is [autobiographical] but I have forgotten what it is all about" (qtd. in Kersley 22). This denial of her life in fiction stems from her uneasiness with the tensions produced by trying to reconcile life and plot.

The clashes between Grand's lived experience, the cultural context in which she wrote, and gender issues become increasingly apparent as the *The Beth Book* moves toward closure, which forms ideology that speaks to the issue of female creative anxiety.[1] Carolyn Heilbrun notes that "true" narratives of female lives can be anxiety-inducing as they deny the comfort of a set "script," whereas romances provide a sense of completion or fulfillment (39). *The Beth Book* reverses this situation, however, for here the pressure of the script, or plot, causes anxiety. Many feminist critics have commented upon the difficulties particular to the female writer. Not only is she encroaching upon a patriarchal tradition of the male author, but in asserting her own right to exercise creative power, she must somehow appropriate existing language and conventions without perpetuating patriarchal ideology (cf. Jacobus, "Difference" 10-11; Gubar 92). As author, Grand confronts this dilemma: how can her female protagonist rebel against oppression without surrendering to the confining structure of the patriarchal romance plot?

Grand's attempt to develop an alternative female story is closely bound up with the idea of the New Woman; *The Beth Book* is in one sense an autobiography of a New Woman. But although Sarah Grand helped coin the term, she by no means controlled the idea behind it.[2] Images of the New Woman ranged from Ibsen's independent heroines to mannish caricatures in *Punch*. The term was and is a site of ideological struggle; hence, Grand's own definition must be clarified. In all of Grand's novels, certain traits reappear in her central female characters and are valorized by the texts: a desire for education, a highly-principled and individualistic questioning of social conventions, a rejection of sexual double standards, and a belief in honest self-expression. Grand designates her New Woman as both morally and intellectually superior to what she calls "the Bawling Brotherhood" ("New" 271). This image of the New Woman is positive and empowering; however, Grand cannot sustain it in her fiction. She may question but she cannot deny social convention.

Sarah Grand's life illustrates her definition of the New Woman. Her early life is much like that portrayed in *The Beth Book*: a sensitive, intelligent girl surmounts oppression from her family and her husband to become a "woman of genius."[3] Yet "Sarah Grand" is as much a construct as her idea of the New Woman. Frances Elizabeth McFall (her middle name later served for her alter ego) consciously adopted the name "Sarah Grand" when she left her husband and child (to save her husband embarrassment, according to her biographer, Gillian Kersley). Grand had several stories explaining why she chose that particular name: it was suggested by her stepsons; it came to her in a dream; she took it from an old woman; she liked it because it was short and memorable. Elaine Showalter, however, sees the name as signifying more than convenience: it represents the "sense of feminist pride and of matriarchal mission" of 1890s feminism (Kersley 64–65; Showalter, *Literature* 29). The Sarah Grand who in print and on the platform spoke to women's issues and who styled herself "Madame Sarah Grand" evokes an image of female power; she is grand in name and deed. As well, "Sarah" means "princess" in Hebrew, so Grand's pseudonym is doubly majestic.[4] Yet by creating a new identity for herself, Grand masks her true self; although the new name provides safety and control over Grand's public image, Frances McFall still cannot speak as herself. She needs the persona of Mme. Grand.

Nonetheless, despite (or perhaps because of) her controversial persona, Grand became immensely popular. Her first novel, *Ideala* (1888), was privately printed because she could not find a publisher, but by 1899 it had gone through seven editions in both Britain and the United States. Her most commercially successful work, *The Heavenly Twins* (1892), was reprinted six times within four years. Heinemann claimed thirty-five thousand sales of the book in just over a year, and family papers show that Grand earned at least £18,000 from it.[5] By 1897, the year of *The Beth Book*, "Sarah Grand" had become a brand name, signifying a specific type of literature on women's issues. Yet Grand's sales cannot be accounted for by any narrow segment of the market for popular fiction. Her popularity suggests that the ideological content of her writing spoke to readers with diverse political attitudes: while her criticism of contemporary gender roles might appeal to those holding "advanced" views, both her adherence to novelistic conventions and her refusal to allow characters completely to defy social morality would appeal to less daring readers.

The different implications of Sarah Grand's image and the conflicting levels of discourse within a text like *The Beth Book* are better understood within wider social contexts. Not everyone shared Grand's enabling vision of the New Woman's potential. In addition to the *Punch* cartoons, magazines of the day carried more elaborately theorized criticisms of the phenomenon. *The Beth Book* was written over an eighteen-month period in 1895 and 1896 which saw a number of important articles dealing with the New Woman. Reviewers consistently condemned New Woman authors and characters for their "unwomanly" desire for autonomy and questioned their sanity, as such desire must be unnatural (Hogarth; Tyrrell; Oliphant). Contemporary critical responses to *The Beth Book* reveal that Sarah Grand confronted these same prejudices, some of which she may have shared.[6]

Indeed, Grand's works reproduce such conflicts. On the one hand, there is the sense of female solidarity (supportive characters recur in different novels), the resistance of oppressive social controls, and the criticism of unworthy men (husbands in most Grand texts). On the other hand, a number of observers note Grand's conservatism in both her novels and her essays, her concern with women's appearance, and her respect for marriage as an institution (Kersley 68–69; Rubinstein 20, 219; Cunningham 56–57). In *The Beth Book*, for example, the heroine does not blame her woes upon marriage, but rather upon the poor husband material available to her. Earlier, the narrator comments: "Beth had been born to be a woman, but circumstances had been forcing her to become a career" (499, 433). Beth's responsibility and right to choose her own destiny are denied her; her life is determined by coincidence and accident. The plot thus attempts to assert Beth's "womanliness," avoiding the potential charge of "unsexing" its heroine (cf. Heilbrun 25, 48). These elements articulate an underlying uneasiness with the more controversial qualities of the New Woman.

The Beth Book begins, however, by describing the rebelliousness of an embryonic New Woman. The young Beth is impulsive, curious, and outspoken, leading her to war against the social conventions enforced by her mother. The narrator intrudes sympathetically to criticize both the lack of education available to girls and the physical tortures daughters undergo to become competitive in the marriage market (114, 119, 225). Beth resists this fate by studying the classics in an attempt to understand the source of male power (274–75). Thus, Grand sets up an equation common in New Woman fiction between reading, knowledge, and power, thereby suggesting that literature (including her own novels) is an educational and empowering tool (cf. Flint). Beth follows Lucy Snowe and Maggie Tulliver, characters who question both traditional artistic constructions of the feminine and the role of fiction as a form of patriarchal control exercised through plot.

Beth, though, is of special interest because of her desire to write. Her comments on writing fiction are interesting, for she rejects those conventions with which Grand wrestles. Beth detests perfect, golden-haired heroines, and she is bored by "plotty-plotty books" filled with coincidences and tangled stories. Most important, Beth refuses to see the love-story as the pivot of any novel, saying scornfully, "as if there was nothing else in life but our sexual relations" (373). It is tempting to apply Beth's remarks to Grand's fiction. Certainly Beth is not the ideal blonde heroine of romance; however, she is portrayed as beautiful to discriminating viewers, and her genius is a type of perfection. Of more interest, however, is her rejection of overly complicated romance plots. Here Beth points to one of the main concerns of Grand's novel: the tension between a woman's "career" and her love life. Beth seeks a career because she is unfulfilled, but once she becomes successful her true reward is love.

Frank Kermode may insist on the necessity of an end to provide meaning to a plot (46), but as Heilbrun says, "women have lived too much with closure" (130). Many critics have commented upon the typical nineteenth-century marriage or romance plot. Generally, such plots construct a heroine as object, denied personal as opposed to social development. The plot enforces a pattern of confinement, as the female character's "progress" is determined primarily by her love options. Such plots are the bearers of ideology that reinforce societal strictures against female self-determination.[7] The romance plot hinges upon closure, which does indeed give it meaning; for fictions that culminate in marriage, or in the celebration of a love relationship, inscribe the emotional subjection of women. *The Beth Book* grafts a romance ending upon a quest plot, and the fruit thereof is at best bitter.

Nevertheless, Grand's novel does contain what Rachel Blau DuPlessis calls "writing beyond the ending," for Beth, who so desires knowledge and an outlet for her talents, is at an early age manipulated by her mother into marrying a seemingly charming doctor. As the text is lengthy, there is plenty of space to analyze the institution of marriage. A husband, or at least the one she acquires, proves to be anything but the answer to Beth's needs. Daniel Maclure is a brute: he installs his mistress in Beth's home, practices vivisection, and runs a Lock Hospital under the Contagious Diseases Act. For Beth, marriage to this man is a form of imprisonment. He has free access to her rooms, he reads her mail, and he pries among her private papers. The narrator frequently empathizes with all wives in Beth's situation. In fact, the text is almost excessive in its denunciation of the potential evils of marriage for innocent girls—it is certainly no recommendation for the marriage plot.

Within the confines of the marriage, however, Beth continues her quest for development in defiance of her husband's tyrannies. In her first attempt at artistic self-expression, she turns to the traditional female art of embroidery. Because she sells her art for profit, her husband intervenes and censors her activities. Her economic independence is an affront to his control. Eventually, in the most significant action during her life with her husband, Beth finds and converts a secret attic room into a private study, finally achieving a room of her own (346–47). This measure of independence within her marriage is, though, somewhat uneasy. A perceptive contemporary book reviewer notes that Beth is pretty much silenced once she marries; that is, the narrative provides little of her internal life ("Two" 622). Both Marianne Hirsch and Showalter point out the claustrophobic and limited nature of development which occurs in such secrecy (Hirsch 23–24; Showalter, *Literature* 208–09, 215). Beth's quest forces Beth back upon herself; she remains pent up as long as she stays with her husband.

Having established the dangers of marriage, the plot continues as a quest. Beth leaves her husband after a clash over social
conventions and exchanges her attic at home for an attic in London. Oddly enough, although this moment seems to signify the
true culmination of Beth's quest, the novel continues for another
forty or so pages. The effect is one of anticlimax. We are told
very little of Beth's activities, save that she is happy and industrious. She anonymously publishes an immensely successful
book of nonfiction, but we know nothing of its contents. Beth's
long-awaited intellectual and artistic development remains a
mystery.

More seriously, the text is highly ambivalent about Beth's
hard-won freedom. Not only are her artistic endeavours largely
dismissed, but the plot maneuvers her into yet another romantic
situation which competes with her chosen career. Her attic
neighbor proves to be a male painter, Arthur Brock, whom Beth
befriends. When he falls ill of some vague, debilitating fever,
Beth proves her "womanly" compassion by freely choosing to
nurse him and ignore her work. Arthur's "highest character
and...perfect refinement" make him a worthy object of Beth's
self-sacrifice (504–05). As a young girl, Beth cut off her hair in a
fit of humiliation (279); this scene is repeated when she sells her
hair to pay for Arthur's medicine, food, and coal. When Arthur
accuses her of joining "the unsexed crew that shriek on plat-
forms," the narrative neither condemns his attitude nor defends
its heroine. Instead, Beth cries because she has hurt his sensibili-
ties (509). This incident completes her subjection in the role of
nurturer; the female artist is lost.

At this point, the quest plot seems to be stalled. In order for
Beth to continue her search for self-expression, she must break
away from Arthur. Since her subjection is self-imposed, the plot
contorts itself through the kind of coincidences that Beth earlier
deplored. A friend appears to take Arthur away to the country,
and when he departs at the end of chapter fifty, Beth collapses
after weeks of self-deprivation—a symbolic death. Angelica Kil-
roy, one of the supportive women who reappear in Grand's
texts, happens to be driving by Beth's rooming house when the
accident occurs, and miraculously restores her. However, the
new Beth does not continue with her writing. In another happy
coincidence, Beth acts as an impromptu speaker at a women's

meeting when the guest speaker fails to arrive and is a great success. But (as with her writing) we are not told what she says; furthermore, once Beth becomes an orator, her words are lost through time, as speech is not necessarily recorded.

Beth's death and rebirth appear to be an escape from the ambivalence and discomfort aroused by her attempts at a writing career. But her story now begins to read as fantasy. Under the patronage of her friends, Beth acquires a beautiful cottage in the country, contact with other women who share her interests and concerns, and a successful career. Once more, however, the plot is not satisfied. Earlier, during her life with her husband, Beth had been heartened by the sight of a horseman who made her think of "a man to be trusted...true and tender, a perfect knight." The narrator quotes from "The Lady of Shalott," implying that the rider is a Lancelot who will save Beth from her depression: "the horrid spell was broken" (433). On the last pages of the novel, we are told that Beth is not satisfied with all that she has achieved. As she looks out over the fields, her final desire is answered: Arthur Brock, "the Knight of her long winter vigil," appears complete with accompanying Tennyson tag (527). The romantic image of Arthur riding toward her in the sunlight appears to give Beth everything at last, a career and a lover.

Heilbrun claims that a woman can only survive romance if it is without closure, that is, if it does not lead to marriage (87). Yet the very open-endedness of Beth's romance with Arthur is in itself disturbing, as it seems to dissolve serious problems in a solution compounded of Tennyson, love, and sunshine. Arthur's name has all the chivalric and romantic associations of King Arthur, but Arthurian legends do not enable women: the knights quest and the maidens wait to be rescued. Arthur has once before stood between Beth and her art; now he seeks her love and nurturance again. Moreover, although the tag from "The Lady of Shalott" aligns Arthur with Beth's unknown savior, it also raises troubling intertextual connections. Heilbrun equates the safety and enclosure of a happy love relationship with the mirror of the Lady of Shalott, an illusory reality (20). If Arthur is Lancelot, then Beth must be the Lady of Shalott; the latter's weaving is related to Beth's own artistic endeavours. This does not auger well for Beth—for once the Lady saw the knight and left her art, she lost her creative vision and died.

Showalter, in her introduction to the Virago edition of the novel, calls Beth "a valuable and unusual heroine" because "Grand allows her to survive and to succeed" (n.p.). Yet the novel contains many fissures, and its ending calls into question the possibility of even a New Woman maintaining an independent artistic career. Beth, like her author, has all the essential qualities of the New Woman, yet their stories are ultimately different. Various determining factors cause the text to reinscribe anxieties about female creativity that Grand seemed to surmount in her own life. The text is a testament to the deep-rooted ambivalence even a successful female writer could experience about appropriating authorial power. The age of the New Woman may have been a fruitful one for the development of women's emancipation, but it was also fraught with tension.

That is not to say, however, that *The Beth Book* and other New Woman novels by women are failures because they are historically determined. It is impossible for the text to resolve ambivalence which has not been resolved by the culture that produced it. Such anxiety might seem self-defeating, but as Boumelha notes, the act of writing can be a protest in itself, and the revelation of existing tensions and conflicts is political in that it bares hidden power relations (66–67; also Beer 80; Miller 356–57; Goode 112–13; Vicinus 21). Furthermore, by exposing the subtle ideologies of the romance plot, such New Woman fiction suggests that men might need to be displaced from the center of women's lives (cf. Flint 61–62). New Woman fiction by women is not only a necessary stage in the evolution of women's writing, but an enabling one. *The Beth Book* may not overcome the anxieties surrounding the image of the creative woman, but paradoxically, those anxieties are empowering. Self-consciousness is the first stage of political awareness and resistance.

NOTES

1. I use "ideology" in the sense of an unconscious articulation of an individual's relation to power structures. My interest in ideology is informed by the early work of Macherey and Eagleton. More recently, I have been influenced by Davis's study of the ideologies of narrative structures.

2. Grand first used the term in an article in the *North American Review*. "Ouida" added the capital letters in her reply article in May of the same year. The acceptance of the term was sealed when *Punch* used it in a facetious ditty. See Rubinstein 15–16 and Jordan 20.

3. Kersley bases much of her reading of Grand's life upon *The Beth Book*.

4. Interestingly, the Biblical Sarah was originally named "Sarai," which means "contentious." This would seem to connect Grand's polemical writing with her regal authority. See Withycombe 263–64.

5. Huddleston 14–15; Flint 60; Cunningham 57; Rubinstein 25; Kersley 87. Details vary according to the source. I follow Huddleston and Rubinstein primarily.

6. "Two Notable Novels" is the most sympathetic review, yet it still censures Grand for a lack of "love" in the novel. "New Novels," appearing in the *Athenaeum* (lampooned in the novel as the *Patriarch*), accuses Grand of "nagging" and calls Beth "a perfectly insupportable bag of fads" (744). An anonymous book review and "Sarah Grand's Latest Book" attack the novel for its "coarseness," implying that both Beth and Sarah Grand are "unwomanly," the one for having desires and the other for writing about them.

7. See brief comments in Heilbrun 77, 121; Cunningham 20; Showalter, *Literature* 180–81; and more generally in the introduction by Abel et al. DuPlessis's first chapter is especially pertinent here.

WORKS CITED

Abel, Elizabeth, et al., eds. *Voyages In: Fictions of Female Development*. Hanover: UP of New England, 1983.

Beer, Gillian. "Beyond Determinism: George Eliot and Virginia Woolf." Jacobus, *Women* 80–99.

Rev. of *The Beth Book*, by Sarah Grand. *Spectator* 79 (1897): 691–92.

Boumelha, Penny. *Thomas Hardy and Women*. Sussex: Harvester, 1982.

Cunningham, Gail. *The New Woman and the Victorian Novel*. London: Macmillan, 1978.

Davis, Lennard. *Resisting Novels: Ideology and Fiction*. New York: Methuen, 1987.

DuPlessis, Rachel Blau. *Writing Beyond the Ending: Narrative Strategies of Twentieth-Century Women Writers.* Bloomington: Indiana UP, 1985.

Eagleton, Terry. *Criticism and Ideology.* 1976. London: Verso, 1978.

Flint, Kate. "Reading the New Woman." *Browning Society Notes* 17.1–3 (1987–88): 55–63.

Goode, John. "Sue Bridehead and the New Woman." Jacobus, *Women* 100–13.

Grand, Sarah. *The Beth Book: Being a Study of the Life of Elizabeth Caldwell Maclure, A Woman of Genius.* 1897. Intro. Elaine Showalter. New York: Virago, 1980.

———. "The New Aspect of the Woman Question." *North American Review* 158 (1894): 270–76.

Gubar, Susan. "'The Blank Page' and the Issues of Female Creativity." *Writing and Sexual Difference.* Ed. Elizabeth Abel. Chicago: U of Chicago P, 1982. 73–94.

Heilbrun, Carolyn. *Writing A Woman's Life.* New York: Norton, 1988.

Hirsch, Marianne. "Spiritual *Bildung*: The Beautiful Soul as Paradigm." Abel et al. 23–48.

Hogarth, Janet. "Literary Degenerates." *Fortnightly Review* 65 (1895): 586–92.

Huddleston, Joan. *Sarah Grand: A Bibliography.* St. Lucia: Dept. of English, U of Queensland, 1979.

Jacobus, Mary. "The Difference of View." Jacobus, *Women* 10–21.

———, ed. *Women Writing and Writing About Women.* New York: Barnes and Noble, 1979.

Jordan, Ellen. "The Christening of the New Woman: May 1894." *Victorian Newsletter* 63 (1983): 19–21.

Kermode, Frank. *The Sense of an Ending.* New York: Oxford UP, 1967.

Kersley, Gillian. *Darling Madame: Sarah Grand and Devoted Friend.* London: Virago, 1983.

Macherey, Pierre. *A Theory of Literary Production.* Trans. Geoffrey Wall. London: Routledge, 1978.

Miller, Nancy K. "Emphasis Added: Plots and Plausibilities in Women's Fictions." Rpt. *The New Feminist Criticism.* Ed. Elaine Showalter. New York: Pantheon, 1985. 339–60.

"New Novels." Rev. of *The Beth Book,* by Sarah Grand. *Athenaeum* 3657 (1897): 743–44.

[Oliphant, Margaret]. "The Anti-Marriage League." *Blackwood's* 159 (1896): 135–49.

"Ouida" [Marie Louise de la Ramée]. "The New Woman." *North American Review* 158 (1894): 610–19.

Rubinstein, David. *Before the Suffragettes: Woman's Emancipation in the 1890s.* New York: St. Martin's, 1986.

"Sarah Grand's Latest Book." Rev. of *The Beth Book. Saturday Review* 91 (1897): 557–58.

Showalter, Elaine. Introduction. Grand. n.p.

———. *A Literature of Their Own: British Women Novelists from Brontë to Lessing.* Princeton: Princeton UP, 1977.

Stubbs, Patricia. *Women and Fiction: Feminism and the Novel 1880–1920.* Sussex: Harvester, 1979.

"Two Notable Novels." Rev. of *The Beth Book,* by Sarah Grand. *Review of Reviews* 16 (1897): 618–22.

Tyrrell, Robert Yelverton. "Jude the Obscure." Rev. of *Jude the Obscure,* by Thomas Hardy. *Fortnightly Review* 65 (1896): 857–64.

Vicinus, Martha. "Rediscovering the 'New Woman' of the 1890s: The Stories of 'George Egerton.'" *Feminist Re-Visions.* Ed. Vivian Patraka and Louise A. Tilly. Ann Arbor: U of Michigan P, 1983. 12–25.

Withycombe, E. G. *Oxford Dictionary of English Christian Names.* 3rd ed. Oxford: Clarendon, 1977.

Forbidden Reading and Ghostly Writing in Edith Wharton's "Pomegranate Seed"

Carol J. Singley and Susan Elizabeth Sweeney

At the beginning of Wharton's ghost story "Pomegranate Seed," Charlotte Ashby pauses on the threshold of her house, half-afraid to enter because she wonders whether another "square grayish envelope" addressed to her husband lies on the hall table within (324). Such letters, which figure prominently in Wharton's fiction and especially in "Pomegranate Seed," have the distinct power to alter male-female and same-sex relationships.[1] Eager and fearful to discover the contents and author of these ambiguous letters, "so alike in appearance that they had...become one letter, become 'it'" (325), Charlotte feels ambivalent about the letter and the opportunities for independent interpretation and expression that it represents. She experiences what we call "anxious power": she covets the power of language, yet feels anxious about the trespass implied by a woman's appropriation of such power.

Charlotte wrestles with the choice between the power of written discourse, traditionally a male domain, and the power of romance, traditionally a female domain. The horror of the story is that on the one hand, she fears she cannot compete with the letter's uncanny power over her husband, Kenneth; on the other, she attempts to master that power by appropriating and reading the letter, but with ambiguous results (she gains a mother, but loses a husband). Charlotte's anxiety extends to her sense of herself as both a typically passive woman and a potential usurper of texts and textual power. She is poised on the threshold between two realms of gendered expectation, a fact underlined by the tale's narrative construction—its supernatural *and* realistic tone, its multitude of indeterminacies, gaps, and absences.

Indeed, Wharton's ghost story brilliantly exemplifies the ways in which ambivalence toward reading and writing shapes women's narrative. In order to show how "Pomegranate Seed" demonstrates anxious power, we read the story in several related contexts: Wharton's life, psychoanalytic theory, reader-response criticism, and feminist theory. In particular, we trace Wharton's lifelong anxiety about reading and writing and relate it to the female Oedipal triangle of her childhood; apply Lacan's reading of Poe's "The Purloined Letter" to "Pomegranate Seed" to show how Wharton's purloined letter represents the power of language and generates a series of triangular relationships among those who attempt to appropriate it; and explain how the many ambiguities of "Pomegranate Seed"—including its title—represent Wharton's ambivalence as well as her readers'. Finally, we show how the story's three female characters— Charlotte and Mrs. Ashby, who fearfully read a letter that does not belong to them, and Elsie, who writes illegible letters from beyond the threshold of the grave—represent the anxious power of female readers and writers. In other words, we read "Pomegranate Seed" as a parable about women's ambivalence toward the power of reading and writing.

I

Leaving Charlotte for a moment, we pause on the threshold of our argument to describe Wharton's ambivalence toward appropriating the forbidden power of language. Indeed, in this image of Charlotte poised expectantly at the doorway, we see two sources of anxiety from Wharton's childhood which are significant in "Pomegranate Seed": fear of crossing well-defined borders of feminine behavior, and ambivalence toward the power conferred by acts of reading and writing. Just as Charlotte hesitates upon her threshold, so, too, Wharton felt anxious about crossing the threshold of her parents' home after her daily outings. And just as Charlotte reads a ghostly letter addressed not to her but to her husband, so, too, Wharton crossed the threshold of her father's library to read forbidden books.

In Wharton's childhood, the threshold of her parents' home suggested the precarious border between the familiar and the unfamiliar which Freud calls the "uncanny." In an autobiographical fragment, "Life and I," Wharton describes the "chronic fear" and "formless horrors" (1079) that haunted her return from her daily walks:

> While I waited on the door-step...I could feel it behind me, upon me; & if there was any delay in the opening of the door I was seized by a choking agony of terror. It did not matter who was with me, for no one could protect me; but, oh, the rapture of relief if my companion had a latch-key, & we could get in at once, before It caught me! (1080)

If crossing her parents' threshold represented security in childhood, in adolescence it evoked ambivalence, representing a need for escape as well as refuge. As Cynthia Griffin Wolff notes in her account of Wharton's adolescence, on her parents' doorstep "the opposing demands of two distinct worlds were visited upon her—the world of adulthood, independence, freedom, and sexual maturity; and the world of childhood, obedience, limitation, and emotional starvation" (173).

In her autobiography, *A Backward Glance*, Wharton again evokes the term "threshold" to describe her anxious desire to read texts in her father's library, especially those forbidden by her mother (64).[2] She remembers "enter[ing] into the kingdom of my father's library" as one of the single most important events of her life: "Whenever I try to recall my childhood, it is in my father's library that it comes to life" (43, 69). She recalls "pulling open...the glass doors of the low bookcases, and dragging out book after book in a secret ecstasy of communion" (69). Her ecstasy was secret because certain books were forbidden: her mother not only decreed "that I should never read a novel without asking her permission," but "almost always refused to let me read it" (65). Although Wharton specifically associates this childhood taboo with novels and ghost stories, from childhood onward she experienced all reading and writing as something forbidden. Elaine Showalter explains her compulsion to "make up" stories (*Backward* 33) as "almost a form of illicit sexual indulgence" (146). And Wharton herself portrays writing as "irresistible" temptation: "I would struggle against it" but "the struggle was always a losing one" (*Backward* 89, 35).

"Pomegranate Seed," the story expressing Wharton's anxiety, includes both Charlotte Ashby, a woman who engages in forbidden reading, and Elsie Ashby, a woman who produces ghostly writing, suppressed and "nearly undecipherable" (363), from beyond the threshold of the grave. The experiences of both women in "Pomegranate Seed" help us to understand Wharton's own struggles with reading and writing. In particular, Charlotte's attempts to read Elsie's mysterious letter, and uncover the identity of the woman who wrote it, reflect not only Wharton's childhood anxiety about reading novels and ghost stories, but her adult anxiety about writing. Indeed, Charlotte and Elsie are doubles—just like the acts of reading and writing which they represent. Their story reveals the extent to which, for Wharton, writing as well as reading is a disturbing, guilty act characterized by the purloining of male power and language and haunted by maternal disapproval.

If "Pomegranate Seed" reflects Wharton's anxiety about forbidden female reading and writing, it also evokes the female reader's anxiety about those same acts. In fact, the relationship between Elsie and Charlotte, mediated by the letter, duplicates the relationship between Wharton and her audience, mediated by the text of "Pomegranate Seed" itself. Thus the first glimpse of Charlotte haunted by a "premonition of something inexplicable, intolerable, to be faced on the other side of the curtained panes" (331) is also a figure for Wharton's reader, poised on the threshold of the story. Because we too want to read the letter, we are implicated in Charlotte's voyeurism and her eventual act of appropriation; and, as female readers in particular, we share her anxiety about seizing the power implied by the appropriation of a man's letter.

II

In order to understand how the letter in "Pomegranate Seed" represents the power of language, we turn to Edgar Allan Poe's detective story "The Purloined Letter" and its analysis by Jacques Lacan. Indeed, similarities between "Pomegranate Seed" and Poe's story are not surprising, considering Wharton's familiarity with Poe and his possible influence on her short fic-

tion. As a child, Wharton would have been familiar with Poe—
"that drunken and demoralized Baltimorean"—if only because
he was one of those writers banished from her parents' library
(*Backward* 68). "Pomegranate Seed" is thus not only the kind of
supernatural literature that Wharton was forbidden to read as a
child, it also reinterprets a famous story by an author who was
explicitly forbidden.[3]

There are several suggestive similarities between "The Purloined Letter" and "Pomegranate Seed." In both, a marriage is
endangered by a mysterious letter whose contents are withheld
and which is addressed—or, in Poe's story, readdressed—in an
oddly androgynous hand. In both stories, the letter creates a
romantic triangle, even though its writer never appears: Poe's
purloined letter is used for actual blackmail, while Elsie's letter
threatens the marriage through emotional extortion. As Lacan
persuasively argues, power depends not on the letter's contents, but on its possession—and on who sees it (and can therefore purloin it). In "The Purloined Letter," Minister D— steals
the letter and gains power over the Queen; the detective, Dupin,
seizes that power when he discovers and steals the letter in
turn. Similarly, in "Pomegranate Seed," Elsie writes letters
which demonstrate her power over Kenneth; and Charlotte
attempts to appropriate that power when she finally opens and
reads the last letter.

Lacan's reading of "The Purloined Letter" illuminates the
connections between reading, writing, and power in "Pomegranate Seed." The purloined letter, Lacan argues, has no intrinsic
meaning: because its contents are unknown, it is a blank which
each character attempts to fill during the course of the narrative.[4]
The letter's very absence of meaning, then, grants it meaning as a
signifier; purloining it—either by reinterpreting it or literally
stealing it—is how characters gain power. Such power is illusory,
however, because the letter is endlessly subject to further purloining. By concentrating on the series of glances in the story, Lacan
shows how each appropriation of the letter creates new triadic
relationships among those who possess the letter, those who purloin it, and those who become aware of its theft:

> Thus, three moments, structuring three glances, borne by
> three subjects, incarnated each time by different characters.

The first is a glance that sees nothing: the King and the police. The second, a glance which sees that the first sees nothing and deludes itself as to the secrecy of what it hides: the Queen, then the Minister. The third sees that the first two glances leave what should be hidden exposed to whomever would see it: the Minister, and finally Dupin. (32)

Lacan's reading also applies to "Pomegranate Seed." In Wharton's story, the fact that the mysterious letter's contents are unknown—or barely legible—establishes it as a floating signifier, which creates shifting relationships among the characters who attempt to appropriate it and discover its meaning. When Charlotte finally reads the purloined letter she, like the Minister and then Dupin, finds that it confers only an elusive and ambiguous power. "Pomegranate Seed" also describes a series of triads like those Lacan finds in Poe's story, beginning when Kenneth, like Poe's Queen, receives an incriminating letter and Charlotte, seeing him read it, wishes to appropriate it for herself. When Charlotte finally does so, with her mother-in-law looking on, a new set of triangular relationships is created among the letter writer, Charlotte, and Mrs. Ashby; and Kenneth, like Poe's Queen, disappears from the narrative altogether. Even after Charlotte reads the letter with her mother-in-law's help, another triangle is generated when she reaches for the phone to involve the police—presumably the letter will next pass into an officer's hands.

Lacan's reading of "The Purloined Letter" is especially relevant to feminist theory. The loss of the letter and the power it represents places each character in a feminized position, "obliged to don the role of the Queen, and even the attributes of femininity and shadow, so propitious to the act of concealing" (44). Indeed, the Queen, the only female character in Poe's story, has neither letter nor power and is barely present in the text. In contrast, in Wharton's story the major characters are female: the narrative action revolves around a woman who appropriates the letter, while the single male character occupies the feminized position in which the letter can be or already is stolen. Similarly, the powerful roles of reader and writer, which Poe assigns to Dupin and the minister, Wharton gives either to Charlotte and Kenneth's mother, or to Elsie, whose "authority is expressed through the actuality of the letters she sends" (McDowell 139). Despite their many similarities, then, "Pomegranate Seed" defines the woman's position in the triad quite differently than "The Purloined Letter." Wharton transforms the masculine world of Poe's story—just as in other fiction she transforms the world of James and Howells, creating "a female perspective that deconstructs that world and gives access to regions beyond the imagination of the male writer" (Schriber 158).

III

Lacan implies a number of triangular relationships among the characters in "The Purloined Letter"—all generated by the elusive letter. In our reading of "Pomegranate Seed," however, we identify these triangular relationships more explicitly in order to understand Wharton's ambivalence toward the power of language and the construction of gender. In particular, Wharton's purloined letter involves her heroine in three separate triangles: the familiar romantic triangle, further complicated by the shifting masculine and feminine roles played by Elsie, Charlotte, and Kenneth; the female Oedipal triangle, in which Elsie and Kenneth play the roles of Charlotte's parents; and the triangle created by the interplay of glances as characters watch each other read the letter. Wharton describes these triangles from a feminine point of view, emphasizing the female child's Oedipal situation. What this means—given Lacan's identification of the letter with an authorial power that the woman always lacks—is that Wharton expresses her ambivalence toward such inappropriate, "unfeminine" power.

Thematically, "Pomegranate Seed" is a love triangle in which the second wife (Charlotte) competes with the first (Elsie) for her husband's love. This conventional triangle is complicated, however, by the androgyny of both the mysterious letter and the woman who writes it. The letter's handwriting—clearly a woman's, yet indicating manly "strength and assurance"—is the first clue that the writer possesses oddly "masculine" traits (301, 324). This apparent androgyny is borne out when Charlotte cannot decide whether the envelope contains a business letter or a love letter. Confident of Kenneth's love, she at first assumes that the letter concerns one of his "nearly always tiresome" female clients, rather than "any sentimental secret." But although Kenneth tells her it is business, she quickly realizes that, whereas he often discussed business letters with her, "concerning this mysterious correspondence his lips were sealed" (328). The letter falls somewhere between the masculine world of business and the feminine world of romance, and its resistance to categorization contributes to its ambiguous power.

Indeed, the woman whose letters now control Kenneth from beyond the grave also controlled him while she was alive. Elsie "absolutely dominated" (327) her husband; he, in turn, had such "great love for his first wife" and "despair" over her death that only "his absorbing professional interests had kept him from suicide" (329). The fact that her letters often arrive when Charlotte and Kenneth return from their holidays—Elsie herself "hated travelling" (355)—demonstrates her attempts to reclaim possession of her home, children, and marriage.

Charlotte, Elsie's antithesis, is stereotypically feminine and compliant: she has won Kenneth's love through patience and understanding; she is good with his children, having "gradually dispelled by her good humour" any doubts about her maternal ability; she passively accepts that her well-paid professional husband "couldn't afford to do the place over for her" (329); and she is so dependent that even being alone is "another way of being with Kenneth" (324). When her letter makes her suspect his infidelity, she comforts him rather than herself: "Poor Kenneth! If you knew how sorry I am for you—" (340). Charlotte even accepts blame for the growing rift between them: "If I'd seen that the letters made you happy...that they gave you something I haven't known how to give...I should have had the courage to hide what I felt" (349).

What Charlotte lacks, of course, is the very confidence and power that Elsie exhibits. However, Charlotte's desire for knowledge progressively competes with her loyalty to Kenneth, until she finally declares: "I don't care what it costs me to find out who it is....If it costs me your love, I don't care!" (341). Elsie's letter thus sets into motion Charlotte's desire for knowledge and the power that it confers. The story suggests, however, that the cost of such knowledge is high: Charlotte must be willing to forfeit not only her domestic role, but her husband.

This rivalry between Charlotte and Kenneth's first wife can also be read psychoanalytically as a dramatization of the female

Oedipal triangle (cf. Zilversmit 300). In a struggle that duplicates a daughter's rivalry with her mother, Charlotte tries unsuccessfully to replace the first Mrs. Ashby and usurp her home, husband, and bed. Yet Charlotte is haunted by anxiety over committing the Oedipal crime, an anxiety which is confirmed by the fact that Elsie, unsuccessfully repressed by the text, does eventually reclaim her husband. This psychoanalytic interpretation of "Pomegranate Seed" is borne out by the title's allusion to the Persephone-Demeter myth, which focuses on mother-daughter relations; by Charlotte's recurrent rivalry with her predecessor; and by the fact that, of the three Mrs. Ashbys, only Charlotte has no children of her own. The end of "Pomegranate Seed," then, represents the triumph of reality over Oedipal fantasy: Kenneth's first wife wins back her husband; Kenneth and Charlotte remain childless; and Charlotte, no longer her mother's rival, returns to the safe role of daughter—significantly, not to the mother whose death she had imagined, but to her mother-in-law, a "proxy mother" (Zilversmit 300).

This psychoanalytic reading of "Pomegranate Seed" also helps us to understand the Oedipal triangle in Wharton's childhood—"the Oedipal crime...acted out by Edith Jones in her father's library" that Paula Berggren notes—as well as Wharton's pornographic sketch "Beatrice Palmato." Indeed, just as Wharton suppresses the fantasized father-daughter incest in "Beatrice Palmato" (which was only published posthumously), so she suppresses a similar fantasy in her ending to "Pomegranate Seed."

Since Wharton associates her own Oedipal situation with the private reading in her father's library forbidden by her mother, it is not surprising that she expresses the triangles in "Pomegranate Seed" not merely in a series of glances, as Poe does, but in a series of scenes in which one character watches another read. Because we are particularly concerned with Wharton's ambivalence toward reading and writing, and because she explicitly identifies the glance with reading itself, we pay special attention to these triangles. The glance, as Freud points out, is fundamentally erotic in nature because the spectator imagines possessing the object of his gaze ("Three" 149–59). Wharton demonstrates her fascination with the gaze's haunting power in an appropriately entitled ghost story, "The Eyes"—which describes the eerie psychological effects on Andrew Culwin, a self-described "spectator" (40), of being himself the object of another's gaze. Wharton identifies this erotic gaze specifically with the act of reading because, as Berggren shows, reading, voyeurism, and forbidden sexual knowledge combine in the primal scene of her childhood: for Wharton, to disobey her mother by reading books in her father's library was "figuratively [to] gaze upon her father's nakedness." Wharton may also associate reading with voyeurism because, as Robert Con Davis says, "the profoundly paradoxical situation of reading" exemplifies the erotic power of the gaze.[5] For Wharton, then, reading is a voyeuristic act—especially reading a letter addressed to someone else, as Charlotte does in "Pomegranate Seed."[6]

"Pomegranate Seed" is structured around a series of glances similar to those that Lacan analyzes in "The Purloined Letter"; but it is significant, given Wharton's association of reading and voyeurism, that Charlotte is unaware of the power of the gaze until it is manifested in reading a text. Her initial glance is as unseeing and unsuspicious as the King's in "The Purloined Letter." Thus she does not recognize the power of the gaze in Elsie's portrait, which follows her "with guarded eyes" from a wall in the library (333); she is not alarmed when Kenneth moves the portrait to the nursery so that the children can grow up "with her looking down on them" (330); nor does she realize that Elsie possesses Kenneth in a "mysterious bondage" (348), "a secret persecution before which he quailed, yet from which he could not free himself" (343). And even when the letters begin to arrive, Charlotte is not suspicious. Although she thinks that she recognizes the handwriting on the envelope which "looked up at her faintly," she is unaware of its gaze until she sees Kenneth's expression as *he* sees it: "she would have thought no more of the letter if, when her husband's glance lit on it, she had not chanced to be looking at him" (326). Now Kenneth—whose glance, in Lacan's terms, "deludes itself as to the secrecy of what it hides"—becomes the object of Charlotte's gaze. And Charlotte, who "sees that the first two glances leave what should be hidden exposed to whomever would see it" (Lacan 32), spies upon Kenneth's exchanges with the letter. Charlotte has not only become aware of Elsie's gaze; she has herself become the voyeur.

Her voyeurism, like Elsie's, reverses the traditional sexual relationship described by Laura Mulvey and E. Ann Kaplan, in which the male subject's gaze focuses upon the female object in order to possess her, project his fears and desires upon her, and define his identity through her. By usurping the male gaze, in fact, Charlotte also begins to appropriate the traditional male role of detective and protector: she wants to "penetrate the mystery" and "help [Kenneth] to bear the burden it implied" (335). She even objectifies Kenneth's physical appearance as a man might a woman's, noticing for the first time that "the upper part of his face is too narrow" (333). And Kenneth, as object of Charlotte's gaze, becomes correspondingly dissipated and feminized in her eyes: he seems "years older...emptied of life and courage," even "unstable" as he pleads headache or fatigue to ward off her "cross-questioning" (326, 340, 337).

Charlotte's suspicion about Kenneth's correspondence is confirmed with the arrival of the eighth letter; she is "almost glad of the sight. It seemed to justify everything, to put a seal of definiteness on the whole blurred business." She realizes that she wants to read the letter herself, to appropriate its contents with her own glance, but she cannot bring herself to violate Kenneth's privacy. Instead, knowing that "she would have no peace till she found out what was written on that sheet" (332), she contrives to watch Kenneth read it, hiding at the threshold of his library in order to "see what happened between him and the letter when they thought themselves unobserved" (333). Just as before Charlotte watched Kenneth read the address on the envelope, she now watches him read the letter in a scene of literary voyeurism that is repeated throughout the story. She tries to read the letter's meaning in his face: "what Charlotte first noted there was a look of surprise....Apparently all the writing was on one page, for he did not turn the sheet but continued to stare at it for so long that he must have reread it a dozen times" (334). Her suspicions about his erotic communion with the "visibly feminine letter" are borne out when, after he reads it, she sees his lips "touch the sheet" (325, 334). Elsie's hypnotizing glance as manifested in her letter, Kenneth's corresponding kiss of the letter he has just read, and Charlotte's own voyeurism all confirm Wharton's connection of reading with the erotic gaze.

And what of the gaze belonging to the reader of "Pomegranate Seed"? The fact that the narrative is limited to Charlotte's point of view forces us to become voyeurs as well, analyzing Kenneth's behavior, accumulating evidence, and imagining the letter's contents. And our desire to read the letter reminds us that we are already voyeurs, watching Charlotte just as she watches Kenneth; that we are, in fact, involved in a similar triangle, trying to discover the contents of someone else's letter by reading about it in the text of someone else's story. Thus the letter in "Pomegranate Seed," like private correspondence which has become public, raises profound questions about the nature of reading and "the real sense in which reading constitutes an act of violation" (Spacks 52).

IV

So far we have read "Pomegranate Seed" in the contexts of Wharton's life and Lacan's analysis of "The Purloined Letter." We now turn to a specific scene in the story in which reading a purloined letter evokes a woman's anxious power. Charlotte's forbidden reading is described as an act of transgression, in which she not only appropriates Kenneth's letter but interprets various absences: the space where Elsie's portrait hung, Kenneth's disappearance, and the letter's text. Instead of standing on the doorstep, "shivering with the premonition of something inexplicable, intolerable, to be faced on the other side" (331), or secretly watching her husband's correspondence with the letter, Charlotte now crosses the threshold, usurping Kenneth's library, desk, letter-opener—and the letter itself. In this climactic act of reading the ninth and last letter, Kenneth's death is implied, the author of the letters is identified, and Charlotte's new relationship with Mrs. Ashby is established. Despite the certainty implied by these resolutions, however, the ending of "Pomegranate Seed" remains ambiguous, evoking ambivalent responses in both Charlotte and the reader.

Charlotte's appropriation of Kenneth's letter completes the gradual shift in their relationship; she has now finally assumed the male role of reader, detective, and penetrator of secrets, as shown by the scene's phallic imagery of authority and rape.

Charlotte first stares at the letter "as if she could force her gaze to penetrate to what was within" (360); but the envelope is "so tightly stuck that she had to hunt on her husband's writing table for his ivory letter-opener." In fact, opening the letter seems to confirm Kenneth's death: when she rummages through his desk, the items on it "sent through her the icy chill emanating from the little personal effects of someone newly dead," and when she opens the envelope, "the tearing of the paper...sounded like a human cry" (363).

But what does Charlotte gain by appropriating Kenneth's letter? The sheet of paper inside the envelope is nearly blank, unreadable: "Her sight must be blurred, or else dazzled by the reflection of the lamplight on the smooth surface of the paper...she could discern only a few faint strokes, so faint and faltering as to be nearly undecipherable" (363). This sentence ironically recalls Wharton's earlier description of the curtains on Charlotte's door, which prevented her from seeing if a letter had arrived because they "softened the light within to a warm blur through which no details showed" (323). Although Charlotte has now crossed the threshold and even read the letter, she is confronted with the same blurred, illegible surface as before.

In a series of triadic relationships, Charlotte had watched Kenneth read the eighth letter; she herself is "watched by Mrs. Ashby" (364) as she tries to read the ninth; and now, unable to comprehend it, she watches her mother-in-law read it in turn. While Mrs. Ashby tries to decipher the almost invisible hand-writing in the lamplight, Charlotte studies her face as if it were the letter, just as earlier she tried to read Kenneth's face. Indeed, she learns more from her mother-in-law's face than from the letter itself: Mrs. Ashby's features, which usually express only "simple and sound emotions," now convey more ambivalent ones: "a look of fear and hatred, of incredulous dismay and almost cringing defiance...as if the spirits warring within her had distorted her face to their own likeness" (364).

Although the letter's contents remain mysterious, Charlotte does discover its author when she asks if Mrs. Ashby recognizes the handwriting. Significantly, she learns the answer not through Mrs. Ashby's words, but through her gaze. Charlotte watches her "anxious eyes" apprehensively scan the room, hesitating to pronounce the name aloud. When Charlotte counters, "'You'd better say it out, mother! You knew at once it was *her* writing?'...Mrs. Ashby looked up; her eyes...were lifted to the blank wall behind her son's writing table" (365). Elsie is thus named by her absence rather than her presence, just as the letter has meaning because its contents are withheld. In fact, Elsie's signature is the "blank wall"—placed, appropriately enough, behind the man's writing table—which resembles her letter: as Charlotte tells Mrs. Ashby, "If even you can see her face on that blank wall, why shouldn't he read her writing on this blank paper?'" (366).

In "Pomegranate Seed," then, Wharton literally represents the act of reading as peering at an almost blank page, as filling in gaps, absences, ellipses. "'No one could possibly read that letter,'" Mrs. Ashby tells Charlotte (366); and after considerable effort, with the aid of a bright lamp and a magnifying glass, Charlotte believes that she can decipher only two ambiguous words: "'I can make out something like 'mine'—oh, and 'come.' It might be 'come'" (363). As readers of "Pomegranate Seed," we must also fill in blanks. The words "mine" and "come" encourage us to construct hypothetical sentences, such as a command addressed to Kenneth ("You are mine; come to me"), or a message addressed to Charlotte, who, after all, is the one who reads the letter and therefore, according to Lacan, its intended recipient ("He is mine, he has come to me"). "Pomegranate Seed" thus defines reading as the production of meaning rather than the discovery of truth. As readers of the story, we, like Charlotte, must make our own decisions and confront our ambivalence about them.

Readers of "Pomegranate Seed" have been confounded by its lacunae since the beginning. Wharton's publisher persuaded her to make the story's ending more explicit (*Letters* 532–33); her editor at the *Ladies' Home Journal* could not comprehend the title; and Wharton was "bombarded by a host" of readers anxious to discover the title's meaning and the means by which the letters were written (Preface ix). Wharton's first readers were especially puzzled by the fact that Elsie, the presumed author of the letters, was never named. Elsie, after all, is identified only by the blank space on the wall: her name, which Kenneth refused to utter (339), is never pronounced aloud, and the pronoun "her, "referring to "the unknown female" writer (328), remains without an antecedent (even if Charlotte's italicized *"her"* suggests one).

Kenneth's sudden disappearance leaves another blank which the reader must explain. His absence, like others in the story, somehow suggests a presence: even after his apparent death, he continues to affect the women's lives. And Charlotte's relationships with the other two Mrs. Ashbys constitute still another mystery for the reader: she and Elsie, although adversaries, seem like the same woman; and the story both celebrates and subverts her "tacit bond" with the mother figure (344).

Finally, the story's title is another mystery that Wharton never explained to her readers. Like her other titles, it "may function as a blank...and point toward a veiled meaning or an implied comment" (Blackall 157). If the simple phrase "pomegranate seed" is an oblique allusion, the myth to which it alludes is even more ambiguous. Yet this ambiguity is appropriate; indeed, it may be why Wharton alluded to the Persephone-Demeter myth to begin with. After all, Persephone—who is both dead and alive, both lost and found, both absent and present, both knowledgeable lover and innocent daughter, like Keats' "still unravished bride of quietness"—is ultimately the very figure of ambivalence, forever poised on the threshold between masculine power and feminine propriety. The literary allusion in Wharton's title thus ironically expresses her own ambivalence toward reading and writing. Persephone's consumption of forbidden fruit in Hades parallels Wharton's illicit reading in "the kingdom of [her] father's library" (*Backward* 43); and Persephone's punishment manifests, for Wharton, her own anxiety about the seductive power of language that she discovered there: in the library, words "sang to me so bewitchingly that they almost lured me from the wholesome noonday air of childhood into some strange supernatural region, where the normal pleasures of my age seemed as insipid as the fruits of the earth to Persephone after she had eaten of the pomegranate seed" ("Life" 1075–76). Indeed, Candace Waid notes that in Wharton's imagination Persephone is always "a figure for the woman writer" (3, 199). Josephine Donovan argues that the myth dramatizes "the question of translating women's private artistic material into public patriarchal discourse," and that Wharton's decision to become a writer is an ambivalent capitulation to that discourse (51).

We suggested earlier that Charlotte, poised expectantly on

her doorstep, was a figure for Wharton's reader, poised on the threshold of "Pomegranate Seed." And when Charlotte finally crosses the literal and figurative thresholds of the story to read Elsie's letter, she evokes, particularly for female readers, divided allegiances that reveal our own ambivalence toward knowledge and power. We can read Elsie's power as either "malevolent" (343) or constructive; we can also read Charlotte's appropriation of the letter as either reprehensible or admirable: as a violation of Kenneth's privacy, or as the justifiable acquisition of knowledge that she has been denied. Indeed, the lacunae of "Pomegranate Seed"—what Kellogg calls "too many explanatory loopholes" (239)—are designed to elicit the reader's collaboration. Wharton's fiction often demands such engagement; she imagines her readers "meeting me halfway among the primeval shadows, and filling in the gaps in my narrative with sensations and divinations akin to my own" (Preface viii). Reading "Pomegranate Seed," we discover not answers to our questions, but new questions that we must answer—just as Charlotte, trying to find out when she and Kenneth will go away together, learns that he has left town and sits "blankly gazing into new darkness" (353).

V

If Charlotte reflects our own ambivalence about reading, then her double, Elsie, reflects Wharton's anxiety about writing. Although feminist criticism may too quickly identify Wharton with her female characters (A. Kaplan 434), the parallels between Elsie and Wharton are obvious. The very ghostliness of Elsie's writing evokes Wharton's own literary creativity, which she describes as an alienating and mysterious process that occurs "in some secret region on the sheer edge of consciousness" (*Backward* 205). It is also characteristic of Wharton to express her anxiety about writing in a ghost story; she often used such tales "as a metaphor of internal fears" (Zilversmit 296).[7]

Elsie can be read, then, as a ghost writer for Wharton herself, her spectral letters indicating Wharton's own "anxiety of authorship" (Gilbert and Gubar 48–49). Elsie's writing not only takes the traditionally feminine form of letters—the "forgotten genre," in Spacks' phrase—it is barely able to communicate. Excluded and repressed, "written as though there were not enough ink in the pen, or the writer's wrist were too weak" (325), her letters are "so faint and faltering as to be nearly undecipherable" (363).

If Elsie is represented primarily by her writing, then her death—an absence that cannot quite be repressed—also signals Wharton's ambivalence toward female art and authorship. If, as Susan Gubar suggests, "the creation of female art feels like the destruction of the female body" (302), then in "Pomegranate Seed" the artist's body, like Margaret Aubyn's in Wharton's *The Touchstone*, is dead and buried before her story even begins. Living female artists in Wharton's fiction fare no better, and are particularly satirized in such stories as "The Pelican," "April Showers," and "Expiation" (A. Kaplan 438–40). Mary Suzanne Schriber concludes that "the younger Edith Wharton was not secure enough in her vocation to draw out of her foundering self a female protagonist who is an artist; the older Edith Wharton, realizing that women novelists were ignored by the culture, purposely did not assign her own gender to an artist, choosing instead to satirize the state of the arts as governed by men" (179). Wharton does depict one successful female writer: Helen Dale, who has authored many bestsellers and calls herself "the greatest novelist...of the age" ("Copy" 276). But even her success is marred by her ambivalence: faithful readers are a poor substitute for the married lover she gave up years ago; and her debate with that lover about using their old love letters as "copy" for forthcoming memoirs implies that female artistic success comes only at the cost of emotional fulfillment.

Wharton's anxious power is also revealed by Elsie's androgynous handwriting—"bold but faint," manifesting "masculine curves" and yet somehow "visibly feminine" (324–25). Elsie's pen(man)ship implies that female authorship and authenticity are incompatible. Indeed, Wharton once appropriated a male identity for herself—the pseudonym "David Olivieri"—to publish her early novel *Fast and Loose*. In addition to granting legitimacy, such masculine disguise provides protection from public exposure. For Wharton, "the author who circulates her name on a title page" is "as vulnerable as the lady of leisure who displays herself as an art object" (A. Kaplan 446). Accordingly, Elsie's authorship, as represented by her handwriting, is contradictory, as if male disguise were necessary for a woman to write at all.

The empty sheet which constitutes Elsie's writing is itself an ambivalent figure, as Gubar's essay on female creativity implies. Woman is traditionally described as a blank page to be inscribed by the pen of the masculine author. Such metaphors—as well as the cultural attitudes that they represent—force the female writer to experience her own authorship as "self-inflicted violence" in which she writes on the blank page of her body with her own blood (296, 303). Elsie's page—an almost "'absolute blank'" which nevertheless bears traces of illegible writing (363)—similarly conveys in a single image both the suppression and expression of her art. If death represents internal and external restriction of Elsie's art, then the fact that her writing transcends death by crossing the very threshold of the grave suggests the strength of her need to express herself—as if writing were more important than being. Elsie's letter, then, like the unstained bedsheet in Isak Dinesen's story "The Blank Page," is "a mysterious but potent act of resistance" (Gubar 305). In keeping with Mary Jacobus' definition of feminist writing, the letter, "though necessarily working with 'male' discourse…work[s] ceaselessly to deconstruct it: to write what can't be written" (10).

Thus Elsie's ghostly writing, when finally deciphered, spells out Wharton's own anxious power. "The conscious mind of Edith Wharton did not break free entirely from her culture's ideology of woman," Schriber explains; "her imagination, however, the driving force behind her fiction, saw well into it and beyond" (82). "Pomegranate Seed" is shaped by this difference between Wharton's imagination, on the one hand, and her fearful acceptance of social convention, on the other. In this ghost story, Edith Wharton purloins both the "letter" and the power it represents; but she also reflects her own ambivalence—and that of the female reader—toward the possession of such power.[8]

NOTES

1. See stories entitled "The Letter" and "The Letters," as well as *The House of Mirth, The Age of Innocence, Summer,* "Roman Fever," and "The Looking Glass."

2. The autobiography's rhetorical structure reproduces Wharton's anxiety about entering her father's domain. She introduces the topic of

the library but then nervously veers away from it with a lengthy digression about New York society. When she finally returns to the topic, she likens it to approaching the library's doorway: "The library calls me back, and I pause again on its threshold" (64).

3. Other stories also bear Poe's imprint (Dwight).

4. Subsequent critics analyze Lacan's own elusive language, demonstrating the same subjective filling-in of gaps that he locates in Poe's story. Derrida equates the Queen's purloined letter with the Law of the Father, or the phallus—in other words, with male language and power.

5. Although we believe that we visually possess a text, we are in fact "focused upon and held by a Gaze that comes through the agency of the object text....We—as readers—then become the object of the Gaze" (Davis 980).

6. Wharton's fiction often conflates letters and voyeurism: in "The Looking Glass," Mrs. Atlee looks away as her mistress reads a forged letter from a dead lover because "you couldn't stare at a lady who was reading a message from her sweetheart" (248), and in *The Touchstone*, reading Margaret Aubyn's published love letters after her death is like "listening at a keyhole" (37).

7. Wharton's letters to publishers at the beginning of her career are replete with self-doubt: "I am not a very good judge of what I write" (*Letters* 31); "perhaps I might...acquire more assurance (the quality I feel I most lack)" (32–33). In 1912, she still referred to herself as a "half-talent," musing, "if only my work were better it would be all I need" (285). Even in 1925, despite considerable success, she confided to a friend: "as my work reaches its close, I feel so sure that it is either nothing, or far more than they know....And I wonder, a little desolately, which?" (483).

8. We thank Clare Colquitt and Annette Zilversmit for generously reading earlier versions of this essay and offering valuable suggestions.

WORKS CITED

Berggren, Paula. "Seeing the Gorgon: Edith Wharton and the Problem of Knowledge." Edith Wharton and Women. Modern Language Association Convention. San Francisco, December 30, 1987.

Blackall, Jean Frantz. "Edith Wharton's Art of Ellipsis." *Journal of Narrative Technique* 17.2 (1987): 145–62.

Davis, Robert Con. "Lacan, Poe, and Narrative Repression." *Modern Language Notes* 98.5 (1983): 983–1003.

Derrida, Jacques. "The Purveyor of Truth." Trans. Alan Bass. Muller and Richardson 173–212.

Donovan, Josephine. "Edith Wharton and the Pomegranate Seed." *After the Fall: The Demeter-Persephone Myth in Wharton, Cather, and Glasgow*. University Park: Pennsylvania State UP, 1989. 43–83.

Dwight, Eleanor. "Edith Wharton and 'The Cask of Amontillado.'" *Poe and Our Times: Influences and Affinities*. Ed. Benjamin Franklin Fisher IV. Baltimore: Edgar Allan Poe Society, 1986. 49–57.

Freud, Sigmund. "Three Essays on the Theory of Sexuality." *Standard Edition of the Complete Psychological Works of Sigmund Freud*. Ed. James Strachey. Vol. 7. London: Hogarth, 1959. 125–244.

Gilbert, Sandra M., and Susan Gubar. *The Madwoman in the Attic: The Woman Writer and the Nineteenth-Century Literary Imagination*. New Haven: Yale UP, 1979.

Gubar, Susan. "'The Blank Page' and the Issues of Female Creativity." *The New Feminist Criticism: Essays on Women, Literature, and Theory*. Ed. Elaine Showalter. New York: Random House, 1985. 292–313.

Jacobus, Mary. "The Difference of View." *Women Writing and Writing About Women*. Ed. Mary Jacobus. Oxford University Women's Studies Committee. London: Crown Helm, 1979. 10–21.

Kaplan, Amy. "Edith Wharton's Profession of Authorship." *ELH* 53.2 (1986): 433–57.

Kaplan, E. Ann. "Is the Gaze Male?" *The Powers of Desire, the Politics of Sexuality*. Ed. Ann Snitow et al. New York: Monthly Review P, 1983. 309–27.

Kellogg, Grace. *The Two Lives of Edith Wharton: The Woman and Her Work*. New York: Appleton-Century, 1965.

Lacan, Jacques. "Seminar on 'The Purloined Letter.'" Trans. Jeffrey Mehlman. Muller and Richardson 28–54.

McDowell, Margaret B. "Edith Wharton's Ghost Stories." *Criticism* 12.1 (1970): 133–52.

Muller, John P., and William J. Richardson, eds. *The Purloined Poe: Lacan, Psychoanalytic Reading*. Baltimore: Johns Hopkins UP, 1988.

Mulvey, Laura. "Visual Pleasure and Narrative Cinema." *Screen* 15.3 (1975): 6–18.

Poe, Edgar Allan. "The Purloined Letter." Muller and Richardson 6–23.

Schriber, Mary Suzanne. *Gender and the Writer's Imagination: From Cooper to Wharton.* Lexington: UP of Kentucky, 1987.

Showalter, Elaine. "The Death of the Lady (Novelist): Wharton's *House of Mirth.*" *Representations* 9 (1985): 133–49.

Spacks, Patricia Meyer. "Forgotten Genres." *Modern Language Studies* 28.1 (1988): 47–57.

Waid, Candace. *Edith Wharton's Letters from the Underworld: Fictions of Women and Writing.* Chapel Hill: U of North Carolina P, 1990.

Wharton, Edith. "Copy." *The Collected Short Stories of Edith Wharton.* Ed. R. W. B. Lewis. New York: Scribner's, 1968. Vol. 1. 275–86. 2 vols.

———. "The Eyes." *Ghosts* 37–65.

———. *Ghosts.* New York: Appleton-Century, 1937.

———. *The Letters of Edith Wharton.* Ed. R. W. B. Lewis and Nancy Lewis. New York: Scribner's, 1988.

———. "Life and I." *Edith Wharton: Novellas and Other Writings.* Ed. Cynthia Griffin Wolff. New York: Library of America, 1990. 1071–96.

———. "The Looking Glass." *Ghosts* 844–58.

———. "Pomegranate Seed." *Ghosts* 323–67.

———. Preface. *Ghosts* vii–xii.

———. *The Touchstone, Mme de Treymes and Others: Four Novels by Edith Wharton.* New York: Scribner's, 1970.

Wolff, Cynthia Griffin. *A Feast of Words: The Triumph of Edith Wharton.* New York: Oxford UP, 1977.

Zilversmit, Annette. "Edith Wharton's Last Ghosts." *College Literature* 14 (1987): 296–309.

PART 3

Developing Narratives of Differences

Willa Cather and the Fiction of Female Development

Judith Fetterley

Willa Cather first spoke to me through *The Song of the Lark*—a book she published in 1915 and revised in 1937, and a book I read in the fall of 1971 when I was experiencing that extraordinary sea change associated in those days with coming out as a feminist and a lesbian. I can still recall the anxiety associated with that reading. I kept expecting something terrible to happen to Thea (just as I expected something terrible to happen to me) because she dared to choose herself and her own development over the love and marriage plot. Climbing in Panther Canyon, Thea insists on continuing when Fred wants to rest. As he warns her to look out for rattlers, I nervously turned the pages, convinced Thea would be bitten for the treason of rejecting Fred's advice. Knowing well what passes in this culture for a woman's story, I imagined a rescue scene in which Thea, recognizing her dependence on Fred, admits her need for marriage, home and family, an offer she has just moments before dismissed as "perfectly hideous" (317). When, instead, Thea reaches the top successfully and Fred looks up to see her standing far above him, I experienced a profound sense of relief and delight.

Rereading *The Song of the Lark* some twenty years later, I find in it traces of the conventional woman's story that suffuse it with an anxiety I overlooked in my earlier reading. Thus as Fred looks up at Thea standing above him, he reflects, "'You are the sort that used to run wild in Germany, dressed in their hair and a piece of skin. Soldiers caught 'em in nets'" (320). We recall also the first song Fred picks for Thea to sing, "Tak for Dit Råd" ("Thanks for Your Advice"). Thea models her interpretation of this song on her Norwegian grandmother's story of a jealous husband who "danced his wife nearer and nearer the edge of the rock, and his wife began to scream so that the others stopped dancing and the music stopped; but Ole went right on singing, and he danced her over the edge of the cliff and they fell hundreds of feet and were all smashed to pieces" (279). Even though Thea doesn't take the advice embedded in her grandmother's cautionary tale, and allows her desire to range beyond the limits of a husband, I was right to be concerned about what might happen to Thea up there on that cliff, since Cather herself casts the net over Lucy Gayheart, her 1937 version of Thea, first by subsuming the story of Lucy's artistic development under the story of her romance with her teacher, and then by killing her moments after it occurs to Lucy that her own development could be her lover.

Yet *The Song of the Lark* still remains for me an exceptional text in its uncompromising portrayal of a woman who grows up to get what she wants. Perhaps for this reason it is one of the least appreciated of Cather's texts while, ironically, *The Professor's House*, which in effect unwrites *The Song of the Lark*—Godfrey St. Peter's disintegration reversing Thea Kronborg's development—is one of the most appreciated. In *The Song of the Lark* Cather asserts the central importance of desire to Thea's development; in *The Professor's House* Godfrey St. Peter loses the magic of desire and wants only to die. Cather offers no explanation for St. Peter's malaise, leaving readers to assume that the story behind her fiction could not be told directly or openly. Others have commented on the possible connection between Louis Marsellus in *The Professor's House* and Jan Hambourg, the man Isabelle McClung married in 1916. Reading both Thea and St. Peter as fictional self-portraits—a reading informed, of course, by my own vision of development—I would suggest that in writing *The Professor's House* Cather registered the devastating effect of losing her primary object of desire, just as *The Song of the Lark* records the wonder, the miracle of discovering and having her desire.

That such an inscription might be attended by anxiety can hardly surprise us. What does surprise us is how little of the anxiety manifested in later texts makes its way into *The Song of the Lark*. In the preface to the 1932 edition of the book Cather comments, "Success is never so interesting as struggle," thereby identifying what she perceives to be "the chief fault of the book." While one could argue that *The Song of the Lark* ends with the end of Thea's struggle and the beginning of her success, let us grant instead Cather's premise that the last two sections of the novel describe "a successful artist in the full tide of achievement," in order to explore the implications of her choosing to locate fictional and personal interest in the story of the adolescent girl and not in that of the mature woman. In this choice Cather duplicates the position of Godfrey St. Peter, who rejects his adult identity in favor of the boy he used to be. St. Peter can find no connection between his original boy self and the man he has become, and he must either kill the man to get back to the boy or kill the boy to survive as the man. Though in *The Song of the Lark* Cather stresses the connection between the child Thea and the adult Kronborg, finding in the experiences of childhood the roots of the artist's later success, by the time of the Preface she has, like St. Peter, lost the thread of that connection and any belief in the value of adult identity. In wishing she had stopped her novel earlier, presumably with Thea's discovery in Panther Canyon of "what she was going to try to do in the world" (307), Cather effaces entirely the figure of Die Kronborg and her own accomplishment in portraying a woman who succeeds in developing. In the context set by this later text, we may then well exclaim that the wonder lies in how freely and clearly *The Song of the Lark*—like Thea's voice which "at the appointed, at the acute, moment...like a fountain jet, shot up into the light" (235)—rises above the chorus of Cather's doubts.

So how does Thea grow? Early in her writing Cather describes "the light-reflecting, wind-loving trees of the desert, whose roots are always seeking water and whose leaves are always talking about it, making the sound of rain. The long, porous roots of the cotton wood are irrepressible" (37). In Thea "the life" is "rooted deep" (218), for she develops by finding the water that is always there for the irrepressible root. In *The Song of the Lark* a root system digs down, takes hold, and nourishes the growing plant. In *The Professor's House* St. Peter, living in an attic that no longer has a house below it, is a plant without roots, and the book describes the slow but inevitable death of such a plant.

In her 1932 preface Cather refers to Moonstone as a "smug, domestic, self-satisfied provincial world of utter ignorance." But in *The Song of the Lark* Moonstone does not appear so monolithically antagonistic to Thea's development. Indeed, at the height of her artistic achievement, Thea claims, "'They save me; the old things, things like the Kohlers' garden. They are in everything I do'" (460), and we are led to believe that had Thea not grown up in Moonstone she would not have been so great an artist. *The Song of the Lark* derives much of its creative energy from the conviction that all places have water, that all places are capable of nourishing the "irrepressible" root. We remember that even in Moonstone Thea acquires a copy of *Anna Karenina*. And we remember as well that when Thea's first teacher, Wunsch, leaves Moonstone he goes even farther "west"—to Concord, Kansas, "the jumping-off place," as Ray Kennedy describes it, "'no town at all. Some houses dumped down in the middle of a cornfield'" (107)—but perhaps even Concord has its Thea who will get what she needs from him. For with his German training and his *Orpheus* score, Wunsch brings to Moonstone, and to Thea, something of that "fourth dimension" Dr. Archie notices on his first trip to New York City. Wunsch provides Thea with a model of artistic excellence, the desire to achieve something beyond the merely "personal," just as Spanish Johnny provides a model of what the love of music can mean in a human life. Cather tells us that "Mexican settlements were rare in Colorado then" (41) and that Spanish Johnny comes to Moonstone accidentally; but she underscores the debt that Thea's development owes to her early contact with the Mexican settlement, achieved in defiance of Moonstone norms, when she brings Spanish Johnny back at the end of the novel to hear Thea sing.

Through Wunsch Thea meets the Kohlers, whose garden forms an oasis to which Thea returns in memory long after she has left Moonstone. Mrs. Kohler's trees are "not American basswood, but the European linden" (24), and her garden brings a bit of her own Rhine village to the sand gulch in Colorado, modelling the degree to which desire and will can transform the desert. Moreover, the Kohlers' house contains, in addition to the mechanical marvels of a cuckoo clock, a real work of art in the "piece-picture" made by Fritz Kohler during his days as an apprentice tailor. However, in taking in Herr Wunsch, Mrs. Kohler gives Thea something more important than garden or house; she gives her a knowledge of the sympathy that those who are artists can excite in others who are not. Cather calls the first section of *The Song of the Lark* "Friends of Childhood," for Thea, like Herr Wunsch, experiences as a child the sympathy and caring that the exceptional can inspire in the unexceptional. Ray Kennedy dies because his fussiness inspires in Joe Giddy only the wish to counter Ray's carefulness with his own carelessness. Thea, on the other hand, has something that inspires Dr. Archie to sew her a healing cocoon and bring her white grapes in the middle of a Moonstone winter, saving her life in the face of her father's apparent indifference and her mother's preoccupation with a new baby. And that inspires Ray Kennedy to take her to the "sand hills"—the part of the Southwest that most tantalizes her with its human and natural history and which in time will come to mean as much to her as the music of Wagner—and to leave her the money she needs to develop beyond Moonstone. Moonstone gives Thea an early belief in the friendliness of the world toward one who possesses the gift of music, that "second self" that can speak to the "second selves" of others; and while Thea eventually loses this belief, having once had it makes her a sympathetic and thus a great artist.

But though Thea manages to make even her compulsory attendance at weekly prayer meeting nourish the artist within her, for a daughter trying to grow up finding food may be easier than eating it. Indeed, in calling the first section of her book "Friends of Childhood," Cather may suggest that for daughters friends are better than mothers, for it is never easy for a daughter to cease to be "dutiful." Look again at the cottonwood image: "The long porous roots of the cottonwood are irrepressible. They break into the wells as rats do into granaries and thieve the water" (37). Coming home on the train from Chicago, Thea listens to the cough of a dying girl and meditates on the difference between their futures. The riddle of why some people fail while others succeed, which haunts Thea with a version of survivor guilt, recurs in the figure of the tramp who poisons the Moonstone water supply. We note that people initially attribute the trouble with the town's water supply to rotting cottonwood roots, and we can feel here the anxiety of the daughter who fears her own success in finding water may be a rat's thievery. When Thea accepts the rare opportunity to sing a major role in Europe rather than return to Moonstone to visit her dying mother, we appreciate the enormity of what is required of the daughter to develop; even so loyal a supporter as Dr. Archie thinks Thea made a mistake in not coming home.

The anxiety of the daughter who does not finally believe in her right to the attic room—that private space in a crowded household—or to the support system that it represents, can be recovered as well from a reading of *The Professor's House*. Professor St. Peter has purposely kept his attic study primitive to disguise the real luxury of his life. During the years of writing his histories, St. Peter has devoted his weekdays to teaching and university responsibilities and his nights, the weekends, and even Christmas Day, to his writing. He has trained his family not to bother him while he works; daughter Kathleen waits half a morning sitting outside his study door, her fingers swollen from a bee sting, for him to emerge. But the luxury of being undisturbed takes second place to the greater luxury of knowing that in the house below him a life goes on that includes him, indeed revolves around him, and which he can enter whenever he wishes: "When he was writing his best, he was conscious of pretty little girls in fresh dresses—of flowers and greens in the comfortable, shabby sitting-room—of his wife's good looks and good taste—even of a better dinner than usual under preparation downstairs" (101). As a man who can assume such support as "natural," St. Peter has indeed "managed to have his luxuries" (27). Yet in connecting St. Peter's loss of desire with the cost exacted of his family by his "luxuries," Cather records her own sense of illegitimacy and fraudulence, her understanding and expectation of betrayal. Behind the pervasive bitterness of *The Professor's House* lurks the daughter's anxiety that she never deserved her success in the first place, and it is within this context that we can realize once again the miracle of *The Song of the Lark*.

When Thea leaves Moonstone for Chicago she carries with her "the essentials, the foundation" (460) of her later achievement. Yet her experience in Chicago brings her as close to failure as she ever comes. Though she meets Harsanyi, a Wunsch without the alcohol, his insistence that she acknowledge her voice forces her to leave his tutelage and brings about an irrevocable break with her family. Confronted with her sister's hostility and her mother's unwillingness to take her side against her sister, Thea loses the illusion that her family cares what becomes of her. When Thea leaves Moonstone the second time, she leaves without that illusion and "forever." And she returns to a world shaped by the antipathetic personality of her teacher, Madison Bowers, whose lack of generosity threatens to convert her sympathetic personality into a version of his own bitterly contemptuous and negative self.

Thea is saved from despair and failure and provided with the context which will enable her to grow by her meeting with Philip Frederick Ottenburg. Godfrey St. Peter, who wishes he had died before he knew his wife, has become someone he no longer recognizes through years of "always consciously or unconsciously conjugating the verb 'to love'" (264), but *The Song of the Lark* without Fred would be a very different book. Fred gives Thea's desire a human dimension; Thea admits she wants him for a "sweetheart." Yet Fred is no ordinary lover. In Fred, conveniently married to a woman he despises and thus emotionally available to Thea while unable to offer her the developmentally dangerous option of marriage, Cather creates a symbol for the role Isabelle McClung played in her life. Temporarily at least, Cather did not have to choose between her love for Isabelle and her own career; and her relationship with Isabelle enabled her to believe in the miracle of human sympathy and the viability of her own desire. It is this story that she tells in *The Song of the Lark*, which she dedicated to Isabelle. In *The Professor's House* Isabelle appears as Lillian, St. Peter's wife, whom he consistently associates with the daughter who has married Louis Marsellus and whom he resents for having found in her relation with Louis a way to continue to develop—something he himself, having lost her, can no longer do. For St. Peter desire has been "the magical element" in life and work, and *The Professor's House* mourns the death of desire. Writing *The Song of the Lark*, Cather still had her desire. She still believed the world contained a "Fred" and that a girl like Thea, or herself, had the ability to find and have a "Fred."

In Cather's analysis of what enables the female artist to develop "there is only one big thing—desire" (76), and she gives this desire a distinctly physical cast. While the love and marriage plot produces phallotropic women—that is, women who view their bodies as objects in a drama staged by phallic persons—a lover like Fred (or Isabelle) gives a woman like Thea (or Willa) the chance to make her own body the foundation of her subjectivity. Desire has shaped Thea from her earliest moments of self-consciousness, providing the secret knowledge that makes her "different" and forming the source of her happiness. As a child she has shared her secret with only one other person. Together she and Wunsch had "lifted a lid, pulled out a drawer, and looked at something. They hid it away and never spoke of what they had seen; but neither of them forgot it" (79). At the end of the novel, Harsanyi identifies this "something" as the passion he claims is every artist's secret, "an open secret, and perfectly safe" (477). But, given the similarity of Cather's language to descriptions of the frequently covert and often subsequently repressed masturbatory experience of adolescent girls, I would identify this "something" as referring equally to Thea's sexuality. When Thea leaves Moonstone, "She was all there, and something else was there, too—in her heart, was it, or under her cheek? Anyhow, it was about her somewhere, that warm sureness, that sturdy little companion with whom she shared a secret" (157). While this "sturdy little companion" can clearly be read as the "warm sureness" of Thea's knowledge that she has a voice, it also suggests Thea's sexuality. Indeed, in choosing a singer as her figure for the female artist, Cather chooses a context in which body and art are inseparable. In Panther Canyon, Thea comes to understand that "with her, at least, voice was first of all, vitality; a lightness in the body and a driving power in the blood" (307). Since Thea's voice comes from her body, to deny her body would destroy her voice and thus her art. In *The Song of the Lark*, then, Cather resolves the opposition, so frequent elsewhere in her work, between women's sensuality and their development, inextricably connecting the artist's passion for her art with the woman's passion for her body and its desires.

Cather gives Thea a body in *The Song of the Lark*, and keeps us aware of this body as a site of desire. At the literal and emotional heart of *The Song of the Lark* Cather places the sun-filled sensual world of Panther Canyon, a world Thea first possesses alone and then shares with Fred. Chicago has made Thea physically and spiritually sick. Fred reads her body language—"her back was most extraordinarily vocal" (291)—and offers her a summer on his ranch in Arizona. In Panther Canyon Thea returns to her first source of happiness, her own body reflected and recovered in a landscape that mirrors it. Cather describes Panther Canyon in language distinctly vaginal:

> The canyon walls, for the first two hundred feet below the surface, were perpendicular cliffs, striped with even-running strata of rock. From there on to the bottom the sides were less abrupt, were shelving, and lightly fringed with *piñons* and dwarf cedars. The effect was that of a gentler canyon within a wilder one. The dead city lay at the point where the perpendicular outer wall ceased and the V-shaped inner gorge began....In this hollow (like a great fold in the rock) the Ancient People had built their houses. (297)

In this hollow that resembles her own body, Thea makes her home, lying hour after hour in the sun, a completely sensuous creature who encounters music for the first time as a completely sensuous form.

Thea bathes every day in a pool in a hollow at the bottom of the canyon. From this daily ritual of precise and loving attention to her own body, she gains insight into the connection between life, art, and womanhood. Years earlier Ray Kennedy told Thea that among the Cliff Dwellers women were the artists, and in the fragments of pottery she finds throughout Panther Canyon Thea proves the truth of this assertion. Bathing, she understands:

> The stream and the broken pottery: what was any art but an effort to make a sheath, a mould in which to imprison for a moment the shining, elusive element which is life itself....The Indian women had held it in their jars....In singing, one made a vessel of one's throat and nostrils and held it on one's breath, caught the stream in a scale of natural intervals (304).

When we recall that etymologically "vagina" means "sheath" and consider the sexism of this etymology—its opposing of passive and in effect dead female bodies to active and life-giving male bodies—we can more fully appreciate the revision Cather accomplishes here. Envisioning her body as the site where she can catch, hold, and shape life into art, and imagining that her Indian predecessors, making sheath-like pots to hold the precious water, achieved a similar connection between a woman's body and life and art, Thea places her sexual and gendered self at the very center of human creativity.

The Indian women with whom Thea identifies provide her with models for her own struggle to become a female artist. With them as her history, she finds herself no longer alone and singular but part of an ancient and deep-rooted pattern. In reconstructing the lives of these foremothers, Thea in effect imagines "mother." As she will later demonstrate when she incorporates the memory of her mother into her portrayal of Fricka, in Panther Canyon Thea learns how to mother herself, generating the history she needs to support her own development.

Panther Canyon serves Thea well because it enables her to resolve the major obstacles to her development. She recovers her body and finds a way to connect desire with personal and artistic growth. And in Panther Canyon she finds a solution to the daughter's guilt over surviving and transcending the mother. Not only does she reconfigure mother as artistic role model, she reintreprets the "hardness" at the heart of human existence. The topography of Moonstone came to Thea entangled with the mentality of smug self-satisfaction which appreciates only the mediocre and hates anything beyond itself. Though Thea finds Panther Canyon intensely inhabited, the people who built the cliff town have vanished, leaving her free to create her own interpretation of human nature and human history from the shards of the past she finds there. The hardness Thea found so troubling in the Moonstone tramp becomes from the perspective of Panther Canyon a universal fact of human existence, not a particular feature of individual lives nor, as in *The Professor's House*, the unnatural hardness of female forms that ought to be soft and nourishing. Resolving her guilt, Thea comes to see that in surviving and succeeding where others fail, she acknowledges and fulfills obligations "older and higher" than those to family and friends, given her by the Cliff Dwellers who have extended her sense of history far beyond Moonstone.

In *The Professor's House* the American Southwest still figures as the site for a profound understanding of human life, but St. Peter, the historian, cannot find in Tom Outland's story a usable history, a history that would enable him to continue to desire. In Panther Canyon Thea encounters a world she experiences as intensely alive, and in it she finds the sources of life—sun, water, and desire. Thus she picks up the stream just where her Cliff Dwellers put it down. But the city Tom discovers appears to him eternally asleep, long ago destroyed and dead still. And in Cliff City, Tom excavates a tomb whose human remains provide evidence for a theory of history far different from that which Thea creates from Panther Canyon. As Father Duchene explains: "'They were probably wiped out, utterly exterminated, by some roving Indian tribe without culture or domestic virtues, some horde that fell upon them in their summer camp and destroyed them for their hides and clothing and weapons, or from mere love of slaughter'" (221). Though Cather places this analysis of the fate of the cliff dwellers in a voice twice removed from St. Peter's, it clearly echoes his interpretation of his own history in which the higher civilization of godly men is wiped out by an alliance of women and Jews.

Though this mesa has its canyons—fringed by cedars, the only living things in the midst of all this death—Tom observes that a tower, "beautifully proportioned...swelling out to a larger girth a little above the base, then growing slender again...was the fine thing that held all the jumble of houses together and made them mean something" (201). In *The Professor's House*, then, Cather accords cultural meaning to the male body and permits no celebration of the female body and its desires. Indeed that desire, the source of creativity in *The Song of the Lark*, appears here in the figure of Mother Eve, the dead woman whose mouth still screams through all these years and whose face still keeps its look of terrible agony. Later the men who discover her speculate that, like the wife in Thea's Norwegian story, she was murdered by her husband who returned unexpectedly and found her, as they delicately put it, in "improper company." Perhaps Tom discovers his own body in Cliff City, but Tom's experience is out of reach of St. Peter. Thea's experience in Panther Canyon centers *The Song of the Lark*, but Tom's story signals the ending of *The Professor's House*. Rereading what Tom once had and lost serves to conclude Godfrey St. Peter's own history of desire.

In 1932, Cather claimed she should not have included the Kronborg section in *The Song of the Lark*. Rereading *The Song of the Lark*, I still love the final section, both for the courage Cather displays in risking a description of Thea's success and for her success in making that description convincing. By the time of *The Professor's House*, Cather no longer dares to describe the histories that have won St. Peter his reputation and his prizes, and she stays even further away from the mysteries of the Outland engine. Though nostalgia—the grief for a youth that was better and is gone—murmurs below the surface of *The Song of the Lark*, Thea's present moment dominates the final section of the novel. Like Dr. Archie and Spanish Johnny and Fred and Harsanyi, we witness what it has all been about. Through Cather's words we see and hear Thea sing. And because Cather has had the courage to describe Thea's singing, we believe Fred when he concludes, "'But take it from me, no matter what she pays, or how much she may see fit to lie about it, the real, the master revel is hers....Anybody with all that voice and all that talent and all that beauty, has her hour. Her hour,' he went on deliberately, 'when she can say, "there it is at last, *wie im Traum ich*—'As in my dream I dreamed it / As in my will it was'"'" (424).

But having changed so much myself in the years between my first reading of *The Song of the Lark* and this later reading, I can now register those features of the text that foreshadow the anxieties of *The Professor's House*. Though Thea can embrace the hardness of human existence in Panther Canyon, she cannot always find hardness inspiring, particularly when it takes the form of betrayal by the one other woman whom she considers an artist and believes shares her artistic commitment. *The Professor's House* describes a world with hardness everywhere, from the dressmaking forms St. Peter cannot bear to surrender, perhaps because they still offer the illusion of softness, to the floor Tom hits when he falls down the stairs in St. Peter's house. Despite the existence of "friends of childhood," Cather sets Thea's development in a context essentially hostile to it. Indeed, Thea's disappointment in Madame Necker identifies how much against the odds Thea's accomplishment has been. Hearing Jenny Lind sing transforms Theodore Thomas from an itinerant violinist to the conductor of the Chicago Symphony, but Cather does not give Thea the immediacy of such models. Indeed, we remember that the female artists of Panther Canyon are long dead. When Thea leaves for Germany, she tells Fred that she is "'going to Lehmann, if she'll take me'" (376), but we never see

Lehmann. Later we learn that in Germany Thea is called "die Wolfin" because she terrorizes the other girls studying with her. Thea has no female mentor and she will not serve as mentor to any other woman.

In fact, Thea has only male mentors, models, and friends. Her first words state flatly, "'Brothers are better'" (7), and she reserves her contempt for other women. The misogyny implicit in these features of *The Song of the Lark* becomes quite explicit in *The Professor's House*. In this later text we enter an intensely gendered world in which heroes are male and women represent all that is vulgar, cheap, and hard. Only Augusta, perhaps Cather's emblem for Edith Lewis, owner of the hard forms who pulls St. Peter back into a life without delight, commands a grudging respect. Returning home from witnessing his older daughter's acquisitive orgy, St. Peter remembers "about Euripides; how, when he was an old man, he went and lived in a cave by the sea, and it was thought queer, at the time. It seems that houses had become insupportable to him. I wonder whether it was because he had observed women so closely all his life" (156). And we can remember that Mother Eve, dead for over three hundred years, still has enough malignant power to send a good pack mule to the bottom of the canyon.

When Wunsch leaves Moonstone, he gives Thea his score of Gluck's opera, *Orpheus*, and inscribes it with the phrase, "Einst, O Wunder!"—thus recalling an earlier moment when Wunsch explained to Thea that only one woman could ever sing the music Gluck wrote. As Wunsch predicts, Thea becomes another wonder, and all concerned in the making of this wonder share Harsanyi's relief when he finally hears her sing: "'At last,' he sighed, 'somebody with *enough!*'" (476). But beneath the relief we sense the strain of such standards, standards that apparently apply only to women, for Harsanyi, a brilliant concert pianist himself, suffers from no such singularity. In creating Thea as a singular wonder in a world of commonplaces and failures, Cather reveals the anxieties that underly both her portrait of Die Kronborg's power and her own sense of power as a writer. Reading *The Song of the Lark* with attention to the anxieties implicit in its accomplishment, we can understand why for Cather *The Professor's House* lay ahead. But for us *The Song of the Lark* can always lie ahead, helping us, like Thea, to realize the power of our desire. "'As in my dream I dreamed it, / As in my will it was.'"

WORKS CONSULTED

Cather, Willa. *The Song of the Lark*. Lincoln: U of Nebraska P, 1978.

———. *The Professor's House*. New York: Vintage, 1973.

O'Brien, Sharon. *Willa Cather: The Emerging Voice*. New York: Oxford, 1978.

Robinson, Phyllis. *Willa: The Life of Willa Cather*. Garden City: Doubleday, 1983.

"How Do We [Not] Become These People Who Victimize Us?": Anxious Authorship in the Early Fiction of Joyce Carol Oates

Brenda O. Daly

When Joyce Carol Oates tells us that "most novelists divide themselves up lavishly in their novels" ("Hostile" 278n), she implies that a writer's imagination enables her to transcend socially determined gender categories. Nevertheless, as I shall show, Oates's early fiction reveals a pattern of authorial self-division that conforms to gender conventions: her male characters, such as Richard Everett in *Expensive People* and Jules Wendall in *them*, assume the right to define themselves, whereas her female characters, Maureen Wendall and Nadine Greene in *them*, merely act out roles in some (male) author's fiction. This probably unconscious projection of Oates's authorial power upon male characters is symptomatic, I believe, of a certain anxious authorship in her fiction in the 1960s, an anxiety rooted more in gender than in social class. Indeed, in the final pages of *them* lower-class Maureen asserts herself more effectively than does her counterpart Nadine from the upper-middle class suburb of Grosse Point, a passive princess whose problems Oates also explores in "How I Contemplated the World."[1]

We see, for example, that the unnamed narrator of "How I Contemplated the World" refers to herself only in the third person, as "the girl," whereas Richard Everett, as narrator of *Expensive People*, begins his memoirs with the bold, "I was a child murderer." Although both are children of wealth, only Richard readily assumes an authorial persona, speaking from the place of a violently preestablished, coherent authorial "I." By contrast, the girl, who has no preestablished I, illustrates Judith Kegan Gardiner's point that female identity is a process that does not conform to the Oedipal myth of a unique, whole, and coherent self (179). Moreover, though Gardiner suggests that women often define themselves through the act of writing, the girl does not. Although both of these privileged adolescents have been educated in elite private schools, only Richard writes well. Moreover, only Richard dares to criticize America. His highly polished memoirs are a savage satire of the values of a consumer society, the same values his parents uphold. Richard's confession that he has killed his mother, not his father, is even more sophisticated satire—an inversion of the Oedipal plot that functions as a critique of the model of identity promoted by the Freudian psychiatrists who, of course, fail in their attempts to "cure" him.

The socially determined personae adopted by both of these adolescents—the male "author" and the female "character"—are ultimately self-destructive. For example, it is apparent from the girl's essay, a disorganized outline of her experience of running away from home, that she is a character still in search of a (male) author, a lover to replace her father; whereas Richard, a mirror image of the girl, is already an accomplished author, but one whose I has been established by violence, by matricide. His satire reeks of aggression, not only against his parents but against most adults, including his anticipated readers. Helplessly acting out the script of the passive female character and the aggressive male author, these adolescents clearly acquiesce to traditional gender roles. Like many other adolescents in Oates's early fiction, as Robert Fossum says, they feel as if they are "actors in a script written and directed by someone else." Both "How I Contemplated the World" and *Expensive People* also illustrate Fossum's point that "repeatedly, Oates's people crave an order associated with 'home' and the loving protection of the father. Repeatedly, this conflicts with the yearning for the 'road' and freedom from the father" (286).

Of course, "lighting out for the territory" is hardly a new metaphor for the struggle for self-definition in American fiction. Huck Finn and Holden Caufield are well-known examples of adolescents who not only run away, but narrate their stories of flight with considerable insight. This male tradition may lead Fossum to conclude that the yearnings of adolescents in Oates's fiction, whether for home or for the road, are "expressions of a struggle to control their own lives against the forces of 'accident,' circumstances, [and] other people" (286). Here Fossum minimizes the desire for relationship implicit in the metaphor of "home," perhaps because his unexamined model of identity formation is, in fact, based upon male experience. This romantic model of identity places emphasis on control and autonomy, almost to the exclusion of connectedness. Yet whether we are at home or in flight, we define ourselves only in relationship to others; even our declarations of independence must be acknowledged by someone, as Jessica Benjamin points out. In both her criticism and fiction Oates emphasizes, as does Benjamin, that the self is socially embedded, or "interconnected." Oates also shares with Bakhtin a belief in the relational nature of consciousness, a conception of the self constructed in and through language. And if we accept the notion that identity is formed through both private and public discourses, it follows that, as Bakhtin says, language "ventriloquate[s]" us. It then becomes apparent why Bakhtin asserts that "we must all, perforce, become authors" (qtd. in Holquist 314). If we do not author language, language authors us.

It is not surprising, however, that Oates's experiences as a woman make her more attentive than Bakhtin to the ways that gender complicates self-definition or self-authorship. In fact, the problem of self-authorship became an "obsession" for Oates, as she says in a 1973 comment about "How I Contemplated the World." She defines this story's theme—which, she states, "so obsessed me that I've treated it half a dozen times, perhaps more"—as the riddle of "why we leave home or make vain attempts to leave home, or failing that, yearn to leave home" (Appendix 542). She adds, "there are many ways of leaving." She intimates that one way of leaving home is literal; another is imaginative. Both ways pose considerably greater problems for young women, as Oates implies in this elaboration of her theme:

> While you're away, trying to map out another life, new parents or stray adults or simply anyone with an I.Q. one point above yours conquers you. They just walk up to you and take hold. That's that. The puzzle is, how do we become these people who victimize us? They are so charming, so much in control of their bitten-off part of the world; they are so very masculine. (542)

This comment betrays a degree of autobiographical anxiety about how Oates herself is to leave home, how she is to leave the house of fiction the "masters" have built. How, for example, is she to use her own high I.Q.? How is she to claim authorial power without becoming one of those who victimize others, one of those "very masculine" authors who are "so much in control of their bitten-off part of the world"?

Yet Oates's remark about those who "just walk up to you and take hold" at least implies a democratic ideal. One might go further and assert that this image of over-aggressive masculinity suggests the need for a more maternal conception of authorial power, power that nurtures rather than controls. Oates also understands that such nurturant power—more a daughter's inheritance than a son's—lacks cultural authority, since it has, historically, been limited to the domestic sphere. As Lynda Boose and Betty Flowers point out, the authority a daughter inherits from a mother is not parallel to that which a son inherits from a father. Oates explores this power disparity in *Expensive People*. She lays bare the gender politics of the Oedipal myth of authorial power by creating a writer who is also Richard's mother. Thus Richard must "kill" his mother, rather than his father, in order to acquire authorial power. Imagining himself a character in his mother's fiction, a violent man in a short story called "The Sniper," Richard literally acts out the part of "the sniper." Eventually, having failed to win his mother's attention, he turns his gun against her, against the mother who is forever abandoning him because, as we learn, she is unhappy with the constraints of her social identity—as Mrs. Everett, wife and mother. Richard's psychiatrists, blinded by their belief in one plot, an Oedipal plot of course, assume that he has fantasized the matricide. Their own gender politics cause them to deny Richard's credibility, as he anticipates many of his readers will also.

But *Expensive People* is more than a satire of Oedipal plots and psychiatric theories of personality. It is also a satire of Joyce Carol Oates's previous fiction. Some of the titles written by Richard's mother, Natashya (Nada) Everett, are the same as those by Oates: "The Molester," for example, and "Building Tension in the Short Story." Why this self-satire? The fact is that, like Nada, Oates has written violent plot lines for her male protagonists. Her first two novels end in suicide—Shar Rule's in

Expensive People, Swan Revere's in *A Garden of Earthly Delights*, and now Richard Everett's, as promised, at the end of his memoir, *Expensive People*. This pattern of violent closure explains why Oates perceives herself, like Nada, as sacrificing her heroes for aesthetic purposes: to "build tension" in her fiction. Significantly, in her next novel, *them*, both Maureen Wendall and her brother Jules physically survive, but they do not escape traditional gender scripts. Indeed, at the end of the novel, they seem fated to reenact old scripts, scripts that transform victims into victimizers.

How do we [not] become these people who victimize us? Oates returns to this question in *them*, once again exploring—through the creation of an alternate self—how to nurture the young. This time she portrays herself as a teacher, a "Miss Oates" who fails a student just as her counterpart, Nada Everett in *Expensive People*, failed her son. In particular, Miss Oates flunks a young woman named Maureen Wendall, a student who attended her English class at the University of Detroit night school. After leaving the class, Maureen writes a letter to Miss Oates which begins positively, "I think I am writing to you because I could see, past your talking and your control and the way you took notes carefully in your books while you taught, writing down your own words as you said them, something like myself" (309). But in a subsequent letter Maureen says bluntly, "You failed me" (314), explaining that on the only paper she had handed in, Miss Oates had written "*Lack of coherence and development*" in blue ink, along with a failing grade (315). Like *Expensive People*, this novel illustrates the failure of an educated adult woman—writer, mother, or teacher—to nurture the young. Oates has yet to create an adult woman who uses her imagination, as Oates herself does, to move beyond powerlessness. Although her novels criticize the socioeconomic system that destroys the human potential not only of "them" but also of "expensive people," they fail fully to elucidate—or transform—their own equally oppressive gender scripts.

In the Author's Note to *them*, however, Oates calls attention to this problem, as if after completing the novel she could finally see the gender issue more clearly. Although Joanne Creighton thinks that most readers will find the author of the Note "indistinguishable in any way from the 'real' author" (65), the distinction is significant. For by making herself a character both in the novel *and* outside it—a strategy that challenges the (masculine) notion of authorial "objectivity"—Oates calls attention to the "fiction" of authorial power. Indeed, she demonstrates her discomfort with that model of authorial power that Foucault historicizes in "What Is An Author?" asking "at what point we began to recount the lives of authors rather than heroes, and how this fundamental category of the-man-and-his-work began" (720). In both *Expensive People* and *them*, through the creation of alternative female selves, Oates seems to posit what Gardiner identifies as "a maternal metaphor of female authorship [that] clarifies the woman writer's distinct engagement with her characters" (179).

In the final lines of the Author's Note to *them*, Oates seems to give her powers of authorship away, not to Maureen or Nadine, but to Jules. She writes, as if merely providing an account of the fates of her major characters:

> We have all left Detroit—Maureen is now a housewife in Dearborn, Michigan; I am teaching in another university; and Jules Wendall, that strange young man, is probably still in California. One day he will probably write his own version of this novel, to which he will not give the rather disdainful and timorous title *them*. (n.p.)

Surely this final comment is ironic. This is not the "real" Joyce Carol Oates, but a gendered alternate self who assumes a male character to be superior to a female author. Yet we know that Oates—as opposed to Miss Oates—is not only a teacher, but also a writer, the author of *them*, a woman whose imagination is superior to her male hero's. She is not simply a character in someone else's plot. Nevertheless, Oates seems uncomfortable with her superiority, as if she wishes to break down the hierarchies between the authorial "I" and "them" through the act of passionate imagining. In naturalistic terms, however, it is highly improbable that Jules, a high school dropout, will write a novel with a title superior to Oates's own "rather disdainful and timorous *them*." As the real Oates knows, this title actually points to the most revolutionary theme in the novel: that "we" are "them," that the grammatical as well as the social boundaries separating us are illusory. "'We are all part of a single human family,'" Jules reads aloud, repeating the words of Vinoba Bhave, who is pictured on the cover of *Time* magazine. "Fire burns and does its duty," reads Jules, whose imagination is fired by these words (95). However, Jules has been so brutalized by his impoverished existence that he understands only those fires set during the Detroit riots; moreover, it is an act of violence—rather than of imagination—which frees him from despair. During the riot, he kills a man, the only way he can find to express his passion, his rage. As Oates sees it, acts of imagination, such as writing a novel, offer an alternative to violence, but because of economic injustices this option is not available to Jules, despite his intelligence and passion.

Indeed, as the Author's Note explains, novel-writing is not an act of detached observation, but of passionate imagining—of dreaming other lives, of experiencing "them" from within. As Oates says of the Wendalls, "Their lives pressed upon mine eerily so that I began to dream about them instead of myself, dreaming and redreaming their lives." At the same time, she adds, "Because their world was so remote from me it entered me with tremendous power, and in a sense the novel wrote itself." This revelation of her writing process is intriguing. On the one hand, she rejects the objective authorial role—and the positioning of the author outside and above his characters—but at the same time she seems to disavow her authority by claiming that the world of the Wendalls "entered" her, a penetration so powerful that "in a sense the novel wrote itself" (n.p.). One might describe this "vaginal" moment as an instance of negative capability, and perhaps it is. Yet for Oates writing is also, clearly, an act of resistance. In *them*, for example, she does not accept the constraints of naturalism, as indicated in the resurrection of Jules after Nadine shoots him. At the end of part 2, she writes, "the spirit of the Lord departed from Jules" (380)—but forty pages later in part 3, called "Come, My Soul, That Hath Long Languished," Jules appears again on the streets of Detroit. The point is, of course, that Jules dies a spiritual rather than biological death.

Although Waller argues that "with Oates, we are never provided with a firm moral perspective; instead we are taken into the maelstrom of feelings" (118), her imaginative entry into another consciousness, however disorienting, *is* the moral act.

She doesn't simply impose a moral scheme from above and out-side the world of the Everetts or the Wendalls, she experiences their world from within. We understand, for example, why as a lower-class child Maureen concludes that the suffering of char-acters in most novels "was greater than her own. How could she or her people be raised to this level of suffering?" (166). We understand why although Maureen is attracted to the quiet order of libraries—as Oates herself was—she dares to dream only of becoming a secretary, never a teacher or writer. The clos-est Maureen comes to the act of writing is as secretary of her class—a position that requires neatness and accuracy, not imag-ination. Because of her training for submission and obedience, virtues appropriate to a future wife, Maureen's loss of the secre-tary's notebook makes her feel as if her life were coming "undone," an experience she likens to "that time her period had begun in school" (157). As a girl, it seems obvious, her fate is even more restricted than her brother's.

Indeed, because Maureen's mother, Loretta Wendall, cannot imagine a fate for her daughter different from her own, she fur-ther victimizes her. She belittles Maureen's efforts to read, accusing her of lying about going to the library, and she behaves as if only Maureen's body can save her from poverty, preferably through marriage, but failing that, through prostitution. Loretta treats Maureen as a prostitute, turning her into the bait with which to keep her second husband, Furlong. When Maureen finally acts upon her mother's training, turning to prostitution and storing her earnings in a book of poetry called *Poets of the New World*, Furlong nearly beats her to death. Thus, the door to Maureen's self-authorship slams shut. By contrast, Maureen's brother, who loses his English notebook and drops out of school, finds a substitute dream: a dream signified by the photo-graph of a girl which he manages to retrieve when the wind grabs it, dashing it into the mud of an expressway. Despite his near-illiteracy, Jules has seen enough movies to imagine himself as "a character in a book being written by himself" (99), author of his own fate. Thus, despite repeated brutal defeats, he contin-ues to think optimistically that he is the hero, the Alan Ladd or Marlon Brando, of a book which he authors himself.

Jules presents himself as a romantic suitor to Nadine Greene, daughter of a wealthy family. When she rejects and abandons him, he continues to love her, imagining that "so long as he owned his own car he could always be in control of his fate—he was fated to nothing. He was a true American. His car was like a shell he could maneuver around, at impressive speeds; he was a second generation to no one. He was his own ancestors" (335). Oates rejects this myth. As Jules's creator, she is anxious not to be confused with authors who give Jules, and thousands like him, an ahistorical, romantic myth to live by. As Oates implies in her portrayal of the female writer in *Expensive People*, we deny our ancestors at our peril. Nada Everett, pretending not to be one of "them," a member of her poor Polish family, ends up writing her son a suicidal plot, a plot which declares that we must kill our fathers (and mothers) in order to be free. This same romantic plot initially gives Jules a sense of freedom, but it is the kind of freedom that repeatedly leads Jules, like Richard Everett, into a dead end.

One such dead end is Nadine herself. In fact, despite the efforts that Jules makes to become a romantic hero—his own ancestor, a self-created Gatsby to Nadine's Daisy—he also loves his family. His loving letters help to heal his dying sister, and at the end of the novel—when Maureen declares her intention to forget "them"—it is Jules who asks her, "'But, honey, aren't you one of *them* yourself?'" The tragedy is that in a society which denies that "we are all members of a single family," Jules continues to dream only a romantic dream. He tells his sister, at the novel's end, that Nadine is still at the center of his yearning: "'I want to marry her, anyway, that woman, the one who tried to kill me, I still love her and I'll make some money and come back and marry her, wait and see—when I come back, a little better off, we can see each other. All right?'" (478). Still the questor, still imagining himself the author of his own story, Jules sets off for California, but he has become, to Maureen, just one of "them." Maureen too has survived, through marriage, but she has sacrificed family and imagination in order to escape the ghetto. By contrast, Jules, however ambiguously, is still fired by the secular scripture, the quest plot often embedded in naturalistic novels.

As Rachel Blau DuPlessis argues in *Writing Beyond the Ending*, social conventions are like "scripts," and "literature as a human institution is, baldly, organized by many ideological scripts" which are not "neutral, purely mimetic, or purely aesthetic." She explains:

> Romance plots of various kinds, the iconography of love, the postures of yearning, pleasing, choosing, slipping, falling, and failing are, evidently, some of the deep, shared structures of our culture. These scripts of heterosexual romance, romantic thralldom, and a telos in marriage are also social forms expressed at once in individual desires and in a collective code of action including law: in sequences of action psychically imprinted and in behaviors socially upheld. (2)

Although Oates certainly protests the secularization of the quest in *them*, she also finds the class and gender archetypes inherent in the romance plot problematic. For if Jules can imagine himself as Nadine's suitor, she continues to regard him as one of "them," as "slime." Despite her desire for Jules, she imagines herself degraded by contact with him: he may have diseases, he may have slept with black women, with "them." If the romance plot is for Jules a potentially liberating script, a model for self-definition, for Nadine it is oppressive, requiring a form of self-annihilation. The same plot that defines the man as a subject requires that Nadine act as an object who exists only for a man. As Nadine says, "'You know, Jules, a man's love creates a woman's love. You've made me the way I am.'" (349).[2]

This very passivity destroys their potential love, as we learn from Oates's romantic description of Nadine. When Jules first sees her, she seems "under an enchantment"; and he describes her simply as "the girl," as "someone's daughter, unassailable" (230-31). When Jules arrives at Nadine's home in Grosse Point, she is like the fairy-tale princess in the tower; Jules longs to be "the carpet beneath her feet" (258). Dressed in white, she reminds Jules of a statue of the virgin Mary, or an aloof nun whom he secretly loved as a boy. Despite the spiritual nature of his quest, he discovers only the nullity of Nadine's innocence. Jules understands that "her sad, evil vision of purity kept him pure. He could not contaminate her with his lust; she seemed to feel nothing" (275). In this implied criticism of Nadine's innocence, her "perverse" and "obscene" purity, Oates locates her own moral vision. The hierarchic moral code which informs the structure of the romance plot—a structure which, as a female writer, Oates has found restrictive—allows for self-definition of the son but only at the daughter's expense. If Jules feels a sense of expansion, of "ballooning," as he acts out the quest plot, the same script provides no such possibilities for Nadine, or Maureen, or any of Oates's heroines, from Karen Herz in *With Shuddering Fall* to Shelley in *Wonderland*. Although these young women—like the girl in "How I Contemplated the World"—try to leave home, try to escape being defined by others, they are unable to become their own authors.

To this puzzle Oates returns again and again. In a critical essay on D. H. Lawrence, she states the problem indirectly, explaining that in Lawrence's story, "The Princess," it is the "father's ethic of the cold locked-in ego [that] dooms her to frigidity" ("Hostile" 278). Nadine's frigidity, or Shelley's "shell," have been created by the Law of the Father, by the sacred or the secular scripture which regards the daughter as the father's property or object. This passive frigidity, as Oates depicts it, drives the lover to violence, against the woman or himself. Given this analysis of the ethics of plot, Oates's question, "How do we become these people who victimize us?" assumes autobiographical significance, not in terms of biology, but in terms of her own psychological struggles as a female writer. For the story of the "princess" parallels Oates's own obedience to the father's ethic, an ethic which shapes the conventions of plot and characterization in the realistic or naturalistic novel. Such conventions, presumed to be "natural," perpetuate the very gender archetypes that Oates finds oppressive, but at this point in her writing career, she has not yet found a way to "write beyond the ending" of the romance plot. Furthermore, even when Oates assumes an adolescent persona, she does not entirely escape traditional gender hierarchies: her male writers, however destructive, more easily assume an inherently violent authorial power.

As a female writer, Oates attempts to resist romantic scripts that victimize the young, but the weight of tradition makes it extremely difficult; perhaps that is why in 1969 Oates described the artistic process in words that suggest victimization. In the Author's Note to *them*, she describes her characters who enter her as lovers enter the bodies of Maureen or Shelley; but she portrays herself as lacking authority over this process: "in a sense the novel wrote itself" (n.p.). Why this refusal to credit herself at least as a co-creator, shaper of dreams, one who trans-forms images into art? Susan Gubar argues that this problem is common to female writers:

> Because of the forms of self-expression available to women, artistic creation often feels like a violation, a belated reaction to male penetration rather than a possessing and controlling. Not an ejaculation of pleasure but a reaction to rending...a painful wounding, a literal influence of male authority. If artistic cre-ativity is likened to biological creativity, the terror of inspira-tion for women is experienced as the terror of being entered, deflowered, possessed, taken, had, broken, ravished—all words which illustrate the pain of the passive self whose boundaries are being violated. (302)

Waller describes Oates in similar terms, as "almost passively open to the tortures and obsessions, the agonies of the particu-lar place and time of America today" (124). But in *them* it is not a woman but her hero Jules whom Oates describes as "torn apart" by his love for his family—"dragged to the bottom of the river by chains of love" (207), just as, during the writing pro-cess, Oates herself is torn by contending voices. By contrast, Nadine doesn't want to be touched, doesn't want to "'get them mixed up with myself, everybody so close'" (265).

This gendered self-division occurs, I think, because Oates projects her authorial powers onto her male character, Jules, and her anxieties about loss of control onto her female characters, Maureen and Nadine. By the early 1970s, in *Marriages and Infi-delities*, Oates escapes monologic (either male or female) gender archetypes by redefining this struggle for authority as both love *and* infidelity to the masters of fiction, both marriage *and* resis-tance to monologic authorial control; but in the 1960s, Oates had not yet satisfactorily defined her own authority, or that of her female characters. The difficulty is, as Sandra Gilbert and Susan Gubar argue, that defining the canon as shaped by Oedipal struggle—with the pen as phallus—creates difficulties for the female writer. Yet as Oates continued to seek a different self, and a new kind of authority, she resurrected "the girl" again and again. In "How I Contemplated the World," for example, she gives a young woman the persona of author and the chance to author herself, but all her dreams lead her either back home or to her tyrannical lover Simon, both of which are "evil" choices. As Oates comments, "It's a story with an evil ending because not only must you return home again (lacking the power, I mean the economic and physical power, to stay away), but while you're away, trying to map out a new life, new parents or stray adults or simply anyone with an I.Q. one point above yours conquers you" (Appendix 542). This comment may apply to either young men or women, but adolescent girls suffer more severely from lack of economic and physical power, as well as the habit of allowing others to dominate them. Men can assume the role of author, of conqueror, whereas women become anxious when they acquire power. If women are to become self-authoring, how should they redefine authorial power? Thus, the young writer of "How I Contemplated the World" enacts Oates's own struggle to leave home, a struggle to re-imagine both conventional characters and conventional endings.

The young narrator of "How I Contemplated the World" begins bravely, but she too is fated to act out the metaphysics of romance plots. She drafts an essay for Mr. Forest, a man she describes as "sweet and rodentlike," who is nevertheless more powerful than she because, she writes, he "has conferred with the principal and my parents and everything is fixed." According to their agreement, and according to convention, her identity is "fixed," stable, already defined. Indeed, in the upper-class "heaven" of Grosse Point, her desire does not exist. In this materialistic world, even her actions, however "bad," have no consequences. Her parents, the principal, and Mr. Forest agree to "treat her as if nothing has happened, a new start, begin again, only sixteen years old, what a shame, how did it happen?" (157). Yet the girl, as she calls herself, desires something. She is hungry for something. She opens her essay with a description of herself before the "fall": "The girl (myself) is walking through Branden's, that excellent store. Suburb of a large famous city that is a symbol for large famous American cities. The event sneaks up on the girl, who believes she is herding it along with a small, fixed smile, a girl of fifteen, innocently experienced" (149). She sees herself, in retrospect, as "innocently experienced," someone who thinks she is in control of events but who suddenly finds herself stealing a pair of gloves. This theft, like leaving home, is a desperate attempt to resist the role of passive virgin. Like Alice in

Wonderland, the girl desires experience, desires a fall. This necessary fall, this journey into the world below—to what she calls "poking around in the debris" of Detroit—appears regularly in the romance, usually as a pattern of descent experienced by the hero. Generally, of course, the role of heroine in a romance is more restrictive: she is more often a victim than an initiator of action, more often concerned with preserving her virginity than with gaining experience, sexual or otherwise (Frye 71–72).

The girl is striving, heroically, to break this pattern, a pattern that Oates also explored in the figure of Nadine in *them*. Nadine acts the part of a passive object to the questor Jules who, despite his lower class origins, has greater freedom to initiate action, and greater freedom of imagination as well. The girl, however, anticipates no response and no changes in her static world; she assumes that her parents and teachers won't hear her. Yet "How I Contemplated the World" also explores ways to alter gender roles in the romance plot, making the young woman the initiator of action, and providing her with a guide to the world below. Clarita, the young black woman who guides her in the world of "them," says, "I can never figure out why girls like you bum around down here," and asks, "What are you looking for anyway?" It is difficult for Clarita, who imagines herself moving up—as she watches television—to imagine someone wanting to move down. Yet Clarita and the girl are both victimized by Simon. A drug addict and a pimp, Simon might have played the part of romantic hero, but having escaped from a world very much like the young white woman's, he says, cynically, "Once I was Huckleberry Finn...now I am Roderick Usher" (152). If he is Roderick Usher, locked in his mad house, the young woman's fate should be obvious to her, and yet she can't seem to resist this mirror image of herself. Behaving like a sacrificial victim, she allows herself to be sexually abused by him and, she tells us, sold to other men for drug money when she was "too low for him." Even so, the girl confesses that she would go back to Simon, if she could. "Would I go back to Simon again? Would I lie down in all that filth and craziness? Over and over again" (158). Like her author, Joyce Carol Oates, she is drawn back to a man like Simon, a man whose apparent capacity for conquest, for the heroic, fascinates her.

Oates tells of this fascination in her 1980 preface to *Three*

Plays, plays she describes as rituals of sacrifice behind "a surface realism and a prose facade" ("Ontological" vii). In these plays it is men who become "mock-saviors and mock-playwrights," and "whose refusal to be mere third-person characters assures them victory" (ix). The problem for a female writer is how to be democratically both, how to be her own author while at the same time a character in the lives of others. Such traditional gendering of authorial power is a puzzle that Oates explicitly acknowledges in a 1982 discussion of her childhood reading of *Alice's Adventures in Wonderland* and *Through the Looking Glass*:

> I might have wished to be Alice, that prototypical heroine of our race, but I knew myself too shy, too readily frightened of both the unknown and the known (Alice, never succumbing to terror, is not a real child), and too mischievous....Though a child like me, she wasn't telling her own story; that godly privilege resided with someone named, in gilt letters on the book's spine, "Lewis Carroll." ("Stories" 15)

Having become Joyce "Carroll" Oates, she found the masculine authorial self a problem throughout the 1960s; she remained puzzled about how to be a female writer without victimizing others, without forcing them to act as characters in a script determined by someone with "godly privilege." Oates managed to solve this riddle, but not before experiencing a personal crisis.

This personal crisis was resolved, according to Joanne Creighton, by writing the story "Plot." Although "Plot" may be read as the story of a young man who commits suicide, it also tells the story of the character's author, who self-consciously identifies with her hero, but at the same time strives to differentiate herself from him. Oates solves her anxiety about authorial power by sharing it with readers, by fully disclosing the writing process, by demystifying it. As the first two lines of the story show, this self-disclosure requires graphic self-division:

> Given: the existence of X. / Given: the existence of myself. / Given: X's obsessive interest in me. / Given: the universe we share together, he and I, which has shrunk into an area about two miles square in the center of this city. (194)

The writer then hypothesizes that X "is on a mission of reclamation, a private detective hired by my father; he is a police agent" (194). Here it becomes apparent that the character is "he," whereas the writer, the I, experiences the character, X, as a paternal agent. He = X = Paternal Agent = Author = Violence. The I imagines she has committed some offense. Could that offense have been to claim the right to be both woman and writer, and furthermore, to write as a woman? This graphic self-division marks the point at which Oates rejects the notion of a unified self—an I in competition with all others—consciously adopting, as part of her writing strategy, Gardiner's notion of identity as process. In "Plot," Oates makes this process visible, opening a space—on the same plane—for a writer's more democratic self-division into all her characters, regardless of gender.

NOTES

1. The full title of this story is "How I Contemplated the World From the Detroit House of Correction and Began My Life Over Again: Notes for an English Class at Baldwin Country Day School; Poking Around in Debris; Disgust and Curiosity; a Revelation of the Meaning of Life; a Happy Ending..." That Oates herself does not regard the ending as "happy" is apparent in her comments in the Appendix of *Cutting Edges*.

2. Oates said in 1973, "When I wrote this part of *them* [where Nadine shoots Jules] I felt Nadine to be the enemy, since I was obviously on Jules' side," but because her sympathies were divided, she related that she also wrote a poem that describes from Nadine's point of view "her befuddlement at her dependence upon a man, upon a man's loving her, from which she will get whatever identity she possesses" ("Transformation" 48).

WORKS CITED

Benjamin, Jessica. *The Bonds of Love: Psychoanalysis, Feminism, and the Problem of Domination*. New York: Pantheon, 1988.

Boose, Lynda E. and Betty S. Flowers. *Daughters and Fathers*. Baltimore: Johns Hopkins UP, 1989.

Creighton, Joanne V. *Joyce Carol Oates*. Boston: Twayne, 1979.

DuPlessis, Rachel Blau. *Writing Beyond the Ending: Narrative Strategies of Twentieth-Century Women Writers*. Bloomington: Indiana UP, 1985.

Fossum, Robert H. "Only Control: The Novels of Joyce Carol Oates." *Studies in the Novel* 7.2 (1975): 285–97. Rpt. *Critical Essays on Joyce Carol Oates*. Ed. Linda W. Wagner. Boston: G. K. Hall, 1979. 49–60.

Foucault, Michel. "What Is An Author?" *Literary Criticism: The Greeks to the Present*. Ed. Robert Con Davis and Laurie Fink. New York: Longman, 1989. 721–32.

Frye, Northrop. *The Secular Scripture: A Study of the Structure of Romance*. Cambridge: Harvard UP, 1978.

Gardiner, Judith Kegan. "On Female Identity and Writing By Women." *Writing and Sexual Difference*. Ed. Elizabeth Abel. Chicago: U of Chicago P, 1982. 177–91.

Gilbert, Sandra M. and Susan Gubar. *The Madwoman in the Attic: The Woman Writer and the Nineteeth-Century Literary Imagination*. New Haven: Yale UP, 1979.

Gubar, Susan. "'The Blank Page' and the Issues of Female Creativity." *Feminist Criticisms: Essays on Women, Literature, and Theory*. Ed. Elaine Showalter. New York: Random House, 1985.

Holquist, Michael. "Answering As Authoring: Mikhail Bakhtin's Trans-Linguistics." *Critical Inquiry* 10:2 (1983): 307–19. Rpt. *Bakhtin: Essays and Dialogues on His Work*. Ed. Gary Saul Morson. Chicago: U of Chicago P, 1986. 59–71.

Oates, Joyce Carol. Appendix. *Cutting Edges: Young American Fiction for the 1970s*. Ed. Jack Hicks. New York: Holt, Rinehart and Winston, 1973. 542–43.

———. "The Hostile Sun: The Poetry of D. H. Lawrence." *New Heaven, New Earth: The Visionary Experience in Literature*. New York: Fawcett Crest, 1974. 43–83.

———. "How I Contemplated the World From the Detroit House of Correction and Began My Life Over Again: Notes for an English Class at Baldwin County Day School; Poking Around in Debris; Disgust and Curiosity; a Revelation of the Meaning of Life; a Happy Ending..." *The Wheel of Love*. New York: Vanguard P, 1970. 149–65.

———. *Marriages and Infidelities*. New York: Vanguard, 1972.

———. "Ontological Proof of My Existence." *Three Plays*. Princeton: Ontario Review P, 1980. vii–ix.

———. "Plot." *Marriages* 196–215.

————. "Stories That Define Me: The Making of a Writer." *New York Times Book Review* 11 July 1982: 3, 15–16.

————. *them*. Greenwich, CT: Fawcett Crest, 1969.

————. "Transformations of Self: An Interview with Joyce Carol Oates." *Ohio Review* 15. 1 (1963): 51–62.

————. *Where Are You Going, Where Have You Been? Stories of Young America*. New York: Fawcett Crest, 1974.

————. *Wonderland*. 1971. New York: Fawcett Crest, 1973.

Waller, Gary F. *Dreaming America: Obsession and Transcendence in the Fiction of Joyce Carol Oates*. Baton Rouge: Louisiana State UP, 1979.

Receiving the Other:
The Feminine Economy of
Clarice Lispector's The Hour of the Star

Deborah J. Archer

The work of Brazilian author Clarice Lispector (1925–1977) is touted as the quintessential example of *écriture féminine* by Hélène Cixous, who dubs her "the greatest writer in the twentieth century" ("Reaching" 7).[1] Before Cixous discovered her, Lispector received a good deal of critical renown; however, this first wave of attention virtually ignored Lispector's feminist content, focusing instead on her unique contribution to Brazilian literature, her phenomenological concerns, and her "humanist" themes.[2] More recently, though, with the growth of feminist literary theory and criticism—particularly the burgeoning interest in French feminist theories—Lispector has begun to be re-examined as a feminist, indeed a "feminine," writer.

Yet feminist theory has not considered Lispector's ambivalence. *The Hour of the Star* (*A hora da estrela*) exposes and explores the self-conscious ambivalence with which Lispector approaches the creation of her protagonist, as well as the writing process itself. It is my contention that this ambivalence indicates Lispector's feminine mode of expression; her hesitancy and indecision reflect her overriding concern with receiving and speaking for the "other," with establishing the proper distance between herself and her protagonist so that Lispector can speak for her (or allow her a voice) without appropriating her.

Further, Lispector's anxiety also reflects the postmodernist concern with the inadequacy of language and the relationship between language and reality. The impossible task which Lispector sets for herself is to make her words fit her protagonist's—the other's—reality, and her self-conscious, halting, introspective narration demonstrates her acute awareness of and extreme sensitivity to the power and imperfection of language.

The Hour of the Star opens, "Everything in the world began with a yes" (11) and closes simply, "Yes" (86). In between (and it seems before and after) is the story of Macabéa, a rendering of the consequences of poverty, and an analysis of the creative process. It is a very small book (only eighty-six pages) about a very small woman (perhaps eighty-six pounds)—an "almost-a-woman," as Cixous calls her. But within this slim little book, a great bit of life is conveyed to us; for Macabéa's existence, which is almost nonexistence, touches the infinite.

It is a painfully difficult task to write about this book because there is everything to say—and nothing. Everything because the text works on so many levels simultaneously, blurring distinctions, traversing boundaries, going beyond. And there is nothing to say about it because, finally, what can I say that will render this text to you? I want to say simply: go to the novel and read it. For it is a gift that has already been given to you, and I can do no more.

This will not suffice, though, for you will need a reason, some proof. I must seduce you to Lispector as I was seduced by her. And therein lies the rub. For seduction implies control: I must presume an authoritative position, enticing you through language to my interpretation of beauty, value, and truth. And I must presume, also, to speak for Lispector, to recreate her text critically without appropriating it for my own purposes. Or is this even possible?

I could say that I am writing this only because what Lispector has to say and the way she has to say it is so important that (I believe) you should know it. But with that statement, now, I've already taken up a position of authority. That is, I've taken that position for as long as you allow me to hold it. You can stop reading. Or you can continue to read but refuse to believe me. And really it isn't at all necessary that you believe me, only that you believe Lispector. Because I am telling the truth: I do believe that what Lispector has to say and the way she has to say it is important. So I will try to give some proof without letting it get in the way of what I want to say, and I will try with the utmost restraint not to impose any more control than is necessary.

The Hour of the Star is about control. Well, actually it is about lack of control, which in this text is both a lack of privilege (the inability to choose, powerlessness) and also a denial of privilege (refusing to choose, relinquishing power). The author, "(in truth Clarice Lispector),"[3] presents herself to us from inside parentheses. Her authority is an afterthought, an aside, a whisper inserted between the lines within parentheses, power displaced by punctuation.

The book doesn't even give us that most familiar element of authorial privilege, a title. Instead, the title page lists thirteen possible titles: *The Blame is Mine*, or *The Hour of the Star*, or *Let Her Fend for Herself*, or *The Right to Protest*, or *As for the Future*, or *Singing the Blues*, or *She Doesn't Know How to Protest*, or *A Sense of Loss*, or *Whistling in the Dark*, or *I Can Do Nothing*, or *A Record of Preceding Events*, or *A Tearful Tale*, or *A Discreet Exit by the Back Door*. Lispector hesitates: How can she bind this text with one name, this text which is more than a text? How can she bind this young woman's life, tie it up and put a title on it?

So we have an author in parentheses and a book with thirteen titles. We also have a narrator, Rodrigo S. M., but even this person entrusted to tell the story does not appear to have control. He repeatedly tells us that he does not know the characters' fates: "As it happens, I have no idea how this story will end" (16). "I don't even know the girl's name" (19). "I have a restless character on my hands who escapes me at every turn and expects me to retrieve her" (22).

The characters themselves are far from privileged. The protagonist, Macabéa, is a nineteen-year-old, indigent, uneducated woman from the backwoods of impoverished northeastern Brazil—"she had been born with a legacy of misfortune, a creature from nowhere with the expression of someone who apologizes for occupying too much space" (26). Her parents died when she was two, so Macabéa was raised by her physically and emotionally abusive aunt—her "only surviving relative in the whole wide world" (27). After her aunt dies, Macabéa moves to Rio de Janeiro to work as a typist, a functionally illiterate typist who is excruciatingly slow and unbearably sloppy. She takes up residence in the slums of the red-light district, subsisting on hot dogs, coffee, and Coca-Cola, chewing paper and swallowing the pulp when she cannot afford food. She has a calcium deficiency, a thyroid deficiency, and a disturbingly conspicuous cough.

Macabéa's destiny was written at her birth; she was "a mere accident of nature" (36). The reader holds out hope, wants Macabéa to become empowered, to take control over her life. That is, the reader wants Rodrigo (in truth Clarice Lispector) to intervene for her, to change her destiny. For as many times as Rodrigo (Lispector) claims no influence over Macabéa or her situation, we want to believe otherwise, we've been taught to believe otherwise—that the author can make the narrator tell any story, that the characters of a novel belong to the author. But Macabéa does not belong to anyone, least of all, perhaps, to Lispector, as indicated by the very ambivalence with which Lispector approaches her writing.

And so no one intervenes to change Macabéa, because this is a feminine text. How do I know this text is feminine? It has little to do with biology; for although the sex of the author is female, the sex of the narrator is male, and yet they both are feminine. It has to do with what Cixous and Irigaray call "libidinal economy"—that is, with one's relationship to the "gift" and to "giving," with the difference between the masculine "gift-that-takes" and the feminine "desire-that-gives."[4]

The Hour of the Star is desire-that-gives; the female author and the male narrator create and offer the text "without loss or repression being incurred in the process" (Armbruster 152), by establishing a feminine relationship to the other. From the opening of the novel, Rodrigo (in truth Clarice Lispector) agonizes over the act of creation: how to, and who should, write Macabéa. He does not "know" her; she is a young woman he saw in the crowded streets of Rio de Janeiro. But he must write about her, he says, "otherwise I shall choke" (17). The problem is to assume the proper distance, to be close enough in proximity to speak for the other, while maintaining enough distance so as not to possess or incorporate the other. It can be said another way: to leave the other intact in all its otherness while still allowing it voice. For one of the first definitions of the "other" is silence—just like the "feminine."

This proper proximity is based on perception, respect, and love, and is facilitated by Lispector's use of a male narrator. For although Rodrigo is feminine, the fact that he is male imbues him with a perspective different from that of the female author;[5] he can establish another kind of relationship to Macabéa than can Lispector. Macabéa, therefore, is perceived and written from more than a single, unified perspective.

Rodrigo tells us that in preparing for this delicate undertaking he has gone without food and sleep; he has given up sex and football, both of which he dearly loves; he has not shaved and has clothed himself in rags. All of this in preparation, out of love and respect, to step into her poverty, to write the truth—because this woman who is no one from nowhere deserves the best.

Rodrigo doesn't even say her name; that is, he doesn't name her. Her name comes relatively late, almost halfway through the text, in part to show her anonymity, to reinforce that there are "thousands of others [like her] who are mere accidents of nature" (36). But also, Rodrigo (Lispector) thus refuses to possess this woman, to appropriate her. The first time the name Macabéa appears in the text is when Macabéa herself says it. She is referred to as "the girl from the northeast," "the typist," and "she," until she meets a young man who asks her name, and she says "Macabéa" (43). Macabéa names herself.

Rodrigo (Lispector) proceeds slowly and patiently to receive Macabéa, for "slowness is the patience needed to wait for, hear, and undergo the approach of the other" (Armbruster 151). And Macabéa is accepted in all her difference and presented to us as a living being; the text "is not simply a narrative, but above all primary life that breathes, breathes, breathes" (13). But this feminine gift of life is not easy to give or to receive, and the entire process produces great anxiety within Rodrigo (Lispector). The narrator's (author's) dilemma is how to make language represent reality and, more particularly, how to make the text's language represent the reality of Macabéa. It makes no sense to Lispector to write a richly-worded, sophisticated tale of a poverty-stricken illiterate; that would be appropriation, a vulgarization and a colonization of the other: "I will give you a voice and you will speak my language"—the bourgeois mentality, the masculine "gift-that-takes."

And so Rodrigo tells us that he will not write anything complicated; the text will be "stark" and the words "unadorned." The language must not be embellished because Macabéa does not "know how to embellish reality" (33). This is how Lispector makes the text more than a text; she relinquishes her privileged position to language so that she may accommodate Macabéa's tiny voice. The effect is a symbiotic relationship between the novel's form and content, as well as a correspondence between author, narrator, and protagonist: Rodrigo's (Lispector's) struggle with language reflects Macabéa's struggle as an illiterate; Rodrigo's (Lispector's) fear and indecision about writing Macabéa's existence reflect Macabéa's own aimless, dire existence. Lispector, Rodrigo, Macabéa are at some moments blurred, at others distinct: the right closeness, the right distance. The feminine body of this text has permeable boundaries,[6] ever shifting and refusing closure, so that its multiple selves and plural speaking subjects move back and forth and in and out of one another without possession, so that the text exceeds the limits of phallogocentric discourse.

But there is yet a perhaps more profound level to Lispector's ambivalence, for she too was from impoverished northeastern Brazil.[7] Lispector might have been born Macabéa, as she tells us, "when I consider that I might have been born her—and why not?—I shudder. The fact that I am not her strikes me as being a cowardly escape" (38). And yet, as Lispector wrote about this impoverished woman with a diseased body who was simply a victim of fate, she was coming to grips with her own diseased body, for she knew that she was dying of cancer. She, too, was the victim of absurd fate.

And it is not only Lispector who is confronted with her own tenuous existence, through the existence of all the Macabéas in this world, but the reader as well. Lispector asks the question which every reader must ask herself: "If one thinks about it carefully, aren't we all mere accidents of nature?" (36). Yes, we all might have been born Macabéa, were in fact, to varying degrees and in different respects, born Macabéa, for we all have some poverty and some disease, have all at some point been a victim of one kind or other. And conversely, that we were not born Macabéa is (un)equally an accident of nature; whatever privilege by race, class, gender, ethnicity, and the like, each of us was born into is simply fortuitous. This is a political revelation of the most personal kind.

And if one catches, if one is touched by, this revelation, then one certainly must understand, and in fact share, the ambivalence and anxiety which permeate this text. It is one thing to intellectualize it: to discuss the relationship between art and life, to discuss, theoretically, receiving the other. It is quite another to accept it: to accept the knowledge of the closeness/distance of the other to one's self.

For as the reader cannot help but consider herself fortunate to have escaped Macabéa's lot, she also cannot ignore Lispector's most pointed and personal questions; the author's self-interrogation becomes the reader's: "Am I a monster or is this what it means to be a person?" (15). To say I am educated, I have an identity and a voice, I understand words and I can write—this other is different, is ignorant, is ugly, is dull—I am grateful that I am not it—I am better than. Is this a monster or is it simply the definition of a person?

This line of interrogation comes close to the truth, but it still can be an intellectual defense mechanism. "Am I a monster or is this what it means to be a person?" is an existential question, one that could scarcely be articulated by Macabéa. In other words, that Lispector and her readers are able to consider such a question may be a way of reaffirming the distance. Intellectualizing is easier than accepting. Writing (and reading) about Macabéa is easier than inviting her to dinner.

Or is it? Is it the closeness or the distance which produces the greatest anxiety?

For Lispector, I cannot say. If I wanted to prove a case I could prove it either way: the closeness of Macabéa to Lispector makes her "shudder"; the distance between them makes her feel like a "coward." For myself, I can only answer by writing an end to this.

Lispector says in *The Hour of the Star* that her "mandate is simply to reveal her [Macabéa's] presence so that you [and I] may recognize her on the street, moving ever so cautiously because of her quivering frailty" (19). And I have seen her. She was walking, hunched in a thin coat through the cold night, as I was on my way to the shopping mall. I told my friend, there is Macabéa. But I didn't stop to offer her a ride or ask if she needed any help. I was afraid of everything not-like-me that she might have been. So instead I leave non-perishable food items at the door of the mission. As Lispector says in one of her titles, *The Blame is Mine*.

For one truth of the story of Macabéa is that I (I cannot speak for you) am complicit with the systems which give birth—and nothing more—to Macabéa. Lispector and her readers can make *A Discreet Exit by the Back Door*, or by the back cover of the text; she/we can step back out of Macabéa's poverty after eighty-six pages. But the discreet exit is also Macabéa's—and the important point is that it is an exit, a departure rather than a conclusion.

Lispector—in her ambivalence, in her relinquishing of power and privilege—does not, perhaps cannot, close the text. For the reality of Macabéa cannot be contained—however scrupulously and tenderly Lispector attempts to represent it—within a system (of language, of choice, and the like) from which she is precluded. Macabéa resides outside of language, beyond this text, so that the best Lispector and her readers may hope for is a brief encounter, a recognition.

It is a re-cognition to which I return again and again because the exit leaves open that possibility, that potential. And while it is true that Lispector and her readers must step back out of Macabéa's poverty, it is not without being forever changed in the encounter.

NOTES

1. The term *écriture féminine* is loosely translated as "feminine writing." I use it here to denote both the theory and the practice (literary, critical, and political) proposed by Cixous in "The Laugh of the Medusa" and *The Newly Born Woman*. Cixous praises Lispector in *Reading with Clarice Lispector*, "Reaching the Point of Wheat," "Extreme Fidelity," and *Vivre l'Orange/To Live the Orange*.

2. Latin American literature scholars such as Fitz (who has written extensively on Lispector) and Pontiero praise her unique voice and stylistic virtuosity as both influencing and exemplifying the shift from regionalism to internationalism in Brazilian letters. Douglass summarizes the critical rift between humanist and feminist interpretations, arguing that the two are inseparable in Lispector's work. Peixoto discusses Lispector's fictions as Bildungsromane.

3. This phrase is from the author's dedication to *The Hour of the Star*. The translation here is by Ann Liddle and Sarah Cornell as presented in Cixous's "Extreme fidelity": "Dedication of the author (in truth Clarice Lispector)."

4. According to Cixous and Irigaray, the masculine libidinal economy is a sociosexual construct and contract based on ownership and appropriation, on the rate of exchange and the rate of return. Within the masculine economy, something is "given" only to get something more in return, hence the masculine "gift-that-takes" (Cixous, *Newly* 87). The feminine libidinal economy, however, is based on multiplicity, variance, and abundance; "everything is exchanged, yet there are no transactions" (Irigaray, *This* 213), hence the feminine "desire-that-gives" (Cixous, *Newly* 99). Both Cixous and Irigaray relate these economies to anatomical difference—man with his monolithic penis, women with lips, breasts, vagina, clitoris—and to sexual difference—for example, orgasmic/pleasure potential and castration anxiety. However, the extent to which such differences are to be viewed metaphorically and/or literally remains slippery. Both Irigaray and Cixous maintain that it is what society (patriarchal culture) has made of these differences which is important, and further, that men are quite capable of assuming a "feminine" position (as Cixous argues that Genet, Kafka, and Joyce do) and women of assuming a "masculine" position. See also Cixous's "The Laugh of the Medusa."

5. Although this may seem paradoxical, men are not inherently precluded from assuming a feminine position in a libidinal economy. While Rodrigo is feminine in that he refuses to appropriate and possess Macabéa, he is still male, and his gender difference (from Macabéa as well as Lispector) creates another viewpoint.

6. The idea of "permeable boundaries" is approached in various ways by a number of feminist theorists. Chodorow, for example, posits that "girls come to experience themselves as less separate than boys, as having more permeable ego boundaries. Girls come to define themselves more in relation to others" (93). Many other feminist theorists, for example Cixous and Irigaray, relate this psychological permeability to women's physical permeability (evident in menstruation, intercourse, pregnancy, and the like), and to the larger question of the relationship between the body and ways of knowing and perceiving. The idea is that "permeability"—psychological and/or physical—indicates a resistance to closure and limitation and a potential for otherness, multiplicity, and difference. See also Kristeva, Ostriker, Suleiman, and Lauter and Rupprecht.

7. Lispector was born in Techtchelnik, Ukraine, while her family was en route to Brazil. For twelve years she lived in Recife, the capital of Pernambuco, in northeastern Brazil; her family then moved to Rio de Janeiro.

WORKS CITED

Armbruster, Carol. "Hélène-Clarice: Nouvelle Voix." *Contemporary Literature* 24.2 (1983): 145–57.

Chodorow, Nancy. *The Reproduction of Mothering*. Berkeley: U of California P, 1978.

Cixous, Hélène. "Extreme fidelity." Trans. Ann Liddle and Susan Sellers. *Writing Differences: Readings from the Seminar of Hélène Cixous*. Ed. Susan Sellers. New York: St. Martin's, 1988.

———. "The Laugh of the Medusa." Trans. Keith Cohen and Paula Cohen. *New French Feminisms*. Ed. Elaine Marks and Isabelle de Courtivron. Amherst: U of Massachusetts P, 1980. 245–64.

———. "Reaching the Point of Wheat, or, A Portrait of the Artist as a Maturing Woman." *New Literary History* 19.1 (1987): 1–21.

———. *Reading with Clarice Lispector*. Trans. and ed. Verena Andermatt Conley. Minneapolis: U of Minnesota P, 1990.

———. *Vivre l'Orange/To Live the Orange*. Paris: Editions des femmes, 1979.

———, and Catherine Clément. *The Newly Born Woman*. Trans. Betsy Wing. Minneapolis: U of Minnesota P, 1986.

Douglass, Ellen H. "Myth and Gender in Clarice Lispector: Quest as a Feminist Statement in 'A Imitaço da Rosa.'" *Luso-Brazilian Review* 25.2 (1988): 15–31.

Fitz, Earl E. *Clarice Lispector*. Boston: Twayne, 1985.

Irigaray, Luce. *This Sex Which Is Not One*. Trans. Catherine Porter. Ithaca: Cornell UP, 1985.

Kristeva, Julia. *Desire in Language*. Trans. Thomas Gora, Alice Jardine, and Leon S. Roudiez. Ed. Leon S. Roudiez. New York: Columbia UP, 1980.

Lauter, Estella, and Carol Schreier Rupprecht, eds. *Feminist Archetypal Theory: Interdisciplinary Re-Visions of Jungian Thought*. Knoxville: U of Tennessee P, 1985.

Lispector, Clarice. *The Hour of the Star*. Trans. with an Afterword, Giovanni Pontiero. Manchester: Carcanet, 1986.

Ostriker, Alicia. *Stealing the Language: The Emergence of Women's Poetry in America*. Boston: Beacon, 1986.

Peixoto, Marta. "*Family Ties*: Female Development in Clarice Lispector." *The Voyage In: Fictions of Female Development*. Ed. Elizabeth Abel et al. Hanover, NH: UP of New England, 1983. 287–303.

Pontiero, Giovanni. Afterword. Lispector 89–96.

Suleiman, Susan Rubin, ed. *The Female Body in Western Culture: Contemporary Perspectives*. Cambridge: Harvard UP, 1986.

"What There Was Before Language": Preliteracy in Toni Morrison's Song of Solomon

Deborah L. Clarke

Literacy long a source of both strength and anxiety in the African American literary tradition, takes on a somewhat different role in Toni Morrison's fiction. While the written text can assume a manipulative power associated with white culture in some of her work—the Dick and Jane passages of *The Bluest Eye* or School-teacher's book in *Beloved*—*Song of Solomon* both highlights and transforms the power of literacy. The novel has relatively few scenes focusing on the acts of reading and writing, but the written text, both as legal and literary document, plays a prominent role. Literacy can be both used and abused, resulting in a rather ambiguous judgment on the power of reading and writing. Yet Morrison's ambivalence toward literacy comes across not necessarily as a negative anxiety because literacy is not necessarily the controlling force in the African American community, where nature and orality modify the power of the written word. This is not to say that literacy is negligible, for the novel ultimately approaches the question of how much literacy is tied to the formulation of language and culture, a frequent concern of those traditionally denied access to reading and writing.

Certainly there is a dichotomy between the written text, generally associated with white power, and oral discourse, the province of the African American community. However, the paradigm of orality versus literacy ultimately falls short as a means of examining Morrison's presentation of language, literacy, and power. What Morrison provides is not an opposition but an interplay between written and spoken discourse, which are differentiated not exclusively by race but also by class. The written word is not inherently exploitative—after all, we're working within the confines of a written text here—but must be subsumed into a new form of language, one based on childhood and on nature. While this practice of turning toward nature, as Margaret Homans argues, is common in female writers, Morrison's use of natural language follows a slightly different pattern. Finding strength rather than death in nature, Morrison creates a language and community based on a different kind of cultural myth. This natural language seems to grow out of female discourse, but Morrison ultimately takes it beyond gender differentiation to a more inclusive language, thereby avoiding the limitations—and much of the corresponding anxiety—of both gendered discourse and literacy.

An examination of Morrison's anxiety about literacy must take into account the position of literacy within the African American literary tradition. Given that it was illegal to teach a slave to read or write, literacy, as Frederick Douglass points out, became the means to achieve freedom and equality; to learn to read was to beat the system of slavery. In Douglass' case, literacy and freedom were literally equated as he finally escaped by writing his own pass, and then gained national prominence by writing his own story. To be literate for Douglass—and after him Washington and DuBois—is to be human. More anxiety surfaces, however, in the work of Langston Hughes, Richard Wright, and Ralph Ellison. Hughes begins his first autobiography, *The Big Sea*, by describing himself throwing all his books overboard as he sets sail for Africa, saying it was like "throwing a million bricks out of my heart" (3). Richard Wright both yearns to read because words were "the gateway to a forbidden and enchanting land" (49), and recalls that publishing his first story cut him off from family and friends. And when Ellison's Invisible Man learns to his sorrow the content of the letters he has naively delivered, he takes the first step toward recognizing how completely he has been co-opted by white society, a realization that only beomes complete when he recognizes the handwriting on yet another letter. The problem lies not in literacy but in what the written text represents: controlling authority.

This summary, however, represents the male tradition. In general, African American female writers tend to place less emphasis on the process of reading and writing. Harriet Jacobs' slave narrative focuses more on sexual abuse than enforced ignorance, and Harriet Wilson's Frado sees school more as a means of escaping oppression at home than gaining an education. Janie, of Hurston's *Their Eyes Were Watching God*, searches for a voice, not a text. Janie's final observations on her search for self privilege experience: "you got tuh *go* there to *know* there" (285). Thus Toni Morrison, who writes out of a tradition with a mixed response to literacy, views it with less anxiety than many of her white counterparts. Joseph T. Skerrett has observed that "Morrison is an inheritor as well as an innovator" of the work of Hurston and Ellison, and as such she looks "very carefully at the way folk processes inform Afro-American life" (193). The sense that so many female writers have of being excluded from literary history is somewhat mitigated by a tradition which also privileges experience, community, and orality.

Clearly, the title of her third novel resonates with textual associations, yet Morrison inverts both the biblical allusion in the novel's title and the characters' biblical names by creating a new Song of Solomon, a children's game. By redefining this archetypal poem into something associated with childhood, Morrison subtly privileges not simply an oral culture, but a form of preliteracy which preempts the Song of Songs. It is important to note that this reconceptualization of the Song of Solomon is precisely that; it is not an eradication of the written text, but rather, a translation into a more fluid form of discourse. Morrison does not simply pit written texts against oral discourse; she creates out of the interplay of the two a discourse based on nature. In so doing, Morrison moves beyond a simple equation of literacy with the white community and orality with the black. The African American community is not plagued by illiteracy, for in the opening chapter we see six-year-old Guitar correct the white nurse's spelling of "admissions." Rather, it is the use—and abuse—of language and written texts that can render the power of literacy ambiguous. In particular, when literacy defines class, it becomes an anxious tool of domination.

The novel opens with a written text, the letter from Robert Smith announcing his flight "from Mercy." Yet there are, in fact, two different versions of this text, one from the narrative and the other from Smith himself.

> The North Carolina Mutual Life Insurance agent promised to fly from Mercy to the other side of Lake Superior at three o'clock. Two days before the event was to take place he tacked a note on the door of his little yellow house:

> At 3:00 P.M. on Wednesday the 18th of February, 1931, I will take off from Mercy and fly away on my own wings. Please forgive me. I loved you all.
> (signed) Robert Smith,
> Ins. agent (3)

No power of credulity is strained by the preliminary passage; someone announces plans to fly—by plane, we assume—from one place to another. The note, however, reveals Smith's intentions to "fly away on my own wings," a significantly different statement. Juxtaposed to the narrative description, the letter reveals the fallacy of the reader's assumptions. If the information of the first sentence comes from Smith's note, the narrator has subtly revised it; the reader's subsequent recognition that the initial paragraph is misleading highlights the importance of careful reading. The note, which announces itself as a written text, offers a more accurate rendition of the situation, thus subtly privileging written discourse even over narrative voice. In this case, the written document proffers truth as long as we read what is there. The ensuing paragraphs call into question this privileging of the written text. Morrison goes on to explain how Not Doctor Street got its name, after the city "had notices posted in the stores, barbershops, and restaurants in that part of the city saying that the avenue running northerly and southerly from Shore Road fronting the lake...had always been and would always be known as Mains Avenue and not Doctor Street." The legal written notice provides, in this case, the opportunity for the community to invert the power of the written word. "It was a genuinely clarifying public notice because it gave Southside residents a way to keep their memories alive and please the city legislators as well. They called it Not Doctor Street" (4). By essentially undoing government bureaucracy the people do not negate the written document so much as transform it into a means of communal expression. Writing, so often the tool of the dominant class, can also serve to mock its pretensions to power and control. By allowing the communal voice to modify written dominance, Morrison suggests the possibility of a discourse which draws on both orality and literacy. In this case, the written text again offers "truth"—for the right readers.

In juxtaposing these two textual examples—the letter and the public notice—in the first two pages of the book, Morrison indicates that textual authority, open to variable interpretations, lacks a stable foundation and thus a controlling position. The result is an atmosphere which conveys not anxiety but fluidity—a mark, Luce Irigaray asserts, of women's language (79). The varying responses to written texts unquestionably convey ambivalence toward literacy, but the multiple interpretations create a more female-based discourse which reduces the controlling power of the written word. Strength lies not in controlling written discourse but in adapting it.

One of the more blatant abuses of literacy and the power of writing surfaces, however, with two women, Corintheans Dead and the white State Poet Laureate, Michael-Mary Graham— women who depend on literacy to enforce class status. Michael-Mary Graham, who writes every morning from ten to noon and every afternoon from three to four fifteen, and in whose home "colors, furnishings, and appointments had been selected for their inspirational value," is delighted to be able to present her maid with a copy of *Walden* for Christmas "rather than that dreary envelope" (191). While Thoreau's wisdom may be priceless, the literature of the great white fathers, given by one who would be a great white mother, is an inadequate substitution for a Christmas bonus. Graham privileges literature in its conventionally white masculine form as a way of privileging her own endeavors and thus imposes a class distinction that suggests one should prefer art to money, a prerogative of the upper classes. The irony of her choice of Thoreau, however, undermines her literate status, as his philosophy of self-sufficiency is foreign to her, suggesting that she herself has either not read or not understood him. Thus Graham damages herself with her own weapons, as her attempt to establish her elitist literary status reveals her ignorance or her hypocrisy.

In this case, Michael-Mary Graham has found an appropriate recipient for her bounty. Corintheans, whose Bryn Mawr education has "unfit her for eighty percent of the useful work of the world" (190), condones this literary elitism by going to work incognito, carrying a copy of *Contes de Daudet* on the bus to disguise the fact that she works as a maid, though once at work she must pretend ignorance of French and of education. She masks this job both through her appearance and her language, telling her mother she works as an

> Amanuensis. That was the word she chose, and since it was straight out of the nineteenth century, her mother approved, relishing the blank stares she received when she told her lady guests what position her daughter had acquired with the State Poet Laureate. (188)

When one uses literacy to protect the appearance of class status, educated language obscures truth rather than communicating it. The word "amanuensis" "was a lie, of course, even as the simpler word 'secretary' was a lie" (188). This literate fallacy not only lacks authenticity, it also marks Corintheans as a woman who has lost touch with her community and its values, and has been co-opted by the "poetry" of Michael-Mary Graham. By disguising her position, she disguises the injustice of the situation, implying that African American women can, in fact, find nonmenial jobs, while also suggesting that the menial jobs which other black women perform are beneath her. Yet in dissociating herself from such labor she comes dangerously close to dissociating herself from the benefits derived from this job: responsibility and love.

It would be easy to conclude that the Michael-Mary Graham incident simply privileges manual labor over literary labor, because Corintheans flourishes through the independence achieved as a working woman and gains a lover in the process, while Graham has given up marriage and children to the demands of poetry. Yet Corintheans' affair with Porter, originated and facilitated by the sentimental verse on a flowery greeting card, redeems, to a certain extent, the place of poetry. The power of literacy is neither inherently exploitative nor classist, though it takes Corintheans a while to come to this realization. When she first receives the card, she wishes "he had signed it, not because she wanted to know his name, but so it would look more authentic—otherwise somebody might think she bought it herself" (194). The desire for authenticity, which is lacking in her own language, suggests that Corintheans views the card essentially as a legal document, requiring a signature to be binding. This need for a signature marks her as trapped in the legalistic power of the document (a power which even the city legislators could not enforce on Not Doctor Street), and indicates that she reads the text the wrong way, too dependent on what constitutes written authenticity. She has, indeed, become Michael-Mary, who gives out *Walden* oblivious to its meaning.

In her quarrel with Porter she equates literacy with worth, as she attacks the less educated women with whom she feels competitive, and demands, "'Why don't you drop a greeting card on one of *their* laps?...You couldn't do that could you, because they wouldn't be able to read it'" (197). For Corintheans, at this point, asserting herself means asserting her literacy, her class—until she realizes that the alternative is a life of genteel emptiness, making velvet rose petals. Rather than spend life engaged in this artificial travesty of women's association with nature, she leaves her concern for literacy-enforced class behind and bangs frantically on "the car-door window of a yardman" (199). Her relationship with Porter, established through a card covered with flowers, defeats Bryn Mawr and Michael-Mary Graham. The flowery card, with its association of language and nature, offers Corintheans a better option than either making velvet roses or reading of Thoreau's solitary sojourn. While these flowers may be no more "natural" than the velvet roses, they accompany a text with a sincere message, and thus offer life while the roses evoke death. By combining the natural and literary in unexpected ways through this greeting card, Morrison creates a kind of natural discourse by merging literacy, nature, and pathos. An elitist dependence on literacy comes close to breaking Corintheans; what saves her is the ability to value a greeting card above Thoreau, to move beyond a dependence on "high" culture. In essence, she leaves behind the discourse of literacy and class, thereby breaking out of her family-imposed isolation and joining the community around her.

In rejecting her class background, Corintheans rejects a family history of misreading the power of literacy. Macon Dead II says of his father, "Everything bad that ever happened to him happened because he couldn't read." This comment appears to support the notion of literacy as power because the first Macon loses his name and his farm due to illiteracy. Yet if we examine the situation more closely, we find that the father's illiteracy is not as heavy a burden as the son feels. True, he loses his name—Jake Solomon—to become Macon Dead, but this also represents a choice: "Mama liked it. Liked the name. Said it was new and would wipe out the past" (54). By becoming "Dead," Macon preempts the whites who murder him, taking his own death symbolically under his own control. And the fact that he may have signed away the rights to his farm without realizing it has little to do with its loss; had he refused to sign, he would have been murdered just the same. Macon Jr., like his daughter Corintheans, places great emphasis on the power of the signature, on writing which conveys legality. But so long as Macon Sr. is viewed as legally negligible, his signature can be manipulated or dispensed with as the whites see fit. Everything bad that happened to him happened because he was an African American in a racist country, not because he was illiterate.

In contrast to his son, Macon Sr. would likely say that the worst thing that ever happened to him was the death of his wife, an event which literacy can do nothing to mitigate. Once again, Morrison subtly undercuts literacy as a determining force, thereby reducing any attendant anxiety. The scene of Sing's death and Pilate's birth adds a further dimension to the already complex portrayal of language and literacy in the text. Homans argues that Western texts are based on the myth "that the death or absence of the mother sorrowfully but fortunately makes possible the construction of language and culture" (2). Thus female writers view language ambiguously, particularly the figurative language associated with men, women being labelled as literal and natural. Morrison, however, inverts the process. The death of the mother—who was literate—leads not to symbolic discourse but to a more natural language. True to the family tradition, Macon chooses a name from the Bible, a written text. But this tradition does not represent a process whereby children are named after prominent biblical figures, thus reinforcing patriarchal biblical authority, for the tradition consists of putting a finger down on a word, any word. We see reverence for the Bible but also a reconceptualizing of its inherent meaning. Macon, in his illiteracy, chooses "a group of letters that seemed to him strong and handsome; saw in them a large figure that looked like a tree hanging in some princely but protective way over a row of smaller trees" (18). The shape of the word attracts Macon, creating a new kind of symbolic discourse, one that privileges not abstract meaning but nature—the letters look like trees. Indeed, the power of this new form of symbolic discourse is so strong that Pilate will grow up to smell "like a forest" (27), sway "like a willow" (30), and look like "a tall black tree" (38).

The name takes on further meaning when Macon discovers its literary referent. When asked, "You don't want to give this motherless child the name of the man that killed Jesus, do you?" Macon replies, "I asked Jesus to save me my wife" (19). Given the inadequacy of Jesus, representative of the written Bible, Macon finds it a fitting response that this name symbolically reaffirms the death of Jesus. Symbolic discourse is not predicated on the death of the mother but on the death of the Son. Morrison recasts the myth of language to undermine both its patriarchal exclusivity and textual authority, yet she goes beyond simply negating the power of the text in killing off the word of God. For to kill Christ is to kill *Logos*—not the written word of God, but the spoken word of God. Thus Morrison undermines not just written discourse but spoken discourse, commanding discourse, the physical manifestation of logos. Pilate, a woman of almost divine strength and understanding, replaces Christ, and her lack of a navel enhances her divinity. Though others later fear that she was not "born natural" (143), she is, in fact, a child whose birth engenders a new kind of logos, one based in nature. Macon's original sense of the visual and natural potential of letters carries more sway than its textual referent, as Pilate resembles not Pontius Pilate but a tall black tree. The biblical word gives way to a new form of language which heals rather than commands. The biblical text is inadequate not because it is written but because it imposes patriarchal authority. Morrison's ability to recast the Bible reduces the dominance of the text and thus lessens the anxiety associated with that dominance.

Pilate's life bears witness to the connections between the textual and the natural. She never gets beyond the fourth grade in school, yet she is fascinated by geography and carries a child's geography book with her throughout her life. In this case, literacy enhances one's relation to the land—to geography—which Pilate further emphasizes by collecting rocks from every state where she has lived. Despite her fourth-grade education, she quotes the Bible "verse and chapter" (208). In fact, as Brenda Marshall points out, Pilate's biblical knowledge goes beyond chapter and verse; she subtly misquotes Matthew 21:2, alluding to the loosing of an ass and colt tied together. She thus gently mocks not only the white policemen but also Milkman and Guitar, the ass and colt needing to be "loosed." Her clever recasting of Matthew parallels Morrison's recasting of the Song of Solomon, once again both validating and transforming textual authority.

While Pilate's language often follows the patterns which Homans sees in female writers, she also undoes, to some extent, the gendered discourse which other women employ. Homans argues that female writers tend to focus on the literalization of the figurative as a means of expressing ambivalence about their cultural exclusion from figurative language:

> Because the relative valuation of figurative and literal language, and of figuration and literalization, is at the heart of gender difference in language, we should expect to find that literary texts concerned with writing and revising myths of gender and language would locate this project first in the structure of their own language, in their own practice with respect to literal and figurative....If literalization suggests a move in the direction of a mother-daughter language, figuration suggests a return to the paternal symbolic. (29–30)

When Pilate hears her father's ghost say, "Sing, Sing," she takes the command literally and begins to sing, which "relieved her gloom immediately" (148). While we may later assume with Milkman that she simply got it wrong—after all, to be a woman is to be literal and thus less imaginative and intelligent—we can also view this response as a process of figuration. By singing, Pilate figuratively recreates her mother, Sing Byrd or Singing Bird. Alice Walker ends her essay, "In Search of Our Mothers' Gardens," with an imaginative recreation of Phillis Wheatley's mother as a village singer, storyteller, poet, or artist. She concludes, "Perhaps in more than Phillis Wheatley's biological life is her mother's signature made clear" (243). Pilate, I would argue, bears the mark of her mother's "signature" in her singing, through making the literal—the mother—figurative. The song does not represent a "return to the paternal symbolic" because Morrison has broken down those categories of gendered discourse. Walker's identification of the mother's signature seems to me to provide an important transformation of the notion of signature as legal authentication held by Corintheans and Macon. The mother's signature does not legalize a written document; it represents her figurative presence, what Coppélia Kahn calls the "maternal subtext" (35).

Thus Milkman must come to terms with this signature as a means of completing his search for self; consequently, his final act is to sing to Pilate. He is led to this moment by his recognition of natural language; as he sits in the Virginia woods, he realizes that what he hears is "what there was before language. Before things were written down. Language in the time when men and animals did talk to one another, when a man could sit down with an ape and the two converse" (281). Here, Morrison equates language with the written word, with literacy, and then sets up a prehistoric ur-language as primary. This prelanguage recalls what Irigaray calls "prediscursive reality," the preverbal communication between mother and child (89). Women, she says, excluded from Lacan's Law of the Father, serve as a reminder of this prediscursive reality and thus threaten and undermine male-centered symbolic discourse. Thus "what there was before language" can be viewed as a particularly feminine prelanguage, a signature of the mother which precedes Lacanian symbolic discourse, associated with the father. In the novel, prelanguage, the language of the earth itself, provides vital information, the knowledge that someone standing behind Milkman is about to kill him. In order to escape Guitar, a member of the Seven Days (a group of men who practice biblical eye-for-an-eye justice), Milkman must learn to recognize the language of Mother Nature, an older, and less "textual," text.

But whereas Irigaray identifies this prediscursive reality as a female discourse, Morrison relates it to men as well. Mother Nature, the age-old symbol of the feminine, takes on a dual gender as Milkman feels "the sweet gum's surface roots cradling him like the rough but maternal hands of a grandfather" (282). While Milkman's original quest is to trace the gold, what he finds is his great grandfather, prefigured in this forest experience. In reconceptualizing language, Morrison moves beyond the Lacanian symbolic discourse, defined as a masculine mode, and then erases the female exclusivity of maternal discourse to formulate a new language which needs neither words nor texts and which unites both masculine and feminine, the signatures of the mother and the father.

If the mother's death leads to a conflation of literal and symbolic discourse, the father's absence leads to a song, the Song of Solomon, which provides the final key to Milkman's identity. The Song of Solomon, both a biblical text and a children's game, evokes the authority of biblical patriarchy yet also provides a link back to the mother, given the common association of women and children. Rather than setting up a dichotomy between paternal and maternal, figurative and literal discourse, Morrison combines the two into a circular pattern in which each leads to the other. In so doing, she challenges linguistic hierarchy and thus defuses much of the anxious potential of language. This transcendence of gendered discourse, accomplished through the communal expression of men, women, and children, redeems the comic androgyny of Michael-Mary Graham, with her dual-gendered name. The answer is not to erase gender but to build upon the difference in order to create a fuller language.

Morrison's final focus on language as a kind of primary or prehistoric communication is interestingly reinforced by the language of childhood when Milkman finds his final clue through a children's game—the kind from which he, as a child, was excluded. For him, as for his sister Corintheans, the isolation of his childhood is erased as he claims, "But I can play it now. It's my game now" (331). Children's language, preliterate by definition, offers a communal identity distinct from textual authority and written discourse, for Milkman, listening to the song without a pen, must memorize it rather than write it down. By transforming a biblical text into a memorized children's game, Morrison decenters the written text, reducing its power without eradicating it as a form of discourse. The text becomes, in essence, the alphabet, one of the tools from which this new language is made, rather than the controlling authority.

Morrison's discourse is predicated not on textual or government authority but on childhood and nature. In emphasizing this preliteracy, she creates a new paradigm to replace the dominance of the written text, so long associated with white authority and denied to African Americans. Henry Louis Gates poses a critical question for African American literature:

> How can the black subject posit a full and sufficient self in a language in which blackness is a sign of absence? Can writing, with the very difference it makes and marks, mask the blackness of the black face that addresses the text of Western letters, in a voice that speaks English through an idiom which contains the irreducible element of cultural difference that will always separate the white voice from the black? (12)

Toni Morrison, I would argue, recasts the "text of Western letters," the Bible. Her refusal to eradicate either Western letters or the black experience unmasks the black face of the African American. By first turning to Mother Nature, then transforming her into Parent Nature, she creates a unique form of nonhierachical discourse, a language for men and women, for blacks and whites. Literacy loses its power to intimidate as it becomes not eradicated but subsumed into a new Song of Songs.

WORKS CITED

Gates, Henry Louis. "Writing 'Race' and the Difference It Makes." *Critical Inquiry* 12.1 (1985): 1–20.

Homans, Margaret. *Bearing the Word*. Chicago: U of Chicago P, 1986.

Hughes, Langston. *The Big Sea*. New York: Hill and Wang, 1940.

Hurston, Zora Neale. *Their Eyes Were Watching God*. Urbana: U of Illinois P, 1937.

Irigaray, Luce. "Cosi Fan Tutti." *This Sex Which Is Not One*. Trans. Catherine Porter. Ithaca: Cornell UP, 1985. 86–105.

Kahn, Coppélia. "The Absent Mother in *King Lear*." *Rewriting the Renaissance*. Ed. Margaret W. Ferguson et al. Chicago: U of Chicago P, 1986. 33–49.

Marshall, Brenda. "The Gospel According to Pilate." *American Literature* 57 (1985): 486–89.

Morrison, Toni. *Song of Solomon*. New York: Signet, 1977.

Skerrett, Joseph T., Jr. "Recitation to the *Griot*: Storytelling and Learning in Toni Morrison's *Song of Solomon*." *Conjuring: Black Women, Fiction, and Literary Tradition*. Ed. Marjorie Pryse and Hortense J. Spillers. Bloomington: Indiana UP, 1985. 192–202.

Walker, Alice. "In Search of Our Mothers' Gardens." *In Search of Our Mothers' Gardens*. New York: Harcourt Brace Jovanovich, 1983. 231–43.

Wright, Richard. *Black Boy*. New York: Harper and Row, 1945.

Literary Tricksterism:
Maxine Hong Kingston's
The Woman Warrior:
Memoirs of a Girlhood Among Ghosts

Bonnie TuSmith

When an ethnic female writer publishes an "autobiography," she is immediately confronted with inappropriate expectations. As readers we must realize, for example, that neither the Ben Franklin paradigm nor the exotic world of Suzie Wong are valid points of reference for interpreting *Woman Warrior*. Ultimately, we must read the work on its own terms. In reading Kingston's "autobiography," we must recognize that the writer is a creative artist who consciously uses a strategy of narrative ambiguity to tell her story.

When Kingston says in an interview that literary forms "reflect patterns of the human heart" ("Talk" 26), she tells us how she views herself as a writer. By connecting form with "heart" rather than "life," she refers to the artist, not the sociologist. For Kingston, artistic form is organic rather than artificial: it is part and parcel of the human spirit. This position directly contrasts with the stated premise of a major study on Asian American literature, which deliberately "emphasize[s] how the literature elucidates the social history of Asians in the United States" (Kim xv). When applied to an artist who consciously manipulates form in order to be true to "patterns of the human heart," the belief that a literary text can and should be used to document an ethnic culture seems misguided. Because many critics have made the same assumption, they tend either to blame or praise *the author* for her naive narrator's interpretation of Chinese American culture.

In *Woman Warrior*, Kingston uses a narrator who has a child's passion for knowing. What is Chinese and what is American? What is real and what is make-believe? Do the Chinese despise women, or do they see them as potential warriors? Since we have an impressionable protagonist/narrator who feels bombarded by confusing stories in her childhood, this desire for definition is appropriate. However, because the young protagonist singlemindedly pursues either/or options and because her voice dominates the book's first part, the unwary reader is easily lulled by her simplistic pronouncements. Due to her confusion, limited knowledge, desire for absolutes, and total subjectivity regarding people and events, her narration is unreliable.

In an interview, Kingston clearly distinguishes herself from this narrator: "Oh, that narrator girl. It's hard for me to call her me....She is so coherent and intense always, throughout. There's an intensity of emotion that makes the book come together. And I'm not like that" ("This" 6). The distinction between the "I" and "that narrator girl" is revealing. The reader must understand that the writer is, in her daily life, neither coherent nor intense, even though her narrative persona epitomizes these traits.

Had Kingston limited her narrative to the protagonist's naive point of view, she might not have advanced significantly from Jade Snow Wong's *Fifth Chinese Daughter* (1945). In contrasting Wong's and Kingston's literary forms, Patricia Lin Blinde categorizes Wong's autobiography with the Horatio Alger paradigm of American success (55). According to Blinde, Wong simply "'repeat[s]' the white world's articulations and expectations as to what Chineseness is or is not." Consequently, autobiography becomes "a public concession as to her place (and by extension the place of Chinese-Americans) in the world and mind of Americans" (58–59). On the other hand, Blinde says, Kingston belongs to a generation with fewer illusions. The pre-World War II faith in a coherent world, "a world that still believed in the truths of its own imaginative constructs" (54), is no longer possible. In fact, the coherence of Kingston's "narrator girl" is drastically different from that presented in Wong's work. Kingston creates an ambivalent narrator who compensates for her insecurities by reaching for absolutes, while the literary artist transcends her naive narrator's limitations through technique. Before delving into these artistic strategies, however, we must first understand Kingston's definition of autobiography.

Blinde's perception that literary form separates Kingston from Wong is provocative. What does it mean to say that two autobiographies are worlds apart because of their forms? According to Thomas Doherty, autobiography is a literary form particularly suited to Americans' "individualistic and optimistic" self-image. Therefore, Franklin's self-portrait as "an aggressive actor in a society of possibilities" is considered the prototype for "autobiographies in the American tradition" (95). Given this definition, ethnic women's stories are anything but "American" autobiographies. The self as a confident actor selecting among various possibilities simply does not reflect the experiences of most women in America. In order to write a prototypical American autobiography, then, the ethnic woman must either conform to the Eurocentric male definition of the genre and produce a seemingly self-effacing, assimilationist work like *Fifth Chinese Daughter*, or she must subvert and redefine "autobiography" in some way. Kingston's own viewpoint on the subject is revealing. In an essay exposing her reviewers' racist assumptions, she explains: "After all, I am not writing history or sociology but a 'memoir' like Proust." She quotes one reviewer who understood this and said that Kingston was "slyly writing a memoir, a form which...can neither [be] dismiss[ed] as fiction nor quarrel[ed] with as fact" ("Cultural" 64).

This distinction between autobiography and memoir is crucial to the Kingston controversy. By evoking Proust's massive *A la recherche du temps perdu*, which Lillian Hornstein calls "an autobiography of the mind" (435), Kingston challenges the static notion of autobiography in the "American tradition." The Proustian memoir emphasizes fluidity and the presentness of psychological time. Memory is a private code of freely-associated images triggered by seemingly insignificant details in one's environment. As such, the memoir is exploratory. Rather than positing a coherent, already-constituted self which only has to be "revealed" through the autobiographical act, it views identity as fluid and constantly evolving. This alternative understanding of the function of autobiography is particularly suited to women. Unlike their male counterparts' texts, as Leslie

Rabine points out, there is no "lost paradise" in *Woman Warrior* and other ethnic women's "semiautobiographical works" (477). In addition, since there is no "it" to return to, the absence of an Edenic past actually structures ethnic women's stories. But how can absence provide structure? In place of a linear, backtracking approach based on community-decline and nostalgia, works like *Woman Warrior* depict continuity through change and creative adaptation.

In identifying her literary form with Proust's, Kingston not only refutes traditional definitions of autobiography and nonfiction but also legitimizes genres such as memoirs, diaries, and journals (all "female" forms, according to some feminist theorists) which have been considered—at least in America—less "literary" than *the* autobiography. Given the value judgments implicit in issues of literary genre, the publication of Kingston's first book as an autobiography, with "memoirs" in its subtitle, suggests conscious manipulation. As we have seen, the two terms are not synonymous. If Kingston believes she has written an exploratory, quasi-fictive memoir, why did she allow her book to be published as autobiography without qualification? If the general public tends to view autobiography as gospel truth, is Kingston somehow responsible for misleading the reader? After all, the absolutist position implicit in "American autobiography" and the text's dominant narrative voice seem a perfect match. When the narrator tells us that her ethnic culture denigrates women—equating females with "slaves" and "maggots" and thus forcing her to "get out of hating range" (62)—should we not take her word for it? And if we do, can we then conclude that Kingston defends the lone female against her oppressive ethnic community?

To address this question, we might consult Ralph Ellison. "America is a land of masking jokers," he informs us. Franklin posed as Rousseau's Natural Man, Hemingway as a nonliterary sportsman, Faulkner as a farmer, and Lincoln as a simple country lawyer—"the 'darky' act makes brothers of us all" (*Shadow* 70). Ellison asserts that the smart-man-playing-dumb role is not the unique province of black culture. Rather, "it is a strategy common to the [American] culture," and "might be more 'Yankee' than anything else" (69). The historian John Ward corroborates this point when he identifies Franklin as a social and literary trickster.

In *The Autobiography*, says Ward, when Franklin offers himself as Representative American, he acknowledges his awareness of this self-conscious pose (93). This observation suggests that the prototypical American autobiography already has the markings of an "invented self" and does not provide the "straight goods" which the general public expects from the genre.

If we realize that masking is, in Ellison's sense, an *American* cultural phenomenon, and that tricksterism is prevalent in American literature, we can then approach a writer like Kingston without misconceived notions of her "difference." Given that autobiography, like any other genre in literature, is an artistic construct, Kingston's ethnicity should not make her work "social history." If we can accept Franklin's pose in this supposedly nonfictional genre, we should be able to read autobiographies by ethnic women writers with the same understanding. Otherwise, our approach is both racist and sexist.[1] The parallel between scholarship on Frederick Douglass and Kingston illustrates this point.

In an enlightening analysis, Henry Louis Gates demonstrates that virtually all of Douglass' biographers have misconstrued their subject by taking the autobiography literally. The self that the famous abolitionist describes in his three autobiographies is a public image carefully crafted to promote his cause (*Figures* 103). As such, it is "fictive" in the sense of "made by design." "Almost never," Gates points out, "does Douglass allow us to see him as a human individual in all of his complexity" (109). In using an intentionally constructed persona as "fact," biographers can only present an external view of their subject, a view which is the conscious manipulation of its trickster creator. In a sense, Douglass and Franklin are Representative Men today because we still believe their autobiographical constructs. While the misreading of both Kingston's and Douglass' autobiographies stems from the same misunderstanding of the nature of literature, Kingston's situation is complicated by the writer's non-great-man status. If we cannot get quick facts about her ethnic culture from her autobiography, as we can from writers like Wong, then why should we even bother with Kingston?

Yet, from the wide readership that *Woman Warrior* enjoys, it seems that many people find the work of value. This, we contend, has a great deal to do with its artistry. In devising a narrative strategy of ambiguity which captures her multivariate ethnic reality, Kingston is a "literary trickster" in the best American tradition.

Critics accurately identify her various boundary-crossing strategies in *Woman Warrior* as ambiguous or ambivalent. Ambiguity plays a prominent role in the text. They miss the mark, however, when they attribute these strategies to the necessity of "bridging two cultures." If we understood that, as they say, "cultures are made, not born" (Nee, qtd. in Newman 53), we would know that Chinese America as an ethnic culture is not a "bicultural" dualism of either/or possibilities. Rather, it is a *new entity* which is neither Chinese nor European. Because many people have difficulty with this concept (since we are so used to thinking in stereotypes and polarities), they sort between "Chinese" and "American" along with the naive narrator. As mentioned earlier, the narrator's sorting does not reflect Kingston's worldview; it is an artistic device used to create thematic tension between the female individual as protagonist and the ethnic community as antagonist.

A key element of Kingston's strategy of ambiguity is to offer alternative, often contradictory versions of a story without value judgment. The narrator usually tells us when she invents; however, we must sort through her various "truths." Because we are on shifting sand, a convenient anchor is a naive narrator who seeks absolutes with life-and-death urgency. The young protagonist's desire for easy answers when confronting her mother's "talk-stories" about China reflects the reader's need for firm ground. This is a literary "trick," though. Active participation in the text almost requires a level of confusion like the protagonist's. In an essay on fiction and interpretation, Naomi Schor defines the relationship between "interpreter" (interpreting critic or reader) and "interpretant" (interpreting character in the text) as one of "narcissistic identification" (168–69). When a literary work features an interpretant, such identification makes distance difficult to maintain. In reading Kingston, however, distance is crucial.

In *Woman Warrior*, the surface discourse is misleading because the struggle between the protagonist and the immigrant community of Stockton is narrated from the protagonist's point of view. This view, as we have said, is naive due to the narrator's limitations. While anti-female attitudes and unusual practices of "the Chinese" are emphasized, limited space is devoted to the cultural mores of European Americans. In addition, the protagonist's white male oppressors are never identified as such; instead, they are given the generic name "boss" and described as "business-suited in their modern American executive guise" (57). Because the narrator identifies her mother's vivid and grotesque stories as Chinese, the reader might conclude that the Chinese are truly barbaric. This unbalanced presentation of cultures should serve as a warning signal to the discerning reader. Why, one might ask, are white male oppressors "bosses" and ethnic male oppressors "Chinese"? In order to understand such seeming distortions, we must examine the text.

In *Woman Warrior*, verbal articulation is necessary to survival. The protagonist shows how acutely she feels this when she tortures the quiet girl. "If you don't talk," she exclaims, "you can't have a personality" (210). People deprived of speech, as are the various crazy women cited in the text, do not survive. Here is the primary dilemma of the Chinese American experience. It is in *America* that survival is an issue for ethnic Americans, where deprivation of speech (a direct result of racist laws) leads to a lack of personality and even the lack of will to live.[2] Storytelling is thus an essential skill in a hostile environment, a skill which ensures the survival of the tribe as well as its individual members. To arrive at this interpretation, the reader must piece together various elements in the text, or what might be called the "subtext." What makes Kingston's "memoirs" so slippery is the implied author's refusal to spell out connections for the reader. Words such as "talk-story," "personality," and "survival" are linked by juxtaposition rather than cause-and-effect logic. The reader must fill in the gaps.

Forcing active reader participation is, of course, a prevalent modernist technique. Nevertheless, a major problem for ethnic writers is the audience's lack of knowledge regarding ethnic American histories and cultures.[3] In *Woman Warrior*, this is problematic since historical information is scattered throughout the text and often is not attached to specific issues. When the narrator tells us that Chinese people are secretive (6), for example, we might not understand why until the fear of deportation is mentioned (214). Thus, the reader is expected to suspend judgment and not jump to conclusions as the narrator does.[4] Kingston's technique of ambiguity, then, requires reconstructive reading skills. While illuminating contexts for the story can be found in the text, only the alert reader can make the necessary connections.

Given the memoir's nonlinear form—that is, its achronological ordering—when Brave Orchid declares, "That's what Chinese say. We like to say the opposite," and the naive narrator inserts "It seemed to hurt her to tell me that" (237), readers need to step back and reconstruct an appropriate context for the exchange. We must realize that we are not witnessing a cultural clash; actually, *both* mother and daughter are Chinese Americans who share a common culture—though of two successive generations—in America. Brave Orchid calls herself Chinese when she wishes to rationalize her behavior. The evasiveness which both the narrator and her mother attribute to the Chinese, as if it were a racial characteristic, is easily explained within the context of Chinese American history. Even the protagonist's grudge against the "emigrant villagers" must be viewed in the appropriate context.

The misogynistic sayings which are repeated throughout the text must be understood in relation to the Chinese bachelor society in America. As a result of the Chinese Exclusion Act of 1882, Chinese women were extremely scarce for several generations in this country. Immigration laws toward the Chinese became somewhat more liberal only with the advent of World War II. This historical fact might have contributed to a brand of male defensiveness (a solidified posture against female encroachment) which is unique to the Chinese American experience. In other words, negative male attitudes toward women—at least as the protagonist experiences them—are partially American-made and, as such, cannot be attributed to the Chinese without locating them in their specific social and historical contexts.

Why is *Woman Warrior* so ambiguous in both its rhetoric and ideology? Some critics attribute the work's ambiguity to Kingston's "bicultural" background.[5] Not all ethnic texts employ ambiguous narrative strategies, however. For Kingston, ambiguity is a conscious choice which has little to do with bridging cultures. In various interviews, she comments on the need to play literary tricks in "nonfictional" works. On a pragmatic level, she wanted to protect her subjects from immigration officers and police; "but what happened," she admits, "was that this need for secrecy affected my form and my style" ("This" 10–11). In other words, ambiguity was necessary as a "cover." A second consideration has to do with the attempt to capture oral culture on the printed page.

As an ethnic female writer, Kingston aligns herself with the Chinese oral tradition of storytelling or talk-story.[6] "Oral stories change from telling to telling," she points out. The written word, on the other hand, is static and finite. "That really bothers me, because what would be wonderful would be for the words to change on the page every time, but they can't. The way I tried to solve this problem was to keep ambiguity in the writing all the time" ("Maxine" 18). This structural ambiguity allows us to *experience* Brave Orchid's changing the story with each telling.

Walter Ong argues that there is no such thing as "oral literature," because "you can never divest the term 'literature' of its association with writing. This association inevitably deforms the study of oral performance" (146). Ong warns us against the habit of viewing oral performance as literature *manqué*. Since Kingston is, above all, a writer, can she be placed in Ong's category of offenders? As she views it, the vitality of her ethnic heritage resides in oral storytelling. The ability to talk-story is equated in both *Woman Warrior* and *China Men* with communal survival and affirmation: it gives talkers like Brave Orchid "great power" (*Woman* 24). For Kingston, to claim her cultural status, the ethnic female writer must make words "change on the page" in the manner of oral performances. Thus *Woman Warrior*, a work which is literary in many respects, thematically privileges orality. Here ambiguity is the creative compromise of a literate mind conveying the improvisational immediacy of oral culture.

By maintaining fluidity throughout the text, Kingston assumes a nonparadigmatic stance and challenges the frequently monolithic Western tradition. In *Woman Warrior*, fluidity between immature and mature perceptions is maintained through two narrative voices: one child, the other adult. "You lie with stories," the child screams at her mother. "I can't tell what's real and what you make up" (235). This accusation suggests that the young protagonist wants certainty in her life. The narrative's conscious, forward thrust seeks clarity—a release from confusing stories and nightmares. This seemingly clear position is undercut, however, by an adult narrator who admits, analyzes, and condones her own fabrications.

After describing in elaborate detail her aunt Moon Orchid's confrontation with her husband, the narrator comments, "What my brother actually said was..." (189). In other words, the story she just told is her own creation. Her next concession—"His version of the story may be better than mine because of its bareness, not twisted into designs"—implies that the reader has the right to choose among versions of the text. The adult narrator's own position, however, is clearly conveyed through a parable:

> Long ago in China, knot-makers tied string into buttons and frogs, and rope into bell pulls. There was one knot so complicated that it blinded the knot-maker. Finally an emperor outlawed this cruel knot, and the nobles could not order it anymore. If I had lived in China, I would have been an outlaw knot-maker. (190)

Why would she have been an outlaw knot-maker? For the mature narrator, simplicity and clarity no longer seem important. Contrary to the "narrator girl's" anxiety about confusing ethnic stories, her unconscious penchant for telling stories "twisted into designs" like complicated knots is now a virtue. The adult protagonist has attained a tolerance for ambiguity.

While presenting herself as an "outlaw," an exile from the Chinese American community in which she grew up, the adult narrator yet seeks a way to return to the fold *on her own terms*. She had to leave, she claims, because she thought that "the Chinese" despised females. Psychologically and spiritually, however, she has not given up her ethnic community. The cycle of departure and return is, as the narrative shows, a new and welcome possibility for ethnic females. Ultimately, women warriors do not ride off into the sunset.

Structurally, each story of the woman warrior—whether of the legendary Fa Mu Lan, the narrator's mother Brave Orchid, or the narrator herself—tests the potential for reconciliation between the individual and her community. The narrator declares, for example, that both she and the legendary swordswoman have "the words at our backs" (63). That is, if she uses her verbal ability to avenge her oppressed ethnic community, might she not also be loved and admired by her people? The parallel between the two "warriors" seems perfect until we realize that Kingston's Fa Mu Lan story is a Chinese American myth and not Chinese history. In the classics, Fa Mu Lan's parents do not carve words of vengeance on their daughter's back.[7] In Chinese culture, the legend serves as an example of a daughter's filiality toward her parents. Kingston's fantasy tale, on the other hand, emphasizes the hazards of crossing gender boundaries: "Chinese executed women who disguised themselves as soldiers or students" (46). Assertion of womanhood—by secretly having a lover and bearing a child in battle—is made a heroic act. These details do not correspond to legendary Chinese heroines who fulfilled the "neuter" role of warriors without strong sexual identification (Rankin 52). Hence, the narrator/author's "'chink' and 'gook' words" (63), as well as Fa Mu Lan's tattoos and male/female assertions, are creative constructs made in America.

Once we realize that the sense of Chinese historical "truth" conveyed in the "White Tigers" section is an illusion, we can question the narrator's next formulation in the same chapter. When she declares, "My American life has been such a disappointment" (54), rather than falling into the bicultural trap of counterpointing "Chinese" heroism against an unheroic "American" life, we might ask: what other life does the narrator have? Since she has never had a Chinese life outside her imagination, the word "American" is meaningless and merely designates "reality." By the same token, when the narrator uses the term "Chinese," the reader needs to substitute "illusion." Because the swordswoman myth is mostly a child's wish-fulfillment, it cannot serve as catalyst for change. The "woman warrior" of the book's title is possibly the trickster's first joke.

Kingston herself has stated that Fa Mu Lan is *her* myth: "But I put ['The White Tigers' chapter] at the beginning to show that the childish myth is past, not the climax we reach for. Also, 'The White Tigers' is not a Chinese myth but one transformed by America, a sort of kung fu movie parody" ("Cultural" 57). Within the text, the mature narrator exhibits the same awareness when she says: "Perhaps I made him up [the retarded man from her childhood], and what I once had was not Chinese-sight at all but child-sight that would have disappeared eventually without such struggle" (239). In a single stroke, all of the naive narrator's insights are dismissed as "child-sight." The titanic struggle between "Chinese" and "American" is now seen as a made-up story. Given this interpretive reversal, what is left?

Portrayals of women in *Woman Warrior* seem to alternate between positive and negative depending on the narrative point of view. Both Fa Mu Lan and Brave Orchid are heroic when the naive narrator describes them, as evidenced in the "White Tigers" and "Shaman" sections. These positive portraits of privileged, exceptional individuals suggest that the warrior image is indeed promoted in the book. When we move to the omniscient narrative of the fourth chapter, however, we find a different view of strong women. Just as we gradually realize that Fa Mu Lan exists only as a fantasy, here we view the "real life" warrior as less than perfect. While the episode between Brave Orchid and her sister Moon Orchid is humorous, it also exposes the destructive side of the rugged individualist. In this chapter, Brave Orchid drives her sister insane. She is culpable, the implied author seems to say, because she cannot empathize with those weaker than herself. This negative judgment is periodically inserted into the text from the third-person point of view: "But Brave Orchid would not relent; her dainty sister would just have to toughen up." There is also intrusive commentary: "She looked at her younger sister whose very wrinkles were fine. 'Forget about a job,' she said, which was very lenient of her" (147).

Even though the text embeds the negative aspects of heroic women such as Fa Mu Lan and Brave Orchid, it also includes an alternative community of women with whom the narrator is identified. In the Fa Mu Lan story, "cowering, whimpering women" on "little bound feet" later form a mercenary army of swordswomen called "witch amazons" (53). While these women are described contemptuously from Fa Mu Lan's point of view ("They blinked weakly at me like pheasants that have been raised in the dark for soft meat"), they also present a vivid image of the downtrodden who ultimately prevail. Throughout the text, a string of oppressed, misunderstood women—including the no-name aunt, the witch amazons, Moon Orchid, the quiet girl, various crazy ladies, and the narrator herself with her "bad, small-person's voice that makes no impact" (57)—counterbalances the superwomen. The protagonist waivers between the weak and the strong, as she does between her outlaw status and her ties to the ethnic community. Her fear of insanity causes her publicly to denounce the rejects, the "Crazy Marys" and "retards," of society. On the other hand, she is closely identified with them in the text—she asks her sister, "do you talk to people that aren't real inside your mind?" (221)—and, in contrast to Brave Orchid, exhibits a deep understanding for this segment of society.

Halfway through *Woman Warrior*, the adult narrator returns home for a visit. The familiar tug-of-war between mother and daughter resumes until the daughter confronts her overpowering mother with the confession, "when I'm away from here, I don't get sick" and Brave Orchid responds with "It's better, then, for you to stay away....You can come for visits" (127). Then the mother calls her daughter "Little Dog," a term of endearment. In this crucial scene, not only does a mother learn to let go of her child, but the two women establish grounds for mutual respect. This hint of reconciliation is extended to the book's symbolic ending. The final story is a collaboration between her mother and herself, the adult narrator informs us. Rather than the usual vying over which version of a story is "truer," we now have two storytellers enjoying equal time without, as Sidonie Smith puts it, "the privileging of one before the other" (172). This final juxtaposition suggests the recognition and acceptance of human diversity, mutual respect, and communal sharing.

As an ethnic woman writer, Kingston employs the narrative strategies of a "trickster" to tell her tale. This approach allows her to explore a naive narrator's ambivalence toward her mother's confusing stories without equating the narrator's viewpoint with her own. If we recognize that *Woman Warrior* is a complex work of art and not a social document, we might begin to appreciate Kingston's attempt to make words "change on the page."

NOTES

1. Oscar Wilde once said, "Give a man a mask and he'll tell you the truth." Kingston could have published *Woman Warrior* under the mask of fiction in order to protect the truth she tells. However, her eth-

nicity and gender complicate the issue. Would her first work be taken as seriously if it were advertised as fiction? In effect, Kingston uses a fictional technique—the mask—in a nonfictional genre to tell the truth of her ethnic female experience. This strategy of expedience must be linked with audience expectations in a racist and sexist society.

2. In *China Men*, the narrator's ancestors find ingenious ways to combat this deprivation while working as laborers in mines and on railroads: they sing, recite poetry, and shout into empty spaces.

3. *China Men* lists immigration laws for eight straight pages as a frustrated response to this ignorance.

4. Kingston makes a point of not intruding and making connections of which her narrator is incapable. A child growing up in a multiethnic urban environment, for example, is bound to sort by color—if not by gender and class. The protagonist stresses the "Chinese" stories through the same lens: as that aspect of her reality which best captures her vivid imagination.

5. For example, according to Blinde, "It is as if the richness of a bicultural life experience cannot be contained within the limits of literary dictates and that a 'spill-over' from one form to another is the only justice that can be done in the rendition of such a life" (53).

6. Kingston picked up the term "talk-story" in Hawaii, where it has become common usage.

7. Historically, it was a male warrior, General Yueh Fei, who had his back tattooed (Lightfoot 65 n.2).

WORKS CITED

Blinde, Patricia Lin. "The Icicle in the Desert: Perspective and Form in the Works of Two Chinese-American Women Writers." *MELUS* 6.3 (1979): 51–71.

Doherty, Thomas P. "American Autobiography and Ideology." *The American Autobiography: A Collection of Critical Essays.* Ed. Albert E. Stone. Englewood Cliffs: Prentice Hall, 1981. 95–108.

Ellison, Ralph. *Shadow and Act.* 1953. New York: New American Library, 1966.

Gates, Henry Louis, Jr. *Figures in Black: Words, Signs, and the "Racial" Self.* New York: Oxford UP, 1987.

Hornstein, Lillian H., et al., eds. *The Reader's Companion to World Literature*. 2nd ed. New York: New American Library, 1973.

Kim, Elaine H. Preface. *Asian American Literature: An Introduction to the Writings and Their Social Context*. Philadelphia: Temple UP, 1982. xi–xix.

Kingston, Maxine Hong. *China Men*. New York: Ballantine, 1977.

———. "Cultural Mis-readings by American Reviewers." *Asian and Western Writers in Dialogue: New Cultural Identities*. Ed. Guy Amirthanayagam. London: Macmillan, 1982. 55–65.

———. "Maxine Hong Kingston." By Arturo Islas. *Women Writers of the West Coast: Speaking of Their Lives and Careers*. Ed. Marilyn Yalom. Santa Barbara: Capra, 1983. 11–20.

———. "Talk With Mrs. Kingston." By Timothy Pfaff. *New York Times Book Review* 18 June 1980: 1, 25–26.

———. "This is the Story I Heard: A Conversation with Maxine Hong Kingston and Earll Kingston." By Phyllis Hoge Thompson. *Biography* 6.1 (1983): 1–12.

———. *The Woman Warrior: Memoirs of a Girlhood Among Ghosts*. New York: Vintage, 1977.

Lightfoot, Marjorie. "Hunting the Dragon in Kingston's *The Woman Warrior*." *MELUS* 13.3–4 (1986): 55–66.

Nee, Dale Yu. "See, Culture is Made, Not Born…" *Bridge, An Asian-American Perspective* 3.6 (1975): 42–48.

Newman, Katharine. "Hawaiian-American Literature Today: The Cultivation of Mangoes." *MELUS* 6.2 (1979): 47–77.

Ong, Walter J. "Oral Culture and the Literate Mind." *Minority Language and Literature: Retrospective and Perspective*. Ed. Dexter Fisher. New York: MLA, 1977. 134–49.

Rabine, Leslie W. "No Lost Paradise: Social Gender and Symbolic Gender in the Writings of Maxine Hong Kingston." *Signs* 12.3 (1987): 471–92.

Rankin, Mary Backus. "The Emergence of Women at the End of the Ch'ing." *Women in Chinese Society*. Ed. Margery Wolf and Roxane Witke. Stanford: Stanford UP, 1975. 39–66.

Schor, Naomi. "Fiction as Interpretation/Interpretation as Fiction." *The Reader in the Text: Essays on Audience and Interpretation*. Ed.

Susan R. Suleiman and Inge Crosman. Princeton: Princeton UP, 1980. 165–82.

Smith, Sidonie. *A Poetics of Women's Autobiography: Marginality and the Fictions of Self-Representation.* Bloomington: Indiana UP, 1987.

Ward, John William. "Who Was Benjamin Franklin?" *Retracing the Past: Readings in the History of the American People.* Ed. Gary B. Nash. 2 vols. New York: Harper, 1986. 1: 90–97.

Different Voices:
The Re-Bildung of the Barrio in Sandra Cisneros' The House on Mango Street

Leslie S. Gutiérrez-Jones

I

> The space of a tactic is the space of the other. Thus it must play
> on and with a terrain imposed on it and organized by the law of a
> foreign power.
>
> —de Certeau, *The Practice of Everyday Life*

Dreaming of a day when she might attain the "American dream" of home ownership,[1] the young protagonist of Sandra Cisneros' *The House on Mango Street* promises herself that if that day comes, she will joyfully accommodate "passing bums" in her attic, because she "know[s] how it is to be without a house" (81). Esperanza's lack of a "real house" to call her own repeatedly troubles this child of the barrio; when a nun from her school incredulously identifies the family's tenement lodgings, the little girl's sense of identity is devastated: "you live *there*? The way she said it made me feel like nothing. *There*. I lived *there*. I nodded. I knew then I had to have a house. A real house" (9). The house of the title, which succeeds this apartment, still falls far short of Esperanza's dreams; it still "isn't it," not "a real house"—one with a yard and a fence and "real stairs, not hallway stairs, but stairs inside like the houses on T.V." (8). Excluded from the suburban standard presented through her father's job and through television, Esperanza has available to her only external models—models she can "rent" but never own. Raised amid annual relocations, shared washrooms, and landlord-tenant battles, Esperanza also experiences her rootlessness on the most literal level; the house she searches for, she anxiously insists, must be one she "can point to." Acutely aware of the disempowerment that results from lacking "a home of one's own," she yearns to stake out an architectural space—one which she implicitly assumes will provide her with the "space" to develop a sense of identity and an artistic voice. But when architecture will not cooperate, she must look instead to her imagination in order to create a sense of place—one which can, in turn, provide a place for her writing.

Esperanza must learn to create for herself, and from herself, a "home" which will be truly hers. She finds—or creates—such a space for herself through her art, through the writing which her Aunt Lupe insists will keep her free. Shifting from a literal to a metaphoric register, her "house" becomes not a structure she can point to, but a spiritual sanctuary she carries within: "only a house quiet as snow, a space for myself to go, clean as paper before the poem" (100).[2] During her year on Mango Street, Esperanza does develop a sense of place and identity: by the work's end, she has found peace and purpose in her writing; she has created for herself the "home in the heart" predicted by the local fortuneteller.

Just as Esperanza must leave behind her dependence on rented spaces and on standards external to her own experience, so Cisneros, a Chicana writer, is faced with the challenge of creating a home in the midst of a predominantly white, predominantly male, literary tradition: that of the *Bildungsroman*.[3] Writer and character both face the conflict between desire for self-expression and fear of being co-opted by the very forms of self-expression available. The individual focus of writing, and particularly of the genre of the Bildungsroman, threatens to betray that aspect of identity which most calls out for expression: membership in a community. Only a fierce loyalty to this connection provides an adequate response, for Esperanza as for Cisneros, to the ambivalences generated by individual artistic achievement. Like her protagonist, who insists that the house of her own *cannot* be "a man's house"—especially "not a daddy's" (100)—Cisneros must insistently remake the conventions and formulas of a patriarchal individualistic tradition, using them in order to transform them, tactically appropriating them in order to make them her own...and, by extension, her community's.

One model for understanding what is at stake in such an appropriation may be found in Michel de Certeau's analysis of the creative art forms of the disempowered, the "subtle, stubborn, resistant activity of groups, which, since they lack their own space, have to get along in a network of already established forces and relationships" (18). For the marginalized writer, the "already established forces and relationships" are represented by the literary tradition of the dominant culture: the genre definitions, the intertextual "lineage," the theoretical frameworks, and the like. Such products of hegemonic culture are ubiquitous, and contact with them virtually inescapable; any writer, then, becomes a "consumer" of sorts. But consumption for de Certeau may become a form of production: creativity may thus be expressed in the Chicana writer's "ways of using," in her "innumerable and infinite small transformations of and within the dominant cultural economy in order to adapt it to [her] own interests and [her] own rules" (xii–xiii). Cisneros, in de Certeau's terms, "poaches" upon the supposedly private reserve of the white male Anglo-European literary tradition, moving like a nomad "across fields she did not write" (174). Like Esperanza, she can neither purchase nor inherit a "ready-made" structure to call home, but instead creates from within a new space, a home in the heart where her fellow transients are welcome.

II

> We advanced none to the rank of Masters but such as clearly
> felt and recognized the purpose they were born for, and had got
> enough of practice to proceed along their way with a certain
> cheerfulness and ease.
>   —Goethe, *Wilhelm Meister's Apprenticeship*

As a ready-made structure for a Chicana writer to inhabit, the Bildungsroman poses some serious problems, and so we should examine the literary territory Cisneros would occupy. On the most basic level, the controversy that surrounds any attempt to define this genre leaves the location of its "walls" quite uncertain.[4] Among scholars of English literature, Jerome Buckley's *Season of Youth* remains the most popular touchstone for revision and debate; but perhaps Randolf Shaffner's study of the apprenticeship novel, which follows Buckley's analysis, illuminates most clearly the strain that would be involved in simply "inserting" a Chicana protagonist into Buckley's master plot.[5] Shaffner begins his study with an explicit statement equating his use of the terms "Bildungsroman" and "apprenticeship novel"—an equation reinforced by his title. The concept of apprenticeship, however, by suggesting its senior counterpart, makes explicit the goals of normative—white, male—"development"; two items on Shaffner's "checklist" of the genre's distinguishing traits make glaringly apparent his model's essential incompatibility with Cisneros' project. According to Shaffner, the *Bildungsroman* presupposes "the belief that a young person can become adept in the art of life *and become a master*," as well as "the prerequisite of *potential for development into a master*" (18, emphasis mine). In Goethe's terms, he must be able to recognize the purpose he was born for. Esperanza may achieve a certain level of control over her life and art, even a certain (heavily circumscribed) sense of power and potential—but the society which constructs and sanctions the identity of "master" will nevertheless deny her this title based on her status as a Chicana. The issue of potentiality (and its corollary, another of Shaffner's presuppositions: "the key notion of choice") sets up the major tension for a female Bildungsroman: if *bildung* is the tradition whereby the "young male hero discovers himself and his social role" (Labovitz 2), and if the sanctioned social role of women still precludes a true search for, or discovery of, an individual "self," how can this young *female* hero hope to experience a counterpart to bildung?[6]

When Esther Labovitz tackles the problematic issue of defining a female Bildungsroman, she astutely identifies a number of the changes such a hybrid would entail, especially concerning distinctions between male and female parameters of rebellion; yet she assumes that the female Bildungsroman evolved naturally during the twentieth century in response to women's improved social conditions, developing belatedly as "cultural and social structures appeared to support women's struggle for independence" (70). The degree to which the "cultural and social structures" cited by Labovitz as supporting women's independence are, in fact, in place for women of color (or more generally for women marginalized and oppressed on account of race, ethnicity, sexual orientation, or socioeconomic class) seems questionable; but, more critically, her analysis of the female Bildungsroman suggests a trajectory which would (and supposedly *should*) parallel the male version, presumably "catching up" at the projected point at which women's independence gains full social support: the point at which a young woman's rebelliousness, like a young man's, could be relegated to a simple and temporary "stage" preceding "mature" acceptance of the established social order. But while the Bildungsroman of a white western bourgeois male—or even, theoretically, of a "liberated" white western bourgeois female—might appropriately provide a dénouement stressing the achievement of "a proper balance between internal individual development and external submissions to group regulations" (O'Neale 26), such a resolution would likely undercut the social critique of a politically self-conscious writer, or protagonist, of color.[7]

Cisneros' narrator does finally achieve a sense of calm resolution, but it is not the resolution of surrender or acceptance; rather, Esperanza insists with quiet determination that she has "gone away to come back" (102). She has left behind her selfish desire to escape, alone, from the barrio of Mango Street, not to return "until somebody makes it better." Realizing "Who's going to do it? The mayor? (99)," Esperanza commits herself to changing, not accepting, the established order—to becoming that somebody who is emphatically not the mayor and who will indeed try to make it better. Esperanza's final determination to return to Mango Street "for the ones [she] left behind. For the ones who cannot [get] out" (102) reflects a crucial point of difference from the sacred ground of the literary genre upon which Cisneros is poaching.

This shift from an individual to a communal perspective marks a significant turn upon the highly individualistic tradition Cisneros would "homestead." The Bildungsroman's emphasis on the individual reverberates with ethnocentric assumptions and political implications, as Susan Stanford Friedman notes, along with other feminist and cultural critics:

> Isolate individualism is an illusion. It is also the privilege of
> power. A white man has the luxury of forgetting his skin color
> and sex. He can think of himself as an "individual." Women
> and minorities, reminded at every turn in the great cultural
> hall of mirrors of their sex or color, have no such luxury. (39)

A strong focus on the autonomous subject (exemplified by Bildungsromane such as Joyce's *A Portrait of the Artist as a Young
Man*) would betray Cisneros' political ideology in writing the
life of a sexually, ethnically, and economically marginalized protagonist like Esperanza. As Esperanza's culture and experience
little resembles Stephen Dedalus', so Cisneros' rendering of her
narrative must distance itself from Joyce's; the Bildungsroman's
privileging of the individual must not negate Esperanza's, and
Cisneros', commitment to the community.

As narrator, Esperanza creates and chronicles her developing identity not through self-absorbed introspection, but by noting, recording, and responding to the lives around her—those
lives for whom almost half of the collection's forty-four "prose
poems" are named, and whose significance is underscored by
Cisneros' title, which situates Esperanza not as a solitary loner
but as she comes to perceive herself: a product and member of a
particular community. Immune to the "privilege of power" associated with glorifying the individual, Esperanza comes to understand that the three strange sisters, and her friend Alicia, are
right: Mango may say "goodbye *sometimes*," but even when set
free from the physical locale, Esperanza "will *always* be Mango
Street" (101, 98, my emphases). Protagonists like Cisneros' might
be outsiders vis à vis the dominant culture, yet they are emphatically not loners. Unlike the traditional "American"[8] hero, who
underscores his independence by isolating himself on the high
seas (Captain Ahab), in the wilderness (Thoreau), in the "territories" (Huck Finn), or on the road (Jack Kerouac), Cisneros' hero
has no such choice. Esperanza has already been symbolically
cast out of mainstream "American" suburbia; her status as outsider is not chosen, but imposed. Yet she does not react to her
exteriority by perceiving herself as "alone against the world."
Rather, Esperanza defines herself as a member of a community—
the community that is Mango Street.

III

Let one forget his reason for being, they'd all droop like tulips
in a glass, each with their arms around the other. Keep, keep,
keep, trees say when I sleep. They teach.
                    —Sandra Cisneros, *The House on Mango Street*

The reconceptualization of identity and individual development found in Cisneros' work radically transforms both the Bildungsroman and the standard wisdom of developmental psychology. Carol Gilligan takes issue with the traditional
"developmental litany" which "intones the celebration of separation, autonomy, individuation, and natural rights" (23). Gilligan cites Nancy Chodorow's claim for differences between
female and male identity formation based on the child's recognition of similarity to (female) or difference from (male) the primary caretaker—most often maternal in our society—in order
to examine both its empirical effects and its theoretical implications. Criticizing conventional notions that reduce development
to a simple linear ordering based on separation, Gilligan instead
envisions separation and attachment as a "reiterative counter-
point in human experience," recognizing both the "role of separation as it defines and empowers the self" and "the ongoing
process of attachment that creates and sustains the human community" (156). She sees a mature stage of development as one in
which the individual recognizes her interconnectedness with
the world, achieving a balance between responsibility to herself
and responsibility to others (155).

Cisneros' Esperanza explores the difficulties—and the possibilities—inherent in the struggle for such a balance, as she
learns that neither self nor community can sustain itself independently; each requires the other. For example, when she
senses the difficulty of reconciling "femininity" with conventional notions of adulthood, she determines "not to grow up
tame like the others" and instead practices her "own quiet war,"
"leav[ing] the table *like a man*, without putting back the chair or
picking up the plate" (82, emphasis mine). But this strategy of
male emulation only shifts the burden to her mother (whose
sacrifices are described in the segment which immediately fol-

lows), and casts herself into the role of the "bad" woman, the villainess in the movies "with red red lips who is beautiful and cruel." Esperanza admires the selfishness of this woman whose "power is her own. She will not give it away," yet when she tries to envision such an identity for herself, the callousness of such power brings her to an abrupt—and disturbing—realization (82). When "the three sisters"—her friends' *comadres*, whose eerie clairvoyance suggests both the Fates and Macbeth's witches—order her to make a wish, she complies, thinking "Well, why not?" But when she is immediately reprimanded, "When you leave you must remember to come back for the others," she feels chastised and guilty: "Then I didn't know what to say. It was as if she could read my mind, as if she knew what I had wished for, and I felt ashamed for having made such a selfish wish" (97).

The sisters recognize that Esperanza is "special," that "she'll go very far," and that she does therefore have a responsibility to herself and her talent, a responsibility which will necessitate her packing her "bags of books and paper." Esperanza likewise realizes the implications of her talents, acknowledging in her final vignette that she will indeed go far: "one day I will say goodbye to Mango. I am too strong for her to keep me here forever" (101). And yet her power and freedom are both circumscribed and expanded through being shared. She will never be like the "tame" women "who lay their necks on the threshold waiting for the ball and chain" (82); but neither will she be like Stephen Dedalus, who sees his art as a function of his own autonomy, necessitating his abandonment of home, fatherland, and church.[9] Esperanza senses her ongoing responsibility: not toward the centers of (relative) power, the fathers and husbands who contribute to the oppression of Mango Street's women by demanding obedience and docility, but toward those to whom Cisneros has dedicated the work: "*A las Mujeres*." Her loyalty is toward the less powerful, the less strong, the less articulate in the dominant language: toward those, the sisters remind her, "who cannot leave as easily as you." Although she recognizes in her closing statement that her achievements might be misunderstood by friends and neighbors, she reassures herself that all will be rectified: "They will not know I have gone away to come back. For the ones I left behind. For the ones who cannot get out" (102). By the end of her narrative, then, Esperanza attains the balanced maturity described by Gilligan.

In order to reach this resolution, Esperanza must juggle her conflicting feelings toward suburban havens ("Sally" versus "Those Who Don't"); toward the onset of sexuality ("Sire" versus "Red Clowns"); toward marriage ("Marin" versus "Linoleum Roses"); and toward fathers ("Papa Who Wakes Up Tired in the Dark" versus "What Sally Said"). Throughout these struggles Esperanza continues to value connectedness; for example, although she first describes her younger sister Nenny as a burden ("Since she comes after me, she is my responsibility" [11]), Nenny provokes more loyalty than resentment. When Nenny reveals her childish ignorance about the mystery of women's hips, Esperanza stubbornly stands by her:

> If you don't get them you may turn into a man. Nenny says this and she believes it. She is this way because of her age.
>
> That's right, I add before Lucy or Rachel can make fun of her. She is stupid alright, but she *is* my sister. (47)

Putting her critical judgments aside, Esperanza asserts her familial loyalty above all. Similarly, her thoughts of her parents are filled not with the hostility and resentment of a sullen adolescent, but with tenderness and gratitude for the emotional security they provide:

> my mother's hair...sweet to put your nose into when she is holding you, holding you and you feel safe, is the warm smell of bread before you bake it, is the smell when she makes a little room for you on her side of the bed still warm with her skin, and you sleep near her, the rain outside falling and Papa snoring. The snoring, the rain, and mama's hair that smells like bread. (10)

Likewise, she does her best to return such comfort, as she later sympathizes with her grieving father:

> my brave Papa cries. I have never seen my Papa cry and don't know what to do....
>
> And I think if my own Papa died what would I do. I hold my Papa in my arms. I hold and hold and hold him. (53)

The continuity between generations will remain unbroken; as her father weeps for the loss of his parent, Esperanza recognizes that some day she will in turn grieve his death—and will herself need to be held and held and held.

Esperanza's compassion extends beyond these ties to her immediate family, to the many abused or abandoned wives of Mango Street: to Rosa Vargas, "who is tired all the time from buttoning and bottling and babying and who cries every day for the man who left without even leaving a dollar for bologna or a note explaining how come" (30), to Rafaela and Sally, whose husbands jealously lock them away (76), to Minerva, with whom Esperanza shares her poems (80). Her intuitive understanding of other, younger women—women closer to her own age—is especially striking, as she attains a sort of omniscience born of empathy:

> Marin, under the streetlight, dancing by herself, is singing the same song somewhere. I know. Is waiting for a car to stop, a star to fall, someone to change her life. Anybody. (28).

> Sally, do you sometimes wish you didn't have to go home?... You could close your eyes and you wouldn't have to worry about what people said because you never belonged here anyway and nobody could make you sad and nobody would think you're strange because you like to dream and dream...when all you wanted, all you wanted, Sally, was to love and to love and to love and to love and no one could call that crazy. (78–79).

In such passages Esperanza's usually simple prose style reaches a lyrical intensity, as she gives voice to the longing for love and striving after dreams which breeds loneliness—and the seeds of dependency ("someone to change her life")—in these young women. In particular, Esperanza grasps Sally's unhappiness, and shares with her the anguish of a home that can never fulfill that term's promise—a home which is not her own, a home where she "never belonged...anyway."

Esperanza bonds with Marin and Sally over the sort of fantasies in which many residents of this barrio indulge; yet even more pervasive on Mango Street, when such escapism fails, is the sense of exclusion. Esperanza feels strongly for all her neighbors who "don't belong": the unhappy Mamacita who speaks no English (74), the eccentric Ruthie who "laughs all by herself" (64), Esperanza's own Aunt Lupe "sick from the disease that would not go" (54), and others. Through her sympathy for these individuals' plights, Esperanza comes to understand the nature of xenophobia, sexism, and bigotry—the fear of difference which excludes, and even ridicules, Mamacita, Ruthie, and Lupe, not for who they are but for how they look and how they speak. Esperanza has herself participated in such injustice, as when she joins her friends in mocking Lupe's infirmity. This cruelty, generated spontaneously from the obliviousness of a childhood game, is unintentional; Esperanza's simple defense is "We didn't know. She had been dying such a long time we forgot." But when her aunt does finally die, the girls take on responsibility for her death, and Esperanza unsparingly shoulders her share of the burden for their communal guilt:

> Most likely I will go to hell and most likely I deserve to be there. My mother says I was born on an evil day and prays for me. Lucy and Rachel pray too. For ourselves and for each other...because of what we did to Aunt Lupe. (54)

Such painful experiences with "difference" elucidate Esperanza's encounters with racial prejudice: with misunderstanding and fear born of ignorance, and with the phenomenon of not belonging.

> Those who don't know any better come into our neighborhood scared. They think we're dangerous....They are stupid people who are lost and got here by mistake.
> But we aren't afraid....
> All brown all around, we are safe. But watch us drive into a neighborhood of another color and our knees go shakity-shake and our car windows get rolled up tight and our eyes look straight. Yeah. That is how it goes and goes. (29)

Esperanza does not learn such lessons as an isolate individual, but rather shares them (as do the weird sisters), as part of a group: as one of three girlhood friends, in the case of mocking Lupe, or as part of a general "we" of Mango Street, in the case of "Those Who Don't." Her budding feminism, like this sensitivity to the dynamics of exclusion, is also gained through interaction and involvement with others. She recognizes the dangers of her gender and refuses the threatened "ball and chain" partly in response to the experiences and warnings of others (for example, her mother in "A Smart Cookie") and partly in response to her own experiences with harassment and abuse, the majority of which either occur in the company of her friends ("The Family of Little Feet"), or result from a betrayal by more "sophisticated" classmates like Sally ("The Monkey Garden" and "Red Clowns"). Bearing out Gilligan's assertions, Esperanza does not experience—or narrate—the harsh lessons of growing up as an autonomous, self-absorbed individual, but as a sensitive and involved member of a community.

This more interactive model for development—what Gilligan refers to as a privileging of "identity as relationship"—may yet precipitate its own anxieties and ambivalences, especially in earlier stages of development, when, according to Gilligan, the sense of responsibility to others may overwhelm a sense of responsibility to oneself. At this stage Gilligan notes the emergence of a pattern of fears based on the "danger" of individual success. While an individual who privileges separation will experience relations with others in terms of a hierarchy, characters like Esperanza, who privilege attachment, may perceive her interaction with others in terms of a "web." These two metaphors imply contrasting goals (respectively, moving up versus staying centered) and contrasting dangers (entrapment born of intimacy versus isolation born of achievement). Rather than the more typically "male"[10] anxiety—"the wish to be alone at the top and the consequent fear that others will get too close"—Esperanza must come to terms with "the wish to be at the center of connection and the consequent fear of being too far out on the edge" (Gilligan 61). By determinedly marching away, yet with equal determination promising a return and reconciliation, Esperanza achieves a sense of balance between her own needs and the needs of her community—to the benefit of both.

IV

> "Something" *different* speaks again and presents itself to the masters in the various forms of non-labor—the savage, the madman, the child, even woman.
> —Michel de Certeau, *The Practice of Everyday Life*

Esperanza's narrative itself attains a similar balance between her needs and the community's. Just as she can understand and express the "voices" of silenced women like Marin and Sally, so too she "knows" and conveys experiences such as those of the anonymous hit-and-run victim, "Geraldo No Last Name." Geraldo died without having met Esperanza (she hears only the barest outlines of the episode, through her friend), and lived a life quite removed from her own, as a non-English-speaking (probably undocumented) immigrant. Yet she intuitively grasps—and communicates—aspects of his life otherwise closed off to acquaintances, doctors, police, and even his own family:

> They never saw the kitchenettes. They never knew about the two-room flats and sleeping rooms he rented, the weekly money orders sent home, the currency exchange. How could they?
>
> His name was Geraldo. And his home is in another country. The ones he left behind are far away. They will wonder. Shrug. Remember. Geraldo. He went north...we never heard from him again. (63)

Esperanza speaks for the excluded, in de Certeau's terms "the various forms of non-labor": the sickly, the deranged, the abused, the anonymous dead and the disempowered; the simple poetry of her prose gives voice to the "cries of the People excluded from the written" (158). She expresses herself as an artist by expressing the struggles of others, establishing her own identity as she conveys the identity of her neighborhood.

Yet even with such a noble project, valorizing the lives of those not generally considered worthy of literary attention, Esperanza is still faced with the potentially alienating effects of artistic achievement: the more her identity becomes that of "the writer," the less she will be an ordinary member of her own community. As an intellectual and artistic enterprise, writing confers upon the writer a certain power: a certain autonomy, control, and *author*ity which is likely to distance the writer from her own *dis*empowered community. De Certeau conveys just such a problematic when he associates the origins of written culture with the privileging of the autonomous individual, with the "mastery" of a hegemonic culture based on rationality, industry, and economic production (154–61). Powerless and placeless, the nonelite consumers of this master culture function as the oral disruption, the voices upon whose existence *and exclusion* the production of writing depends.

Esperanza (and, by extension, Cisneros) undercuts this alienating *authority*, evading its threatened division from the community by expressing herself and her subjects in prose which eschews the conventions of formal literary language. The simple, childlike poetry of *Mango Street* does *not* stifle "the cries of the People excluded from the written" to provide a monologic narrative or an omnipotent narrator; rather, Esperanza gives expression to "a kind of speech" which emerges as "what 'escapes' from the domination of a sociocultural economy" (de Certeau 158), from the tyranny of the written word. With the informal eloquence of a storyteller, she captures rhythms of speech and dynamics of conversation, conveying the oral element(s) of the barrio's voice(s). Quotation and explication are interwoven smoothly, with no quotation marks to isolate and contain other voices; for example, her own and her mother's voices are allowed to flow and alternate without interruption:

> Today while cooking oatmeal she is Madame Butterfly until she sighs and points the wooden spoon at me. I could've been somebody, you know? Esperanza, you go to school. Study hard. That Madame Butterfly was a fool. She stirs the oatmeal. Look at my *comadres*. She means Izaura whose husband left and Yolanda whose husband is dead. Got to take care all your own, she says shaking her head. (83)

Similarly, free indirect discourse conveys the distressed and disjointed rhythms of Marin's narrative, even when Esperanza's retelling of it shifts pronouns into the third person.

> And how was she to know she'd be the last one to see him alive. An accident, don't you know....And he was just someone she danced with. Somebody she met that night. That's right.
> That's the story. That's what she said again and again. Once to the hospital people and twice to the police. (62)

At times Esperanza's narrative voice drops out altogether and she is heard faintly (even lost) among a chaotic chorus of children's voices, as in the segment made up entirely of dialogue (or multiple monologue) entitled "And Some More":

> There's that wide puffy cloud that looks like your face when you wake up after falling asleep with all your clothes on.

Reynaldo, Angelo, Albert, Armando, Mario...
Not my face. Looks like your fat face.
Rita, Margie, Ernie...
Whose fat face?
Esperanza's fat face, that's who. Looks like Esperanza's
ugly face when she comes to school in the morning. (35)

Such a blending of competing voices would elicit anxiety
and resentment from a narrator like Stephen Dedalus, but for
Esperanza this cacophony produces only light-hearted (and
self-critical) humor, as Nenny's catalogue of cloud names finally
intersects—and comments on—the bickering of the group:

Your ugly mama's toes.
That's stupid.
Bebe, Blanca, Benny...
Who's stupid?
Rachel, Lucy, Esperanza, and Nenny. (36)

The competing voices eventually blend to produce a sort of harmony—even a simple wry wisdom—in a way that a monologic
narrative would not allow. Such rhetorical instances mark yet
another aspect of Esperanza's unique development toward an
artistic voice and a sense of self which would achieve an ongoing balance between connection and separation. Esperanza does
not need either to indulge in self-imposed exile nor to inhabit
externally-imposed, rented spaces that can never be her own;
instead she creates a true home—a home in the heart—by
absorbing and embracing the voices of her community.

The House on Mango Street, then, despite its apparently "sin-
gle" narrator, expresses the multiplicity of focus found in many
recent works of fiction by women: Alice Munro's *The Lives of
Girls and Women*, Gloria Naylor's *The Women of Brewster Place*,
Joan Chase's *During the Reign of the Queen of Persia*, Louise
Erdrich's *Love Medicine*, Nicholasa Mohr's *Rituals of Survival*,
Alison Lurie's *Only Children*, and Amy Tan's *The Joy Luck Club*.
Telling a communal story diffuses the problematic ideology of
individualism, and allows female writers the opportunity to
explore (and potentially to resolve) tensions between group
involvement and individual autonomy—tensions that cannot
be addressed within a literary tradition glorifying a single protagonist. The genre of the Bildungsroman, then, provides a par-

ticularly treacherous, yet particularly rewarding, ground for Cisneros' "poaching." As the young Esperanza must create an identity for herself in a fictional world which denies selfhood to members of her sex, her class, and her ethnic group, Cisneros must create her own space, and assert her own voice, within a culture not historically open to her; her tactic of poaching upon the Bildungsroman provides an opportunity, as it were, to renovate and remodel the rented cultural space of this patriarchal genre, in order to make it her own.

NOTES

1. McCracken astutely justifies the apparent "selfishness" of Esperanza's material ambition as "not a sign of individualistic acquisitiveness but rather represent[ative of] a basic human need." Her overall argument provides an important corollary to my own, placing many issues I discuss into the larger context of Cisneros' reception history.

2. Interestingly, de Certeau's term *"propre"* undergoes a dual translation in Esperanza's narrative: her wished-for "proper" place is to be both "clean" (as paper) and "her own."

3. More specifically, since Esperanza is also the artist of the work she narrates, *Mango Street* would belong to a subset of Bildungsromane, that of the Künstlerroman.

4. The term's breadth of meaning is a source of ongoing debate between critics in German and English literature. For the former, see *Michigan Germanic Studies'* special issue, especially the foreword by guest editor Amrine. I draw upon the broader sense of the term, as used by scholars of English literature. I would note that the lack of any consensus definition may have its advantages; to press my analogy, such "floating" walls might lend themselves well to "remodeling."

5. For a summary of this "master plot," see Buckley 17–18.

6. Beddow's argument for a broader definition of the genre at first seems to alleviate this gender bias; he attempts to shift critical work on the Bildungsroman away from a focus on individual development, claiming that such themes operate within the genre not as ends in themselves, but to "offer insights into human nature." But his proposed alternative genre title, *"Humanitätsroman,"* betrays its gender bias when he slides quickly from the more neutral "nature of humanity" to the (not so) universal masculine, "vision of man" (5–6).

7. O'Neale rightfully insists that the conventional Bildungsroman resolution, in which the hero abandons adolescent rebellion upon recognizing the "validity in the established order," would be a "repudiation of historic ethnic aspiration in this country." "To allow a character to surrender to dominant group mores which exclude his [sic] humanity or to validate an established order that wants to destroy him [sic]," O'Neale asserts, "has never been the choice for protagonists within the protest canon" (26).

8. I use the term "American" as per standard academic usage, to designate canonical literature of the United States, but distance myself from such usage with quotation marks since in actuality the United States constitutes only a single aspect of the culture of the Americas, and the canon only one aspect of United States literature.

9. "I will tell you what I will do and what I will not do. I will not serve that in which I no longer believe whether it call itself my home, my fatherland or my church: and I will try to express myself in some mode of life or art as freely as I can and as wholly as I can, using for my defense the only arms I allow myself to use—silence, exile, and cunning" (Joyce 246–47).

10. I use quotation marks here to distinguish abstract categories from biological givens. Gilligan stresses that hers is not an essentialist model, that her distinctions between these two "voices" are characterized by theme rather than gender. Her association of different voices with women or with men is an empirical observation (presumably brought about by traditional gender-based child-rearing roles) and is not to be interpreted as necessary or absolute.

WORKS CITED

Amrine, Frederick, ed. *Michigan Germanic Studies* 13.2 (1987).

Beddow, Michael. *The Fiction of Humanity: Studies in the Bildungsroman from Wieland to Thomas Mann.* Cambridge: Cambridge UP, 1982.

Buckley, Jerome. *Season of Youth: The Bildungsroman from Dickens to Golding.* Cambridge: Harvard UP, 1974.

Chase, Joan. *During the Reign of the Queen of Persia.* New York: Ballantine, 1983.

Chodorow, Nancy. *The Reproduction of Mothering.* Berkeley: U of California P, 1978.

Cisneros, Sandra. *The House on Mango Street*. Houston: Arte Público, 1986.

De Certeau, Michel. *The Practice of Everyday Life*. Trans. Steven Rendall. Berkeley: U of California P. 1984.

Erdrich, Louise. *Love Medicine*. New York: Bantam, 1984.

Friedman, Susan Stanford. "Women's Autobiographical Selves: Theory and Practice." *The Private Self: Theory and Practice of Women's Autobiographical Writings*. Ed. Shari Benstock. Chapel Hill: U of North Carolina P, 1988. 34–62.

Gilligan, Carol. *In a Different Voice: Psychological Theory and Women's Development*. Cambridge: Harvard UP, 1982.

Joyce, James. *A Portrait of the Artist as a Young Man*. Ed. Chester G. Anderson. New York: Penguin, 1968.

Labovitz, Esther Kleinbord. *The Myth of the Heroine: The Female Bildungsroman in the Twentieth Century*. New York: Peter Lang, 1986.

Lurie, Alison. *Only Children*. New York: Avon, 1988.

McCracken, Ellen. "Sandra Cisneros' *The House on Mango Street*: Community-Oriented Introspection and the Demystification of Patriarchal Violence." *Breaking Boundaries: Latina Writing and Critical Readings*. Ed. Asunción Horno-Delgado et al. Amherst: U of Massachusetts P, 1989. 62–71.

Mohr, Nicholasa. *Rituals of Survival: Woman's Portfolio*. Houston: Arte Público, 1985.

Munro, Alice. *The Lives of Girls and Women*. New York: New American Library, 1983.

Naylor, Gloria. *The Women of Brewster Place*. New York: Penguin, 1983.

O'Neale, Sondra. "Race, Sex, and Self: Aspects of *Bildung* in Select Novels by Black American Women Novelists." *MELUS* 9.4 (1982): 25–37.

Shaffner, Randolf P. *The Apprenticeship Novel: A Study of the Bildungsroman as a Regulative Type in Western Literature with a Focus on Three Classic Representatives by Goethe, Maugham, and Mann*. New York: Peter Lang, 1984.

Tan, Amy. *The Joy Luck Club*. New York: Putnam, 1989.

PART 4

Reading and Writing Empowerment

Ambiguous Benefits: Reading and Writing in Feminist Metafiction

Gayle Greene

I

The publication between 1972 and 1974 of Margaret Drabble's *The Realms of Gold*, Margaret Atwood's *Surfacing*, Margaret Laurence's *The Diviners*, Erica Jong's *Fear of Flying*, and Gail Godwin's *The Odd Woman* indicates that by the early seventies a new genre, feminist metafiction, had come into existence: the protagonist looks to the literary tradition for answers about the present, speculates about the relation of "the forms" to her life and her writing, seeks "an ending of her own" which differs from the marriage or death to which she is traditionally consigned, and seeks freedom from the plots of the past. Behind these novels are the major works of Doris Lessing, *The Golden Notebook* (1962) and *The Children of Violence* (1952–1969), prototypical *Künstlerromane* and *Bildungsromane* of contemporary women's fiction, in which questing protagonists seek "something new": and something new, a term which recurs in Lessing's works, means more than individual freedom or fulfillment—it means something radically oppositional to "the nightmare repetition" of the past.[1]

Metafiction is a form of literary criticism, a fictional expression of critical positions and assessments, and feminist metafiction is a form of feminist literary criticism. As feminist critics undertake what Annette Kolodny calls a "re-visionary rereading" of the literary inheritance,[2] feminist writers also embark on "re-visions"—though critics reenter old plots to reevaluate them, and novelists reenter them to rewrite them or to "write beyond" earlier endings, in Rachel Blau DuPlessis's suggestive term for the project of twentieth-century female writers.

Like early feminist critics—Mary Ellmann, *Thinking About Women*; Kate Millett, *Sexual Politics*; Carolyn Heilbrun, *Toward a Definition of Androgyny*; Annette Kolodny, *The Lay of the Land*; Judith Fetterley, *The Resisting Reader*—the protagonists of feminist fiction critique images of women and the plots of the past. "'Did you believe that stuff when you were little?'" asks a character in Atwood's *Surfacing*; "'I did, I thought I was really a princess and I'd end up living in a castle. They shouldn't let kids have stuff like that'" (66–67). Jane Clifford of Godwin's *The Odd Woman* "ransacks novels for answers to life," only to find that survival depends on eluding "already-written stories" (29, 50). Jane Gray of Drabble's *The Waterfall* seeks understanding of her affair with her cousin's husband in "old-fashioned" novels (*The Mill on the Floss, Jude the Obscure, Jane Eyre, Therese Racquin, Nana*), only to realize that their punitive morality would have killed her for less (138). Lessing's Martha Quest reads "like a famished person," "starved," only to discover "a gap between her self and the past" (*Martha* 200, 27, 10): "Is it really conceivable that [women] should have turned into something quite different in the space of about fifty years? Or do you suppose they didn't tell the truth, the novelists?" (*Proper* 205). Mira of Marilyn French's *The Women's Room* seeks "books she could find herself and her problems in. There were none…nothing helped. Like the person who gets fat because they eat unnourishing foods and so is always hungry and so is always eating, she drowned in words that could not teach her to swim" (29). Atwood in *Lady Oracle* and Fay Weldon in *The Fat Woman's Joke* similarly associate unsustaining fiction with unnourishing food, and in Marge Piercy's *Braided Lives* the protagonist's mother reads with "a vast hunger for something. That same hunger that terrifies her in me" (12).[3] Feminists write fiction to fill the "gap" between past and present, to satisfy women's "hungers" with more nourishing words.

Feminist novelists, like feminist critics, engage in re-visions of the tradition. "Re-vision" is, as Adrienne Rich says, "more than a chapter in cultural history: it is an act of survival" (35). But re-vision is *also* a chapter in cultural history, and a chapter in social history as well—specifically, in the history of the women's movement. Feminist fiction was produced by feminism—though it also produced feminism—and feminist metafiction, which focuses on women as readers and writers, points to the key role of reading and writing in the women's movement. As Rich and others suggest, feminism is a renaming of the world: "in order to change what is, we need to give speech to what *has been*, to imagine together what *might* be" (260).[4] As women who knew the power of reading began writing fiction, they wrote about reading and writing—which is why feminist metafiction emerged at this time.

That reading and writing emerged as key issues, and often as problematic issues, had to do with the paradoxical situation of women in the postwar period, as they found themselves caught in the crossfire of conflicting signals, in the clash between increased socio-economic opportunities, on the one hand, and a restrictive domestic ideology, on the other. "In the 1950s, one of the surest ways forward for an intellectual young woman from the provinces, for a socially disadvantaged young woman from the provinces, was through Oxford, through Cambridge," says the narrator of Drabble's *The Radiant Way* (86); and Drabble's protagonists here, as in *A Summer Bird Cage, Jerusalem the Golden*, and *The Waterfall*, seek "escape through university" (141). In the United States, an expanding postwar economy allowed women to regain some of the ground they had lost since the second decade of the century, whereas in England new opportunities were created by social legislation: "at eighteen the world opened for them and displayed its riches, the brave new world of Welfare State and County Scholarships, of equality for women, they were the elite, the chosen, the garlanded of the great social dream" (88). Sheila Rowbatham describes "a lot of feminists...from working-class families, who had gone to university for the first time, or...from a lower-middle-class uneducated background...a lot of us were in this process of class transition"(38); Sally Alexander describes herself as "a child of the welfare state...born into the right to education, subsistence, housing and health—that birthright gave my generation the confidence to expect more" (91). Angela Carter refers to the 1944 Education Act, which provided all children with the right to education, as "the most single important cultural event in recent British history": it "granted the ambiguous benefits of a grammar-school education to certain children of the upper working and lower middle class such as myself who might otherwise have driven trains and delivered milk" (32).

"Ambiguous benefits" is right, for although education raised women's expectations, it also made many of them unhappy, creating ambitions that were frustrated by the domestic ideology that urged them back into the home, the ideology described by Betty Friedan as "the feminine mystique." When women's aspirations clashed with this ideology, the result was the malaise—"the problem that has no name"—that produced the ferment that made the women's movement. The protagonists of Drabble's *A Summer Bird Cage*, Atwood's *The Edible Woman*, Sylvia Plath's *The Bell Jar*, Sue Kaufman's *Diary of a Mad Housewife*, Alix Kates Shulman's *Memoirs of an Ex-Prom Queen*, Sheila Ballantyne's *Norma Jean the Termite Queen*, Godwin's *The Odd Woman*, Lois Gould's *The Final Analysis*—all have college degrees that are useless to them. The second wave of feminism in the late sixties and early seventies, in America, Britain, and Canada, was created by middle-class, college-educated women who had learned to want more—who, like the protagonists of this fiction, had expectations their worlds were not meeting: "from books I learned there is something else and I want it bad," says the protagonist of Piercy's *Braided Lives* (9); "books had betrayed her, leading her to want what she could not approach," says the protagonist of Piercy's *Small Changes* (29).

These protagonists turn to reading for validation of themselves and escape from their circumstances. Martha Quest reads seeking answers, and Lessing suggests that her search is typical and that, contrary to the ivory-tower aestheticism prevalent in the fifties, writers have a responsibility to it:

> For she was of that generation who, having found nothing in religion, had formed themselves by literature....And so she knelt in front of a bookcase, in driving need of the right arrangement of words....Which suggests that it is of no use for artists to insist, with such nervous disinclination for responsibility, that their productions are only "a reflection from the creative fires of irony," etc., etc., while the Marthas of this world read and search with the craving thought, What does this say about my life? (*Proper* 61–62)

Tina of Kaufman's *Diary of a Mad Housewife*, a "mad housewife" with a B.A. from Smith, keeps copies of Chekov, Mann, Flaubert, Austen, Marvell, and Forster on her bedside table, using them as "a way of calming myself without pills or booze"; she finds the means of terminating an unfortunate affair in an Elizabeth Bowen novel—"God bless you, Elizabeth Bowen" (50–51, 267). For Norma Jean, who has a B.A. from Berkeley, reading is a source both of discontent and strength; as her husband complains, "she reads everything. They're stacked to the ceiling next to the bed: women's lib, ancient Egypt, sociology, the newspaper"; they "take her places where I have no access" (120). Sasha of *Memoirs of an Ex-Prom Queen* finds in her father's library escape from her "baffling life" ("they made me forget I was a piece of meat, albeit a prime piece according to specifications of my mounting pile of *Seventeen* magazines") and finds in philosophy temporary relief from an imprisoning self-consciousness (51–52, 146).

Often, however, what the protagonist finds in the culture's texts is reinforcement of the very stereotypes that entrap her, for if "the tradition" inspired woman's aspirations, it also frustrated her dreams by marginalizing and denigrating her. "I have been suspecting for a while now that everything I ever read was lies," says the narrator of *The Women's Room* (210). Jong's Isadora takes "refuge behind books" as though they were "a bullet-proof shield, an asbestos wall, a cloak of invisibility," while also lamenting that she has been taught to see "through the eyes of male writers":

> Of course, I didn't think of them as *male* writers. I thought of them as *writers*, as authorities, as gods who knew and were to be trusted completely.
>
> Naturally I trusted everything they said, even when it implied my own inferiority. I learned what an orgasm was from D. H. Lawrence....I learned from Shaw that women never can be artists; I learned from Dostoyevsky that they have no religious feeling; I learned from Swift and Pope that they have too *much* religious feeling....I learned from Faulkner that they are earth mothers....I learned from Freud that they...are ever "incomplete" because they lack the one thing in the world worth having: a penis.
>
> But what did all this have to do with me...? (*Fear* 14, 154)[5]

Atwood catalogues "stereotypes of women...from the Western European literary tradition"—the "old Crones, Delphic Oracles...Three Fates, Evil Witches, White Witches, White Goddesses, Bitch Goddesses, Medusas...Mermaids...Snow Queens... Medea...Lady Macbeth...Eve...and Mother," "the Whore of Babylon, the Whore with the heart of gold...the Scarlet Woman, the Red Shoes, Madame Bovary...Molly Bloom and her chamber pot and her eternal yes, Cleopatra and her friend the asp"—concluding, "what do I have to do with thee?" ("Curse" 219–21). Piercy's Jill tries to "adjust novels and biographies...to invent roles for myself," but "a female Hamlet or a female Count of Monte Cristo taxes my inventiveness. Hamlet gets to hog the whole play" (*Braided* 21). Morag of Laurence's *The Diviners* wonders what the lady in a poem by John Donne "might have said of *him*" (191); a character in Edna O'Brien's *Girls in Their Married Bliss* wonders if Shakespeare isn't part of her friend's tragic end: "Oh, Shakespeare deepest and powerfulest of friends, father of us all. Father—the crux of her dilemma" (531). It is remarkable how similar such critiques are to those being voiced by feminist critics during these same years.

Feminist writers and critics especially critique the love story, "the old story"—though, as Godwin's Jane Clifford admits, "that is the story we still love most....Even 'emancipated women'...love to hear the old, old story"; Baba of *Girls in their Married Bliss* also calls it "the old, old story" (387, 459). These protagonists may "love" it, but they nevertheless realize that it is likely to leave them dead (in the old versions) or confine them to living deaths (in contemporary versions). Martha Quest, who "sees herself...through literature" (7), expects to find her "end" and deliverance in a man, only to discover that marriage consigns her to ancient and inexorable patterns of repetition, biological and social. Sasha of Shulman's *Memoirs of an Ex-Prom Queen* "wallowed in fable, searching for guidance" and "read every romance as a parable for the future," only to find herself "at thirty...without income or skill, dependent on a man and a fading skin"—it was "there in all the texts I'd ever studied," "the fulfillment of a curse!" (24, 285, 293). Mira of French's *The Women's Room* also feels cursed: "It had all happened anyhow. Oedipus couldn't escape his fate, and neither could she. The scenario had been written before she was even born" (99); so too does Miriam of Piercy's *Small Changes* (397). In *How to Save Your Own Life*, Jong's Isadora protests,

> all of the greatest fiction of the modern age showed women falling for vile seducers and dying as a result. They died under breaking waves, under the wheels of trains, in childbirth. *Someone* had to break the curse, *someone* had to wake Sleeping Beauty....*Someone* had to shout once and for all: Fly and live to tell the tale! (236)

II

The critique of romance is a critique of the ending, for the love story allows woman one end: her "end," both in the sense of "goal" and "conclusion," is a man. Feminist critics have analyzed marriage as the one plot available to woman, her sole means of success or survival, the quest and vocation that absorbs all possible *Bildung* and defines her transition to adulthood. Marriage symbolizes her integration into society; death symbolizes her failure to negotiate that entrance, as well as the culture's failure to imagine her existence apart from marriage—to allow her "something else to be," in Toni Morrison's phrase (52).[6]

Jane Clifford rejects what she calls the "Emma Bovary syndrome"—"literature's graveyard positively choked with women who...'get in trouble' (commit adultery, have sex without marriage; *think* of committing adultery, or having sex without marriage) and thus, according to the literary convention of the time, must die" (Godwin 302). The nightmarish power of this plot is suggested by a passage in Alice Walker's *Meridian* which is reiterated three times, as though in a spell: "She dreamed she was a character in a novel and that her existence presented an insoluble problem, one that would be solved only by her death at the end." The reiteration suggests the compulsive and obsessive nature of this "dream," and "even when she gave up reading novels that encouraged such a solution—and nearly all of them did—the dream did not cease" (117).[7]

Some of these writers contrast the neat shapes of fiction to the muddles of "real life." Martha Quest's reading has taught her to assume that her life will be shaped by the dramatic dénouements of fiction, but Lessing thwarts her expectations by the slow, shapeless series form of *The Children of Violence*. Mira of French's *The Women's Room* protests:

> In the great literature of the past you either get married and live happily ever after, or you die. But the fact is, neither is what actually happens. Oh, you do die, but never at the right time...and you don't live happily ever after, but you do live. (211)

Even Woolf got it wrong, French claims, in envisioning a "violent and apocalyptic end" for Shakespeare's sister:

> I knew that isn't what happened. You see, it wasn't necessary...there are so much easier ways to destroy a woman. You don't have to rape or kill her; you don't even have to beat her. You can just marry her. You don't even have to do that. You can just let her work in your office for thirty-five dollars a week. (64–65)

Ella Price laments, "We don't get chopped down like redwoods, we wither....And we don't jump in front of trains. We just keep going. Not dead but alive. And nobody ever knows. That's what's so awful, that no one knows" (Bryant 84).

Though French complains "you could never go beyond the end" (24), contemporary women writers do write beyond the end, beyond the telos of romance and its "regimen of resolutions," in DuPlessis's term (21). Though Ella Price's friend calls Nora's ending "'absurd. You can't do that. Just walk out, without a job, without any knowledge of the world, leaving the children. It just can't be done'" (91), Ella and other contemporary protagonists do it. In *Bodily Harm* Atwood redefines "terminal" (a word much on the mind of her protagonist, who has just had a mastectomy) to mean not "the end of the line, where you get off" but "where you can get on to go somewhere else" (264).

But "somewhere else" is not so easy to imagine, since few narratives, as Carolyn Heilbrun says, take their protagonists past such revelations and dramatize their new freedoms from old plots (42–43). The protagonist of Barbara Raskin's *Loose Ends* would like "to write a novel about an American woman who, after a lifetime of psychological dependency upon men...moves out front alone, on her own," but does "not know yet what form such an experience takes...because it hasn't happened yet"

(312–13). Thus *Loose Ends* concludes, like *Ella Price's Journal* and Atwood's *Bodily Harm, Surfacing,* and *The Edible Woman,* with the protagonist poised on the brink of an unimaginable future. Shulman's 1969 *Memoirs of an Ex-Prom Queen* ends with Sasha poised on the threshold—"'I'm leaving,' I said from the doorway"—overcome by *ennui*: "It all sounded vaguely familiar, like snatches of an old play" (225-26). It had struck Martha Quest as "an old play" years before this, in Lessing's 1952 *A Proper Marriage*: "there's something so *vieux jeu*...in leaving like Nora to live differently!...One is bound to fall in love with the junior partner, and things will begin all over again" (274).

Martha was right, things do "begin over again." Martha, Sasha, and Isadora leave one husband for another; and, reading beyond the endings of Jong's *Fear of Flying,* French's *The Women's Room,* Raskin's *Loose Ends,* to the follow-ups of these successful first novels—*How to Save Your Own Life, The Bleeding Heart,* and *Hot Flashes*—we find the most amazing recuperation of romantic fantasy: "how to save your own life" turns out to be—find a new man.

Clearly, leaving home is not enough: change requires more than moving out, resolution, or will: it requires a process of re-envisioning which allows an evolution and alteration of desire and consciousness, both protagonist's and reader's—a "working through" like that which occurs in psychoanalysis.

III

Since the available forms do not accommodate something new, feminist novelists forge new forms that render the process of change. The most convincing of this fiction—Lessing's *The Children of Violence* and *The Golden Notebook,* Drabble's *The Waterfall,* Laurence's *The Diviners,* Atwood's *Lady Oracle*—places the end of the affair or marriage at the beginning or in the middle and devise narrative modes that enact working through.[8] A brief analysis of *The Waterfall* indicates how Drabble accomplishes this form.

The Waterfall is Drabble's most self-consciously intertextual work, a metafiction that draws attention to problems of finding a style and making an ending, a writerly text that invites the reader to participate in the production of meaning and renders the process of "working through." Abandoned by her husband as she is on the verge of delivering a baby, Jane Gray withdraws to her bed, "empty, solitary, neglected, cold" (8), frozen into an "ice age of inactivity" (7), sunk into near-catatonic stupor. But what is born in the opening pages is not only a child but a passion—for James, her cousin Lucy's husband—as, "delivering" a child, she is herself "delivered" (10, 16, 159); and as "submit[ting]...helplessly to the current" (39), she is saved by love, Sleeping Beauty awakened.

But Jane is not only a woman abandoned by one man and saved by another: she is also a poet and novelist who uses "the power of the pen" to repudiate "the old novels" in which "the price of love was death" (256) and to define a new relation to the myth of romantic salvation. As a first-person narrator who is writing a novel about herself in the third person, Jane uses fictional form to sort out her feelings about her affair with her cousin's husband; and though she enlists romantic precedence to justify this affair, she also interrogates her stylized, romantic fictionalization by means of an analytical first-person critique. From this processive re-vision of "I" by "she," and "she" by "I," she forges a new "system" and "morality" (47, 53) and a "feminine ending"—open, irregular, indecisive, unpunishing—which accommodates transgression.

Taking her metaphors where Jane finds her salvation—in female sexuality and maternity—Drabble makes *jouissance* the source of an alternative discourse with the revolutionary implications of *écriture féminine*, "writing the female body." Moreover, Jane creates her new system from a verbal medium reconstituted by recombinations of words according to principles that subvert conventional relations between subject and object, by means of which she shakes words free from their usual meanings and liberates them from their customary positions in a discourse inscribing hierarchy and possession. A complicated series of wordplays extends throughout the novel and shakes words free of their usual associations, liberating words such as "do," "have," and "make" from syntax which describes possession and product—something one person does to another—and making them not only describe but reflect processes of reciprocity and mutuality: "she was his, but by having her he had made himself hers" (159) is an image of "impossible possession" (125) which transforms "have" from something one person does *to* another, to something two people do *with* each other, mirroring, in the circularity of its construction, a process which is endless. The wordplay transforms enclosures to openings, limits to limitlessness, endings to endlessness. *The Waterfall* is—in Hélène Cixous's terms—"a new insurgent writing" that "wrecks partitions, classes, rhetorics, regulations and codes" and "change[s] the rules of the old game" (256).

NOTES

1. The term "something new" occurs in *Martha Quest* 53, 141, 216; *Landlocked* 117; and *The Golden Notebook* 61, 353, 472–73, 479. "The nightmare repetition" is from *A Proper Marriage* 77, 95.

2. Showalter also describes feminist criticism's "tasks of revision and rediscovery" (437); Gilbert refers to "the revisionary imperative" as an "attempt to reform 'a thousand years of Western culture'" (32).

3. Gelfant describes the "hungry woman" "in fiction written by women about women," the woman who "believes that books will give her power, and so she reads compulsively—looking for ways to change her life" (207–08).

4. Daly says, "Women have had the power of naming stolen from us" (8); Christ refers to the "role of language in articulating and shaping women's experiences of new being" (81).

5. See Rich: the girl who turns "to poetry or fiction looking for *her* way of being in the world" "comes up against something that negates everything she is about: she meets the image of Women in books written by men…but precisely what she does not find is…herself" (39).

6. Miller distinguishes between the "euphoric text" and the "dysphoric text" (*Heroine's* xi). See also DuPlessis 1–19. Miller also discusses the laws of probability and possibility that govern closure as a kind of "contract" between writer and reader ("Emphasis" 36).

7. This ending persists in contemporary women's fiction—in O'Brien's *Girls in their Married Bliss*, Spark's *The Driver's Seat*, Didion's *Play it as it Lays*, Rossner's *Looking for Mr. Goodbar*, Rubens's *Go Tell the Lemming*, Oates's "Where Are You Going?" and Lessing's *The Grass is Singing* and "To Room 19."

8. I discuss these works in *Changing the Story*.

WORKS CITED

Alexander, Sally. Interview. Wandor 81–92.

Atwood, Margaret. *Bodily Harm*. New York: Simon and Schuster, 1982.

———. "The Curse of Eve—Or What I Learned in School." *Second Words: Selected Critical Prose*. Boston: Beacon, 1982. 215–28.

———. *Surfacing*. New York: Fawcett, 1972.

Ballantyne, Sheila. *Norma Jean the Termite Queen*. Harmondsworth: Penguin, 1986.

Bryant, Fanny. *Ella Price's Journal*. Berkeley: Ata Books, 1972.

Carter, Angela. "The State of Fiction: A Symposium." *The New Review* 5.1 (1978): 31–32.

Christ, Carol P. *Diving Deep and Surfacing*. Boston: Beacon, 1980.

Cixous, Hélène. "The Laugh of the Medusa." Trans. Keith Cohen and Paul Cohen. *New French Feminisms: An Anthology*. Ed. Elaine Marks and Isabelle de Courtivron. Amherst U of Massachusetts P, 1980. 245–64.

Daly, Mary. *Beyond God the Father: Towards a Philosophy of Women's Liberation*. Boston: Beacon, 1973.

Didion, Joan. *Play it as it Lays*. New York: Bantam, 1972.

Drabble, Margaret. *The Waterfall*. New York: Fawcett, 1977.

DuPlessis, Rachel Blau. *Writing Beyond the Ending: Narrative Strategies of Twentieth-Century Women Writers*. Bloomington: Indiana UP, 1985.

French, Marilyn. *The Women's Room*. New York: Jove Publications, 1977.

Friedan, Betty. *The Feminine Mystique*. New York: Dell, 1983.

Gelfant, Blanche H. "Sister to Faust: The City's 'Hungry' Woman as Heroine." *Women Writing in America: Voices in College*. Hanover: UP of New England, 1984. 205–224.

Gilbert, Sandra. "What Do Feminist Critics Want? A Postcard from the Volcano." *The New Feminist Criticism: Essays on Women, Literature, Theory*. Ed. Elaine Showalter. New York: Random House, 1985. 29–45.

Godwin, Gail. *The Odd Woman*. New York: Warner, 1974.

Greene, Gayle. *Changing the Story: Feminist Fiction and the Tradition*. Bloomington: Indiana UP, 1991.

Heilbrun, Carolyn G. *Writing a Woman's Life*. New York: Norton, 1988.

Jong, Erica. *Fear of Flying*. New York: Signet, 1973.

———. *How to Save Your Own Life*. New York: Signet, 1977.

Kaufman, Sue. *Diary of a Mad Housewife*. New York: Bantam, 1970.

Kolodny, Annette. "A Map for Rereading: Or, Gender and the Interpretation of Literary Texts." *New Literary History* 3 (1980): 451–67.

Laurence, Margaret. *The Diviners*. New York: Knopf, 1974.

Lessing, Doris. *The Golden Notebook*. New York: Bantam, 1973.

———. *The Grass is Singing*. New York: New American Library, 1976.

———. *Landlocked*. New York: New American Library, 1966.

———. *Martha Quest*. New York: New American Library, 1964.

———. *A Proper Marriage*. New York: New American Library, 1970.

———. "To Room 19." *A Man and Two Women*. New York: Popular Library, 1963. 278–316.

Miller, Nancy K. "Emphasis Added: Plots and Plausibilities in Women's Fiction." *PMLA* 96.1 (1981): 36–48.

———. *The Heroine's Text: Readings in the French and English Novel, 1722–1782*. New York: Columbia UP, 1980.

Morrison, Toni. *Sula*. New York: New American Library, 1973.

Oates, Joyce Carol. "Where Are You Going, Where Have You Been?" *The Wheel of Love*. New York: Vanguard P, 1970. 34–54.

O'Brien, Edna. *Girls in Their Married Bliss*. *The Country Girls Trilogy*. New York: New American Library, 1968.

Piercy, Marge. *Braided Lives*. New York: Fawcett Crest, 1982.

———. *Small Changes*. New York: Fawcett Crest, 1973.

Raskin, Barbara. *Loose Ends*. New York: Bantam, 1973.

Rich, Adrienne. "Motherhood: The Contemporary Emergency and the Quantum Leap."*On Lies, Secrets, and Silence: Selected Prose, 1966–1978*. New York: Norton, 1979. 259–73.

Rossner, Judith. *Looking for Mr. Goodbar*. New York, Simon and Schuster, 1975.

Rowbotham, Sheila. Interview. Wandor 28–42.

Rubens, Bernice. *Go Tell the Lemming*. New York: Pocket Books, 1983.

Showalter, Elaine. "Literary Criticism in the Wilderness." *Signs* 1.2 (1975): 435–60.

Shulman, Alix Kates. *Memoirs of an Ex-Prom Queen*. New York: Bantam, 1972.

Spark, Muriel. *The Driver's Seat*. Harmondsworth: Penguin, 1974.

Walker, Alice. *Meridian*. New York: Washington Square P, 1977.

Wandor, Michelene, ed. *Once a Feminist: Stories of a Generation*. London: Virago, 1990.

Letters From Nowhere: Fanny Howe's Forty Whacks and Feminine Identity

Johnny Payne

The shocking announcement of the death of that man of letters and leading exponent of experimental fiction—just as he seemed to be entering his prime—took place a decade or so ago. He had many aliases: Pynchon, Coover, Barth or Barthelme, Mailer. Despite his deceptively sturdy and boyish looks, he was hounded to death by accusations of dandyism, dilettantism, social irrelevance and moral philandering, with scarce notice taken of his bursts of political conviction. His opponents vehemently denied and derided his social engagement, while his supporters swore by his penetrating powers of observation. The conflict has yet to be resolved. But odder still is the strange case of his accomplished female counterpart, who had also tried her hand at fictional innovation, in secret, and who passed her short years less criticized than simply unnoticed. In the best marital tradition, she was tossed on the pyre of her husband's widely-skimmed and largely-unread books, without malice, simply as a matter of course, before the question of her social engagement could even be raised. Engagements, like obituaries, are meant to be read once in the papers, and promptly forgotten. So it goes with "women's fiction."

Her premature, unmourned death can be accounted for in part by this fact that "engagement" has a double valence; in her case, it seems more to suggest that intimate but ultimately public preliminary social contract made between a woman and a man, often a prelude to the woman's overwhelming sense of her own inexistence. In her epistolary novella *Forty Whacks*, and in her description of her long correspondence with the late literary lion Edward Dahlberg, Fanny Howe, by creating a "woman of letters," takes exception to the unceremonious psychic burial of women, and of female writers of experimental fiction. She employs the conceit of the letter to explore the onset of an ontological indeterminacy which arises, almost symptomatically, in the context of cultural resistance to a normative patriarchy. In the case of *Forty Whacks*, social and sexual repression become almost synonymous, such that inexistence bears a close relation to gender. Howe uses the epistolary genre to take up questions of social annihilation, locating them on the terrain of domestic betrothals and betrayals.

In *Forty Whacks*, writing and sending letters to a man is precisely what produces a woman's inexistence. Cut off from the social realm, the woman seeks approval and affirmation of her being through the more private, yet potentially social, medium of correspondence. But the epistolary missives in her fiction serve, conversely, to reinforce a precarious dependency on a hostile patriarchal social structure which, if unaltered, can only lead to the woman's effacement. The malleability of her subjectivity, and the misogynist social construction emphasizing her relationality, both foster and preclude her aspiring to possess a unitary ego, that fiction on which liberal republicanism and the modern state are founded. She is asked to believe and participate ardently in the domestic manifestations of a "democratic" society, whose definition depends on her exclusion. The letter thus becomes a hopeless, oppressive dystopian device, encouraging her "communication," even making it a precondition of her acceptance within the patriarchal social structure, but circumscribing that attempted communication within manipulative masculine designs. The letters in Howe's novella attest to the lacerating difficulty of assembling even a minimal feminine (or feminist) identity, and conjoining it to its social medium in a manner which will not, like a marriage of true minds, be annulled or nullified.

The title *Forty Whacks*, evoking the familiar rhyme about Lizzie Borden's parricide, suggests the literally murderous extremity out of which that identity has to emerge. The "I" of this epistolary novella can only begin to engage in self-refashioning after killing a couple—a researcher in zoology and his wife, whom the narrator self-consciously casts in patently Freudian maternal and paternal roles vis-à-vis her "self." Attempting to recover from an implied psychiatric institutionalization, she has lodged with them as a temporary research assistant and housekeeper. But despite the novella's domestic setting, a description of *Forty Whacks* as a fractured Oedipal family romance is inadequate. It rather must correlate that romance to the political state within which it exists. Richard Feldstein and Judith Roof, in critiquing that feminist psychoanalytic criticism which has remained within the "comfortable, suspicious, but conveniently indeterminate norms of human relations," conclude that "the apparently binary balance of the heterosexual romantic couple masks the brooding omnipresence of multiple 'other' terms, such as the state or religion, which create, sanctify, and otherwise control the couple's existence" (3). *Forty Whacks* stages a local enactment of that omnipresence.

The patient's prescribed "rehabilitation," her recuperation into the familial and social bosom, is contingent on her coming to a normative understanding of how a "healthy" person should behave. And this understanding, in turn, depends on, and is framed formally by, her one-way correspondence with her psychiatrist, one Dr. Weed, to whom she sends letters—or rather all the letters in a single packet—describing the "progress" she is making.

Howe's novella consists of two framing letters, to which is appended a month-long series of the narrator's journal entries. But the journal entries themselves function overtly as letters, a public writing meant to allow Dr. Weed to keep a close eye on his patient's progress from far away. "I enclose my diary to prove to you that I have been doing what you suggested—that is, recording my experiences, not by rote but with an analytical eye." And in case she is prosecuted, and he must testify as to her mental competence, "here is my confidential record of the events preceding the tragedy. Do, please, respond" (3–4).

In his absence, Dr. Weed remains vividly present, "responding" even in his textual silence. The letter, the most intimate of documents, serves as confession, as proof, making public the most "confidential" of processes to a confidant whose approval (and, of course, chastisement) the woman must seek if she is to be acknowledged. She values the journal because "it replaces my appointments with Dr. Weed" (14). The structure of Howe's novella implies the withholding or deferral of approval through the absence of Dr. Weed's letters. Yet the vivid austerity of this would-be correspondent becomes apparent (and he a parent) in the narrator's constant, anxious references to him in her letters:

> Above all, I must keep an honest record of events and impressions, according to Dr. Weed's prescription. I do miss him. (5)

> I could identify with Rose as much as I could with Arthur, which was sure proof of my mental health....I know that Dr. Weed would approve. (13)

> If I think of what Dr. Weed would say, it only confirms my conviction that sexual repression is unhealthy. (16)

Jerry Aline Flieger addresses the question of the "multivalence" of the psychoanalytic situation, the mutual vulnerability of patient and analyst. But she also acknowledges that given "the neurotic origin of the transference," and also its relation "to the experience of normal love...the powerful position of the analyst in this drama is obvious. The therapist is parent, original love, and authority object" (197). In *Forty Whacks*, it is the very illusion of an equal, mutual correspondence between patient and liberal analyst that enables the female's epistolary subjugation, equating this structural subjugation with a desirable personal transference.

The second letter, the one which begins (and beguiles) at the beginning, describes the nameless narrator's arrival in California and her adjustment to her new life—in a studied prose meant to convey her cheerfulness and newfound self-control, and to persuade Dr. Weed that she can, after all, be trusted to behave as any woman deserving of the name should. The letter begins "Dear Doctor Weed: I guess I should tell you everything," and then recounts a plan of action reminiscent, in its woodenness, of a list of resolutions, of "Things To Do," penned by an over-eager high school senior who vehemently aspires to the status of co-ed by taking correspondence courses. She resolves "(a) to learn from Arthur...so that...I'd be an able research assistant in biology (b) to read the classic works of literature (c) to apply the information I had acquired in your office to my new life (d) to prove myself independent" (2).

In the pursuit of this "independence," the letter and the journal entries also employ the happy-talk of psychology's "up-front" jargon—"the new language"—as the narrator strives to manufacture a manageable, acceptable self-presentation on paper, even while she enters ever deeper into the domestic bizarreness and jealousies of Arthur and Rose, her employers, and experiences aggressive sexual fantasies about Arthur. The narrator, eager to prove her mastery of self-analysis (thus of self), belabors elementary, "significant" connections which are meant to prove that she possesses enough self-awareness to control her former deviant behavior and parricidal rage. Remembering a hunting trip with her father on the day of her journey to California, she remarks, in what might aptly be called a Dick-and-Jane psychiatric prose, that "only once did I want to kill him and that was when he gave me this pearl-handled revolver as a present, obviously a substitute phallus" (3). Elsewhere, comparing Rose's standing between her and Arthur to the way her mother stood between her and her father, she observes that "It's fortunate I can see these things, otherwise I would be the victim of disturbing emotions...I will *not* be bogged down by unknown infantile feelings" (19).

But this transparent (or at least translucent) auto-placation serves only to veil—like an onionskin sheet of tracing paper—the epistolary script of patriarchal legitimation in which the narrator remains circumscribed, and its exacerbation of her "dysfunctionality." Not only does she participate fully in the "therapeutic" letter/journal writing designed to serve as the very mechanism of her quiescent acquiescence in the domestic confines of a paternalistic state; she also, in becoming an unbidden reader of Arthur and Rose's personal letters, which she discovers while cleaning their room, replicates the invasive voyeurism to which she herself is rendered subject.

> I sat on the floor to read them and had a flash of anxiety (misplaced sexual tension, no doubt) which I was unable to analyze away at the time. It immobilized me, a sensation of fever and withdrawal. I thought of the two alternative actions confronting me: either I leave the space that created the neurosis (that is, stop reading the letters on the floor of the closet) or else stick with it. I decided on the latter. (11)

Deciding on the latter—on the letter—entails an interpretation of her own reading process which, rather than truly resolve any of the analysand's dim unease about the normative, oppressive confines of her open-letter method of treatment, of therapy-by-correspondence, instead subsumes that unease within the category of her supposedly dysfunctional sexuality. The source of her deviance, in the official psychiatric explanation, lies not with any flaw in the terms under which her sexual and social identity within a patriarchal state are allowed, but rather with her libido, and thus can be cured by the onanistic sexual release afforded by the "healthy" act of voyeurism. Only by reproducing the very terms of her victimization and subjugation can she furnish herself with a socially acceptable identity. She resolves the dilemma, in this case, in the officially satisfactory manner, emphasizing the woman's relational destiny as a function of "her" man, and thus failing to challenge the ontological basis of her social construction.

> If I left, the closet might occupy my mind excessively and bring on more symptoms of anxiety; whereas if I stayed, I would come to terms with the problem and lick it right there. Consequently, I read every letter....The most stimulating were from Rose to Arthur and vice-versa....I can see now that my so-called anxiety was a reaction of sexuality toward their relationship....I would give anything to have a man like Arthur writing me letters like the ones he wrote to Rose. So once again he revealed to me, indirectly, what I will want from a man in the end. (11–12)

In answer to Freud's question, "What does a woman *want?*" the narrator seems at this juncture to answer, "Someone who will wear the pens in the family." In making this decision, the narrator subscribes to the heterosexual imperative. Psychoanalysis has tended to define a normal and mature woman as one ready for the role of wife and mother, and thus amenable to the ends of patriarchy. Thus, the narrator is compelled to conceive of Rose as an impediment to her rehabilitation, who stands between herself and the consummation of her heterosexual and social actualization. Her energies become increasingly directed toward the "conquest" of Rose's husband and lover. During a dinner party, amidst drunken talk of "the revolution," the narrator reflects on her "feeling of power and...a calm sensuality that made me appreciate my femininity. The balance of powers had shifted according to my expectations: I had Arthur's respect and John's sexual interest" (21).

This fervent resolve and striving to become a good girl finds its expression too in the frequent reminders to herself to "write home" (35). The weekend she is left alone in the house and discovers the forbidden letters begins, in fact, with missives of a more dutiful kind: "I've taken advantage of the weekend (they are in L.A. visiting friends) by writing letters home" (9). As with Dr. Weed, in whom paternalistic authority resides, her filial fulfillment depends on her unfailing execution of the imperative to correspond, to render a full epistolary account of her adjustment to the social structure. Each activity reinforces the other.

Yet for all the self-analytical reassurance, would-be wifely heterosexuality, and self-imposed admonishments to write home, a profoundly resonant note of irony lingers over the rote proceedings. Her desire to become transparently self-identical with her oppressive medium gives way to the suppressed suspicion that self-annihilation is to be the real outcome of her epistolary devotion. The socialization she's encouraged to accomplish so fully that she will perform its routines automatically—all by rote—gives way to her inkling that she is moving ever closer to the phrase, "That's all she wrote." However vehemently she wills herself to participate in her domestication, the narrator cannot completely fend off the uneasy awareness that her dissolution is in progress. The first letter she comes upon, an unmailed one to a friend, written by Rose—"expressing what she calls 'despair'"—awakens a vague discomfort in the narrator in its reference to Rose's marriage.

> [Rose] described her state of mind in tiny, shaky writing—"I'm always scared! We hardly ever touch, and it's probably my fault. I jump awake at least three times a night—one of those catastrophic, electric leaps—but it's really the way I feel all day." What is her problem? She has everything a girl could want. I must say, at that point I felt some confusion myself. (10)

Rose and the narrator, to some extent, share a status as "inklings," as compulsive (compelled) and unanswered letter writers who formulate only vaguely the hunch that they are complicitous in the denial of their own being, or in a tightly hemmed-in definition of it. Rose's taboo letter remains, significantly, unsent, tucked beneath sloppy piles of dishes and papers to be graded. It only finds a destinee by accident, haphazardly. Even then the narrator remains constrained by the parameters of her femininity. This ideology encourages her contempt of Rose's "despair" (and later, contempt of the lost identity signalled by Rose's doodling of lower-case "roses" on the Yellow Pages). She fails to grasp the letter's desperate valences. In the narrator's misguided interpretation of such written clues, she ends up cribbing, in so many words, a line from Blake, and tries to dispense with her rival by concluding "O Rose, thou art sick!" Unfortunately, rather than compare Rose's situation with her own, the narrator instead wishes that she, too, might be eaten by the invisible worm, that its dark secret love might her life destroy.

But the writing is on the wall, or at least on the closet floor, and its import gradually steals over the narrator. Her instructions to write home disintegrate little by little, eventually relegated to the first item of a bizarre shopping list—confusing familial, cosmetic, and pharmaceutical notions—which makes up her October 3 journal entry:

> write home
> Ortho Novum
> familia
> stockings
> Diorissimo
> gum

This note of reminder to herself, with its latinate quality of a poorly "rote" religious litany, signals the coming-apart of the seamless new language of epistolary psychiatry which she has employed up to this point. The very next journal entry announces that

> I've finally broken all ties with my parents....Mother wrote me a letter signing it with hers and father's names. It's so lazy and just plain insulting of her to do this, I've decided to cut off all communication with them. If they can't even write me separate letters, they are not worthy of my time. I don't care if Dad is a day sleeper, he could write me from the factory at nights. (35–36)

Her aspirations of establishing a direct, satisfactory correspondence with the absent patriarchal figure; of believing in the sacredness of the Oedipal triangle, accepting the enabling claims of liberal psychoanalysis, investing this familial triad with its avowed significance in order to overcome it through an epistolary transference; of circumventing the epistolary mediation of other women, who represent for her obstacles to her full integration as the equal, feminine co-respondent of the masculine realm—all these aspirations are hereby declared as null and void as her selfhood. Like Arthur and Dr. Weed, her father has no actual need to respond or to integrate her, since she is doing such an impeccable job of manufacturing her own fictive, illusory sense of participation and acceptable femininity. Her potential real correspondents—Rose and her mother—remain equally distant because they, like her, are busy replicating the ideology requiring their feminine malleability and mutual wariness or hostility.

The novella's brilliant understatement is achieved through the narrator's cheerful tone of complacent yet anxious, vaguely wary self-delusion, coupled with her unrelenting, critical "analysis" of others, her wholehearted acceptance of Freudian principles and her reasonable, if elementary, understanding of them, as well as her specious application of them to her own situation. By accepting and even seeming to endorse the premises of a modern, liberal state committed to the psychosocial being and "well-being" of its inhabitants, then carrying them to their absurd, fatal, and plausible extremes, Howe creates a dystopian commentary on power and gender relations. The narrator's "parricide" indeed appears as the inevitable outcome of her rehabilitation. In the patient's wholehearted acceptance of patriarchal Freudian doctrine, with its insistence on the patient's latent wish to slay the father, her act seems a ringing endorsement of that doctrine's characterization of her—a sign that she has completely assimilated, correctly albeit crudely, its fundamental precepts. Or, to put it in the narrator's words, from her pen-ultimate journal entry, her final attempt at writing her way into normalcy before the murder, "All we ever really need is time and silence so we can regain our self-consciousness. However, as Dr. Weed would say, 'You can't escape your unconscious'" (46).

The murder, at the same time, throws the narrator completely back into the category of the "dysfunctional" patient, since the nightmare of any espoused form of social logic (and that which exposes its contradictions) is the too-literal application of it by an overzealous disciple. One of the keen ironies in the narrator's relation to Dr. Weed is that her letters, which represent the measure and mechanism of her social control and self-control, neither prevent her from murdering Arthur and Rose, nor are sent to the analyst—to the "authorities"—until after the reprise of "aberrance" has occurred.

The novella's formal structure, presenting letters and journal entries as a single packet, a single outpouring, belies the careful, gradual re-socialization implied by the day-to-day diary installments. Dr. Weed, powerless to change the outcome of the story once it's told to him, becomes the narrator's "captive" audience. Out of this reversal—a potential always implicit in the ideological fiction of psychiatric transference as a two-way correspondence—arises the ambiguity of power and mutual vulnerability between analyst and analysand which can arise within the psychoanalytic drama as a narrative act. As Flieger puts it, Freud's later explanation of the origins of this psychic drama

> tends to give the patient the active, creative role of psychic subject, who 'leads the analyst on' with her tales, a latter-day Scheherazade who captivates her accomplice in the countertransference. For the analysand...is above all a storyteller, and the analyst, however powerful, is an audience, a recipient. Both positions contain aspects of power and passivity—which Freud sometimes elides with masculinity and femininity—and both positions imply mutual implication and mutual vulnerability. (198)

Like the modern state, the psychiatry which helps legitimate it contains the contradictions which hold the potential to subvert it. The letter of confession, once the narrator has completed it—and the rash act in which it culminates—is sent by post, posthaste, but its chastising, paternalistic reply, if there is one, can only arrive postmortem. Therapy-by-correspondence (transference), psychiatry's perfected form of social control, has failed.

The novella's very first letter, which reprises verbatim as its very last—written in the second case as part of the final, October 8, journal entry—presents the narrator and the narration as unrepentant. It is an epistle which negates from beginning to end the self-improving, acquiescent, good-girl prose of the installments which succeed (and precede) it. The novella begins with the sentence "I'd do it again." The defiance of this terse announcement signals an emergence of sorts, a reconstruction of selfhood that can only begin "when the sickness is past and the swooning is over" (1).

Yet one need not overemphasize the text's "subversiveness" of the patriarchal order, its status as, in the words of Ellen Friedman and Miriam Fuchs, "a hopeful alternative...to the failed master narratives" (27). *Forty Whacks*, in advocating the reconstitution of feminine or feminist consciousness, tempers its instant of exuberance (occurring only in the brief, hallucinatory space and time between the carnage of a double murder, not only of Arthur but of Rose, and an implied sure reprisal) with a consciousness of the agonizing difficulty of any satisfactory transformation issuing out of such a dystopian landscape, where "the almond tree has withered and the lamps are smashed in the living room; and my gun is rotting there" (10). The grim, but not impossible, prospect of refashioning the epistolary dynamic of sexual and social oppression into a social contract or conjoining which will not ultimately obliterate feminine identity is succinctly captured in the first/last framing letter. In it, the narrator employs a stuttering epistolary prose in order to assert her being, and her rejection of her status as dysfunctional patient, to her absent interlocutor, Dr. Weed.

> The sun is warm.
> Dear Doctor W
> Dear
> Dearest Doc
> Dear Doctor Weed I am severely
> Dear Doctor Weed
> I am se
> Dear Doctor Weed
> I am severely
>   ALIVE (1)

Her form of address suggests that though Dr. Weed stands as her designated addressee, she does not necessarily stand still as his designated oppressee. His name remains at the head of the letter, but in flux. Nonetheless, language here, a language under renovation, shatters perforce into its basic, almost inarticulate components, as the speaker struggles to gather it into the constituents of a tenable, minimal identity. The attempt to abdicate the narrator's former, Freudian, epistolary form of communication gives way to what can almost be described as aphasia. But *Forty Whacks*, in its allusion to Lizzie Borden's refrain, returns its narrator to the childlike beginnings of speech so that they might, just possibly, serve as a point of departure for a revivifying encounter with language.

The precarious nature of epistolarity came to bear not only on Howe's conception of *Forty Whacks*, but on her emergence as a female experimental writer during the sixties. In her 1985 "Artobiography," her description of her "excruciating" correspondence with novelist Edward Dahlberg during that time attests to another instance of epistolary paternalism, in the form of "mentoring" through letters, a situation not unrelated to the oppressive transference considered in Howe's novella. Though Howe insists that, in the end, the encounter with Dahlberg proved fruitful, providing her "first conscious encounter with a linguistic morality," she portrays him as a manipulative, misogynist correspondent, whose therapeutic exchange with his vulnerable, youthful literary charge has an erotic overdetermination:

> By chance, when I was 22, I wrote a letter to Edward Dahlberg after reading his book *Because I Was Flesh*. This correspondence was to continue over a span of seven years and culminate abruptly and furiously. The letters he sent me were very similar to most of his published letters, except, as he said himself, he had never before attempted to instruct a young woman. This at-the-time young woman had never sought instruction from anyone and took it, when it came, with a surprising lack of suspicion. ("Artobiography" 200)

But this virgin attempt to "instruct a young woman," whatever its intellectual content, seems to have borne a salacious S.W.A.K. on Dahlberg's part—because he was flesh—which he insisted on equating with his mission as Howe's artistic guru. And the sophisticated, intelligent, inquiring Howe, for her part, was therefore cast in the role of the wary, yet sufficiently trusting, object of literary lust, a kind of Little Red Writing Hood à la Bruno Bettelheim:

> I carried his letters on my person, to jobs, movies, everywhere, devouring them over and over again. I was quickly conscious that I was in the presence of a sexist and racist tyrant. But this awareness did not deter me from perceiving, in his aesthetic credo, an important truth which I was privileged to receive personally....He would try to prove to me, towards the end, the connection between life and art—that is, I must love him, if I loved his work. (200)

Howe remarks that this final sophistry failed, and Dahlberg no doubt felt he had one more sorrow to add to his earlier literary litany of *The Sorrows of Priapus*—the lessons of which the remonstrating author, however, had obviously failed to learn himself. For Dahlberg, in that earlier jeremiad, had employed his linguistic morality to assert that

> man must be classed among the brutes, for he is still a very awkward and salacious biped....Primeval natures wallowed without thought, but as soon as men began thinking how pleasant it was to rub themselves and have deliriums from mud, they employed their minds to achieve what paleolithic mankind did without being lascivious....He is the most ridiculous beast on earth, and the reason for this is his mind and his pudendum. (277)

In the intellectually goatish attitude typical of many such exchanges between older, established male mentors, and less established women writers who try to fashion an intellectual identity for themselves in a masculinist-pervaded literary culture, Dahlberg's mental chastity—with its attempt to set up a strict ethical opposition between mind and pudendum—turns out to be intimately related to the thinking-man's licentiousness which he decries. Dahlberg himself stands as a vibrant example of the "bad writing," symptomatic of "moral torpor, dishonest energy, fraud," which Howe says characterize his espoused ethos. Like the ostensibly neutral or chaste correspondent-therapist, Dahlberg encourages a normative epistolary voyeurism, and stakes overt moral or ethical claims for his intellectual dirty-mindedness, while attempting to relegate his female correspondent to a complementary role in a hierarchical power relationship.

Howe remarks how in the course of this correspondence she was "chided, and even verbally abused by him," and wonders in retrospect "why I had the need or desire for such a harsh instructor" ("Artobiography" 201). One might answer, without lapsing too heavily into the "artobiographical" fallacy, that Howe, like the nameless narrator of her creation (only with a much more encouraging outcome in the author's case) felt she had to write Dahlberg before she could begin to write him off. This socially-induced "need or desire" to enter into a verbally abusive contract, another version of epistolary transference—seeking the validating contempt of an older, avowedly "sexist and racist male tyrant" representing a literary culture largely contemptuous of women's experimental writing—fairly begs to be called something like "the hysteria of influence."

This tongue-in-cheek denomination in no way implies the necessity, the legitimacy, or even the tenability of such "influence"; the questionable, even pernicious, concept of acquiring a mentor or guru remains at best a useful fiction, though it's not always clear to whom the usefulness redounds. Nor am I putting forth the critically suspect notion that Howe's early (and to some extent, continuing) admiration of Dahlberg attests to some "real life" familial, Oedipal anxiety which she worked out through her relationship with Dahlberg. An attempted "psychoanalysis" of Howe would not only completely sink into autobiographical fallacy; it would replicate the misogynist underpinnings of the psychoanalytic drama under scrutiny here.

Rather, I'm asserting that, much like the "rehabilitation" of the narrator in *Forty Whacks*, the consent of female writers to self-destructive, quasi-Freudian mentoring arrangements, as a validation of their own writing, draws encouragement from the broader notions of gender and vatic/phallic initiation in contemporary society. This "need or desire" for such epistolary transference, for libidinal investment in such a literary relationship, is manufactured (not inherent or necessary) toward the ultimate end of female writers' exclusion. Even Howe's abbreviated description of her correspondence with Dahlberg hints at this kind of vatic mentoring with which numerous female writers can doubtless identify.

Experimental novelist Christine Brooke-Rose describes a canon as "very much a masculine notion, a priesthood (not to be polluted by women), a club, a sacred male preserve...or a heroic son-father struggle, in Harold Bloom's terms. But a body, a corpus, something owned. And not only a male preserve but that of a privileged caste." But despite the dependence of this libidinal, secular/sacred caste on the periodic entry of outsiders for replenishment, "women's writing does not seem ever to have had that role of 'tonic' or outside remedy, nor does it today" (55–56).

Still, in a democratic, upwardly-mobile society such as the United States of the sixties, everybody, even untouchables, had the ostensible right to speak, and to be touched if necessary. As was the case with psychotherapy, democracy and literature assumed more "open" and therefore viable guises while retaining their hieratic hierarchies. Thus Dahlberg, in the role of therapist-guru-correspondent, consents to administering to his silent, no doubt hysterical literary charge what might be dubbed "the writing cure." He sees the repressed content of Howe's wish for paternal seduction as enacted in her "symptomatic" writing.

Howe's illness might be described by Dahlberg as her delusion of herself as a writer, her desire to enter the male canon, a symptom of her "natural" but repressed erotic longings. As a female writer, her version of the Bloomian father-son struggle must find its embodiment as a fantasy of literary-paternal seduction—the hysteria of influence. But as with most illnesses, even serious ones, there is a cure.

Dahlberg, as analyst/father, moves the subject away from the body and into language by compelling her to write/speak, while he listens. But the goal of the writing cure in Dahlberg's case is to initiate the "patient" into a normative understanding which, despite her movement into language, inspires and compels a chastened silence, a realization that when it comes to the sacred caste of literature, the way is narrow and few (especially women) may enter the vatic enclave. He transmitted, says Howe, a "message about the sanctity of literature....He set a goal which was literally impossible to achieve....His own style, an atavistic vernacular, was the end result of a seven-year self-imposed 'silence,' during which time he immersed himself in reading the classics, Scripture, and studies of the same" ("Artobiography" 201).

In a homiletic homage to the anti-feminist Milton—no doubt one of Dahlberg's anxiety-producing influences—he recommends to Howe a course of action which requires prolonged silence. The writing cure thereby becomes the negation of writing. But despite these monkish imprecations, including the recommendation that she "take the vow of poverty," Dahlberg's continuation of their correspondence for the biblical seven years paradoxically encourages an erotic turn in the analyst-analysand relationship, which culminates in his offering a different paternal cure for the hysteria of influence, and a different sort of vatic-phallic initiation. If she loves his work, she must love him. She must not only be his appendage, but love his appendage.

In Dahlberg's autobiography, *Because I Was Flesh*—the book which initiated his and Howe's correspondence—he provides a telling insight into the vatic and sexual nature of his approach to epistolarity, in recounting the postscript to his sexual relations with a young woman whom he pursued and finally "conquered" during his college days at Berkeley. After many Sundays during which "Angelica twined about me her chestnut tresses" while "I wanted to fall at her feet and chastely press my lips upon her nude body," Dahlberg precipitously decides to "quit" Berkeley in favor of Columbia, in the process leaving behind his cherished Angelica, her nude body, and her chestnut tresses. He remembers the written aftermath with the delicious remorse which only the vatic-phallic conjoining of mind and pudendum can accomplish: "What epistles did Angelica later pour out of her sweet flesh, and how many times she called me Christ....How shall I atone for the beloved Angelica, the bereaved one, the interred one, save as every Edgar Allan Poe, who must bury his seraph?" (153).

Given the exquisite options of angelic burial or reply mail, the choice is easy. But Dahlberg, the avid albeit mobile student, sets forth an eyebrow-raising version of "writing the body." He learns early on the erotic charge of correspondence, the place where letter meets sweet flesh—a lesson he later wishes to teach Howe. Despite the avowed similarity between his published letters and those he sent to Howe, his correspondence with his male counterparts is of a different order, however similar the language. In his self-conscious literary exchange with Sir Herbert Read, in which Dahlberg devotes himself to skewering and vilifying the work of Joyce, Lawrence, James, Graves, Eliot, and

Pound, both he and Read assume the tone of literary oracles making sacred pronouncements from an impermeable enclave, which provides them protection against a diminished, feminized age. The first letter begins

> Dear Herbert:
> It is my fear that in this century of woe and panic literature may pass away, and that after the terrible hecatombs to come, it will be harder to find good books than the body of Osiris. These letters to you are poor oblations to the Muses, for like the Athenian women sacrificing at the tomb of Tereus, I offer you gravel instead of barley groats. (11)

When Dahlberg finds himself among his masculine equals, he executes the real business of epistolary exchange, namely the shoring up of a misogynist priestly literary phallocracy. In this prolonged correspondence with Read, tellingly published under the pious title *The Truth Is More Sacred*, he defends his tendency to censure literary works, by exclaiming, in overtly phallic prose, "I prefer a virile negation to a comfortable, flaccid yea." Dahlberg does not find it amiss, as he aptly proves in undertaking his long postal "instruction" of Howe, "to give a caveat to the raw apprentices of beauty." But the terms of the tutelary agreement are clear: worship of the vatic-phallic principle: "There can be no just words well arranged without vigor. 'I swear upon my virility,' testifies François Villon." The novels of Flaubert, Proust, Lawrence, Joyce, and James, all of which Dahlberg—also the author of a literary autobiography—strangely condemns as "personal memoirs," strike him as too effeminate. Such writing "is an occupation for the lagging ear, and not for a potent intellect." Joyce's *Ulysses*, the worst of the lot, qualifies as "a street-urchin's odyssey of a doddering phallus." Joyce "cannot father a virile sentence"; thus his book "is not rich evidence of manhood." Dahlberg concludes his initiating epistle to Read with a fervid resolution that "what we need in America are more chaste books and more whorehouses" (11–21). As in his exchanges with Howe, the mind, the pudendum, and the epistolary remain inextricable, a holy trinity and a ménage à trois. And in the Read-Dahlberg-Howe triangle I've been describing here, the proper place of each is clearly marked.

Howe's rejection of this scenario found its expression in her negation not only of Dahlberg's prosaic insinuations, but also of his insinuating prose. She began to read authors as heterogeneous as Zora Neale Hurston, Edmond Jabès, Richard Wright, and Flannery O'Connor, "none of whom are on Dahlberg's original list to me." And simultaneous with her mentored correspondence, she also made incursions into the strictly secular, non-vatic realm of popular women's fiction. At the very time she was writing Dahlberg (and *Forty Whacks*), Howe engaged in writing "pulp books for money"—three of them: *West Coast Nurse, East Coast Nurse,* and *Vietnam Nurse.* The omission of this professional detail in her letters to Dahlberg, like the epistolary narration of *Forty Whacks,* leaves itself open to interpretation as either a rejection of her literary filiality or a timorous reinforcement of it; a local abdication of identity, or part of the process of its reconstitution. "These three books," she says, "were written under the pseudonym Della Field. I never mentioned them to Dahlberg" ("Artobiography" 203).

The sustained critique of the drama of epistolary transference in Howe's fiction, and in her "artobiography," exposes the pernicious, socially constructed, and potentially paralyzing nature of that drama. It strips the hysteria of influence of its essentialism, its talismanic power to characterize a woman's desire and her need to write as literary dysfunctionality, as a need to slay the father. The writing of "Dear Edward"—the production of a dead letter—does not necessarily stand as a prerequisite to the writing of a live one.

WORKS CITED

Brooke-Rose, Christine. "Illiterations." Friedman and Fuchs 55–71.

Dahlberg, Edward. *Because I Was Flesh.* Norfolk: New Directions, 1959.

———. "From *The Sorrows of Priapus.*" *Writers in Revolt.* Ed. Richard Seaver, Terry Southern and Alexander Trucchi. New York: Frederick Fell, 1963. 277–85.

———, and Herbert Read. *The Truth is More Sacred.* London: Routledge, 1961.

Feldstein, Richard, and Judith Roof, eds. Introduction. *Feminism and Psychoanalysis.* Ithaca: Cornell UP, 1989. 1-10.

Fleiger, Jerry Aline. "Entertaining the Ménage à Trois: Psychoanalysis, Feminism, and Literature." Feldstein and Roof 185-208.

Friedman, Ellen, and Miriam Fuchs, eds. *Breaking the Sequence: Women's Experimental Fiction.* Princeton: Princeton UP, 1989.

Howe, Fanny. "Artobiography." *Writing/Talks.* Ed. Bob Perelman. Carbondale: Southern Illinois UP, 1985. 192–206.

———. *Forty Whacks.* Boston: Houghton Mifflin, 1969.

Scripted, Conscripted, and Circumscribed: Body Language in Margaret Atwood's The Handmaid's Tale

Sheila C. Conboy

Musing on the formative years of contemporary American feminism, Susan Suleiman describes how a "call went out to invent both a new poetics and a new politics, based on women's reclaiming what had always been theirs but had been usurped from them: control over their bodies and a voice with which to speak about it" (7). In response, there emerged internationally a complex corpus of writing—theoretical and imaginative—which articulates women's relationship to language. Though rejecting the pessimism inherent in Lacanian theory,[1] the works Suleiman examines—by Luce Irigaray, Hélène Cixous, and Monique Wittig—nonetheless embrace part of Lacan's revision of Freud: his theory of the female subject's "privileged relation to the real."[2] Calling for or inscribing new forms of writing which "break open chains of syntax, escape from the repressiveness of linear logic and 'story-telling,' and allow for the emergence of a language 'close to the body'" (Suleiman 16), these feminist writers demand a more materialist conception of language, a new "body language," with which to express their experience.

In her introduction to a collection of essays entitled *Literature and the Body*, Elaine Scarry explains that "a materialist conception of language ordinarily has two companion assumptions":

first, that language is capable of registering in its own contours the contours and weight of the material world; second, that language itself may enter, act on, and alter the material world. The two tend to be inevitable counterparts: the first attributes to language the features it has to have in order to fulfill the claims of the second. Only the substantiveness or weight accorded language by the first endows it with the force it must have to make an impression on the resistant surfaces of the world. (xi)

Although Scarry is concerned here with the human body—not specifically the female body—her definition of a materialist conception of language must necessarily resonate beside the feminist injunction, "Reclaim your body!" (Suleiman 12). For while Scarry separates materialism from feminism, she links both to a current interest in "the reclamation of the material world" (xxv), thereby also contrasting both to much structuralist and post-structuralist theory.

Margaret Atwood's *The Handmaid's Tale*, which inscribes a similarly materialist conception of language, reflects in an imaginative mode many issues central to contemporary feminist theory. Significantly, however, Atwood's novel—variously labelled a "dystopia" or "cautionary tale"—qualifies the optimism of that theory, suggesting that the female writer may (and perhaps should) have profound ambivalence about appropriating the power of any communication thus grounded in the body. Language, as Atwood's narrator discovers, can oppress as well as express. Ultimately, *The Handmaid's Tale* is striking in its explicit and implicit expression of female ambivalence toward writing and reading. To the same extent that the first-person narrative within the novel (also entitled "The Handmaid's Tale") reveals the narrator's contradictory thoughts about liberating her own body from the burden of other people's texts and representing her text as body, so the complete novel, with its appended "Historical Notes," suggests the author's ambivalence about the future of feminist reading in the academic setting.

Indeed, the "Historical Notes" clearly undermine the intimation of the preceding tale that although the politically powerless narrator is trapped by the texts or interpretations of others, her insistence on the reader's identification with the place of her body empowers her to create an "ideal" reader, one who reads her oppressed position sympathetically. Because the narrator, Offred, uses the body as the figure for her text and as the locus of her anxiety about representation, *The Handmaid's Tale* calls into question both the nature of Offred's narrative control and the ability of the patriarchal academy to read her story. Just as Offred's literal body is appropriated by her culture for compulsory service, so too her text—represented as scripted body and directed toward her ideal reader—is finally conscripted by the patriarchal academic institution to serve its own needs. By circumscribing the tale with this frame, Atwood pessimistically suggests that the narrator's apparently powerful language—which engenders the "body" of her tale—has failed to affect the reader *inside* the text, Professor James Darcy Pieixoto. Disempowering the narrator again, this representative of the future academy insists on reading only the "tail" of her body, thus reinforcing anxiety in the reader *outside* the text over continued misconstructions of the female body and misreadings of the female narrative.

IMPOSITION AND COMPOSITION: WRITING THE BODY AS TEXT

Although men in *The Handmaid's Tale* seem to have no apprehension about appropriating language—even when their usage curbs the freedoms of others—the female narrator shows clear ambivalence: she vacillates between a desire to "compose herself" (66) and a longing to shatter the neatness of her composition to make her language reflect her fractured experience. From the beginning, the narrator indicates the extent to which restrictions placed on her literal body result from the texts and interpretations of the fundamentalist theocracy in which she lives. The men in Gilead, not unlike Adam in the Genesis story, have been given the power to name women, and their lack of anxiety about such authorship is indicated by the proprietary names they assign to handmaids: Ofwarren, Ofglen, Offred. But the narrator's designated name literalizes her sense of entrapment and lack of control: she is both "Of Fred" and "Offered," a kind of fertility sacrifice in a sterile household.

While the men are only implicitly Adam figures, they explicitly employ Genesis to authorize control over female identity and to restrict the female body in its most threatening and powerful capacities: sex and childbirth. Official sex becomes "The Ceremony," in which the biblical story of Rachel and Jacob is reenacted literally. Just as Rachel instructed her husband to have sexual relations with her handmaid "that [she might] also have children by her" (Gen. 30:3), so does the wife attempt to control the relations between husband and handmaid. Fully dressed, the handmaid lies between the wife's legs, symbolically fusing the two women into one body, while the husband performs his part in this ritual which the narrator promises "is not exciting" (94). Ironically, the symbolic union implied by the scriptural passage is never realized in the literal act; in fact, the result is not fusion but disembodiment for the women involved, and this parody of female community produces only mutual hatred born of mutual need. As Offred admits after the sex ceremony, Serena Joy speaks to her with "loathing in her voice, as if the touch of my flesh sickens and contaminates her" (95). This biblical interpretation thus deprives the female body of its natural function and pleasure, and sex becomes a matter of mere tolerance, without true intimacy and certainly without love.

Childbearing also becomes a depersonalized rite as the birth takes place in strict accordance with the words of Genesis: Rachel's idea that her maid "shall bear upon my knees" (30:3) translates into a bizarre birthing stool on which the wife sits above the handmaid, framing the pregnant woman with her knees. Once again, this apparent union of women serves only to divide the classes of "wife" and "handmaid" even further. Wives despise handmaids for reminding them of their own infertility; handmaids hate wives for removing children from their wombs—for naming them and calling them their own. What the reader first notices in the sex scene and the birth scene are the differences between the wives' and handmaids' bodies; but even more powerful is the fact that both have been appropriated by patriarchy. Not only have men imposed their biblical interpretations on the women's bodies, but they have forced women themselves to internalize their new culture's expectations: Offred, for example, admits, "Each month I watch for blood, fearfully, for when it comes it means failure. I have failed once again to fulfill the expectations of others, which have become my own" (73).

Yet even as her body submits to the given role of procreation in her present life, it betrays her through its continued commitment to the past. She ambivalently keeps alive, in her mind as well as in her text, the very memories of "before" which both threaten and assist her intention to survive her present conditions. The patriarchal government imposes on the narrator's body texts which are interpreted univocally, and thus ensures the essentially material capacity of words to inflict pain. But the narrator's equivocal wordplay, which often reinterprets those texts, ultimately materializes in a more capacious composition of her body, one which she invites us to read otherwise. For example, as she explains, her "real" name, which the reader never learns,[3] is an alternative text about identity:

> My name isn't Offred, I have another name, which nobody uses now because it's forbidden. I tell myself it doesn't matter, your name is like your telephone number, useful only to others; but what I tell myself is wrong, it does matter. I keep the knowledge of this name like something hidden, some treasure I'll come back to dig up, one day. I think of this name as buried. The name has an aura around it, like an amulet, some charm that's survived from an unimaginably distant past. I lie in my single bed at night, with my eyes closed, and the name floats there behind my eyes, not quite within reach, shining in the dark. (84)

For the narrator, a name is a physical presence: she believes that it embodies the material connection between signifier and signified, whereas the patronymic "Offred" is merely a debased signifier of her current status, which she considers "unreal."[4]

Offred also finds ways to suggest the limited nature of biblical interpretation in her regime. Grimly remembering the fate which might await her if she fails to produce a child, she recites Rachel's words, "Give me children or else I die," adding "there's more than one meaning to it" (61). Whereas the Gileadean regime employs the Bible to enforce a passive acceptance of the "law" of God, Offred explicitly insists on an interplay between language and action, thus mirroring feminist theory's political content, its activist exhortation to change—or break—the law. Viewing the household Bible, Offred thinks,

> The Bible is kept locked up, the way people once kept tea locked up, so the servants wouldn't steal it. It is an incendiary device: who knows what we'd make of it, if we ever got our hands on it? (87)

On the night of the Ceremony, after the commander reads the "mouldy old Rachel and Leah stuff" (88), Offred hears the closing of the Bible as "an exhausted sound" (90); yet her recognition of language's potentially inflammatory nature intimates that she has not yet exhausted the possibilities for interpreting that book—that (as her friend Moira sings comically) "there is a Bomb in Gilead" (218), and telling her story may detonate it.

However, at the same time that the narrator constructs a text grounded in the body, she admits her ambivalence about faithfully recording her own bodily experience: "I avoid looking down at my body....I don't want to look at something that determines me so completely" (63). In one respect, this ambivalence results from the body's needs, which force the narrator to feel unfaithful to her past life. By bridging past and present, her body betrays her—betrays the people and the promises of her former life—as it requires comfort and fulfillment in the present. Yet her new life seems to promise only disembodiment for the narrator. In a society in which her interchangeability with other handmaids erases her individuality, she knows that there have been other "Offreds" and that even if she successfully bears a child there will be others in the future. In addition, her admission of repressed sexual desire—her loneliness at the apparent impossibility of future relationships—denies the body even as it awakens it. Feeling as unreal as the flickering ghosts from her past, she asks: "Can I be blamed for wanting a real body, to put my arms around? Without it, I too, am disembodied" (104). Her narrative, another bridge between past and present, often seems similarly generated by drives beyond her control. In the same way that she fears looking at her body, Offred repeatedly avoids looking at her past, saying about her most painful memories: "I don't want to be telling this story" (225).

In another respect, her ambivalence reflects doubt about her narrative control, her ability to remember the body in her text:

> It's impossible to say a thing exactly the way it was, because you can never be exact, you always have to leave something out, there are too many parts, sides, crosscurrents, nuances; too many gestures, which could mean this or that, too many shapes which can never be fully described, too many flavors, in the air or on the tongue, half-colors, too many. (134)

Indeed, she often asserts a curious connection between physical experience and word—a connection which reverses the ordinary relationship between signifier and signified—saying, for example, that women in old Humphrey Bogart films "wore blouses with buttons down the front that suggested the possibilities of the word *undone*" (25), that summer gardens provoked "the return of the word *swoon*" (153), and that sexual desire made her own body "feel like the word *shatter*" (103). Such assertions imply her use of a materialist conception of language, her sense that (as much current feminist theory proposes) language *contains* bodily experience.[5] Yet such a conception may exacerbate her ambivalence about using language, for in recuperating her body through her text, she must record not only the pain inflicted by others, but also the pain generated by her own memory. Challenging the limitations placed on her body through the seemingly limitless nature of her text, Offred makes the body her book[6]—one which she both reads and writes in a new mode. In fact, she recreates herself in her text: "My self is a thing I must now compose, as one composes a speech. What I must present is a made thing, not something born" (66).

SCRABBLE AS KINKY SEX: WRITING THE TEXT AS BODY

For Offred, then, not only does language corporealize the body's experience, but the body gives birth to the linguistic artifact. One of the clearest links between language and the body occurs at the novel's structural center—chapter 23—when Offred explicitly connects sexuality and textuality. Following a request from the Commander that she meet him in his study— "this forbidden room where I have never been, where women do not go" (136)—she admits that she expected

> something unspeakable, down on all fours perhaps, perversions, whips, mutilations? At the very least some minor sexual manipulation, some bygone peccadillo now denied him, prohibited by law and punishable by amputation. To be asked to play Scrabble, instead, as if we were an old married couple, or two children, seemed kinky in the extreme, a violation in its own way. (155)

Yet in this society, where language is, for women, as illicit as unauthorized sex, Scrabble is itself "unspeakable." That the narrator may employ the game in the serious business of rediscovering her voice seems clear from the first word she spells, "Larynx," but from this point on, she also complicates the interplay between language and the body, revealing that if texts can control bodies, bodies may also provide figures for texts. Rather than demonstrating how the body can feel like a word, she here tests the textures of words themselves: "I hold the glossy counters with their smooth edges, finger the letters. The feeling is voluptuous. *Limp*, I spell. *Gorge*. What a luxury" (139).

So sensuous is the quality of language that Offred can actually taste the letters; they are "candies, made of peppermint, cool like that....I would like to put them in my mouth. They would also taste of lime. The letter C. Crisp, slightly acid on the tongue, delicious" (139). In some ways, the Scrabble game represents in miniature the narrator's text: she employs many words which reflect her bodily restrictions or desires (larynx, zygote, limp, gorge, quandary, sylph); then she liberates herself as she shapes and tastes the words that she can substitute for those that have been put in her mouth ("Blessed be the fruit," "May the Lord open," and other phrases approved for her utterance).[7]

In the larger narrative, too, Offred refigures the body *through* the text, as she imagines the narrative as a metaphorical body. Alluding specifically to the shape of her story, Offred apologizes that it is "in fragments, like a body caught in crossfire or pulled apart by force" (267). This textual body, "this sad and hungry and sordid, this limping and mutilated story" (267–68), replicates the narrator's literal body, which is cut off from her free mind: both body and text are experienced as parts which do not always cohere, as shattered wholes. Yet the very complexity which makes this fragmented tale difficult to read might also empower the narrator to produce an ideal reader who can "share her bewilderment and disorientation" (Greene 14).

This ideal reader is one who responds to the text's extensive allusions to the female body, one who is capable of "rereading as a woman," as Nancy K. Miller puts it—one who can "imagine while reading the place of a woman's body" (355). As Offred herself suggests, her pain in telling the tale is assuaged by the conviction that "I want you to hear it, as I will hear yours too if I ever get the chance." In fact, Offred goes so far as to declare that she is creating her reader: "By telling you anything at all I'm at least believing in you, I believe you're there, I believe you into being. Because I'm telling you this story I will your existence. I tell, therefore you are" (268). Thus, her bodily experience shapes not only her narrative, but also the reader's experience of her narrative.

By shaping the reader's complex identification with her experience, Offred helps the reader to find hope in certain gaps in the narrative structure. For unlike the literal body, the narrative body suggests, if only occasionally, power, choice, and possibility. In spite of the narrator's reminders of her limitations—her frequent assertion that "this is a reconstruction"—the insistent present tense of her story provides a sense of immediacy, a sense of possibilities beyond the restrictive circumstances of her surroundings. For example, when Offred tells her reader what she believes happened to Luke after their attempted escape, she gives three different versions: he is dead of gunshot wounds; he lives as a political prisoner; he escaped to freedom and works with the resistance. Admitting that these versions "can't all be true," she still believes in all of them so that "whatever the truth is…[she'll] be ready for it" (106). Her contradictory beliefs open rather than close textual possibility for the reader.

Like the mutually exclusive accounts of Luke's fate, Offred's conflicting reports of her sexual relations with Nick leave the reader with an optimism which opposes most of the fictive circumstances she recounts. Meeting Nick with help from Serena Joy, the narrator gives what seems to be a straightforward (if somewhat romanticized) account of their relations. Yet the narrator immediately confesses, "I made that up," and then provides an alternate sketch, almost like a take from a Bogart or Brando film, in which the no-nonsense Nick, answering the door in his shirt sleeves (complete with cigarette) moves from sexual banter, to caresses, and finally to sex, first extracting the promise of "no romance." In spite of her nostalgia for such playful talk, Offred realizes what it is for, "what it was always for: to keep the core of yourself out of reach, enclosed, protected" (262).

To some extent this enclosed and protected "self" ensures the partner's eroticization of the unknown, and the true account of this meeting is likewise eroticized because kept "out of reach": the narrator finally denies this second version of the story, too, claiming "It didn't happen that way either.…All I can hope for is a reconstruction" (263). By leaving the reader with nothing but an imagined affair (as well as the knowledge that she went back "time after time, on...[her] own"), the narrator calls into question the representational nature of her text. The narrative body may, finally, be a mirror no more reliable than the glass hanging on the wall in Serena Joy's house, which pictures the narrator's body as "a distorted shadow, a parody of something, some fairytale figure in a red cloak" (9). But if Offred's feminist body language optimistically shows her narrative to be the "word made flesh," it is in part because the reader is willing to imagine the possibilities, is willing to nurture the textual body by keeping those possibilities alive.

THE UNDERGROUND FRAILROAD:
READING THE FEMALE BODY

Although Offred's narration invites the reader to identify with her position, Atwood's "Historical Notes"—part of her novel, though not part of Offred's narrative—question whether such reading will be possible in the future. In what might be called an "afterword," Offred's already futuristic narrative is contextualized by a conference which considers that narrative—"The Handmaid's Tale"—in its historical setting. Here, Atwood destroys the hope that Offred has succeeded in creating an ideal reader, for as the keynote speaker begins to analyze her text, he makes a direct sexual innuendo concerning the female professor who introduced him: "I am sure we all enjoyed our charming Arctic Char last night at dinner, and now we are enjoying an equally charming Arctic Chair. I use the word 'enjoy' in two distinct senses, precluding, of course, the obsolete third (*Laughter*)." (300). The third sense of the word is clearly not obsolete, as it amuses the crowd; and only the reader is left with the irony that in spite of the narrator's plea for identification—in spite of the body-focused language which worked to create a reader who might read the place of a woman's body—the future holds still more readers who will read for their pleasure in and exploitation of the female body. Indeed, Professor Pieixoto's talk—hardly to be called "scholarship," especially considering that he himself refers to it as "my little chat" (300)—seems specifically designed to counter the feminist form and content of Offred's tale.

Whereas Offred speaks as a woman to readers who might read "as women,"[8] Pieixoto speaks, in Miller's construction, "as...[a man] to other men...the better to neutralize...the disruption that feminism promises" (355).

Even more ironically, the reader can remember one of Offred's analyses of her restrictive surroundings: "I sit in the chair and think about the word *chair*. It can also mean the leader of a meeting. It can also mean a mode of execution. It is the first syllable in *charity*. It is the French word for flesh. None of these facts has any connection with the others" (110). Offred's reluctance to imagine connections where there are none apparently indicates her lack of control, her sense of incoherence. In contrast, Pieixoto does not hesitate to exert his linguistic control by playing on the word "enjoy" in connection with the French word for flesh, by punning on "the archaic vulgar signification of the word *tail*" in the title of the text at hand, and by referring cynically to the female rescue mission of the Gileadean Period as "The Underground Frailroad" (301). While his playful language is not *entirely* unlike Offred's call for an opening of textual possiblity, such misogynistic usage clearly opposes Offred's anxious trust that someone will truly "hear" her: "Dear You" (40), she addresses her reader, hoping that her voice embodies herself. She recalls early in the narrative "a quaint expression you sometimes hear, still, from older people: *I hear where you're coming from*, as if the voice itself were a traveler, arriving from a distant place. Which it would be, which it is" (11). Which it is not, for Professor Pieixoto—whose glee over his clever language reminds us that feminists are to respond at least with good-natured groans, or they have no sense of humor.

In addition, Offred's text now fulfills only one of the "companion assumptions" of Scarry's definition of a "materialist" conception of language: while it does, in effect, register "in its own contours the contours and weight of the material world" of Offred's experience, it ultimately fails to "enter, act on, and alter" Pieixoto's world. He indicates that the *material* of Offred's story does not *matter*, that he even wishes she had written a different text, one which would tell him more about the men in her world: "many gaps remain. Some of them could have been filled in by our anonymous author, had she had a different turn of mind" (310). This afterword implies that contemporary feminist reading may be remembered as an "underground railroad" of sorts—one which sought to rescue women's texts from their minor position in the male-dominated canon, but failed to change academic power structures in lasting ways.

If feminist theory seeks in part to free the female reader from her trained identification with a male point of view—her readerly conscription into the service of the patriarchy—Atwood's picture for the future of such reading is bleak. By framing the story with the male-centered proceedings of this conference, Atwood circumscribes our initial optimism—demonstrating how the need for control, closure, and irony makes some readers assemble the textual body that the narrator shows to be in pieces. Conceivably, then, as a cautionary tale, *The Handmaid's Tale* warns that although we must continue scripting, refiguring, and reembodying woman, our ideal readers are too few, and our anxious power, perhaps, illusory.

NOTES

1. Silverman persuasively undermines Lacan's insistence that the female subject is excluded "from symbolic authority and privilege" (188). She argues that "the female subject's linguistic inauguration must be seen as locating her, too, on the side of meaning rather than being," and adds that "female sexuality would seem to be even more exhaustively and intensively 'spoken' than is male sexuality, to be a site where numerous discourses converge" (189).

2. Silverman summarizes Lacan's theory of female subjectivity, explaining that "the female subject neither succumbs to as complete an alienation from the real, nor enjoys as full an association with the symbolic as does the male subject....The female subject escapes that 'castration' which alone assures the male subject his symbolic potency" (186). This "escape" is itself negatively defined, for Lacan goes on to say that woman "lacks lack." But Silverman argues that "woman as plenitude and woman as lack are merely two alternative cultural projections by means of which man can always be assured of having the phallus—in the first instance through appropriation, and in the second through an oppositional definition" (188).

3. Bergmann argues that "the narrator never tells us her name directly, but the list of names at the beginning of the novel, whispered at the Red Center, indicate that it is probably 'June,' since every other

name in the list is assigned to a character." While I find her specula-tion interesting, she does not give sufficient textual evidence to sup-port her contention that the name becomes "a kind of password" (853). It seems to remain more of a "buried treasure."

4. Offred's belief about the material significance of her name opposes Saussure's principle that "the bond between the signifier and the signified is arbitrary" (67).

5. Scarry cites John Donne as an example of a writer who "affirms the continuity between the materiality of the world and the immateri-ality of language by reconceiving language in terms of physical attributes" (xiv).

6. The title of Scarry's own essay in her volume—"Donne: 'But yet the body is his booke'"—suggested the multiple meanings of this phrase.

7. Interestingly, Offred also finds ways to revise texts—to come up with a "new testament" of her own. See, for instance, her revision of the "Lord's Prayer" (194).

8. This phrase originates with Culler, but Miller remarks on her own uneasiness about male critics appropriating feminist language in order merely to speak to one another—an uneasiness which she notes that Elaine Showalter elsewhere calls the "anxiety of recuperation."

WORKS CITED

Atwood, Margaret. *The Handmaid's Tale*. Boston: Houghton Mifflin, 1986.

Bergmann, Harriet. "'Teaching Them to Read': A Fishing Expedition in *The Handmaid's Tale*." *College English* 51 (1989): 847–54.

Culler, Jonathan. *On Deconstruction*. Ithaca: Cornell UP, 1982.

Greene, Gayle. "Choice of Evils." Rev. of *The Handmaid's Tale*, by Mar-garet Atwood. *Women's Review of Books* July 1986: 14–15.

Miller, Nancy K. "Re-reading as a Woman: The Body in Practice." Suleiman, *Female* 354–62.

Saussure, Ferdinand de. *Course in General Linguistics*. Trans. Wade Baskin. New York: McGraw-Hill, 1966.

Scarry, Elaine. Introduction. *Literature and the Body: Essays on Popula-tions and Persons*. Ed. Elaine Scarry. English Institute New Series 12. Baltimore: Johns Hopkins UP, 1988. vii–xxvii.

Silverman, Kaja. *The Subject of Semiotics*. New York: Oxford UP, 1983.

Suleiman, Susan Rubin, ed. *The Female Body in Western Culture: Contemporary Perspectives*. Cambridge: Harvard UP, 1986.

———. "(Re)Writing the Body: The Politics and Poetics of Female Eroticism." Suleiman, *Female* 7–29.

Discourse as Power: Renouncing Denial

Diane P. Freedman

> [Marie Curie] died a famous woman denying
> her wounds
> denying
> her wounds came from the same source as her power
> —Adrienne Rich, "Power"

> The majority of women who go through undergraduate and
> graduate school suffer an intellectual coercion of which they are
> not even consciously aware. In a world where language and
> naming are power, silence is oppression, is violence.
> —Adrienne Rich, "Conditions for Work:
> The Common World of Women"

Long before I embarked on a project to seek out and characterize feminist strategies in literary writing, I was aware of the connection between words and power, though I did not see the possible wounding effect of certain kinds of words or discourse. I
accepted blithely the classical notion of discourse as power: to
survive in Athenian democracy, where (male) citizens argued
their own cases and lawsuits were a way of life, men had to
become adept orators. If they couldn't speak well enough, they
hired a coach or speech writer to augment their education in
reading, writing, and oratory. I thought I should be prepared for
my days as citizen—study English or attend law school, or both.

I hadn't yet recognized that as a woman I was alienated by
both tradition and temperament from conventional argumentative discourse; I sensed only vaguely why it was an emotional
struggle for me to read and write in what I later found out has
been called the "male" or "logocentric" or even "phallogocentric" mode. I believed I could use what I took to be my increasing
facility with language to give voice to whatever "wounded" or
excluded me. I never thought it might be the language and laws

363

of patriarchy that did the wounding and excluding. I didn't ask whether "mastering" the dominant and societal discourses would be self-effacing rather than empowering. Like Marie Curie in Rich's poem, I denied that my wounds might come from the same source as my power, that there was a cost for conventional power. In Curie's case, the source was radium, that odd element which both cures and causes cancers. In my case, it was language. Language can liberate but it can also oppress.

It was only later that I saw the possibility of non-exclusive, non-combative language—what has been called the "female" mode, a style associative, nonhierarchical, personal, and open-ended. As Thomas J. Farrell puts it, "The female mode seems at times to obfuscate the boundary between the self of the author and the subject of the discourse, as well as between the self and the audience" (910). Such writing "follows the shifting perspectives of the writer's mind" (Huber 356). Writers in the female mode use language not to gain power but to create intimacy (Thorne et al.)—intimacy often achieved though self-reflexive statements on the why and how of their practice. Such self-conscious or metadiscursive comments commonly announce the substitution of unconventional or multiple genres for the traditional essay, argue for personal over fixed forms.[1] Further, many feminists speak about refusing to be silenced, not only historically and by patriarchy generally, but within the privileged enclave of academia and its discourses, to which at least some feminists have had illusory or token access. As Rich asserts, no woman is an insider in the institutions fathered by masculine consciousness.

Contemporary feminists want their voices heard in the academy as well as in society, but they write and speak increasingly on/in their own terms, in language denouncing dominant institutions and their discourse(s) while renouncing self-denial. Such writing refuses to deny its author's many voices; it speaks *of* as well as *from* the self, thus demonstrating the power engendered by feminist discourse(s) while rejecting "male" versions of powerful discourse.[2] So Gloria Anzaldúa refuses to deny her many voices: "I will no longer be made to feel ashamed of existing. I will have my voice: Indian, Spanish, White. I will have my serpent's tongue—my woman's voice, my sexual voice, my poet's voice. I will overcome the tradition of silence" (59). Elsewhere, she suggests that the hybrid form of *Borderlands/La Frontera: the New Mestiza*—which mixes English and Spanish dialects, literary genres, and disciplinary discourses—is an extension of her hybrid or mixed-blood identity (77). As Susan Griffin claims, "Why we write, as feminists, is not separable from our lives" (220).

If why and how women write is not separable from their lives, it is also not separable from a history of silence and of nonacademic forms of expression that served lives formerly (and formally) circumscribed:

> The women of the twentieth century who write speak out of a tradition of silence, a tradition of the...personal, revelatory language of diaries and journals. Our style, therefore, does not conform to the traditional patriarchal style we have been taught to regard as "literary" and "correct." (Penelope and Wolfe 125)

The histories of silenced and censored women—including modern American women who allegedly were given access to literary education, the vote, the press, and professorships—became fully known to me only after I became a doctoral candidate in English and began to ask: What kinds of discourse yield (or reject) what kinds of power?

Before I decided to pursue a doctorate in English, however, I considered attending law school, gaining power through conventional oratory. I worked at a university with a law school and one weekend, in order to learn what law school and the practice of law would be like, I attended a symposium on Women and the Law. Of the many activities in which I took part that weekend, one stands out as offering a matrix for explaining and exploring my alternately assertive and ambivalent views of the power of discourse(s), of the power of analysis versus narrative—or legal jargon and generalities versus the language of personal experience.

For an hour or two, I joined a small group in role-playing situations that lawyers who are committed to women's rights might face. What if a manufacturing company notorious for discriminatory hiring and promotion practices asked a feminist law firm, of which we were members, to conduct a one-day workshop on sexual harassment? We and our partners knew the workshop would bring in a big fee, and we were short on the funds needed to help the clients to whom we were most committed—women and children on welfare, the homeless, rape victims. But we also knew the workshop was just a public relations move for the company. It was unlikely that management would follow through or support victims of sexual harassment. Would we do the workshop anyway?

Many women said they would always refuse to work for such a firm; their valuable time would be wasted, especially since no program was planned as a follow-up to the workshop. But I felt strongly that the women in the unenlightened corporation—not to mention the *pro bono* cases the workshop fee would make possible—needed our help. Women furnished with language describing their oppression would be empowered to stop harassers, I argued. Many women don't even know the term and therefore don't have the concept of "sexual harassment." They might know they feel uncomfortable when pressured by a male coworker or supervisor for sex, but, ignorant of the word for it, they might not know how many others are fighting similar situations. Sexual harassment is an institutional, not merely individual, phenomenon; the term itself, like the workshop, signals that there are laws against it and measures that can be taken against those who "sexually harass."

However, empowering though the term sexual harassment may be, it denies the depths and details of the particular—unless the naming process is a prelude to a narrative one, that important exchanging and validating of individual stories and voices. Women may learn more through narrative—their own and others'—than through an argumentative discourse based on generalities and abstractions.[3] So I confided at the symposium that when I was a sophomore in college, a male professor had in fact harassed me, but I didn't know how to speak of it to my friends, male or female. (I was sitting in a stiff wooden chair in his office, discussing the opportunity for a grant for summer fieldwork, when he strode over to me from behind his desk and silenced me with a sudden violent kiss, after which I sputtered awkwardly that I had to go.) I thought it was my fault. I was helped along in my silence by my profound embarrassment and the fact that I needed the grant, but I soon thereafter changed my academic major. When harassed again, if more subtly, by two other male professors, I still couldn't generalize from the first experience, lump the incidents together under one rubric, one name. If I had had a term for this phenomenon, however, I feel sure I could have not only stopped these men from future acts of harassment but felt less anxious and confused.

As I was to read later in an interview with poet Marge Piercy, "When you're a woman before there is a language of feminism, trying to understand what it's like to be a woman, you have no concepts, no vocabulary for even understanding your own situation" (*Parti-colored* 323). Those hypothetical women of our workshop—and others like me at nineteen— needed to know the term "harassment," needed to recognize and acquire the power of naming rather than denial. And they needed also to share their stories. As Griffin notes, "silence leads to more silence" (186). Audre Lorde agrees: "Your silence will not protect you" (41).

I see now that we would have received a better education in naming at the hands of a feminist critic than a lawyer, since the dictionary defines harassment as merely "annoyance" or "vexation." Dominant language can help, because it does foreground the transgression better than silence and it makes possible group knowledge, group response. But it is still somehow inadequate for the hustling/hassling scandal of a person in power taking advantage of someone socially, economically, physically, and verbally unempowered. I wish I had had access to Rich's analysis, which came too late for me (1978) but clearly narrates my experience:

> Most young women experience a profound mixture of humiliation and self-doubt over seductive gestures by men who have the power to award grades, open doors to grants and graduate school, or extend special knowledge and training. Even turned aside, such gestures constitute mental rape, destructive to a woman's ego. They are acts of domination, as despicable as the molestation of the daughter by the father. (*Lies* 242–43)

My decision to research and then apply to law school came from the anger I'd felt at being denied a voice even in the world of the English major (in classes with male teachers, as a public and private-school teacher, as an underpaid freelance editor and proofreader, and as a poet myself—a role considered by others flaky, out of touch with reality), as well as from the conviction that I could "master" the law and its language. I believed I could help save others both with and from legal language. Like Rich, I was someone for whom language [had] implied freedom, while I nonetheless recognized that others "have had language and literature used against them, to keep them in their place, to mystify, to bully, to make them feel powerless" (*Lies* 62–63). I supposed back then that learning the terms of the system was the first step toward surviving under it, and that survival was required for change from within or without.

I had always been an advocate—someone who helped stage a moratorium against the Vietnam War in junior high school, tried to suspend classes in high school to hold a symposium called "Future Week," built a "free school" within the physical structure and curriculum of the high school, took buses to Washington, DC, for impeach-Nixon and anti-nuclear rallies. I was also a rather irritable consumer advocate, one who wrote angry but businesslike letters to manufacturers whose products failed me (I was a consummate capitalist even as I railed against bureaucracy and greed). I returned damaged goods—even spoiled milk—to stores, held onto warranties, called the police on neighbors who refused to silence their dogs' late-night barking, denounced women's exploitation in the fields of teaching and publishing, and improved my status and salary at work (by ensuring that my position, no longer merely secretarial, was reclassified). It would seem, on the surface, that I was a master of self-assertion: I had even been asked to lead an assertiveness-training workshop for college students, primarily women.

But much of my letter-writing, manager-hating, and hand-wringing was basically self-destructive. To borrow Emily Dickinson's words, "I aimed my Pebble—but Myself / Was all the one that fell." I couldn't sleep at night for the angers which seethed within me; my preliminary businesslike requests were soon followed by demands and tears. I could neither accept nor stop the noises next door. It occurs to me now that like children who lack language to describe their abusers and abuse, but who nonetheless, according to child psychologists, "tell," I had been acting out what I felt to be the abusive dimensions of being a woman/consumer/alienated worker in western society.

I was a parody of the diligent homemaker; because I wasn't in a position to bake, can, quilt, or garden, I shopped for bargains and tried to perform what I took to be my material duties as a grown-up woman—in the form of consumer activism. While I might eventually receive an apology from a mail-order house or obtain the petition that I needed three other annoyed neighbors to sign against the offending one, I had no real power, and the military-industrial complex as well as male neighbors with Doberman pinschers and red Corvettes—which I somehow linked together—would do damage again, not only to me.

I thought if I were trained and accredited in the law, I would have power over all my harassers. I didn't know that such power sometimes eludes even female attorneys[4] or, more important, that attempts to overpower another are nothing if not self-destructive. Moreover, I didn't yet see, as Griffin did, that "the culture which educates me and whose language I speak wants to silence women" (186). At the law symposium, I glowed with pride as workshop participants asked whether I was already a law student, intimating that I should be, I spoke like a lawyer, and so forth. I was proud, too, when I was subsequently accepted into that conservative, prestigious law school after proving once again my linguistic powers (and the power of language)—on the entrance exam and essay.

Clearly I hadn't yet read and recognized Lorde's conviction that *"the master's tools will never dismantle the master's house"* (112). When I did read Lorde's essay I questioned the logic of her image even as I relished its rhetorical ring: Why can't the master's tools dismantle his house? The tools are nothing without their worker. And yet: Maybe the image isn't right, but the sentiment surely could be. In my case, my tool was language, but even harboring the notion of mastering language was proof that I was stuck in the "master's house." Like it or not, I was already implicated in, even a privileged member of, the master system. Rich observed in 1987 that "white women are situated within white patriarchy as well as against it" (*Blood* x): the greater facility I had with the master's language, the more closely I was allied with the system I considered dismantling. This hierarchical system grants power to women or others angry at their oppression only so long as they acquiesce in perpetuating the patriarchy.

But I was not willing to accept only the power accorded those who don't make waves, what Elizabeth Janeway calls the "power of the weak." I didn't believe that I could manage silence sweetly and subversively, or even that I could sweet-talk or street-walk my way around men, but what other alternatives to legal action and language were there? I couldn't make my way to a powerful man's heart through his stomach (nor did I want to). And I didn't have a women's group for support and Janeway's "effective action"; I had only the words I worked at alone as a writer—until, that is, I read such feminist writer-critics as Rich, Anzaldúa, Lorde, Griffin, and Piercy, whose powerful prose blending personal narrative and theory or politics and poetry inspired me to write both about them and like them.

I was plagued by proliferating questions. Can power be truly positive? Even what is called "power-within" (as distinguished from "power-over") can intimidate those without it. Surely some of the male academics who verbally intimidated me tried not to, but it happened anyway: does asserting the self necessarily mean denying another? Can parachuting away from one kind of discourse (closed, legal, patriarchal, academic, impersonal, elitist) to another (open, revolutionary, feminist, quotidian, personal) solve such a problem? Is it possible to write and speak differently, after all? And if so, would we still (or finally!) get published? Would we be heard? Would we lose our jobs, be denied tenure? Where would the difference(s) reside—in new genres, new grammar, new voices, new imagery? The feminist writers I read answer or continue to ask these questions in many ways.

Rich determinedly rewrites the very definition of "power":

> The word *power* is highly charged for women. It has long been associated for us with the use of force, with rape, with the stockpiling of weapons, with the ruthless accrual of wealth and the hoarding of resources, with the power that acts only in its own interest, despising and exploiting the powerless—including women and children....But for a long time now, feminists have been talking about redefining power, about that meaning of power which returns to the root...to be able, to have the potential, to possess and use one's energy of creation—*transforming power*. (*Blood* 5)

Like Rich, Anzaldúa also clearly believes creative power, which is indispensable, is tied up in personal power: "a lack of belief in my creative self, is a lack of belief in my total self and vice versa—I cannot separate my writing from any part of my life. It is all one" (73). Both Rich and Anzaldúa imply that power of a certain sort ("transforming," "creative") is both good and separate from exploitative kinds of power. They echo other feminists like Nancy Hartsock, who in 1981 wrote: "a feminist definition of power—power as energy, effective interaction, or empowerment—contrasts with and challenges the assumption of power as domination or control" (qtd. in Thorne et al. 19).

Janeway suggests that too often women are oppressed by their fears of reinforcing the power system, and that perhaps they should dismiss such questions as:

> Suppose I make a breakthrough; what will I get that's worth the hassle? Won't I have to commit myself to masculine goals and techniques for doing my work that I both dislike and resent, personally and in principle? How can a woman get anywhere without following Henry Higgins's suggestion and being more like a man? Do I want to pay that price in order to lay my hands on power? In fact, do I really want to lay my hands on it at all? (326)

But I can't afford to dismiss this question of being thus assimilated, positioned as I am in the academy—first a doctoral student and, as of this writing, an assistant professor of English. I agree with Rich's assertion that "at the bedrock level of my thinking…is the sense that language is power.…But this notion hangs on a special conception of what it means to be released into language: *not simply learning the jargon of an elite, fitting unexceptionally into the status quo*" (*Lies* 67, emphasis mine).

Rich obviously found a way to use language powerfully without "fitting unexceptionally into the status quo"; I felt great relief when I read her ideas, as well as the nonconventional forms (personal narratives, journals, poems-in-prose) and ideas of such feminist writers as Griffin, Anzaldúa, Lorde, Piercy, Alice Walker, Louise Bernikow, Cherrie Moraga, and Judy Grahn. I felt I'd finally uncovered a language and history, not only for physical harassment, but for the extremely efficient if not obvious silencing I'd experienced for years. But almost immediately I was told, by those concerned for my academic welfare or by the examples of those who were not, not to write like them. My protectors and critics realized, with Jane Tompkins, that "to break with conventions is to risk not being heard at all." English feminist Michelene Wandor, who writes in a variety of genres, sometimes in the same work, admits that she feels "a continual uncertainty that [her] voice may not be heard, because it does not run smoothly into any single, clear channel" (86).

And yet I speak of these matters because now I do believe powerful—because unconventional—feminist discourse is possible. Rich and those others I've mentioned inspire still other women to write in their own voices ("follow your own path; it's okay to do that," Rich said at the 1988 University of Washington Roethke Memorial Reading). I speak of these matters in an academic context (the law school symposium, the harassing professors, the question of tenure), because that is where I find myself and where at least some of these questions about language are being discussed. Moreover, I speak of these matters in the manner of a story because women may well have different ways of knowing, that is, through narrative, than men.[5] The narrative or testimonial mode is one of those features of feminist essays I find personally indispensable.[6] In fact, feminist writer-critics' reliance on narrative, testimony, anecdote, poetry—on a self-conscious mixture or patchwork of genres—is one powerful way of revising the conventional academic modes they would criticize.

Obviously, something happened between the time I was accepted to law school and this writing. I deliberated long about leaving a job I liked—helping administer a university writing program—to learn instead legal language and go into deep debt. I formally deferred my admission for a year as I thought about where I could best be myself.

Rich has lectured, "refuse to give up your capacity to think as a woman, even though in the graduate schools and professions...you will be praised and rewarded for 'thinking like a man'" (*Blood* 4–5). I knew, because I had visited several classes, that I would be appalled by the lack of emotional and moral content in legal lectures; I would miss the poetic (word) "justice." Being a law student might simply be another way of acting out the harassment I felt I was always receiving at the hands of a patriarchy. (When asked why I was applying to law school, I told several friends I felt a need to "sue everybody," certainly no solution to my general feeling of powerlessness.) Perhaps what I needed was a kind of double literacy—legal or patriarchal terms for patriarchal ills (employment discrimination, harassment, sexual assault) and institutional attempts at cures (equal-opportunity employer, no-fraternizing clauses, comparable worth, welfare) as well as woman-centered words of personal experience and re-vision. But I was most desperate for the latter.

I too had been a poet, though it was doubtful if in my ongoing self-doubt I still was, yet I was still making my own coinages in stolen moments, without much recognition (which to me meant without much success), when I applied to law school. I admit that part of me wanted to prove to my former classmates that I was not merely a poet (in their minds, an apolitical, alogical anachronism). I also wanted to earn more respect and money than that accorded academic literary specialists or writers, especially those without teaching appointments. I wanted to merge the creative writer and the intellectual, the dreamer and the doer. I had been hurt by all the law school-bound men I knew in college who habitually had excluded me from their farmworker/social-democratic/Marxist dialogues and diatribes. I recall being both angry and cheered when I read what I took to be a description of my plight in Marge Piercy's poem, "In the men's room(s)":

> When I was young I believed in intellectual conversation:
> I thought the patterns we wove on stale smoke
> floated off to the heaven of ideas.
> To be certified worthy of high masculine discourse
> like a potato grater I would rub on contempt
> suck snubs, wade proudly through the brown stuff on the floor.
> They were talking of integrity and existential ennui
> while the women ran out for six-packs and had abortions
> in the kitchen and fed the children and were auctioned off.
>
> Eventually of course I learned how their eyes perceived me:
> when I bore to them cupped in my hands a new poem to nibble,
> when I brought my aerial maps of Sartre or Marx,
> they said, she is trying to attract our attention,
> she is offering up her breasts and thighs.
> I walked on eggs, their tremulous equal:
> they saw a fish peddler hawking in the street.

Now I get coarse when the abstract nouns start flashing.
I go out to the kitchen and talk cabbages and habits.
I try hard to remember to watch what people do.
Yes, keep your eyes on the hands, let the voice go buzzing.
Economy is the bone, politics is the flesh,
watch who they beat and who they eat,
watch who they relieve themselves on, watch who they own.
The rest is decoration.

With such women's wisdom in my ears, I convinced myself I would be truer to myself—and the language around me would be truer to my experience—if I put off law school and applied to doctoral programs in literature instead. It seems another one of my motivations for applying to law school had been a desire to prove I could succeed at a conventional task for a middle-class Jew: going to professional school. I had proven I could compete.

Yet such an attitude makes me wonder: How could I have been afraid that law school would mold me into a member of the ruling class when I was so clearly a person of privilege before I'd even been admitted? How can I remove the blinders my privileged upbringing brought me and instead seek what Rich calls "a common language"? How could Rich? We both grew up the daughters of Jewish doctors and gentile mothers, were Ivy League-educated, wrote poems, married young and ultimately unsuccessfully. She is a mother, lesbian, and widely recognized public figure, which I am not, but we share ties and tensions with the father, his laws, the politics of language. We share the urge to forge new forms and new communities. We both weave from poetry to prose.

Many years later, I feel far more empowered by feminist writer-critics than I imagine I could ever have been by law school. Their alchemizing their lives into poems and prose, admitting as they do their inner conflicts and contradictions, inspires me to do the same, to respond in kind to their words, to try to frame my experience poetically, narratively, unabashedly, to find alternatives to both legal and strictly academic utterance. To be a creative, unconventional critic.

Having passable memories of obtaining two masters' degrees (one in teaching writing, one in writing poetry), I hoped that when I came to the University of Washington for a Ph.D. I could learn how female poets can change the master discourse(s) of academic writing, a discourse that, oppressive as it is, is nonetheless more open than the law to revision. How radically it could be revised and whether I wanted to be that radical was an open question, one that I continue to address at Skidmore College, where I now teach. Luckily, many female writers and even some early (mostly male) poet-critics and several poststructuralist, reader-response, and composition theorists had paved the way for my writing and reading differently.[7] But it is the journeys and journalizing of contemporary American feminist mixed-genre writers I want most to join. It is they who are most confiding of their compositional methods, their lives, their relation to language. They write poetically, narratively, yet conversationally. They encourage readers to respond in kind.

Tompkins summarizes well what I've been working toward these years in Seattle and Saratoga Springs:

> The criticism I would like to write would always take off from personal experience, would always be in some way a chronicle of my hours and days, would speak in a voice in which I can talk about everything, would reach out to a reader like me and touch me where I want to be touched. (173)

I believe very deeply in practicing (as in "rehearsing" as well as "carrying-out") a feminist aesthetic of personal responses to literature—and my literary education. Diverse as contemporary feminist writer-critics may be, they all presuppose that liberation from patriarchal values and practices must take place, if not begin, in language itself. My models are those feminists whose writing embodies the refusals, revisions, fluidities, alchemies, collages, quilts, gardens, border-crossings, crosshatchings about which they speak. Their *essais* try, experiment, make forays into different genres, sashaying into the world of academic rhetoric and back out again, making and registering changes and challenges as they go.

But more than experimental language, we need experiential language, that self-empowering joining of the personal and political, the private and the public. Most feminist critics share my objective if not my self-confessional methods: we must renounce the self-denial implicit in the old language(s) of criticism and gain the power present in writing the self. We must name rather than deny both our wounds and the nature of our powers.[8]

NOTES

1. For a close reading of exemplary practitioners of self-reflexive, genre-bending forms, see my "Writing in the Borderlands." See also *An Alchemy of Genres*, from which this essay is excerpted.

2. As Cixous writes, "Everytime I say 'masculine' or 'feminine,' or 'man' or 'woman' [or 'male' or 'female'], please use as many quotation marks as you need to avoid taking these terms too literally (1)." "Male" here is to be equated with conventional academic discourse, that which DeShazer describes as "formal, detached, pontifical" (118), Farrell as "framed" or "contained" (910), and Annas as "linear" and "abstract"(12, 10). See also Juncker and Gilbert.

3. I find very useful here Bruner's distinction between "paradigmatic" and "narrative" modes of thought, the one "seeking generality and the second uniqueness," as Belenky et al. sum up (n.113). Belenky and her coauthors go on to speak of "connected knowers" as those who learn that "if one can discover the experiential logic behind... ideas, the ideas can become less strange and the owners of ideas cease to be strangers"; this empathy makes possible an expanded "experiencial base" and expanded knowledge (115). Combining Bruner and Belenky et al., I call this learning and knowing through others' and one's own stories "narrative knowing."

4. Consider the example of University of Oklahoma law professor Anita Hill at the confirmation proceedings of United States Supreme Court nominee Clarence Thomas, October 1991.

5. See note 3 and also Ryan's assertion that a thesis or literary-critical endeavor "is also, inevitably, a story, and that [her] thesis will be a story of [her] own involvement in particular kinds of female experience and its representation" (4).

6. Christian asserts that people of color have always theorized "in forms quite different from the Western form of abstract logic...often in narrative forms, in...stories" (336).

7. Though it is beyond the scope of this essay to discuss such analogues and/or predecessors, I have in mind writers from Whitman and William Carlos Williams to Charles Olson and Robert Hass; from Mallarmé to Roland Barthes to Jane Gallop; and from Louise Rosenblatt to Norman Holland and Peter Elbow.

8. This theme is articulated repeatedly, from Olsen's observation that women "who write are survivors" (39)—which is itself quoted over

and over—to Rich's comment that Grahn's original "Common Woman" poem sequence is a study in "power and powerlessness" (*Lies* 255).

WORKS CITED

Anzaldúa, Gloria. *Borderlands/La Frontera: The New Mestiza.* San Francisco: Spinsters/aunt lute, 1987.

Annas, Pamela J. "Silences: Women's Language Research and the Teaching of Writing." Caywood and Overing 3–17.

———. "Style as Politics: A Feminist Approach to the Teaching of Writing." *College English* 47 (1985): 360–71.

Belenky, Mary Field, et al. *Women's Ways of Knowing: The Development of Self, Voice, and Mind.* New York: Basic, 1986.

Bishop, Elizabeth. "Faustina, or, Rock Roses." *The Complete Poems, 1927–1979.* New York: Farrar, 1983. 72.

Caywood, Cynthia, and Gillian R. Overing, eds. *Teaching Writing: Pedagogy, Gender, and Equity.* Albany: State U of New York P, 1987.

Christian, Barbara. "The Race for Theory." *Cultural Critique* 6 (1989). Rpt. *Making Face, Making Soul/Hacienda Caras: Creative and Critical Perspectives by Women of Color.* Ed. Gloria Anzaldúa. San Francisco: aunt lute, 1990. 335–45.

Cixous, Hélène. "Reaching the Point of Wheat, Or, Portrait of the Artist as a Maturing Woman." *New Literary History* 19.1 (1987): 1–22.

DeShazer, Mary. "Creation and Relation: Teaching Essays by T. S. Eliot and Adrienne Rich." Caywood and Overing 115–21.

Dickinson, Emily. *The Complete Poems.* Ed. Thomas H. Johnson. Boston: Little, Brown, 1960.

Farrell, Thomas J. "Male and Female Modes of Rhetoric." *College English* 40 (1979): 909–21.

Freedman, Diane P. *An Alchemy of Genres: Cross-Genre Writing by American Feminist Poet-Critics.* Charlottesville: UP of Virginia, 1992.

———. "Writing in the Borderlands: The Poetic Prose of Gloria Anzaldúa and Susan Griffin." *Women and Language* 12.1 (1989): 1–4. Rpt. *Constructing and Reconstructing Gender.* Ed. Linda Perry, Lynn Turner, and Helen Sterk. Albany: State U of New York P, 1992.

Gilbert, Sandra. "Feminist Criticism in the University: An Interview with Sandra Gilbert." By Gerald Graff. *Criticism in the University.* Ed. Gerald Graff and Reginald Gibbons. Chicago: Northwestern UP, 1985. 111–23.

Griffin, Susan. *Made from this Earth.* New York: Harper, 1982.

Huber, Carole A. "Review of *Teaching Writing: Pedagogy, Gender, and Equity.*" *College Composition and Communication* 28.3 (1987): 355–57.

Janeway, Elizabeth. "Women and the Uses of Power." *The Future of Difference.* Ed. Hester Eisenstein. Boston: G. K. Hall, 1980. 327–44.

Juncker, Clara. "Writing (with) Cixous." *College English* 50.4 (1988): 424–36.

Lorde, Audre. *Sister Outsider: Essays and Speeches.* Trumansburg, NY: Crossing, 1984.

Olsen, Tillie. *Silences.* New York: Dell, 1978.

Penelope (Stanley), Julia and Susan J. Wolfe. "Consciousness as Style; Style as Aesthetic." Thorne et al. 125–39.

Piercy, Marge. "In the Men's Room." *Circles on the Water.* New York: Knopf, 1982. 80.

———. *Parti-Colored Blocks for a Quilt.* Ann Arbor: U of Michigan P, 1986.

Rich, Adrienne. *Blood, Bread, and Poetry: Selected Prose 1979–1985.* New York: Norton, 1986.

———. *On Lies, Secrets, and Silence: Selected Prose 1966–1978.* New York: Norton, 1978.

———. "Power." *The Fact of a Doorframe.* New York: Norton, 1987. 255.

Ryan, Barbara. "Chrysalis: A Thesis Journal." Diss. University of Washington, 1988.

Thorne, Barrie, Cheris Kramarae, and Nancy Henley, eds. *Language, Gender, and Society.* Rowley, MA: Newbury, 1983.

Tompkins, Jane. "Me and My Shadow." *New Literary History* 19.1 (1987): 169–85.

Walker, Alice. *In Search of Our Mothers' Gardens.* New York: Harcourt, 1983.

Wandor, Michelene. "Voices are Wild." *Women's Writing: A Challenge to Theory.* Ed. Moira Monteith. Brighton, Sussex: Harvest, 1986. 72–89.

NOTES ON CONTRIBUTORS

Deborah J. Archer is a Ph.D. candidate at the University of Nebraska, where she concentrates on women's studies and literary theory. In addition to her work on Lispector, she is interested in the dialogue between French feminist theory and feminist archetypal theory.

Elizabeth L. Barnes, Assistant Professor of English at the University of Michigan, specializes in American literature and feminist theory. Her essay is drawn from her dissertation about the influence of eighteenth-century seduction novels on nineteenth-century American domestic novels.

Martha Tomhave Blauvelt, Associate Professor of history at the College of Saint Benedict, has been a Mellon Fellow at the University of Pittsburgh and a Fellow at the Institute for the Editing of Historical Documents. Her most recent publication is "Women, Words and Men: Excerpts from the Diary of Mary Guion," in the *Journal of Women's History.* In addition to editing Guion's diary for publication, she is researching the differences between men's and women's diaries in the years 1760–1820.

Deborah L. Clarke is Assistant Professor of English and women's studies at Pennsylvania State University. In addition to her research in contemporary African American literature, she has published essays on gender, race, and language in *Light in August* and *Absalom, Absalom!,* and won a National Endowment for the Humanities Summer Stipend for her feminist reading of Faulkner's novels, *Robbing the Mother: Women in Faulkner.*

Sheila C. Conboy is Associate Professor of English at Stonehill College, where her research focuses primarily on constructions of the feminine in the history of the novel. She has traced this topic in "Fabric and Fabrication in Richardson's *Pamela*," "Exhibition and Inhibition: The Body Scene in *Dubliners*," and "The Limits of Transcendental Experience in Doris Lessing's *The Memoirs of a Survivor*." She is now writing a book on language and the body in Atwood's fiction.

Brenda O. Daly, Assistant Professor of English at Iowa State University, is completing a book entitled *Daughters in the Fiction of Joyce Carol Oates*, and has published essays on Oates in two collections: *The Intimate Critique: Autobiographical Literary Criticism* and *Feminism, Bakhtin, and the Dialogic*. She co-edited another collection, *Narrating Mothers: Theorizing Maternal Subjectivities* (University of Tennessee Press, 1991).

Terri Doughty teaches English at Malaspina College, British Columbia. She holds an M.A. in Victorian Studies from York University, and won a fellowship from the Social Sciences and Humanities Research Council of Canada for her dissertation on nineteenth-century ideologies of medievalism. She plans to expand her research on Sarah Grand to include other New Woman writers.

Judith Fetterley, Professor of English at the State University of New York, Albany, has published many essays on Cather, other female writers, and the American literary tradition. She is also the author of *The Resisting Reader: A Feminist Approach to American Fiction* (Indiana University Press, 1978), and of "Reading about Reading," an essay comparing representations of reading in narratives by men and women which appeared in *Gender and Reading*.

Diane P. Freedman is a poet, critic, and Assistant Professor of English at the University of New Hampshire, where she teaches American literature, African American literature, and literature by women. Her essay is drawn from *An Alchemy of Genres: Cross-Genre Writing by American Feminist Poet-Critics* (University Press of Virginia, 1992). She is also the co-editor of an anthology entitled *The Intimate Critique: Autobiographical Literary Criticism* (forthcoming from Duke University Press).

Julia Giordano teaches English at New York University and at Columbia University, where she is writing a dissertation on Fulke Greville. Her interests include feminist theory, and issues of equality in seventeenth-century religious and political poetry. A published poet as well as a critic, she won the 1990 Van Rensselaer Prize at Columbia.

Gayle Greene, Professor of English at Scripps College, has published many essays on Drabble, Lessing, and Atwood, and co-edited *Making a Difference: Feminist Literary Criticism* and *The Woman's Part: Feminist Criticism of Shakespeare*. This essay is part of her book on contemporary narrative by women, *Changing the Story: Feminist Fiction and the Tradition* (Indiana University Press, 1991).

Leslie S. Gutiérrez-Jones is a Ph.D. candidate in English at Cornell University, where she specializes in twentieth-century fiction, African American literature, and literature by women. Her essay is drawn from her dissertation on gender, ethnicity, and the construction of the autobiographical voice, entitled "Through the I of a Child: Personal Politics in the *Künstlerroman* of the Marginalized Woman."

Patricia Hannon, Assistant Professor of French at Catholic University, specializes in seventeenth-century literature, female writers, and literary criticism. Her essay is part of a larger work that compares male- and female-authored fairy tales in seventeenth-century France, a subject on which she has published two other essays.

Debra Humphreys, a Ph.D. candidate at Rutgers University concentrating on feminist theory and American popular culture and film, has taught women's studies at Rutgers University, Towson State University, and at the University of Maryland, Baltimore County. In addition to her writing on American literature and popular culture, she is currently working on a project on feminist film theory and Hollywood spectatorship.

Patricia E. Johnson, Assistant Professor of humanities and literature at Pennsylvania State University, Harrisburg, specializes in nineteenth-century British literature and female writers. She has published essays on Brontë and Dickens, and is completing a book entitled *Masters and Men and Women: The Mobilization of Gender in the British Industrial Novel.*

Kathryn R. King is Assistant Professor of English at the University of Montevallo. She has edited Thomas Hardy's *Wessex Tales* for Oxford University Press, and has published essays on Hardy's poetry and fiction. She is now working on a book on Jane Barker and the emergence of the novel.

Christine Moneera Laennec is Assistant Professor of French at Illinois State University. Her scholarly interests center on gender issues, particularly in medieval literature. Her essay "Unladylike Polemics: Christine de Pizan's Strategies of Attack and Defense" is forthcoming, and she is currently working on the body and writing in de Pizan.

Johnny Payne is Assistant Professor of creative writing and literature at Northwestern University. He has published essays on Latin American fiction and the language of dictatorship; his book, *Conquest of the New World: Experimental Fiction and Translation in the Americas,* is forthcoming from the University of Texas Press. His stories and translations have appeared in many magazines, and he is presently writing a novel.

Carol J. Singley, Assistant Professor of literature and American studies at The American University, is past president of the Edith Wharton Society and author of *The Meaning of Longing,* a book on Wharton's relationship to her own intellectualism and to patriarchal religion and philosophy. Her research interests include romance, female initiation, and the gothic. She has published essays on Catharine Maria Sedgwick, Sarah Orne Jewett, and Emily Dickinson.

Susan Elizabeth Sweeney, Associate Professor of English at Holy Cross College and past president of the Vladimir Nabokov Society, has published essays on feminist criticism, self-reflexive narrative, and detective fiction and literary theory. Her forthcoming essays include "Edith Wharton's Case of *Roman*

Fever," on Wharton's identification of reading and writing with carnal knowledge, and "Anne Tyler's Invented Games," on made-up games as paradigms for narrative structure and fiction-making.

Bonnie TuSmith is Assistant Professor of English at Bowling Green State University. Her research includes "ethnic woman-ist pedagogy," the use of color imagery in ethnic literatures, and the theme of community and individualism in contempo-rary fiction. Her multicultural study, *All My Relatives: Commu-nity in Contemporary Ethnic Literatures,* will be published by the University of Michigan Press.

Wendy Wall, Assistant Professor of English at Northwestern Uni-versity, has published essays on poetic prefaces, Isabella Whit-ney, and Alice Walker. Her book, provisionally entitled *The Politics of Publication in the English Renaissance: Authorship, Gen-der and Print,* is forthcoming from Cornell University Press.

INDEX

A

Absence: of closure, xv, 22, 26–27, 208, 260, 324–25, 358–60; of Edenic past, 282; of female author, 94–96, 198, 209–10, 213; of female subject, 60, 95; of feminine text (*See* Feminine text); of male body, 58, 59 (*see also* Body: male body as text); of self (*see* Identity, loss of)

Acker, Kathy, 27

Adolescence: female, 223, 225–26, 228, 235–38, 242, 246–48, 284, 287–88, 298–99, 301–3, 306; male, 235–38, 242–43, 298–99, 301, 306; as metaphor for artistic development, xxi, 235–50, 280. *See also* Bildungsroman; Development, artistic

Alexander, Sally, 317

Ambiguity, strategy of, 27, 279–81, 283–84, 286–87, 291

Ambivalence: definition of, 74; toward authorship, 35, 36, 37, 44, 45, 46, 91, 93; toward education, 318–19; toward female artist figure, 179, 191, 193; toward feminist reading, 26, 350; toward ideology of narrative structure, 74, 75, 81, 86; toward language, 20, 27, 355; toward literary work, 126, 129, 130–31, 139; toward mother, 161, 225–26, 227, 242; toward narrative authority, 22–23; toward oral tradition, 291; toward other, 258–59; toward pleasure, 181, 182; toward

reading and writing, ix, xiii, xiv, 20, 25, 197, 198, 203, 211, 212, 214, 256, 265, 350, 351, 355; toward romance, 152; toward romance plot, 185, 186, 193; toward strong women, 84, 290; toward success, xxi, 35, 226. *See also* Anxiety, sources of; Authorship, obstacles to

Androgyny, 203–4, 213, 276. *See also* Gender roles

Annas, Pamela J., 4

"Anti-writing," xvi, 27, 35–36, 46

Anxiety, sources of: appropriation of other, 253, 254, 256–57, 259; conformity to misogynist tradition, 41; female reading and writing, ix–x, 52, 197, 198, 200, 212; gender roles in fiction, 238, 243, 249; inadequacy of language, 46, 253, 257; liminality, 198; publication, xvi–xvii, 51, 68, 92, 100, 131, 174, 213; successful female development, xxi, 221, 222, 225, 226, 232, 233. *See also* Ambivalence; Authorship, obstacles to; Emotion

Anxiety of authorship, ix, xvi, xvii, 19–20, 51, 68, 91–93, 212, 235

Anxious power, x, xiii, xiv, 28, 107, 111, 112, 125, 126, 198, 208, 214, 360; definition of, ix, 197; experience of, xiv–xv, 3–10; expression of, xiv, 19–28

Anzaldúa, Gloria, 364–65, 370, 371; *Borderlands,* 365

Appropriation: of embedded text, 24, 202, 208–10; of female body, 52, 351; of language, 186, 197, 198,